The Bible and Astronomy

To

James C. Sentell

with the author's compliments
and best wishes

2 February 2003 A.D.

Gustav Teres. S.J.

Gustav Teres, S. J.

THE BIBLE
AND
ASTRONOMY

The Magi and the Star in the Gospel

15
19

3rd Edition

Solum Forlag
Oslo 2002

Gustav Teres, S.J.: The Bible and Astromy.
3rd Revised and Enlarged Edition
Solum Forlag A.S, Oslo 2002
ISBN 82-560-1341-9
Library subject index cards: Astronomy, Babylon, Bible, Cosmology

Frontispiece: The Tower of Babylon reconstructed after the excavations,
and in the background the map of the northern sky with constellations
which are visible during the autumn nights over the horizon of the
latitudes between 30 and 50 degrees. (Cover design by *Gustav Teres*)

ACKNOWLEDGEMENTS

My thanks to the rev. *George V. Coyne, S. J.*, Director of the Vatican
Observatory, who has carefully read the manuscript and promoted the
publication of this book. Most of all I wish to express my deepest
appreciation to Rev. *Olaf I. Waring* from the Diocese of Oslo, Norway,
and the USA, for the many hours he has graciously spent going over and
improving the text of the final version. Particular thanks to **Rev. Randall
M. Smith O. Praem** for his kind assistance.

The author and publisher are grateful to professor David Hughes and
Konradin Ferrari d'Occhieppo for permission to use some illustrations
from their quoted works, and thanks the Vatican Museum and the British
Museum for permission to reproduce the photographs as requested.

Distributed in the U.S. by
International Specialized Book Services, Inc.
5824 N.E. Hassalo St., Portland, Oregon 97213-3644

and in Europe by
Lavis Marketing
73, Lime Walk, Headington, Oxford OX3 7AD

Printed in Norway by Preutz Grafisk A.S, Larvik

CONTENTS

ILLUSTRATIONS

PREFACE

Two billion people were preparing for the anniversary of the second millennium of our era. What exactly were they preparing for? Older people perhaps expected that some catastrophe prophesied long ago would now occur. Younger people seemed more inclined to expect the coming of an age of universal peace and social well-being. But both groups were destined to be disappointed to some extent. The truth is probably going to be found somewhere in between these two ideas.

The leaders of Christian states and churches payed little attention to prophecies. Instead, they encouraged their peoples to cooperate in order to bring about the renewal of social justice and peace and to befittingly celebrate the two thousandth anniversary of Christ's birth.

Some historians and astronomers have proved that our era is most probably seven years late, if we want to determine the date exactly from the year Jesus was born. All researchers will agree that the Christian calendar established in the 6th century is late, if we take into account the evidence provided by historical dates. However, there are still some people who argue about the dates and there are others who consider this question unimportant. Nevertheless, various Church organizations agreed that the commemorative year of Christianity will be the year 2000 of the traditional calendar.

When we were children, the preparation for the Christmas season used to be a happy time. We enjoyed the Nativity plays. In the evenings we used to dress up as kings, shepherds and angels. We went from house to house singing folk songs and carrying the Nativity crèche and the big star. On January 6, the day of Epiphany, we were happy to carry the holy water while escorting the parish priest, who went round the village blessing each house and home. With a piece of white chalk he used to write the date and the initials of the Three Holy Kings on each door. This is what he would have written in the Jubilee Year:

$$20 + G + M + B + 00$$

As children it never occurred to us to ask who Gaspar, Melchior and Balthasar were. We were used to hearing and repeating their familiar sounding names at Christmas time and we thought of them as generous and holy kings, who were there to protect our homes from all misfortune in the forthcoming new year.

Tempus fugit (time flies). But life is half spent before we know what it is all about. We had to spend a great deal of our time studying hard and we have become neither shepherds nor kings. First I studied mathematics and physics and then philosophy and theology, until I realized that without the knowledge of cultural history it was hardly possible to understand and evaluate the scientific progress of our age.

The Heavens and the Bible, two inexhaustible fields of research lie open to us. Astronomy and biblical exegesis are both endless and never boring subjects. According to the Scripture the story of our universe begins with the first words of the Creator: "Let there be light!" And what we want to find out today is what light is and how it comes into being. We compare scientific theories with what the Bible says about the beginning and end of the universe. There are scientists who say man should not believe in anything else but physical theorems. Others claim that science as a whole is uncertain and only the Bible is infallible. Who is right? Is there anybody who understands the language of the Prophets and the language of Mathematics equally well?

Believers and non-believers will agree that the most epoch-making event of the history of mankind is the birth of Jesus Christ. As it is closer to us than the creation of the world, let us talk about it first. A lot of people get stuck right at the beginning of the story: Could it be possible that a few Magi of the East found out where and when Christ would be born just by studying the position of the stars? Why did the apostle Matthew think that those Wise Men had found the Messiah in Bethlehem by observing the motions of the stars?

There is perhaps no other chapter in the Bible that has been so widely discussed and written about ever since the first century as this account of Matthew. Moreover, it is a writing which today seems to be of ever increasing interest to people all over the world. We have been sent letters from India, China and even Japan, asking: What exactly was the star of Bethlehem? Is there a scientifically verified explanation for its existence?

Twenty-nine years ago Patrick J. Treanor, S.J., former director of the Vatican Observatory, gave the following answer to the above question, an answer which retains its validity even today:

> In recent years there have been several explanations, scientific studies as well as popular writings published concerning this question, but not all of them contain factual information. Some popular explanations, lacking the information contained in the latest Biblical studies, oversimplify this problem and cause only confusion and discontent. The historical value of Matthew's account is minimized or even reduced to zero by these explanations. However, it is impossible to correctly interpret the original text if we fail to take into consideration the evidence drawn from literature, theology, cultural history and astronomy. In the present brief study we shall outline only the astronomical arguments which could convince astronomers of the authenticity of the chapter about the star of Bethlehem. We have no intention of overemphasizing the importance of these arguments versus traditional explanations, but we think they are worth serious consideration of biblicists as well (*Osservatore Romano*, January 6, 1971).

Father Treanor had a profound knowledge of the original language of the Bible as well as history and astronomy. Supported by his fellow Jesuits, he showed that the star of Bethlehem was most likely Jupiter in 7 BC when it was in conjunction with Saturn for three months. I have been engaged in this research myself in the course of twenty-five years. The new data I found in the libraries of the Vatican Observatory and the Biblical Institute of Rome have convinced me of the value of the astronomical arguments concerning Matthew's account. I delivered several lectures on this theme, and the audiences had many questions to ask, which shows that this subject is of great interest to the general public as well as to the scholar. My treatises on the results of my research have been published in a book by the Springer Scientific Publishers in Hungary, and partly in special journals in Germany, Norway and England.

I have received a number of requests asking me to write about this subject in English. But if I were to publish just a brief summary of my researches only those well acquainted with the formulas of astronomy and exegesis would understand it. I want to reach a larger audience because there are so many people who have been exposed to confused and controversial ideas about the star of Bethlehem. In this work I would like to provide a secure answer to the many questions which continue to be asked.

From the first century onwards the feast of the Revelation of Christ the Lord (*Epiphania Domini*) on January 6 was one of the major festivals of the Christian world, a day when three events were celebrated:

1. the birth of Jesus in Bethlehem; the revelation of Christ the Lord to the simple shepherds of Israel, who, faithful sons of their nation, were expecting the advent of the Messiah as promised by the prophets;

2. the visit of the Magi to Bethlehem; the revelation of the Lord Savior to the representatives of the nations which like Israel also sought the Messiah;

3. the baptism of Jesus in the water of the Jordan; the revelation of the Son of God to the first disciples, who could hear a voice from heaven saying "This is my Son".

At the end of the 4th century the bishops of the Church in the East and West decided by common consent to celebrate the birth of Jesus on 25 December although it was uncertain whether the 25th was indeed the exact date of the event. In the Greek-Roman Empire December 25 was originally the day of the "Unconquered Sun", a festival described as *Dies Natalis Solis Invicti*, which followed the *Saturnalia* lasting from 17 to 24 December. On this day, when after the winter solstice the lengthening of daylight became apparent, people celebrated the victory of light over darkness. So it was naturally suitable for conversion into a Christian festival. The traditional popular festival was thus endowed with a new meaning, that of the birth of Christ, who, in a spiritual sense, had declared: "I am the light of the world".

The 6th of January was to continue to commemorate the visit of the Magi and to this day the opening liturgical prayer for the feast is the following: "Almighty, eternal God, you revealed your Son to the nations by the guidance of a star. Lead us to your glory in heaven by the light of faith". The significance of the prayer goes beyond the limits of our earthly existence. How did the revelation "by the guidance of a star" take place? To understand this it is necessary to find the correct interpretation of this strange chapter of the Gospel.

I was asked many questions about the writing of this book, the first and last always being: "What is your real purpose in writing and for precisely which audience is the book intended"? My aim is clearly defined by the table of contents, and the title of the book precisely indicates the readers to whom the writing is addressed. Unfortunately, biblicists and astronomers are hardly familiar with each other's terminology, and those who do not belong to either of these special fields, will, of course, require even more detailed explanations than the specialists themselves. This circumstance has not made the author's task easy. I trust however, that the reader will muster up the necessary understanding and tolerance even if he or she is not able to agree with some aspect or other. Nothing in this world is so perfect that it cannot be further improved!

Rome, 6th January 2000.   *Gustav Teres, S. J.*

PREFACE TO THE THIRD EDITION

My thanks to the astronomers and theologians who have written reviews of my book and recommended it to "all men and women who wish to find a better conformity between the results of modern scientific research and the religious message of the Bible". I was even more delighted at letters from people of different professions who wrote to say "we have with interest read your enjoyable book, although it also contains some difficult chapters". I would like to suggest that my readers begin the chapter which most of all is of interest to them. My work is addressed also to those who do not believe in the Bible or do not like mathematics. They will surely not oppose my intention to share with my readers the spiritual treasures which I have come across in the course of my many years of research. This is my humble contribution to the contemporary dialogue between science and religion.

Rome, 25th January 2002.   *Gustav Teres, S. J.*

GENERAL OUTLINE

The relation between the Bible and Astronomy came into focus as the subject of heated debates for the first time in the 17th century, when the discoveries of Kepler and Galileo were already widely known. Since that time, scientific research has reached new heights and new profundity, both in astrophysics and in exegetics.

The authors of biblical texts do not teach pragmatic history nor positive science. It is obvious, however, that they describe historical events, and that they present the scientific conception of the world of their own time. Thus the hagiographers of the Old Testament give a profound insight into the development of the human spirit and culture when they write of the religious and moral laws of ancient monotheism. The better we understand their original language, the more we can appreciate their writings. Therefore, it is part of the task of a biblicist to study the works of the prophets and of the evangelists also from a critical historical and literary viewpoint.

At the very beginning of this century two famous astronomers, Giovanni Schiaparelli (1903) and Edward Maunder (1908), wrote detailed essays on the astronomical expressions and observations which are found in the Hebrew Bible. But nowadays, modern cosmological theories about the origin and the structure of the universe have emphasized the question: How can those biblical texts be appreciated and interpreted in the light of our new astrophysical knowledge ?

Philological research sheds light on the original meaning of Hebrew and Greek expressions which have hitherto been unknown or obscure. Archaeological finds make possible the verification of historical data and the identification of old place names as well as names of stars mentioned in the Bible.

The star of Bethlehem is a case in point. The account of the Magi in Matthew's 2nd chapter seems to be an item of secondary importance, but on examining it closely we find that it is in perfect harmony with the whole Bible, and it alludes to modern questions which are of great interest in our time. For instance, an ever increasing number of books dealing with ancient magic are being published today, and millions of people believe in astrology. What explanation is there for magic being linked to scientific knowledge and religious practices ? The star of the Magi will, in this present study, be a guiding star which help us to orientate ourselves in the cross-roads of astronomical and biblical research.

In recent years the star of Bethlehem has become a matter of common interest throughout the world. Its story has been on the program of the largest Planetaria from Berlin to New York. The astronomical interpretation of the phenomenon is generally correct, but the additional historical explanation is largely inadequate or mistaken. Unfortunately, the inaccurate translations of the original text of Matthew give it a legendary or mythical sound. Some scholars are of the opinion that the passage of the Bethlehem star is a *Midrash*, i.e., a story without a real historical value. However, the literary form of Matthew's second chapter is not yet defined unequivocally. Conclusions drawn from recent archaeological, philological, historical and astronomical research show that Matthew in his 2nd chapter relates an actual event.

The principal facts concerning this matter can be summarized in the following points:

1. King Herod the Great died in the Roman year 750 AUC (*ab urbe* [Romae] *condita*) = 4 BC, that is, four years before the beginning of the Christian era. According to Matthew, Jesus had been born during the reign of King Herod, and after the visit of the Magi, Herod had all the male children in Bethlehem killed who were two years old or under (Mt 2:16). Most researchers today assume that Jesus was born in 7 BC. This is confirmed by the writing on the Roman *Monumentum Ancyranum* of Caesar Augustus, which gives 746/47 AUC = 8/7 BC as the date for the first census, which is mentioned in Luke's Gospel at the time of the birth of Jesus.

2. In 7 BC a very rare and significant astronomical phenomenon was visible: during nine months the two giant planets, Jupiter and Saturn, moved together within the constellation of Pisces, and their western standstill occurred simultaneously near the northern apex of the zodiacal light cone, when it was visible in the meridian of Jerusalem and Bethlehem. At the same time the astronomical point of the vernal equinox moved over from the constellation of Aries into that of Pisces, and, according to an ancient tradition, this event denoted the beginning of a new era.

3. The Magi were astronomers and priests of the Babylonian Marduk temple. In the years of the exile, 598-538 BC, the two great prophets, Ezekiel and Daniel, were active in Babylon. Daniel was appointed as chief counselor by the Chaldaean kings, and he was given the rank of supreme magus (Dn 4:6; 5:11). Early Christian works of art represent the Magi with these two prophets; the Magi are depicted as coming away from them, that is to say from the East towards Jerusalem. Thus they would have known the prophecies about the long expected Messiah, especially the prophecy of the Assyrian magus Balaam, "a star will rise from Jacob, a scepter will come out of Israel" (Num 24:17).

4. Archaeologists have found the archives of the Magi under the ruins of the Babylonian temple. Among the cuneiform tablets are also the star almanacs which give exact astronomical data for the year 305 of the Seleucid era, that is, from 2nd April 7 BC to 18th April 6 BC. Several decades before the birth of Christ the Chaldaean astronomers had precalculated the aspects of Jupiter and Saturn also for the year 7 BC. Modern calculations verify their data. With the aid of electronic computers and planetarium projectors we can reconstruct the celestial phenomena which occurred 2000 years ago.

5. The expressions used by Matthew to describe the rising and the apparent standstill of the star are to be found in ancient astronomical works, both in Babylonian cuneiform writings and Old Greek text books (*Aratos, Geminos*). These help us to understand better the sentences in Matthew's original text which cannot be correctly translated without knowing the language of ancient astronomy.

6. The particular language and matter of Matthew's 2nd chapter allow us to conclude that his primary source could be an original account by the Magi, which he tells in an abridged version but without changing the relevant facts. He writes, namely, of things which could only be known to the Magi; they alone could have used those terms which give adequate expression for the evening rising and the apparent standstill of the star.

7. Today several exegetes agree with the opinion that Matthew relates a natural phenomenon, that is, he is speaking of an actual star and not only of a miraculous event. In the text of *The New English Bible* they have translated the Greek word *magoi* into "astrologers" who "observed the rising of his star" (Oxford University Press, 1970). Those Magi, however, were not ordinary astrologers, but in the context of the Gospel they were learned priests or "wise men", who were not there to cast a birth horoscope for the awaited king.

8. Modern astronomers agree that the Chaldaeans or Babylonian priests were in possession of very advanced mathematical and astronomical knowledge, and as described in the Gospel the Magi could have seen the conjunction of Jupiter and Saturn while they traveled from Jerusalem to Bethlehem. Nevertheless, the Star of Bethlehem in a wider sense was not only an astronomical event, such as the Jupiter-Saturn conjunction. From a theological point of view it may be considered the concurrence of all the historical, cultural, psychological and astronomical factors of that epoch. It is in this concurrence of all these factors with the birth of Christ that we can recognize, if we wish, a divine intervention.

In the following chapters I will attempt to explain and support all these statements as briefly and clearly as possible, in spite of the complexity of the subject. The various opinions of some biblical scholars will be discussed in the subsequent sections entitled "Star of the Messiah" and "Literary Criticism". Among the astronomical assumptions regarding the star of Bethlehem, the conjunction of Jupiter and Saturn is taken as the most probable hypothesis. It has already been supported by several outstanding astronomers such as L. Ideler (1825), J. Hontheim (1908), H. Kritzinger (1925), and P.J. Treanor (1970). Recently two professors of astronomy, Konradin Ferrari d'Occhieppo (1965, 1977, 1978, 1991) and David Hughes (1979), have refuted the comet and nova hypotheses. They have presented all possible evidence to show that it is only the conjunction of Jupiter and Saturn in Pisces that can be accepted as a true astronomical phenomenon occurring at the time of the Magi's visit in Bethlehem. In the present work this hypothesis will be confirmed by a detailed philological and grammatical analysis of the respective expressions in the original text of Matthew (Mt 2:1-9).

The **Supplementary Explanations** give answers to the questions which are left open in the preceding chapters. These explanations also contribute to the contemporary dialogue between scientists and theologians, and should be very instructive for those who wish to deal more in depth with this matter. The smaller *bold faced numbers* in parentheses in the text refer to these supplementary explanations.

Fig. 1: This mosaic can be seen in the church of S. *Apollinare Nuovo* in Ravenna (Italy). It is the work of an anonymous Byzantine artist between 545-550 AD. He has portrayed the Magi as Persian priests.

CHAPTER ONE

THE GOSPEL AND
ITS TRANSLATIONS

Exegesis and Scientific Research

Today the Greek word *Euangélion*, rendered *Evangelium* into Latin and *Gospel* into English, is known in all parts of the globe, but there are only a few people who understand its true meaning. Most people think perhaps that it is an ancient writing which relates the life and teaching of a great Prophet and Wonder Worker. However, the word *Evangelium* does not refer to a kind of text book, nor does it denote an ordinary biography. Since the time of Homer the word *Euangélion* denoted the good news of the victory over the enemy. Later it was used in the emperor cult, where it denoted news of any great imperial event, as the birth of an heir, or his accession to the throne, or new decrees for the good of the people.

When the apostles began to preach "the power and the coming of our Lord Jesus Christ" in the Roman Empire, they filled the old expression with a new sense. They affirmed that it is a true *evangelium* in which nobody will be disappointed. The word Gospel comes from the Old English *gód spel*, which means good tidings preached by Christ; the Good News of Salvation (Gal 1: 6f; 2 Pet 1: 16).

In the oldest codices and manuscripts Matthew is placed first and only his title is *Euangélion*. The Fathers of the Church have spoken of *one gospel* in which four messengers complement each other; their concordance alludes to a common source, and the divergences show their own experiences. St. John Chrysostom, bishop of Antioch (390 AD) says in his commentary: "Matthew rightly calls his writings *Evangelium*, because he preaches salvation for every believer, the remission of debts and the forgiveness of sins; death ceases, and heaven opens. What can be compared to such good things ?" (*Comment. in Matth*. I. 1-2).

According to the ecclesiastical tradition dating from the 2nd century, Matthew was the first apostle who wrote down the Discourses (*Logia*) of Jesus. With reference to the apostolic tradition the bishop Papias (60-130 AD) testifies that Matthew composed his work "in the Hebrew tongue", that is in Aramaic, for the disciples of Christ in Galilee. Under the persecutions the original Aramaic text was

1

lost, but we have its Syriac and Greek translation which is supposed to have been made when Peter and Paul preached in Rome, about 20 years after the ascension of Christ.

The approved Latin translation of the Gospel was prepared by St. Jerome (347-420 AD), who was one of the first great Fathers of the Church. He knew the Greek and the Aramaic and the Old Hebrew languages perfectly. In 382 AD he participated in the pontifical synod in Rome. He was secretary to Pope Damasus, who entrusted him with the preparation of the Latin translation of the complete Bible. This text has been accepted and used in the whole Church of Western Europe, and it is called *Vulgata Versio*.

In 386 AD St. Jerome left Rome and settled in the Holy Land, where he continued his work as translator and interpreter of the biblical texts. In Syria, in the library of Caesarea, he found an Aramaic Gospel, which he also translated into Latin. The few fragments which remained of this work show that it was in accord with the Greek Matthew, and the Fathers of the first centuries, such as Ignatius of Antioch and Clement of Alexandria, considered it to be the original work of the apostle Matthew.

It is not an easy task to translate the old oriental languages of the Bible to modern literary languages. The proper sense of many Hebrew and Greek expressions can only be rendered by circumscriptions or with complementary words. Moreover, the mode of expression of the living languages is continually in the process of formation. Thus in the course of time the meaning of some words will be changed in current use. From time to time these circumstances necessitate new translations of the ancient Sacred Books, and every translation is also an interpretation.

Although the deviations between the translations do not touch the great truths of faith, they still trouble readers and give rise to misapprehensions. These difficulties should be solved by the work of the United Bible Societies which is a world wide fellowship of national Bible Societies working in more than 180 countries. They attempt to present the biblical message in an everyday English version which does not necessarily follow the vocabulary and style found in the historic Bible versions.

The apostle Peter had advised his friends not to distort the meaning of biblical texts, since there are some subjects "hard to understand; these are the points that uneducated and unbalanced people distort" and this is "a fatal thing for them to do" (2 Pet 3: 16). Now we are all the more in danger of misinterpreting some biblical texts, as the Bible has the widest circulation in the world. More that 300 million copies have been printed and distributed during the last decades, and more than 2000 million people are reading them. Actually the Gospel of Christ is the book which makes the greatest impression on millions of

2

non-Christian people; it has been translated into 1530 different languages. Thus the great task of our age is to compose a collective Bible translation in a standard language, and to give a uniform interpretation which will be approved by the Church's Teaching Authority and accepted by all Christians in full agreement with each other. The successors of the apostle Peter had repeatedly encouraged the biblical scholars to collaborate for the sake of the cause. The year 1993 marked the 100th anniversary of the publication of the Encyclical *Providentissimus Deus* by Pope Leo XIII, in which the Pope stressed the importance of a correct and uniform Bible translation, and repelled anticlerical and atheistic attacks. Fifty years later, in 1943, Pope Pius XII wrote an encyclical on the necessity of a new Bible translation taking into consideration the latest findings of scientific research.

On the occasion of these anniversaries the Pontifical Biblical Commission has elaborated and published a document of great importance with the title: "The Interpretation of the Bible in the Church" (Vatican, 15 April 1993). Pope John Paul II has approved this document, and at the audience for the members of the Biblical Commission he has spoken the following encouraging words:

> This document can impart a new impulse to the interpretation of the Bible in the Church, which will benefit the whole of mankind and make the sun of truth and of brotherly love rise at the daybreak of the third millennium... The importance of this task demands a wide-ranging international collaboration. We are living in an age when scientific research is getting more and more important, and it is therefore absolutely necessary that the science of exegesis stands at an adequate level (*The Interpretation of the Bible in the Church*. pp.7-12).

Actually it was Pope Pius XII who introduced a new age in the history of the biblical research. In his Encyclical, *Divino Afflante Spiritu*, he takes as his point of departure the fact that "the Scriptures inspired by the Divine Spirit" are among the most important sources for the eternal truths which serve the life and prosperity of mankind. Therefore, the Pontiff asked biblical scholars to improve the former translations and to find proper answers to the questions which are not quite solved. In order to carry out this task it is necessary to study the ancient oriental languages and in this way to find the literal sense of the Scriptures. The Pope says:

> ...frequently the literal sense is not so obvious in the words and writings of ancient oriental authors as it is with the writers of today. For what they intend to signify by their words is determined not

only by the laws of grammar and philology; it is absolutely necessary for the interpreter to go back in spirit to those remote centuries of the East, and to make proper use of the aids afforded by history, archaeology, ethnology and other sciences, in order to discover what literary forms the writers of that early age intended to use... In many cases in which the sacred authors are accused of some historical inaccuracy or the inexact recording of some events, it is found to be a question of nothing more than those customary forms or styles of narrative which were current in human intercourse among the ancients. A just impartiality therefore demands that when these are found in the word of God, which is expressed in human language for man's sake, they should be no more stigmatized as error than when similar expressions are employed in daily use. Thus a knowledge and careful appreciation of ancient modes of expression and literary forms will provide a solution to many of the objections made against the truth and historical accuracy of Holy Writ (*Acta Ap. Sedis,* Vol.35, 1943, pp.313-323. Trans. by C.Carlen).

At the same time the Pope warns exegetes against the exaggeration of allegorical explanations. He refers to the first Fathers of the Church, in particular to St. Jerome and Origen, who had a thorough grounding in the sciences of their own age, and thus they were able "to defend the infallibility of the Holy Writ both in its entirety and in its parts". The same teaching has been repeated and confirmed by the Bishops at the Second Vatican Council in the *Constitution on Divine Revelation* (1965):

Since God speaks in sacred Scripture through man in human fashion, the interpreter should carefully investigate what meaning the sacred writers really intended, and what God wanted to manifest by means of their words... Those who search out the intention of the sacred writers must have regard for literary forms. For truth is proposed and expressed in a variety of ways, depending on whether the text is history of one kind or another, or whether its form is that of prophecy, poetry, or some other type of speech... The Holy Scripture must be read and interpreted according to the same Spirit by whom it was written. Therefore, serious attention must be given to the content and unity of the whole of Scripture. Also the living tradition of the whole Church must be taken into account along with the harmony which exists between elements of faith. It is the task of exegetes to work according to these rules toward a better understanding and explanation of the meaning of sacred Scripture, so that through preparatory study the judgement of the Church may mature (*Constitution on Divine Revelation,* 12).

These new instructions have defined the right methods of historical and literary criticism in modern biblical studies. The precursors of these methods were the Dominican, M. Joseph Lagrange, founder and leader of the Biblical School of Jerusalem (1890-1938), and the Jesuit, Xavier Léon-Dufour, former president of the French Biblical Commission and editor of the Dictionary of Biblical Theology. The scholars of the Biblical School in Jerusalem in 1956 published the new French translation which was made from the Hebrew or Aramaic and the Greek ancient texts, supplied with occasional short footnotes. The English Jerusalem Bible is its equivalent, first published in London in 1966. In this new edition there are still some doubtful and uncertain points, as for example the Star of Bethlehem in the 2nd Chapter of Matthew.

The French scholars in 1956 still noted that the evangelist had presumably thought of a miraculous star, and "it is futile to look for a natural explanation". But in the edition of the New Jerusalem Bible (1985) this statement is omitted from the notes, and the Magi are described as astrologers who have observed a natural star.

The exegetes are still uncertain about the nature of the star of Bethlehem as well as about the literal sense of Matthew's account. Recent research shows that this state of uncertainty can best be resolved through a proper philological and grammatical analysis of the ancient texts. Let us first read the passage in question as it is rendered into English in The Jerusalem Bible (Mt 2: 1-12):

After Jesus had been born at Bethlehem in Judaea during the reign of King Herod, some wise men came to Jerusalem from the east. "Where is the infant king of the Jews ?", they asked, "We saw his star as it rose and have come to do him homage." When King Herod heard this he was perturbed, and so was the whole of Jerusalem. He called together all the chief priests and the scribes of the people, and inquired of them where the Christ was to be born. "At Bethlehem in Judaea," they told him "for this is what the prophet wrote: "And you, Bethlehem, in the land of Judah, you are by no means least among the leaders of Judah, for out of you will come a leader who will shepherd my people Israel". Then Herod summoned the wise men to see him privately. He asked them the exact date on which the star had appeared, and sent them on to Bethlehem. "Go and find out all about the child," he said, "and when you have found him, let me know, so that I too may go and do him homage." Having listened to what the king had to say, they set out. And there in front of them was the star they had seen rising; it went forward and halted over the place where the child was. The sight of the star filled them with delight, and going into the house they saw the child with his mother Mary, and falling to their knees

5

they did him homage. Then, opening their treasures, they offered him gifts of gold and frankincense and myrrh. But they were warned in a dream not to go back to Herod, and returned to their own country by a different way.

In comparison with the Greek original we may immediately note that this English text is not quite a word for word translation, and it does not render the complete literal sense of Matthew's narrative.

Mistakes and Fallacies

The Fathers of the Church designated as literal any sense the words of Scripture communicate. According to their doctrine the Bible had both a divine and a human author, and the deeper meaning of divine inspiration could not always be known to the human writer. By the literal sense today is meant "the sense which the human author directly intended and which his words convey" (Raymond E. Brown 1968; JBC. 71: 10-14).

The first rule for finding the literal sense is a correct word for word translation and the determination of the literary form the author is employing. This task presupposes the knowledge of the biblical languages, Hebrew and Greek. In addition to this, there is need for auxiliary knowledge, such as history, archaeology and geography. Therefore, it is a fallacy that anyone should be able to understand and interpret a scriptural passage only on the basis of a translated text. Not without reason have the bishops of Rome advised scholars about vernacular translations of the Scriptures.

Until the 16th century the ancient Greek codices of the Bible were available only to a few theologians. Desiderius Erasmus published the first printed edition of the New Testament in a faulty Greek and Latin edition at Basel in 1516. He also urged the national translations, but he himself did not attempt this work, because he was aware of the linguistic difficulties.

Martin Luther prepared the first complete German translation of Scripture, using the Greek and Latin edition of Erasmus. The German New Testament appeared in 1522, and the first edition of Luther's complete Bible was printed at Wittenberg in 1534. As a result of Luther's work there appeared several other translations of the entire Bible into various national languages. These were not lacking in errors and there were often difficulties of a traumatic nature, connected with their publication.

These difficulties are clearly seen in the history of the English Bible. Until the 17th century in England the authorities strictly prohibited translations of the entire Bible into English. William Tyndale (1536) and John Rogers (1555) were put to death because of their translations which were printed in Germany and smuggled into England. The first authorized version known as the King James Version was published in 1611. Since then coming from both Britain and the United States there have been 14 authorized versions and some 80 private versions.

Today the Bible is the most widely distributed book in English speaking countries. The bishops of the Second Vatican Council (1964) firmly insisted that "the faithful shall have access to Sacred Scripture, because it is an excellent tool for the attainment of that unity which the Savior offers to all men" (*Constitution on Divine Revelation*, 21-22).

From the first translation of the Scriptures into English by John Wycliffe (1382) to the New Jerusalem Bible (1985) and the Revised Standard Versions, biblicists have made many emendations, but they admit that there is still need for further improvements.

The opinion today is that the 16th century translations of the Bible were premature in that the reformers, while not lacking in determination, were nevertheless poorly equipped with the necessary language skills. Until the end of the 19th century Latin was still a prevalent part of ordinary education, and the Vulgate Version of the Bible was widespread. Great mathematicians and physicists, such as Isaac Newton and Friedrich Gauss, wrote their scientific works in Latin, but they were not familiar with the language of the Gospel, because they never had studied the early Christian traditions.

We may now ask: Why were the former translators not able to render the proper literal sense of Matthew's account of the Magi and the star ? What could be the cause of their mistakes? Certainly it was not the author's fault. He described all the events which he held to be important regarding the divine person of Jesus. Neither should we accuse those biblicists who did not have access to the relevant sources of history and literature. It seems that their mistakes came mainly from linguistic difficulties.

Besides the linguistic problems, the reason for mistakes was that the translators did not have a solid knowledge of the history and culture of the ancient Near East which was composed of Babylonian, Hebrew and Greek traditions. The Christian Gospel brought unheard of teachings which seemed to be quite contrary to the religious cults of that age. At the same time it was deceptive that there was a certain similarity between the form of expression of some scriptural passages and mythological narratives. Scholars often misunderstood also the intention of the first Church Fathers who had exaggerated the allegorical interpretation of the star of Bethlehem. (1)

In those centuries the nations were living in a world of mythology and astrology, so they believed that their fate was determined by the stars. The practice of astrology belonged to magic, and people were afraid of the magi, thinking them to be sorcerers who possessed mysterious forces or secret powers.

The Christian priests tried to free their faithful from those fatal views and condemned the false magi and astrology. The Fathers of the Church were of the opinion that the Magi were not, in fact, able to predict the Savior's birth from their knowledge of the stellar constellations. But the Old Testament prophets had predicted that kings would come from the East to Jerusalem bringing gold and frankincense for the Messiah. Throughout the centuries the exegetes followed this tradition, and they saw only the fulfillment of the prophecies in Matthew's narrative. The faithful were more and more accustomed to the beautiful story: Some kings came from the eastern countries to Jerusalem to worship the newborn king of the Jews, while a star went before them and stopped over the grotto of Bethlehem.

In this form the story resembles an oriental star saga, but it does not correspond to the original text of the Gospel. This incorrect interpretation was the reason for the many objections which have arisen since the 18th century concerning Matthews's account. The objections some scholars made were based on incorrect translations, and these were in part legitimate.

The most important objections were the following:

- As history testifies, kings from the eastern countries never went to Jerusalem to pay homage to a king of the Jews.
- If they were astrologers, then it was nonsense that they sought in Jerusalem the king whose star they had seen in the East. Why would they then go to a western city ?
- If they saw an actual star, it could not go ahead of them and finally stop above a place.
- If it was a mysterious light phenomenon, they would not call it a star.
- From a theological viewpoint it is incorrect or even superstitious to see any connection between the birth of Christ and the course of the stars. Moses and the prophets condemned any theory that the stars could be deities who steered the destiny of men.
- Astrology has still many disciples, and if Matthew's text should be interpreted astrologically, it would nourish superstition. (2)

In consideration of these objections, or rather because of certain mistakes, scholars came to the conclusion that the 2nd chapter of Matthew does not have real historical value. They supposed that Matthew himself, or his Greek interpreter, had given this popular literary frame to the birth of Jesus, like the narrative midrashim in rabbinic literature.

Other scholars would save the authenticity of Matthew's narrative by interpreting it in a figurative sense or taking it for a divine wonder. It is always easier to think of an inexplicable wonder than to seek a scientific explanation for a rare natural phenomenon. But the writers of the Gospel were not naively credulous men. They controlled their sources carefully, and they reported events faithfully. When they wrote of an event which had taken place through an immediate intervention of God, they made this quite clear. Thus also Matthew emphasizes the preternatural birth of Jesus, as a fulfillment of Isaiah's prophecy: "He was conceived by the power of the Holy Spirit and born of the Virgin Mary". The star of Bethlehem, however, is described as a natural phenomenon, and in this context Matthew does not refer to the prophets, but only to the Magi from the East.

When it is possible to find a natural explanation of an event on the basis of the literal sense of the narrative, then it is not necessary to interpret the event from the point of view of the miraculous. On the other hand, we can, indeed, see in natural events a figurative or symbolic significance which gives rise in us to a sense of awe and admiration. In the language of Scripture there are various metaphors and many symbols. Readers are often confusing these modes of expression, and so they misinterpret the meaning of revelation. For example the Psalmist sings: "The heavens declare the glory of God, and the firmament proclaims his handiwork" (Ps 19). The Psalmist did not personify the stars and the heavens. But here the visible heavens and the firmament are natural symbols which actually represent and declare the power of their Creator. The "glory" and the "hand" are metaphors, that is applications of terms to God, to whom they are not literally applicable, but they figuratively describe the activity of an invisible Supreme Being.

Xavier Léon-Dufour wrote of this matter in the preface to the Dictionary of Biblical Theology:

There is a difference between metaphor and a biblical symbol. The biblical symbol is rooted in divine revelation. God speaks to us through his creation and also by means of the very history which he governs. The Bible does not know two different heavens, one material and another spiritual, but the visible firmament reveals the mystery of its Creator and his work. The Scriptures declare that the first heaven and the first earth shall pass away, but so long as they subsist, their impression on us is indispensable, because at the same time they reveal both the transcendence and the immanence of God. The stars and the earth, the light and the darkness, all the natural phenomena retain their complete symbolic sense in divine revelation. However, the deepest meaning of the cosmic symbols will be fully clear only when they are understood in connection with the history of Christ. When the Son of God was born in order to live among us in a human body, he definitively established the truth of the symbolic language of the divine revelation. The human imagination transforms the realities into metaphors, but Christ reveals the true value of each natural phenomenon which occurred already before his birth and which proclaimed him. The heavens and the earth are not everlasting realities, they have not final value in themselves; the true meaning of their existence is that they proclaim Jesus Christ for us (Léon-Dufour 1970).

In this sense we can understand that a certain configuration of stars might have proclaimed the birth of Christ. But how would such a phenomenon have to be viewed in the light of the literal sense of Matthew's account?

The Original Text and Its Literal Sense

Studying the Greek and Syriac texts of Matthew, we quickly realize that the manner of expression found in the narrative about the star of Bethlehem differs from the style of the subsequent chapters. This shows that the author drew his material from an original source. He spoke about an event to which neither he or the other apostles could have been witnesses. However, what Luke says in his prologue is also valid for this author's work. He wrote down what he "had closely looked into from the beginning"; in other words, what had been verified by the harmonious testimony of various witnesses.

There would have been many living witnesses to the Magi's visit, since their arrival was a very rare event compared to the frequent arrival of caravans of commerce. Matthew emphasizes that they were observed by "all Jerusalem". They were recognized by their distinctive garb and news also spread that they spoke about some star in connection with the birth of a king. All the more did this remain in the people's memory, given that the slaughter of the infants in Bethlehem was also linked with their visit. This is witnessed to by an Essene manuscript from the beginning of the first century which reports that at Herod's command "there followed a massacre of children and the elderly like the one which occurred in Egypt at the time of Moses' birth" (*Assumptio Mosis*, 6: 22; this refers to Pharaoh's murder of the male children born to the Hebrew women immediately upon their birth, as in Exod 1: 22).

All this, however, could not have been sufficient reason for Matthew to accept the story. Who could have convinced him that the Magi really visited Jesus in Bethlehem? And who saw the star they spoke about ? Besides the visitors from the East, the following people play a role in the event: Herod, the chief priests, the scribes, Joseph, and Jesus' mother. Still, the only completely credible witnesses to the entire event were Joseph, Mary, and the Magi themselves. It was certainly Joseph, as head of the family, who received the mysterious visitors from the East and let them into the house. Matthew, however, does not even mention him in this scene; only Jesus' mother is named as principal witness: "They saw the child with Mary his mother" (Mt 2: 11).

Joseph was no longer alive when the account of Jesus' life and teaching was written. But Mary had been familiar with Joseph's personal life, including his dreams, recorded by Matthew, through which he received the angelic message. They certainly must have looked up in the sky and seen the star the Magi pointed out one night upon their arrival in Bethlehem. Obviously Jesus' mother was the most reliable eyewitness to verify the Magi's visit and their statements concerning the star. The star would never have found its way into the Gospel if she had not acknowledged the veracity of this tradition.

Nevertheless, no one could have given such a precise and expert account about the star except one of the Magi mentioned in the text. At the time of Jesus' birth astronomers like them were only found in Babylon. Their knowledge and authority were recognized throughout the cultural world of their day. Neither Herod nor the scribes thought of doubting their assertions that a king had been born in Judaea, even though they did not believe that he would be the prophesied Messiah. The words of the Magi, as quoted by Matthew, show that they had observed "his star" months before; and when they saw it again on the road to Bethlehem "they rejoiced exceedingly with great joy" (as literally in the Greek text: *ekhárêsan kharàn megálên sphódra*, Mt 2: 10). All this concerns their own personal experiences which others could not have known about. Only they could have spoken about these events using such typically Eastern expressions. (3)

It is apparent that Matthew tried to shorten the account of the witnesses. He only recorded what he considered important for understanding what was to follow. Nevertheless, he accurately recorded the astronomical expressions with which every educated person of those times was familiar. It is not his fault if later translators misunderstood a few of his sentences.

We are now going to take a closer look at those sentences which are connected with astronomical expressions (Mt 2: 1-2 and 7-9). On the basis of the three most ancient versions we are going to look for the original and complete meaning of the words. The following English translation was prepared by comparing the Greek, Syriac and Latin texts (4):

1. *Now when Jesus was born in Bethlehem of Judah in the days of Herod the king, Magi came from the east to Jerusalem*
2. *saying: "Where is he who has been born king of [the clan of] Judah for we saw his star in its [evening] rising and have come to pay him homage".*
7. *Then Herod secretly summoned the Magi and ascertained from them the time the star [even then still visible] appeared;*
8. *and he sent them to Bethlehem saying: "Go ...."*
9. *When they had heard the king they set out, and lo, the star which they had [previously] seen in its [evening] rising went before them, while, in its course it halted above [in the direction] where the child was.*

The numbering of the sentences agrees with that typically found in critical editions. The words between brackets are not found in the original text, but they can be inferred from the context and a linguistic analysis of various words. Taken in itself, a strictly literal translation does not help us too much, since some expressions would remain unintelligible for those who are not familiar with either linguistics or astronomy. For this reason some linguistic analysis and explanation are required to demonstrate that the translation is correct.

1. *"from the East"*: Here the Greek word is in the plural (*àpo anatolôn*). Some think this is so because it refers to several countries, as if the Magi had been men of differing nationalities. However, the plural actually originates from the observation that not just the Sun, but also the Moon, and the stars as well, are seen to rise in this direction on the horizon. What is more, in Greek the plural is used to signify this direction of the compass, given that in the singular the word (*anatolê*) refers just to the rising of a star. Syriac and Latin use the singular to signify both; the meaning of the word is determined by the preposition which stands in front of it.

There was no other civilized country in the East at that time except Babylon, which always remained in contact with the people of Judah, who, hearing the word East, would, therefore, immediately have thought of Babylon. The exile which their people experienced there lived on in their memories. They read the story over and over again in the books of the prophets Ezekiel and Daniel. They sang the Psalter: "by the waters of Babylon, there we sat down and wept" and cursed "the daughter of Babylon" (Ps 137). Matthew knew this very well and in his first chapter he mentions the Babylonian Exile four times. Perhaps he does not mention the city here because it was considered the center of wickedness and idolatry from which, in the people's mind, good magi could not possibly have come.

2. *"Where is he who was born king of [the clan of] Judah?"* They were looking for one whom they knew to have been born king in Judah; but obviously they did not want to pay homage to the son of King Herod. The expression "king of [the clan of] Judah" (*basileùs tôn Iudaiôn*) refers to the place of birth, rather than to the king of a certain country. This is verified both by the interpretation of the star and the prophecy quoted in the text. According to the prophets, the Messiah was to arise from the tribe of Judah and was to be born within its territorial confines.

Judah was one of Jacob's twelve sons and the territory around Jerusalem was in the possession of his tribe. The Magi from the East would also have known this, but they were not familiar with Bethlehem. The scribes in Jerusalem enlightened them: Bethlehem was the princely city of Judah because David, the first king of all the tribes of Israel, came from there and according to the prophet Micah, the Messiah-King would also be born there (Mic 2:6).

The Aramaic and Syriac texts of the Gospel do not name Judaea as an independent country. During the Greek and Roman empires the whole of Palestine was designated Judaea. Jerusalem was its Capitol and, by the good graces of Augustus Caesar, Herod the Great was King of Judaea.

St. Jerome, in his explanatory notes to the Vulgate Version mentions more than once that he translated several expressions into Latin from the Hebrew text, when he considered them more accurate than the Greek version. He makes the following comments concerning the sentences cited above:

> It is to the disgrace of the Judaeans that they found out about the birth of Christ from foreigners. The star rose in the East, and they could have known about its coming from the prophecy of Balaam whose successors they [i.e., the Magi] were. See The Book of Numbers, "A star shall rise of Jacob, and a man shall come forth out of Israel" [Num 24:17]. Accordingly, the Magi came to Judaea at the beckoning of the star. The Judaean priests would no longer be able to claim they had not known about Christ's birth, given that the Magi had asked them where the Messiah was to be born. For they said, "in Bethlehem of Judaea". But this is an error which is attributable to the copyists (*librariorum error*) for we suppose the Evangelist to have written "Judah", as it appears in the Hebrew, not "Judaea". Besides Judaea what other country had a city named Bethlehem, thus requiring that such a distinction should be made ? Judah, however, was mentioned because there was another Bethlehem in Galilee. See The Book of Joshua [19:15; there was a village named Bethlehem which belonged to the tribe of Zebulun]. Finally, there was the certainty provided by the prophecy of Micah:

13

"and you Bethlehem land of Judah" (St. Jerome, *Comment. in Matth.*, 1: 2-5).

The old translation (i.e., "Where is the newborn king of the Jews" or "the infant king of the Jews") is wrong and misleading. Who were the Magi looking for anyway? At that time the Jewish nation and state did not exist in the way that we understand them today. The Hebrew attributive adjective *jehùdi* which means Judaean (*ioudàios* in Greek and *iudaeus* in Latin) derives from the noun *Jehudah* which means Judah. Its anglicized form is *Jew* which has, since the Middle Ages, been generalized to include all the Israelites who are now living in European and American countries. In this way the word lost its original biblical meaning. The distinction between "Israel" and "Judah" is apparent throughout the entire biblical period.(5)

The meaning of the Magi's question goes far beyond the infant king or newborn king of a nation. The word "infant" or "newborn" is not even found in the original text of Matthew. The expression *ho tekhteìs basileùs* means the one born king. (*Tekhteìs* is a participle which, set off by the definite article, is an attribute of the king.) The Magi were looking for the one who had actually been born king. They came to this conclusion, as they say in the following sentence, by observing the heavens: "for we saw his star in its evening rising". The New English Bible renders the question of the Magi in this very literal sense: "Where is the child who is born to be king...?" Commenting on the passage of the loaves (Jn 6), Archbishop Fulton J. Sheen says: "When Jesus had shown his Divine Power in multiplying the bread, the people would proclaim him as King, but they could not make him King; He was born a King. The Wise Men knew this" (Sheen 1977, p.135).

For the eastern peoples the kingly office carried with it the dignity of high priest. But only one who received from heaven the power, the innate ability, to exercise the office of king and high priest could accept this dignity. The apostle Paul explains this in his letter to the Hebrews: "Nor did Christ give himself the glory of becoming high priest, but he had it from the one who said to him: 'You are my son, today I have become your father'". Even at the Annunciation, before his birth he was called "the Son of the Most High" that is of the Heavenly Father (Heb 5: 5; Lk 1: 32).

The priests and scribes of Jerusalem understood the Magi's question only too well. Nevertheless they remained silent because they were afraid of Herod. They remembered how he had already had more than 600 scribes imprisoned, and several hundred priests executed; how, a year before that, he had had his wife and two sons killed in his fear to preserve his own power. This was the reason that the Magi's undisguised question caused such alarm throughout the entire city.

It was no mere coincidence that the scribes cited the prophet Micah who, 700 years earlier, prophesied where the Messiah would be born (Mic 5: 1-4; Mt 2: 6). The prophet did not speak about the king of the Jews. Rather, he spoke about one who, despite the fact that he would come from Bethlehem of Judah, would, nevertheless, be the high priest of all Israel, that is, of the new chosen people. At the same time, the prophecy emphasizes that the time and place of his birth restricts neither his origin nor his person; for he is to come from eternity with his almighty power. Here the Hebrew speaks of the Messiah's "origin" with the same expression it employs to describe the Suns rising and its course; for the Sun rises higher and higher and its rays fill the entire world.

"For we saw his star in its evening rising and have come to pay him homage": This sentence is one of the highlights of the narrative for it sheds light on the meaning of the entire event. The Greek text is as follows:

eìdomen gàr autû tòn astéra en tê anatolê kaì êlthomen proskynêsai autô.

This sentence is not isolated from the preceding question, since the conjunction *gàr* (for) serves to connect explanatory and causal subordinate clauses. The Magi's explanation is as follows: We have come here because we observed the star of the one born king here; and we want to pay him our homage.

It is very significant that every noun is proceeded by the definite article, and the possessive pronoun (*autû tòn astéra*) is emphasized: it was his star which we saw. This is determined even more precisely by the expression *en tê anatolê*, i.e., in its evening rising; that is to say, they saw it in the company of other stars. They reexperience the same phenomenon on the road to Bethlehem, and this fact emphasizes its importance even more.

In this context the word *astér* does not stand only for a single star. Rather, it indicates a certain arrangement of stars or even a constellation. The expression *en tê anatolê* usually indicates the rise of a wandering star, i.e. a planet, in a specific constellation, which occurs precisely at sunset or shortly thereafter. Both the Hebrews and Greeks appropriated these astronomical expressions from the Babylonians.

With the exception of this passage from Matthew's 2nd chapter, the expression *en tê anatolê* does not occur anywhere else in the Bible. However, it is often found in its plural form when it refers to the eastern directions (*apò anatolôn* as in the 1st verse). It is not at all inconsistent that in Greek the plural indicates the eastern direction, since the point where the Sun and the planets rise shifts a few degrees across the horizon over the course of the four seasons. The point of sunrise between the Summer solstice (June 23) and the Winter solstice (December 23) moves from Northeast to Southeast.

In the Latin expression there is no definite article and *oriens* means both the eastern direction and the rising of the stars. The meaning depends on the context and on the particle *ab*: *ab oriente* means "from the east", whereas *in oriente* can mean either "in the rising" referring to a star, or otherwise "in the east".

In the Syriac expression the word is found in the singular and its meaning is more definite: *men madneha* = from the east, and *be-madeneha* = in the rising. St. Jerome understood this well. In the text quoted above he clearly says: *oritur in oriente stella,* that is "the star rises in the east", (he says "in the east", because the Magi had first observed it in Babylon, east of Jerusalem). But in the Vulgate version of the Gospel the ambiguity of the Latin word obscures the meaning of the original text. Unfortunately the following faulty translation is still found in many editions of the Bible: "We have seen his star in the East". The first literal translation of this astronomical expression appeared in 1956 in the French edition of the Jerusalem Bible: *l'astre vu a son lever.* Since then subsequent translations have for the most part followed suit, without, however, specifying that it was a question of the star's evening rising. In accordance with Babylonian tradition Greek astronomy uses a separate word to indicate the early morning rising of a star (as *epitolê* or *phàsis*), whereas the expression *en tê anatolê* specifies the position and time of a star's rising at dusk. This distinction is very important for the proper understanding of the following sentence:

7. *"Then Herod... ascertained from them the time the star [even then still visible] appeared".*

Those who are acquainted with the terminology of ancient astronomy will notice at once that here too the original text betrays underlying astronomical expressions. The eyewitnesses surely gave more detailed accounts of the phenomenon, which the author in turn summarized in a few words. Even the first translators might have experienced difficulties when reading the original Aramaic text. What was it that Herod wanted to determine so accurately from the Magi? And what was their response to him?

The Syriac language is closely related to Aramaic and, therefore, helps to explain certain Greek expressions which are otherwise difficult to understand. Comparing the texts we see that here too St. Jerome relied on the Aramaic text when translating this sentence into Latin:

Greek: *tòn khrónon toû phainoménou astéros* =
the time of the appearing star;
Syriac: *beajnà zabnà etehezi lehún kaukebá* =
what time (date) the star appeared to them;
Latin: *tempus stellae quae apparuit eis* =
the time (date) of the star which appeared to them.

In the Syriac as well as in the Chaldaean language the verb *etehezi* specifies the first occasion after a lengthy intermission that a planet appears over the horizon immediately before sunrise, when the Sun's rays have not yet obscured it. In Greek astronomy this phenomenon was described by the verb *phainomai* and its various forms (*phaìnestai, phàsis, epháne*) which can mean to be seen or to shine forth, and as is the case here, to appear. In the sentence cited above, the participle (*phainoménos*), which modifies the word "star", also refers to the early morning appearance of a planet. Moreover, this present participle corresponds to the imperfect (*praesens participium imperfectum*), thus signifying that the star was still visible on a nightly basis when Herod spoke with the Magi.

The other interesting thing about the Syriac text is that the word *kaukebá* (star) exactly corresponds to the word *kakkabu*, its Babylonian equivalent, and to its Hebrew counterpart *kokheba*. In colloquial usage this word did not usually refer solely to a star; rather it was the name of the brightest planet, Jupiter. *Astér Phaéton* (Glistening Star) is the Greek equivalent of the Accadian *Kakkabu pizu*, and the Greek name of the other bright planet, Saturn, was *Astér Khronou* (Star of Time) or *Phaínon* (Sparkler). From a philological and astronomical point of view it is possible that these designations were condensed into the three Greek words *khrónon phainoménou astéros* in the text of Matthew. Thus the original narrative's full meaning could have been as follows: Herod asked the Magi at what date they first saw the "Glistening Star" (Jupiter) in its early heliacal rising, that is, when its first dawn rising took place.

Why did Herod want to know this date ? What was the Magi's response to him? This is found in verse 16 where it is said that after the Magi's return home, Herod had all the male children killed who were "two years old and under, according to the time (date) he had ascertained from the Wise Men" (i.e., from the Magi).

Herod probably thought the visitors from the east were Chaldaeans who would be ready to do his bidding for the right price. That is why he told them to: "Go and find out all about the child, and when you have found him, let me know" (Mt 2: 8). Like any other ruler in those days, Herod believed in common astrology according to which the date for a king's birth was determined when Jupiter, the "Star of kings", first rose just before the rising of the life-giving Sun. The Magi certainly did not lie to Herod, but they would not have given him any of the particulars either. The only thing they might have said is something like this: "his star first appeared at the end of last year". Detailed astronomical explanations will be given in Chapter Three. Now we must content ourselves with tracing out the most important facts. The data for Jupiter's phases was discovered on cuneiform tablets in Babylon. According to these data, which our astronomical calculations have shown to be accurate, Jupiter's first early morning rising would occur in the 12th month (i.e., in mid-March) of the 304th year of the Babylonian calendar. However, when the Magi arrived in Jerusalem they had the star's last evening rising in mind, which, according to their calendar, occurred in the 6th month (i.e., in mid-September) of the year 305. In both the Jerusalem and the Babylonian calendars the first day of the new year was marked by the first New Moon in Spring. That year the first day of the first month (Nisanu 1st) was April 2nd. It is understandable, therefore, that Herod only had the boys killed who were under two years of age. (If the Magi had arrived two years after Jesus' birth, Herod would have killed the two-year-olds as well). "They were warned in a dream not to go back to Herod, and returned to their own country by a different way....Herod was furious when he realized that he had been outwitted by the Wise Men..." (Mt 2: 12 and 16).

It most likely took two or three months before Herod finally realized that he had been outsmarted and resolved to put the children in Bethlehem to death. Thus the Holy Family had plenty of time for the flight into Egypt. But Herod could not even have known whether the Magi had found the child "born to be king" who threatened his power and rule. In any case, from their response to his question he concluded that the child was born the previous year, that is, he would by then have been more than one year old. This is why he had every male child killed who was "two years old or under". He thought the king Messiah was surely among them. Thus Matthew's two pieces of information, namely the time of the star's appearance and the fact that the children were under two years of age, implicitly contain the Magi's answer to Herod's question.

Let us now, however, return to the road leading to Bethlehem, for the account of the events which unfolded there proves to be the most difficult part of the narrative:

9. "...they set out, and lo, the star which they had [previously] seen in its [evening] rising went before them, while in its course it halted above [in the direction] where the child was."

It is easy to sense from the dense style of this verse that it is also a compressed version of a more detailed account. The same "star" is both the subject and the object of the sentence. The dependent clause is directly connected to the main sentence: "...they set out, and lo,...". In other words, the whole event happens on the road from Jerusalem to Bethlehem, and this direction is important. The predicate and the participle are in a specific time which is called the historic past (the Greek *aorist* tense) and which is also used to describe periodic astronomical phenomena. In the following excerpt of the Greek text the English equivalent of each word is placed underneath:

eporeuthêsan kaì idoù ho astér,
they set out and lo the star

hòn eîdon en tê anatolê,
which they had seen in its rising,

*proêgen autoùs héôs **elthôn** estàthè*
went before them while **in its course** it halted

epànô hoû ên tò paidìon.
above where the child was.

The expression *kaì idoù* is both adverbial and conjunctive. As a result, it functions here to connect the assertion which follows it to the preceding clause, while calling our attention to the fact that this assertion is obviously true. This demonstrative particle occurs often in the Gospel but not always with the same meaning. It usually has one of the following two meanings: "Here is / there are" or "Lo and behold" (*idoù* is a part of the verb *ideîn* = to see). In eyewitness accounts, however, the word is always a call for attention: look! hey!

It is in this context that the word *idoù* agrees in meaning with the Babylonian *tammar* which has to do with the observation of stars. This particular meaning of the word is indicated by the relative clause: "...which they had [previously] seen in its [evening] rising". They recognize it as the same star they had seen months before and whose course, with all probability, they had already calculated in advance. We arrive at this conclusion from their statement several verses earlier: "we saw his star". Now, in the present verse, they are referring back to this, and, as a result, we end up with a verb form expressing the distant historical past, i.e., "...the star which they had seen"; *eîdon* is the active aorist pluperfect of the verb *ideîn* = to see, which can also mean to observe.

The expression *ho astér proêgen autoùs* is rendered as "the star went before them" (Revised Standard Version); or "it went forward"

19

(Jerusalem Bible). What is its literal sense? *Proêgen* is the historical continous past tense (aorist imperfect) of the verb *proêgéomai* which in itself can signify: "to go before", "to go forward", "to go ahead", "to precede", or "to proceed". Here it is followed by the personal pronoun (*autoùs*) which is in the accusative case, as it is in the Vulgate Latin text: *antecedebat eos* = it preceded them. That is to say, it was not going ahead of them (or it was not proceeding in front of them), since in this case St. Jerome would have said; *ibat ante eos*.

The corresponding Syriac text: *kaukeba âzel huà qedâmajhùn* literally means "the star went before them", but in the language of astronomy this signifies a shift in a planet's position in a given direction, as viewed by an observer on the Earth. According to the customary translation the star "went ahead of them" which is often interpreted to mean that it guided them. Of course, even this is comprehensible, if taken figuratively, but in this context such a figurative interpretation is not satisfactory.

Here we are face to face with expressions that belong to ancient astronomy and which, in turn, can only be correctly explained by astronomers. What we are dealing with here is the apparent motion of heavenly bodies. When we walk along a straight path in the evenings and look up into the cloudless sky the stars seem to proceed in front of us, and when we stop, they do too, (for if they were moving in front of us in the same way, say, that a distant car might proceed in front of us then, if we went fast enough we would eventually reach them). Even children know this is just an illusion. Matthew, too, knew it, as did those eastern travelers who, making their way from Jerusalem to Bethlehem, saw the bright star in front of them in the twilight sky.

What did the Magi mean by saying that "the star went before them"? Archaeological finds witness to the fact that Babylonian astronomers precalculated the courses and positions of the planets. So the Magi could have known that in November of their 305th calendar year the positions of Jupiter and Saturn would coincide and together they would move westwards until they reached their turning points or stationary points; that is to say, until they halted above in the west. In standard language one says then that the planets came to an apparent standstill.

The Magi also knew that this rare phenomenon could be better observed in the West, say, from Jerusalem's 700 meter-high hill than in their own homeland. If they were astronomers, as indeed they were, then their travel agenda probably provided for such observations. The road from Jerusalem to Bethlehem runs southwards. Stars ascending over the horizon reach their highest point in the South. So as the Magi were nearing their destination, only a few kilometers from the village, they could have seen the star above the hills of Bethlehem. Precisely in this sense they could have said that the star went before them, or preceded them.

Those who had not the slightest familiarity with astronomical expression and phenomena completely misinterpreted the text here in question. They imagined that the star really proceeded southward in front of the Magi like some sort of guide who lights the way. The original text does not envision anything of the sort. What the Magi are saying is that the star was already visible there just as they were nearing Bethlehem. Viewed from Jerusalem it was there before them, i.e. previous to them. It went before them in time (not in space).

The statement "while in its course it halted" or came to a standstill, emphasizes this even more. The adverb of time, *héôs*, does not just signify the end of a period of time, i.e., "until"; it can also signify simultaneity, i.e. "while". The same is true of the Syriac *edama* and the Latin *usque dum* (*usque* = continuously, *dum* = during the time that; taken together they mean "while"). The grammatical structure of the sentence indicates simultaneity. The adverb of time is followed by a present participle and a verb expressing the continuous historical past (the aorist tense in Greek and the imperfect subjunctive in Latin).

Héôs elthôn esthàthê: the key word here is the adverbial participle *elthôn* (in Syriac *dethá* and in Latin *veniens*), the meaning of which is "coming", or "going"; that is to say while moving. When referring to the stars, the best English translation seems to be "in its course".

The form of the verb *érkhomai* (to come, or to go) which expresses the historical past is *elthein*, from which the adverbial participle *elthôn* is derived. Therefore, we have the sentence: "in the star's continuous course [among the fixed stars]"; that is to say "in its motion". The word *elthôn* had been omitted in most translations because it was not understood, or else it was misunderstood and translated as "the star... arrived". *Estàthê* (it halted) is the indicative historical past (passive aorist indicative) of the transitive verb *histánai* (to stop) and as such it always expresses a temporary stopping. The indicative mood shows that we are dealing with an event that really happened. The predicate *estàthê* gives the result of the motion indicated by the preceding participle *elthôn* using a passive grammatical structure; i.e. the star had just come to a standstill in its course, but not of its own accord. Rather, this was due to the laws governing its motion. The Syriac version says exactly the same thing: *edama dethá qam* (while it went it stopped). Likewise the Latin: *usquedum veniens staret* (while coming it halted). Here the subjunctive mood (*conjunctivus imperfectum*) gives us the feeling that the star apparently came to a temporary stop in its continuous motion. In astronomy this entire statement serves to describe the planets' seasonal forward and backward motion. By modern astronomical terms those motions are defined as direct, namely from west to east, and retrograde, from east to west across the sky, as compared to the fixed stars (see Fig. 13: p. 87).

The word *epànô* (above) is also connected to the adverbial participle *elthôn* which proceeds it, and together they function as an adverb of time and direction. If followed by a place name in the genitive case then it is to be translated: "above the place". In the ancient versions, however, there are no place names to be found. The Syriac *leel men ajkà* and the Latin *super ubi* both indicate direction. In other words, the star while moving stopped over there, i.e., in the direction where the Magi were going. Here the Syriac *men ajkà* is the clearest: *men* = from, and *ajkà* = where; taken together they mean "from where". The final relative clause, that is: "where the child was", understood in the present context, likewise refers to the general direction of the Magi's final destination.

Based on all of this, the specific meaning of the sentence is as follows:

the star, in its apparent backward motion, came to a standstill, seen from Jerusalem, just over Bethlehem.

This translation and linguistic analysis is convincing in its own right, and it shows the authenticity and originality of the gospel account, because:

- the chronological order of the events and the astronomical phenomena is consistent and it conforms to reality;
- heavenly phenomena, which were of special importance to ancient astronomers, are recounted with expressions which are known to have been used in Babylonian and Greek astronomy (6);
- the author of the gospel writes down the events from the perspective of the Magi, who were eyewitnesses to all that happened, and for this reason, he departs from his otherwise customary style and uses unique expressions when quoting the Magi's own words: "they rejoiced exceedingly with great joy" when, on the road to Bethlehem, once again they saw the familiar star in the right direction.

Having examined the original biblical text, we would like to know more about who these mysterious visitors from the East were, when they arrived in Bethlehem, and what they saw in the sky.

True Story and Legend

How can one distinguish a true story from an invented legend? This is often a problem when we have to judge the historical value of ancient narratives. The original works of ancient historiographers were lost, some of them remained only in much later copies, and the copyists could have added some legendary elements to the factual story. For example, Tacitus was the most famous historiographer of the first century, but the oldest copy of his works is only preserved in fragments of the 9th century.

The authors of the Gospel also wrote their accounts in the first century, and from the second century onwards the copies of their writings are left to us in very good condition. From the viewpoint of the history of literature the New Testament is one the best preserved and most authenticated writings of antiquity. Notwithstanding, in the 20th century, biblical researchers began to apply the methods of literary and historical criticism in order to determine the literary form, the historical value and the literal meaning of the Gospel narratives. The most important questions are the following: Who is the author and what is his intention in relating a certain story? Why is it set in this particular context within the Gospel? What meaning does the Evangelist attach to it?

The author of the first gospel is Matthew the apostle, otherwise known as Levi, son of Alphaeus. His name is mentioned seven times by the evangelists and to his story are also dedicated particular chapters, which indicates the importance of his personality. He was a tax collector in Capharnaum, by the road along the northern bank of the Sea of Galilee. When Jesus saw him sitting by the customs house, he said to him, "Follow me". And leaving everything Matthew got up and followed him. Then in Jesus' honor he held a great reception in his house, and with them at table was a large gathering of tax collectors and others (Lk 5: 27).

Although the tax collectors were educated scribes, the Pharisees took them as public sinners, because they often used to demand more taxes from the people than was prescribed by law. At that time Jesus was already an accepted master (*rabbi*), and the Pharisees reproach him because he was at the same table with those sinners. Matthew also mentioned this story in his writings, and he quoted what Jesus said to them in reply: "It is not the healthy who need a doctor, but the sick. And indeed I did not come to call the virtuous, but sinners" (Mt 9: 12).

Matthew's name can always be found among the twelve apostles who permanently followed Jesus in his three years of teaching. Among the others he was the best educated and the most skilled, as the others were only fishermen. So he proved to be the most suitable for the responsibility of being the first to gather and put into writing all the traditions related to Jesus' life and all the events to which he was an eye witness. According to the bishops of the first centuries he wrote in Aramaic, and in his Greek text some Hebraisms can also be found, which show a specific Aramaic usage. He follows a style like the historiography of the Old Testament, and thereby he expresses his intention with the writing: he will report historical facts, that is, events which really happened, and prophecies which are fulfilled.

From the very first statement to the last he wants to prove that Jesus of Nazareth is the Messiah whose coming the prophets have foretold. In His person and work all the messianic prophecies were fulfilled. Like the Old Hebrew historiography he begins his gospel with "a genealogy of Jesus Christ, son of David, son of Abraham...." Its aim is to show how Jesus is connected with the leading recipients of the messianic promise, i.e. with Abraham and with David's royal line. However, the continuity of physical descent is broken by the last member: "and Jacob was the father of Joseph the husband of Mary; of her was born Jesus who is called Christ". In the following verses Matthew explains that Joseph was Jesus' legal father only. The reason is that according to ancient mentality legal paternity (adoption or levirate) is sufficient to confer all hereditary rights; the rights here are those of messianic line. "His mother Mary was betrothed to Joseph; but before they came to live together she was found to be with child through the Holy Spirit... Now all this took place to fulfill the words spoken by the Lord through the prophet: The virgin will conceive and give birth to a son and they will call him Emmanuel, a name which means God-is-with-us" (Mt 1: 16-23; Is 7: 14).

With this revelation Matthew begins his gospel as a dramatic account in seven acts of the coming of the Kingdom of God ("Kingdom of the Heavens" in Matthew). The second scene of the first act is the visit of the Magi in Bethlehem. This scene is worth special attention, because it precisely explains the importance of the events to come. According to the Fathers of the Church this narrative enlightens the central message of Matthew's gospel: (1) Jesus as the Savior was born for all men, and (2) he is the Lord of the entire cosmos. Let us now look closer at these two points. While Israel does not recognize the Messiah in Jesus and the chief priests reject Him, the Gentiles not only recognize Him but also accept Him happily, and Christ also accepts them, because He is the Savior King of all people and nations. To prove this Matthew cites the sermons given by Christ in Judaea and Jerusalem, where He kept preaching that His Kingdom is open to all the nations: "many will come from east and west to take their places with Abraham and Isaac and Jacob at the feast in the kingdom of heaven; but the subjects of the kingdom will be turned out into the dark" (Mt 8: 11). This is because the scribes and the Pharisees of Judaea despise the other nations and they also condemn Jesus. They are waiting for a Messiah, who based on a great political power will free Israel from Roman rule. He derides them for their mistakes and He warns them with clear parables: "I tell you, then, that the kingdom of God will be taken from you and given to a people who will produce its fruit" (Mt 21: 43). Finally, just before His ascension, He takes leave of His friends with these words: "All authority in heaven and on earth has been given to me. Go, therefore, make disciples of all the nations..." (Mt 28: 18).

All the nations and all men knew and still know what is the "kingdom of heaven" where everyone can live, healthy and satisfied, where righteousness, love and peace rule permanently. This is so specific to the writing of Matthew that it was later called the "Catholic Gospel". According to the meaning of the Greek word *katholikos*, it is an invitation addressed universally to all people.

Christ also leads the people towards Himself by the phenomena of nature, especially the scientists, who are really seeking Him, as He is the supreme Lord of the entire cosmos. There is no use in arguing whether Matthew consciously intended to show also this with the account of the Star of Bethlehem. The inspiration which lead him in his writings obviously meant this as well. (On page 9 we quoted the reflections of Léon-Dufour, which support this).

The Magi coming from the east represent not only the nations but also the best scientists of that age. They are actually helped by astronomical observations to find Jesus, while the uninstructed shepherds are lead to Him by the angels (Lk 2: 8).

The unexcelled knowledge of Jesus, about which the apostles unanimously testify, is best emphasized in the Gospel of Matthew. St. Paul states that "in him all the treasures of wisdom and knowledge are hidden" (Col 2: 3). According to the thinking of that age, real knowledge is wisdom and power which show up in deeds. Matthew, as an eye witness, convincingly shows that Jesus is not only a doctor who is able to heal all illnesses; not only a teaching master, who precisely knows and understands the Scriptures; he also knows the forces of nature, and keeps them under his power: the bread and fish multiplied in his hands are enough to feed five thousand people, then he walks on the water of the Sea of Galilee and calms the storm, and the admiring people say, "what sort of man is this, that even the winds and the sea obey him" (Mt 8: 27; 14: 13-33). Jesus clearly foresees future events. He foretells to his disciples his crucifixion and that "on the third day he will rise again" (Mt 20: 19). He foresees also coming wars and earthquakes, the fall of Jerusalem and the end of the World: "Immediately after the distress of those days the sun will be darkened, the moon will lose its brightness, the stars will fall from the sky and the powers of heaven will be shaken" (Mt 24: 29). The "powers of heaven" mean the stars and all other celestial forces, or the gravitation which holds the elements of the universe together. With all his words and deeds Christ shows that He has power to save men from death: "All authority in heaven and earth has been given to me." Words such as these must capture the interest of people in any age.

The flourishing interest in astrology aside, we live now in the great age of astrophysics. Modern astrophysics has become the peak of the natural sciences. It encompasses our entire knowledge of mathematics, physics and chemistry. We are making ever larger telescopes (such as the Hubble Space Telescope), and we study the most remote stars through the use of space craft. What is the point of all this research, enormously expensive as it is? We shall address this question in another section. For the moment let it be said that the celestial bodies are like individual laboratories and we benefit from observing the processes in the atmospheres and structures of the stars and planets. Our life and well-being on earth can be improved through these observations. Indeed these improvements have always been the driving force behind scientific research. Essentially this motivation was the same down through antiquity. Our ancestors sought to find a relationship between human life and the celestial bodies, but we see this relationship in a different way from that of our ancestors.

The phenomenon of the star of the Magi is integral to the narrative of Matthew and to understanding the true sense of his second chapter. Interest and belief in the stars was a dominant feature of life at that time not only in the surrounding nations but also in Israel itself. The motion of the stars played a more important role in the everyday life of the people of that time than is the case with us today. Indeed time computations were always and everywhere carried out by astronomical observations. So the star of the Magi has its place within the central cultural scene of that time.

In any case, we would like to know whether we can trust the authors of the Gospel and what is the historical value of the events related. Has everything happened in the same way as they wrote about it? We can judge the historical value of certain chapters based on the analysis of their literary form. On the other hand, it is important to evaluate the early Christian tradition which had developed before the Gospel was written. It is interesting to observe that this tradition was unanimous in relation to some major events in Jesus' life. This is backed up by the letters of the apostles and also by the writings of the Apostolic Fathers. The major parts of this early Christian tradition are well preserved also by the Apocryphal Gospels. These Apocrypha were written by anonymous authors, beginning in the 2nd century, under the name of one of the apostles, but were never included in the canonical books of Scripture, because analysis has proven that some legendary elements have been included in their narratives.

Those who report about historical events usually relate the flat facts and they note exactly the time and place of the happenings. Thus Matthew writes at the beginning of his narrative that at the time of King Herod, when Jesus was born in Bethlehem of Judaea, Magi came from the East to Jerusalem. Then he refers to Archelaus, the son of

Herod, who reigned in Judaea at the time when the Holy Family returned from Egypt to Nazareth of Galilee. These are historical individuals and places, which also correspond to the data coming from other sources of that age.

But at the same time a true story may well be colored by the exaggerations of an artistic imagination and with characterizations drawn from legends. This is what happened to the account of the star of the Magi from the beginning of the 2nd century. A good example of this is the so called "Protoevangelium of James". This was probably composed by a Greek Christian in Egypt, with the title: *Genesis Marias Apokalypsis Jacob*. This tells about Mary's childhood, her engagement to the widower Joseph, and the dramatic circumstances of Jesus' birth up to the massacre of the Innocents in Bethlehem.

During the 3rd century it was translated into Aramaic, Syriac and Coptic. Later its Latin version spread under the title *Protoevangelium Jacobi*, and it was accorded great respect by Christian people. The original version was gradually extended by the copiers, and as a result 30 different manuscripts have survived. Some parts of it were accepted by the ancient Churches, and these have had great influence on feasts such as Christmas and feasts in honor of the Virgin Mary, and also on religious poetry and art in the second century.

Protoevangelium of James

Let us compare the restrained and objective voice of Matthew with the language of James. The description of the birth of Jesus in the Protoevangelium, begins in chapter 18: "Now there went out a decree from the king Augustus that all inhabitants of Bethlehem of Judaea should be enrolled". (This really happened in the time of Augustus. The apostles, however, knew that he was not a king but Roman Emperor and that his decree for a census was directed to the entire empire and not only to Bethlehem). Then Joseph also went to Judaea together with Mary, his betrothed, who was with child. They took refuge in a cave near Bethlehem, and Joseph "went to fetch Hebrew midwives", because the time came for Mary to have her child. Then he said: "I, Joseph, looked up to the sky and I saw something wonderful. When I looked there I saw the top of the sky [?] as it stopped there and the birds of the heavens [stars?] were motionless there". (Here it is obvious that he speaks of the star of Bethlehem, which according to Matthew stopped in its course, and also Joseph was an eyewitness to it. But James did not understand what they had seen in the sky). Chapter 19 tells that when Jesus was born "a great brightness spread through the cave, so that the eye could not bear it". Then the midwife exclaimed: "A maid gave birth without losing her virginity". Chapter 21 gives a popular description of the Magi's visit:

> And behold, Joseph prepared to go forth to Judaea. And there took place a great tumult in Bethlehem of Judaea. For there came some Magi saying: Where is the king of the Jews? For we have seen his star in the east and we have come to worship him. When Herod heard the chief priests and the scribes saying that the Messiah was to be born in Bethlehem, he questioned the Magi: What sign did you see concerning the new born king? And they said: We saw how an indescribably greater star shone among these stars and dimmed them, so that they no longer shone and so we knew that a king was born for Israel. And Herod said: Go and seek, and when you have found him, tell me, that I also may come to worship him. And the Magi went forth, and behold, they saw stars in the east, and they went before them, until they came to the cave. And it stood over the head of the child...

These last statements were interpreted to mean that a star had entered the cave and stood over the child's head. The scene was represented in this way in some old icons. This is obviously a misinterpretation of the primitive text in the Latin version. The dialogue between the Magi and Herod does not render the sense of the question and answer regarding the star, which is clearly stated in the account of Matthew.

The Protoevangelium ends with the following words: "I, James, wrote these events in the time when Herod died and great disturbance arose in Jerusalem." But on the other hand it comes out in the previous chapters that the author had never been to Jerusalem, and he barely knew anything about the geography and history of Palestine. The setting of the geographical places and the chronological order of the events are always inaccurate and vague. Moreover, certain mythological elements are to be found in this popular text of James. This is the reason why the Church Fathers of the West have never accredited it with true historical value.

The aforementioned English translation was made on the basis of a Latin version. It is taken from the New Testament Apocrypha (Hennecke and Schneemelcher 1963, Vol. 1). It is mainly due to this widespread Latin version that from the sixth century on the star of Bethlehem fell into the obscurity of the legendary world. In the meantime the biblicists have found the oldest Greek manuscript of James' Protoevangelium known as the Papyrus Bodmer V (Testuz 1958; De Strycker 1961). This Greek text is probably a 3rd century copy of the original, and is of much more value than the many later manuscripts used as a basis of previous editions. The verses of chapter 21 which relate the story of the Magi can be rendered literally as follows:

And a great tumult occurred in Bethlehem land of Judah, because some Magi came there and said, Where is the King of Judeans, for we saw his star in the [evening] rising and have come to do him homage. When Herod heard this he was troubled. He sent officers and summoned the Magi, and they informed him about the star... And so, they saw stars in the evening rising, and they went ahead of them, while they [the Magi] came to the cave. And he [Joseph] stood at the head of the child. When the Magi saw the child there with Mary his mother, they took from their bag gifts, gold and frankincense and myrrh. And being warned by an angel they returned to their own country by another way (De Strycker 1961; *Protoevangelium Jacobi* 21).

This Greek third century manuscript indicates Egyptian sources besides the account of Matthew. As he reports, the Holy Family had to stay in Egypt at least for three more years in their flight from Herod. The events that were related at the time by Joseph and Mary regarding the birth of Jesus certainly went on by oral tradition among the Israelites in Egypt. At the beginning of the 2nd century the first Christian communities had evolved from these people, as is proven by some finds of Egyptian papyri. In Zeitoun, a northern quarter of Cairo, one can still see the church which had been built above the house where the Holy Family lived. Clement of Alexandria refers to the Egyptian traditions concerning the date of Jesus' birth.

In the Protoevangelium of James we have Joseph as the witness to these happenings. He is the responsible protector of the family and therefore he is the one who welcomes the mysterious visitors from the east. It is Joseph who stands at the head of the child, not the star. It is even more important to note that this manuscript refers to more than one star occurring in one and the same evening rising, and states that these stars went ahead of the Magi. In this text the recording seems to be accurate as compared with the imaginative embellishments of the later versions. The literary form of this passage is in the usual genre of the ancient infancy narratives. (7)

The Legend

Matthew's record has been even more deformed and colored by the poetry and art of the Middle Ages. The Magi became kings, and the star of Bethlehem was represented as a comet. This corresponded to the atmosphere of that age in which kings were converted and nations christianized. Comets also could be seen more often at that time than nowadays.

In 1301 Halley's Comet appeared extremely bright and for three weeks it was a wonderful sight in the skies of Europe and Asia. This phenomenon was the source of inspiration for the Italian artist, Giotto di Bondone, who had portrayed the Magi as three kings, and painted a great comet above the house in Bethlehem. Painters and sculptors followed Giotto's example for centuries. Their kings always appear in the pompous clothing of their own age with golden crowns and long cloaks with ermine collars. The old gray haired Gaspar represents Europe, the swarthy faced Melchior represents Asia and the black skinned Balthasar stands for Africa.

These names come from Syrian and Egyptian records. A Latin manuscript preserved at the National Library in Paris is the one which first took these names in the 5th century from a Greek chronicle. (*Manuscripta Latina* No.4884, fol.51). Their diffusion is due to the anonymous Byzantine artist who composed his famous mosaic pictures on the wall of the church *S. Apollinare Nuovo* at Ravenna about 550 AD. These mosaics give proof of an authentic tradition. Here the Magi are not dressed in royal pomp, instead they wear the characteristic suit of the Persian scholars and priests, in the same way as they appear on the oldest Christian reliefs. They all have their names written above their heads together with the capital letters SCS (abbreviation of *Sanctus*) which shows that they were venerated as saints.

In 1370, John of Hildesheim, a German Carmelite wrote the "Legend of the Three Kings", on the basis of previous Latin and French sources. The Legend briefly tells the following: At the mouth of the river Euphrates, on the hill of Vaus, twelve astronomers observe the rising of an extremely bright star. At the same time, as led by a marvelous providence the kings of the "three Indias" meet each other and decide to go directly to Jerusalem. They arrive there with incredible great speed, and henceforth everything happens in the same way as Matthew has told it. But the legend continues to recount that, after the first feast of Pentecost the apostle Thomas visited the three kings in India, and he also baptized them. All three of them lived more than a hundred years and they died as saint kings. Their bodies remained uncorrupted "whole even unto the hair and skin" in their adorned sarcofagi. St. Elena, the mother of Constantine the Great, found their tombs and she took their bodies to the Cathedral of Constantinople. When the governor Eustorgius was appointed bishop of Milan by the emperor, he took their bodies from Constantinople to the Basilica of Milan built in honor of the Three Magi Kings in the year 343 AD.

Frederick Barbarossa, the German emperor, conquered Milan in 1164 and he took the relics of the Saint Kings to the Cathedral of Cologne. These relics are still venerated there preserved in a magnificent golden shrine behind the high altar. The names of the Three Kings and the date of their deaths are written there: "...in the month of January in the 54th year of our Lord..." The relics have never been identified. Today nobody believes that those belonged to the Magi of Matthew. The legend may reflect the belief that the golden shrine of Cologne contains the earthly remains of those eastern kings who in the first century accepted the Gospel and Baptism of Christ.

The book of John of Hildesheim became widespread all around Europe as one of the genuine pearls among the mediaeval legends. Its Latin text and its German translation were republished. (Christern 1960). This writing belongs to the genre of historical legends and within this to the legend of the saints. It narrates true stories with a language adapted to the understanding of the common folk, using vivid and amusing wording. The aim of the legendary exaggerations is to raise the interest and amazement of the readers with the influence of the attractive example of the heroes.

The "Legend of the Three Holy Kings" gave ideals to be followed by the rulers of the Middle Ages, a thing that they really needed. But the people also needed motivation to obey and respect their king. The Church, therefore, tacitly accepted that the faithful believed in this legend. But the researchers began to lose their patience and confidence. Supposing that the account of Matthew is a simple legend, where then is the historical value in the whole of his Gospel? Men of modern times can only believe historical facts. Is it necessary to demythologize the Gospel? Some exegetes of the 20th century tried to overcome this problem by stating that: "The legend in Matthew's 2nd chapter does not float in a vacuum, because it is based on historical preconditions. But this does not make it a historical report. The historical precedents must not be contested if the entire passage is a legend. Let us accept its statements without looking for its historical value" (Grundmann 1968). This judgment seems to give a sort of forced solution concerning the question of belief in the Gospel. However, the new results of literary and historical criticism together with philological, archaeological and astronomical research have confirmed the historicity of Matthew's account. (8)

The Year of Christ's Birth and the Christian Era

The Magi related that they had already observed the rising of the star of the "one born king" in their eastern country and that arriving in Bethlehem they had seen the same star again. Several months had obviously passed from their first observations to the time of their arrival in Bethlehem. This indicates that they spoke of a certain astronomical phenomenon which had been going on for months and was observable in the region of 31 and 32 degrees latitude.

How can we obtain an accurate date for Christ's birth? Since we do not possess the necessary data, we cannot calculate the exact month and day of his birth. Nevertheless, there are sufficient proofs for the determination of the year of his birth and knowing the year it is not so difficult to calculate the celestial phenomena which the Magi could observe in the skies of their country and of Bethlehem.

Astronomers who have previously dealt with this matter usually approached it from the opposite end, i.e., from the dates of the constellations to the date of birth. However, this cannot be accepted by the biblicists, as long as the historical evidence is missing. All agree that only astronomical time computations can obtain accurate dates. But the question remains: To what extent is it possible to prove that an astronomical and a historical event took place simultaneously, e.g., a Jupiter-Saturn conjunction and a birth, which occurred two thousand years ago?

The first scientifically supportable answer concerning the beginning of the Christian era was given by Johannes Kepler. It is to his merit that he demonstrated the historical and astronomical basis of our chronology, and that he called our attention to the great conjunction of Jupiter and Saturn which occurred in the 7th year before our era. However, he did not take this planetary conjunction as a sign indicating the year of the birth of Christ. He supposed that in the year 6 BC a new star or *nova* might have arisen as an effect of the conjunction of the three superior planets, Mars, Jupiter and Saturn, and he thought that this *nova* might have been the star of Bethlehem.

Kepler's supposition turned out to be false, but the year that he found for the birth of Christ was later confirmed. In his book entitled *Stella Nova* he describes the way in which he arrived at this result. He quotes in detail the early historical sources, from which we can deduce the year of Jesus' birth. In the first place Kepler proves that Herod the Great died four years before the beginning of our era, and he refers to Matthew and Luke who state quite definitely that King Herod was still alive at the time of Jesus' birth.

According to the Israelite historian, Josephus Flavius, Herod received his kingship from Octavian, later Caesar Augustus, and he reigned 34 years. In the last year of his life he was diseased in body and mind. Josephus reports in detail Herod's serious illness "that became more and more acute". He died shortly before the feast of the Passover, that is, before the first spring full moon. In connection with these events Josephus mentions a lunar eclipse before the Passover. This is the only eclipse recorded in his work, and this makes it possible astronomically to determine the year of Herod's death. This lunar eclipse was also associated in the minds of people with the execution of the high priest Matthias and his companions who removed the Roman Golden Eagle from the Temple's gate. Josephus writes: "As for the other Matthias, who had stirred up the sedition, Herod had him and some of his companions burnt alive, and on that night the Moon darkened" (*Antiquitates Iud.* 17: 6-19; *Bellum Iud.* 1: 33).

In the days of Kepler many scholars had contested the reliability of Josephus' record. Therefore, to control his data Kepler calculated backward the dates of the full moons and found that an eclipse occurred 23 March 5 BC, but this might not have been the one mentioned by Josephus, because it occurred simultaneously with the vernal equinox. The next vernal lunar eclipse which was visible in Jerusalem occurred 13 March 4 BC at 10 past 3 a.m., and the Passover full moon occurred on 11 April that year. Kepler says at the end of the chapter *Sylva Chronologica*: "Therefore Herod died eight or nine days before Passover in the fourth year before our era. So even the Heavens justify Josephus."

This result is confirmed also by the fact that Herod five days before his own death had his eldest son Antipater killed, and Archelaus became ruler or ethnarch of Judaea and Samaria from 4 BC to 6 AD. Matthew too mentions this: "Archelaus succeeded his father as ruler of Judaea" (2: 22). The majority of modern scholars agree with the opinion that the spring of 4 BC is the true date of Herod's death.

In the next chapter of his treatise Kepler looks for the date of the enrollment or census mentioned in St. Luke's Gospel at the time of Jesus' birth. He quotes the Greek text and renders it word for word as follows: "It came to pass in those days, that there went out a decree from Caesar Augustus that all the empire should be enrolled." This enrollment, the first, took place while Quirinius supervised the Syrian cities (Lk 2: 1-2).

Luke was born in Syria and he studied in Antioch. Thus he knew Roman history well, and he would have seen the monument of Augustus in Antioch which also recorded the dates of the imperial enrollments. Moreover, there was in Antioch a memorial in honor of Quirinius, put up by the inhabitants of the city. (These finds were discovered at the beginning of the 20th century among the ruins of Antioch called nowadays Antakya in South Turkey.) St. Luke was an extremely cultivated Greek scholar and doctor who in 48 AD became a true follower of the apostle Paul. Luke accompanied him on his journeys and stayed by him during his captivity in Rome from 60 to 64 AD. Paul mentioned him in his letters: "Greetings from my dear friend Luke, the doctor" (Col 4: 14; 2 Tim 4: 11). He was the one who started Christian historiography with his work entitled "The Acts of the Apostles". He recorded also the second census in Judaea, which provoked the revolt lead by Judas the Galilean (Acts 5: 37). According to Josephus Flavius this census took place "in the 37th year of Caesar's victory over Antony at Actium", that is, in 6 AD (*Antiquitates Iud.* 18: 1-2).

Unfortunately, Luke does not specify the exact year of Jesus' birth. What can we deduce from his record? Kepler himself had already noticed some linguistic difficulties. He thought that the meaning of the expression "first census" might have been its first occurrence in Judaea's history, that is, for the first time there was such a census. The Greek word *apographê* meant the enrollment of properties and incomes of all taxable individuals. It was not the same as a national census in the usual sense. The gospel translations talk usually about "a census of the whole world", while *oikuménê* meant only the whole of the Roman Empire.

Another difficulty in the translations is that Quirinius was neither governor nor procurator of Syria during the census in question. Luke did not use the noun "governor", but he described the office of Quirinius by a participle: *hêgemoneúntos tês Syrias Kyrêniou*, that is to say "while Quirinius was supervising the Syrian cities". The misunderstanding is due to the usual meaning of the Greek verb *hêgemonein*: to reign and govern. However, the dictionaries define this verb as to supervise, to preside, to lead, or to rule. Luke himself used the same expression for Tiberius Caesar's reign (as a noun: *hêgemonia*) and similarly for Pilate's procuratorship in Judaea. St. Jerome in his Latin Vulgate showed clearly the differences: *praeside Syriae Cyrino (Quirinio), imperii Tiberii Caesaris, procurante Pontio Pilato* (Lk 3: 1). Thus, Quirinius was a president.

This distinction clarifies the question put so often by some researchers. How can we make Luke's concise descriptions consistent with the historical data of the Roman writers? Kepler was ahead of his time also in this respect. He solved this problem excellently four hundred years ago. He quoted the writings of Tertullian, Tacitus and Dio Cassius. He referred also to the monument of Augustus in Ankara (*Monumentum Ancyranum*) of which only some fragments were known at that time.

Tertullian (about 200 AD) investigated the archives of Rome, and he defended the authenticity of Luke against the heretic Marcion, saying that "the census under Augustus, the data of which are preserved in the Roman archives provide the most trustworthy proofs for the birth of our Lord... In Judaea the census was organized by Sentius Saturninus" (*Adversus Marcionem* 4: 17-19). Saturninus was the imperial governor of Syria from 8 BC to 6 BC. Thus Tertullian narrows down the year of Jesus' birth, although he knew well that Quirinius was the legate of Caesar Augustus for 20 years in the eastern provinces of the Empire.

Why did Luke not mention Saturninus ? Who was Quirinius, and what was his rank? According to Roman sources Sulpicius Quirinius was Consul in Rome in 12 BC, and afterwards he was sent to Syria as commander in chief of the Roman Army Corps. He was the best general of Augustus' army, who suppressed the revolt of the Homonades in 9 BC, occupied their fortresses in the Taurus mountains, and then joined Cilicia to Syria. After this victory the greatest triumphal decorations were conferred upon him. Between 1 BC and 4 AD he was counselor to young Gaius Caesar, grandson of Augustus, during his mission to the East. In 6 AD Quirinius was the governor of Syria, and in the same year he came to Judaea to make an inventory of the possessions of Archelaus. By order of Augustus he divested Archelaus of his ruling power, and then he joined Judaea to Syria. (Cf. Tacitus, *Annales* III,48; Dio Cassius, *Rom.Hist.* Libri 53-56; Josephus, *Antiquitates Iud.* 17-18: 2). Thus it should be clear why Luke refers to Quirinius and not to Saturninus. The reason is that his name was widely known even in the first century, both in Judaea and throughout the Roman Empire. The memory of Saturninus was thus overshadowed by the greater figure of Quirinius.

Kepler quotes the proposition of his contemporary Polish historian, Laurentius Sysliga:

> Some scholars used to bring the objection that Luke refers not to the census of Saturninus, but to the one of Quirinius. The answer to this objection is that Tertullian's observations fit in very well with Luke, because Luke does not say that Christ was enrolled under the census of Quirinius, but he says that the census in Judaea took place at first when Quirinius was the president of Syria. Roman history bears out this explanation of the event. Sysliga adds that in the year in which according to the monument of Ankara the census was taken by Augustus alone, Quirinius might have been commissioned to initiate it in Syria and then Saturninus could have continued it (Kepler, *De Stella Nova. Sylva Chron.* pp. 26-28).

A general census would have been possible only when there was peace in all the provinces of the Empire. After Augustus' victory in Hispania and Gallia, a monumental marble altar (*Ara Pacis*) was raised on the Mars Square in Rome. The inauguration of this Peace altar took place 30 January 9 BC, and during the following 12 years there was peace in the Empire. Augustus himself recorded all these events in his memorandum, and he indicated the year of each census by consular dates. Thus we can calculate exactly that there was a census in the years 28 BC, 8 BC and 14 AD. It is remarkable that Augustus in his records gives us only the number of Roman citizens for the census of 28 BC and 14 AD, while for the census of 8 BC he records all subjects of the Empire.

Kepler remarks that the registration of the Roman subjects is not the same as the census of the entire empire, which includes all the individuals living in the provinces. Dio Cassius states that this new law of census with a view to taxation was ordered by Augustus in the 20th year of his reign, that is, in 9 BC. Tacitus also refers to a memorandum which was written by the emperor as a survey of the entire Empire (*Breviarium totius Imperii*): "It contained the state property, the number of the citizens and allies in arms, the number of fleets, kingdoms, provinces, tributes, property and income taxes, fixed payments and donations. These were all recorded by Augustus himself" (Tacitus, *Annales* I: 11).

Finally, concerning a proper chronology Kepler refers to the coincidence of the following events: In 7 BC Saturninus came to Jerusalem to interrogate Herod and probably to initiate the census for the next year. In that year (7 BC) Herod had put to death his two sons, Alexander and Aristobulus, because they were descendants of the Maccabees, born of his Jewish wife Mariamne. He had lost the favor of Augustus, and from that time the Jewish officials had to take a direct oath of fealty to the Emperor. All this throws light upon Matthew's statement: when Herod heard of the birth of a new king "he was perturbed, and so was the whole of Jerusalem" (Mt 2: 3).

Kepler concludes his study by saying:

Thus we are lacking at least 4 or 5 whole years in the chronology used in Europe. Therefore, the year which we reckon as 1606, when I am writing these things, is really 1610 or 1611. But for all that nobody must think that the calendar which we have used for centuries should be rejected; it is enough to know that it begins with the 5th or 6th year of Christ (*Sylva Chron.* p. 35).

In his later studies Kepler definitely states that there is a time lag of six whole years in our Christian chronology (*De vero anno*, 1614). On the one hand it is granted that Christ was born before Herod's death (4 BC), on the other hand after his birth "in Bethlehem Herod had all the male children killed who were two years old and under, according to the time that he ascertained from the Magi" (Mt 2: 16). He was then convinced that Christ was among those children. Consequently, Jesus must have been born at least 2 years before Herod's death. The conjunction of the three superior planets also occurred in 6 BC, and according to Kepler's view this conjunction could have produced such a new star as the one observed by him in 1604. (9)

Today we have more accurate astronomical and historical data, and with the aid of these we can give correct answers to the questions which are still open. In which year was the first census begun in Judaea? Was a new star or *nova* observable in that year? If the early

Church Fathers intended to count the years accurately from the date of Christ's birth, who is then to blame for miscalculating the beginning of the Christian era? There are people who think that these questions are quite unimportant from the standpoint of theology and religion. All the same there are scholars who find it important for scientific and historical research, and they keep on debating the probability of certain suppositions. Still others contest the historical value of Matthew 2, but the interest for this subject has never been more intense than nowadays, as we now approach the 3rd millennium.

Concerning Kepler's suppositions let us begin with the fact that the conjunction of the planets never produces a new star, what we used to call *nova* or *supernova*. It is understandable that lacking knowledge of nuclear physics and astrophysics Kepler could not explain this phenomenon. *Nova* literally means new, but a nova or supernova is an existing old star which suddenly emits an outburst of light. In such an explosion a star increases its luminosity by thousands to millions of times, and it appears to be a new star. Novae appear unexpectedly and they remain very bright for a few days, then gradually fade. Astronomers can never predict when and where a *nova* will appear.

Between 8 and 5 BC it is certain that such a nova did not appear. In those times regular observations were made. These are preserved in several Babylonian, Egyptian and Chinese records. In some of these tablets we can find the great stationary conjunction of Jupiter and Saturn in 7 BC, but there is no mention about any extraordinary new star. Neither Matthew's description nor the early Christian tradition support the nova hypothesis as an explanation for the star of Bethlehem. This explanation proposed by some modern researchers was definitively refuted by many excellent astronomers (e.g., Ferrari d'Occhieppo 1977, Hughes 1979).

The accurate date of the census in question is a much more important item. Luke was not satisfied with the uncertain time setting: "in those days". He was trying to set accurate dates and, therefore, he followed the Greek historians' way of giving the names of emperors, governors, kings, princes and high priests. It was useless to specify years and months, because there were several different calendar styles in the provinces, and it was difficult to find the connections between them. However, by means of our modern historical and chronological tables and comparison methods it is possible to calculate the years of the reign of given kings and other rulers.

St. Luke himself says in his Prologue to the Gospel: "After carefully going over the whole story from the beginning , I have decided to write an ordered account", that is, to tell the events in the right chronological order (Lk. 1:3). In any case, by mentioning the first census in Judaea Luke gives us an important hint, and his description reflects very well the usual course of a taxation census. After the new order of Augustus the registration was made at the place where the taxable individuals had their landed properties, or where their families originated. Women from their fourteenth year to their sixtieth were liable to registration. We can safely assume that the mother of Jesus herself related the situation which we find in Luke's record: "When I gave birth to my son, I wrapped him in swaddling clothes, and laid him in a manger because there was no room for us at the inn" (Lk 2:7). This shows that the census was still in progress. When Mary and Joseph arrived in Bethlehem, the little inn was already full of rich families and Roman officers. Dio Cassius tells that Augustus assigned powerfully mandated revenue officers for each town and village, and that they were independent of the kings and governors (*Rom.Hist.* Lib. 56: 28).

How long did the census last? The Roman revenue officers respected the national customs in the eastern provinces and they considered also the weather conditions. This is why the registration and the property assessment were going slowly. From the time the imperial order was given it might take two years to complete the census in a province. In this context Luke's expression may be taken as a good approximation.

In the last centuries several documents were discovered which deal with the census ordered by Augustus. Let us quote only the two most important finds: *Lapis Venetus* and *Monumentum Ancyranum*. The so called *Lapis Venetus*, tombstone of the Roman General Aemilius Palatinus was found in Venice, in 1880. The undated inscription gives evidence of a census which supposedly began in 8 BC in Syria:

> In compliance with the order of Sulpicius Quirinius, the supreme commander and legate of Caesar Augustus, I took a census in Syria, in the city of Apamea counting 117 thousand citizens, and likewise by Quirinius' order I captured the fortress of the Itureans on the hill of Lebanon...

The *Monumentum Ancyranum* is a document of decisive importance regarding our subject. A copy of this memorandum was first observed in Ankara by the Hungarian Bishop Antal Verancsics, in 1555, when he paid the sultan Suleiman II a call in the mission of the Emperor Ferdinand. He read the clear Latin inscription on the wall of the ancient temple:

...RERUM GESTARUM DIVI AUGUSTI...

The text engraved into the old and broken stone table is like the one mentioned by Tacitus. Augustus had registered with his own hand all his achievements since he was nineteen. The original was lost, but Tiberius Caesar had several copies made, engraved on stone tablets,

Fig. 2: The first lines of the Monumentum Ancyranum, found in Caesar Augustus' temple in Ankara. (from H. Kähler 1958)

and these were located in the temples of the Divine Ceasar. The largest fragment of this memorandum was found in the ruins of the temple in Ankara, and so it received the name *Monumentum Ancyranum*. Its other parts were discovered in Antioch, in 1914. It took several decades before researchers succeeded in reconstructing the entire Latin text. The critical edition was published and commented upon by P. A. Brunt and J. M. Moore (Brunt and Moore 1973). The superscription is of Tiberius:

> Below is a copy of the achievements of the Divine Augustus by which he placed the whole world under the sovereignty of the Roman people, and of the amounts which he expended upon the State and the Roman people.

Augustus' own text then follows. His orders and achievements are dated with consular years according to the Julian Calendar. In his paragraph 8 we find the statement which gives a conclusive proof for the year of the census in question: "In the consulship of C. Censorinus and C. Asinius I took a census alone, without a colleague, in virtue of consular power given me by a decree of the Roman Senate" (*Res Gestae* § 8:3, cf. note p. 46).

According to the data in the Consuls' Inventory (Degrassi, *Fasti Consulari*) and the chronological tables Censorinus and Asinius were Consuls from 1 January to 31 December in the year 8 BC. This was the year when, according to Luke, "Caesar Augustus issued a decree for a census of the whole empire to be taken". Historical data show that the execution of the order or the enrollments used to begin in September. It is stressed in Augustus' statement that this census was conducted by him alone. This means that it was the first general census which was connected to his name, and which bound all the taxable individuals in each province, also in Judaea. (In the Edition of Brunt and Moore, 1973, the number of Roman citizens in this census is not given.)

Thus we can come to the conclusion that this census began in the autumn of 8 BC and it lasted till the spring of 6 BC. The Romans conducted the assessment of property in the autumn and winter months, not to disturb the agricultural works. The civil year began both in Syria and in Judaea with September, regardless of the fact that the Roman assessment also started on the first of September (every fourteenth year). On the basis of these data it is most probable that the year of Jesus' birth is to be reckoned from mid-September 8 BC to mid-September 7 BC. This result is confirmed by the early Christian tradition that Jesus was 40 years old when he was crucified, and his crucifixion occurred in the 33rd year of our era. (Cf. Corbishley 1975). The oldest and the most reliable tradition about Jesus' age is preserved in the book of Bishop Ireneus written in the 2nd century against the heresies (*Adversus Haereses* II.22: 46): Jesus had completed his fortieth year before he suffered. The apostolic Fathers (*Seniores*) bear witness to this fact, since they were personally acquainted with the apostle John and heard the accounts of the others. St. John mentions in his gospel the dispute between Jesus and the Pharisees in Jerusalem when they said to him: "You are not yet fifty" (Jn 8:57). In the ancient East the age was usually given in round numbers which denoted an entire decade. So they meant that Jesus was in his forties.

Such a round number is used by Luke as well: "Jesus was about thirty years old when he started to teach" (Lk 3: 1 and 3: 23), and this was in the fifteenth year of Tiberius Caesar's reign, that is 29 AD . In the same year Jesus had himself baptized in the Jordan's water by John the Baptist who then presented him to the people. Thereafter he taught the people for three years as a well respected master (*rabbi*). By convention thirty years of age was considered to be the minimal age for exercise of a public function, both in the Roman Empire and in Judaea. Thus the meaning of Luke's expression might be that Jesus was in his thirties, that is, he was then old enough to exercise a public ministry. (Cf. Num 4: 3; 1 Chr 23: 3).

We can now by means of astronomical calculations determine the accurate dates of Christ's crucifixion and resurrection. The writers of the Gospel clearly specify those two days according to the Jerusalem calendar: In that year the first day of the Passover was a Saturday (sabbath); the crucifixion of Jesus took place on "the Preparation Day", that is, on Friday, and his resurrection occurred on "the first day of the week", that is, on Sunday (Jn 19: 31-20: 19). (10) According to the Law of Moses the Preparation Day of the Passover was always the 14th day of the first spring month, i.e. Nisan 14. In other words it was the 14th day after the new moon, the day of the first vernal full moon.

The only remaining question then is: How do we determine the year in which the spring full moon was on a Friday, 14th Nisan?

Jesus began his public teaching in 29 AD. His condemnation and execution took place under Tiberius Caesar's reign, and Caiaphas, the high priest of Jerusalem, and Pontius Pilate, the Roman governor were involved. Tiberius died in 37 AD; Caiaphas and Pilate exercised their functions till 36 AD. In this period, between 29 AD and 36 AD, there are only two possibilities: in the year 30 AD the first vernal full moon occurred on 6th April, and Friday was 7th April. In the year 33 AD the full moon occurred on Friday, 3rd April, exactly on 14th Nisan, the Preparation Day. Granted that Jesus' public ministry lasted three full years, his crucifixion on a Friday could only occur in 33 AD on 3 April, and his resurrection on Sunday, 5 April. According to the apostolic Fathers, in this year Jesus was already 40, which shows that he must have been born in 7 BC. Moreover, the singular star phenomenon, the great conjunction of Jupiter and Saturn was observable precisely in that year from April till December.

What about the mistake in calculating the beginning of the Christian era? We have mentioned this problem above. The editors of the new Jerusalem Bible remark on the 2nd and 3rd chapter of Luke:

> Jesus was born certainly before Herod's death, possibly in 8-6 BC. The Christian era, established by Dionysius Exiguus in the 6th century, is the result of a false calculation: the 15th year of Tiberius was 782 after the foundation of Rome, and Dionysius subtracted 29 full years from this, thus arriving at 753 for the beginning of our era.

The astronomer Kepler was the first scholar who investigated all the historical sources to explain the mistake in calculation of the years after Christ. Biblicists do not refer to his chronological treatise, although his statements are very relevant even today. It is worth quoting Kepler's answer to this question as to the reason for the mistake in our chronology:

> Regarding the circumstances of Christ's birth, the early Church Fathers did not consider it necessary to investigate all its details. At that time it was not yet customary to base the designation of time on Christ's birth... As to the view of those scholars who today wish to add one or two years to the age of Christ, they are not mislead by the Fathers, but by the mistakes of the church community in the 6th century. It is not at all surprising that the Abbot Dionysius writing six centuries later, was not familiar with the customs of the Romans, and therefore he mistook the 15th year of Tiberius' reign, not realizing that it had ended in September. He thought that it had

ended in November. It seems that this was the first mistake. But neither would it be surprising if Dionysius could have interpreted the expression of St. Luke in the meaning that Jesus was baptized in November, in Tiberius' 15th year, when he had just completed his 29th year and had begun his 30th. The graver this mistake is, all the more is it excusable, because there are many disputes about this subject even today, in spite of the clearness of the available writings. In addition to these mistakes, the history of the Romans and Judaeans was neglected, but this can likewise be understood in a century which had hardly recovered from the effects of invasions of the Barbarians. This neglect is also the cause of the doubt shown by those outstanding men of our time who have plenty of books and leisure. Can our conjecture prove to be false regarding the mistake of Dionysius? Had he perhaps differently interpreted the expression of St. Luke? Could he reckon 30 years back from the 15th year of Tiberius, which he had determined correctly, but then he did not separate it correctly from the years of Diocletian which had been used up to that time? Was he confused by the complicated sequence of consuls and emperors? However it may be, the mistake of Dionysius is excusable, as even the early Church Fathers did not have any certain and common knowledge about the year of Christ's birth (Kepler, *De vero anno; Sylva Chron..* pp. 6-8).

We really can not blame Dionysius for the mistake. He did not even intend to specify the exact year of Christ's birth, because he was aware that it was impossible on the basis of the available data at that time. He insisted that the Incarnation of the Lord denoted the beginning of a new era, and that after the lapse of 500 years it was time to designate the years "from the Incarnation of Our Lord". (Hence the abbreviation AD = *Anno Domini*, i.e. in the year of the Lord, and BC = Before Christ, the denotation of the number of a year before the beginning of the Christian era.)

The Abbot Dionysius reached this conclusion when the bishops entrusted him with calculating the dates of the Paschal Full Moons and Easter Sundays for 95 years on. He solved the difficult problem excellently, and nobody could find miscalculations in his work. He sent the new Paschal Tables to Petronius, the patriarch of Alexandria, and he dated his explanatory letter as follows: "in the year of Christ 525, with indiction 3 under Consul Probus".

Those who have thoroughly studied the original works of Dionysius, may clearly see both his intention and his method of reckoning. As it is evident from the dating of his letter, he used the consular dates and the number of the year according to the old Roman calendar "from the foundation of the City" (*ab urbe condita* = AUC).

The foundation of the City Rome must be dated as 753 BC, if one follows Dionysius' reckoning.

In agreement with the bishops he confined himself to the statement of St. Luke that Jesus was about thirty years old in the fifteenth year of Tiberius who succeeded Augustus on 19 August 767 AUC. His 15th year of reign, therefore, was from 19 August 782 to 18 August 783 AUC. The Christian ecclesiastical year however began on 25 March, the feast of the Annunciation and Incarnation, (it was the date of the vernal equinox in the Roman Empire). That is why Dionysius took 783 AUC as the starting point for his calculation, and since Jesus at that time was about (*quasi*) 30 years old: 783 minus 30 is 753 AUC. Thus the year 25 March 753 - 24 March 754 AUC was the initial year of his ecclesiastical calendar. He did not use Christ's actual date of birth as a starting point, he never mentioned this in his work. He spoke consistently of the incarnation which meant the time of the conception (25 March) and not the birth. According to the dating of his letter Dionysius carried out his work under Consul Probus, "in the year of Christ 525". In fact we find in the Consuls' Inventory this datum: Probus Junior Consul in Rome, under the Emperor Theoderic in the civil year 1278 AUC (cf. Degrassi 1952), and 1278 minus 753 full years gives 525 as the number of years reckoned "from the Incarnation of Christ". At that time the main concern of the bishops was that the Christians both in the East and in the West should celebrate the crucifixion and resurrection of Christ, and the so-called movable feasts, uniformly on the same day: the Ascension on the 40th day after Easter Sunday, and Pentecost Sunday on the 50th day. In view of this purpose the bishops accepted the Paschal Tables and the whole calendar of Dionysius Exiguus, and by the end of the eighth century all the Christian kings had officially introduced his chronology. (11)

The Anglo-Saxon scholar, Bede the Venerable (673-735 AD), wrote a supplementary study to the calculation method of Dionysius, entitled *De ratione temporum*, and in his historical writings he dated the events according to this chronology. At the end of the 8th century Charlemagne became monarch in Western Europe, and Pope Leo III crowned him Roman Emperor. The day of his crowning is dated in the Latin Chronicle as follows: *Octavo Kalendas Ianuarii Anno Octingentesimo Domini*, that is, on the 8th day before the first of January of the eight hundredth year of the Lord. This was not on Christmas Day in 800 AD, as it was generally misinterpreted, but it was 25 December 799 in the Julian Calendar, given by the new dates of Dionysius.

The earliest traditions about the date of Christ's birth were noted down by Clement of Alexandria (190 AD) with the Egyptian dating method. He mentioned five different days, which converted into

Julian calendar dates were 2 or 6 January, 29 or 30 April, and 5 May in the 28th year of Augustus' reign. He did not take sides regarding these days, because he did not trust his sources ("according to some... others say ... still others relate"). All the same he gave important information saying that "from the birth of our Lord till the death of Commodus there passed in all 194 years and 1 month and 13 days" (Clement of Alexandria, *Stromata* I. 21: 145-146).

The Emperor Commodus was murdered on the night of 31 December 945 AUC (192 AD). If we subtract the given period from this, namely 194×365+30+13 = 70853 days, we will get 6 January 752 AUC. It was on the basis of this result that some historians stressed, against Kepler, that Dionysius had committed an error of only two years in his calculation. They failed to consider that Herod died in 750 AUC. This was not known in Alexandria in the 2nd century, and nobody knew the accurate date of the first census taken in Judaea.

Ferrari d'Occhieppo (1965) investigated thoroughly the statements of Clement of Alexandria, and he made the necessary chronological calculations. Thus he arrived at the result that the year of Christ's birth given as the 28th year of Augustus' reign must have been a misunderstanding or the copyists' error. It is very probable that they have mistaken the Greek figure 8 for the 3 in the old manuscript, and this resulted in writing 28 instead 23. The conversion of the Egyptian and Alexandrian dates into Julian dates shows that these would have been correct for the 23rd year of Augustus. The years of the era of Augustus were reckoned from 724 AUC, the victory in Actium, because from that time on he was the Emperor of Egypt as well. He had received the title of Caesar Augustus three years later, 16 January 727. However, it is possible that some reckoned his reign from the victory of Illyricum, in 719 AUC, and thus his 28th year would be 747 AUC (7 BC).

The dates from April and May given in the work of Clement were certainly based on astrological calculations. There were some Christian people in Alexandria at the end of the 2nd century who were well acquainted with the system of Ptolemy. According to the Egyptian view the celestial sign of the birth of the Messiah was the first conjunction of Jupiter and Saturn in the constellation of Pisces. If we use the tables of Ptolemy and calculate with his system, this conjunction occurred really between 29 April and 16 May, though not in 752, but in 747 AUC, in the 23rd year of Augustus' reign (7 BC).

There are some correct suppositions regarding Jesus' birth year in the writings of Clement of Alexandria, in spite of the mistaken dates. This uncertainty in the early Christian tradition shows that it would be useless to look for the determination of his birthday. The Babylonian astronomers, 200 years before Ptolemy, had calculated exactly the time of the coming great conjunction of Jupiter and Saturn, but they were not able to predict the birthday of the awaited Messiah. It is enough for us to know what is supported by historical and chronological research, viz., that Christ was born between 6 January and 15 September in the 23rd year of Caesar Augustus' reign, that is, in 7 BC. At any rate, on the basis of Matthew's account about the star and by means of astronomical calculations we will attempt to find the date of the Magi's arrival in Bethlehem. Finally, let us hear a very cautious conclusion in the epilogue of David Hughes:

It is highly probable that Jesus was born in 7 BC. The month in the year is less certain but the majority of the indications guide us to August or September. The choice of a specific day is really stretching the evidence too much, but if one day has to be selected I think we would be safest with the day that the Magi probably chose, the day of the acronychal rising (i.e. the evening rising of Jupiter and Saturn). This means that Jesus was born on the evening of 15 September 7 BC (Hughes 1979).

CHAPTER TWO

THE MAGI
AND THE STAR

Babylonian Priests and Astronomers

The ruins of the Tower of Babel were being excavated at a time when the cannons of the First World War were thundering in Europe and millions of victims were being buried. Was this a matter of some strange coincidence? By then it had become common usage to refer to a Babylonian confusion of languages. From the books of the Hebrew prophets and Greek historians all educated people had learned something about the unbelievable greatness, prosperity and wickedness of that ancient city. What in the last century was but a legend, has in our century become historical reality.

From 1534 the ancient land of Babylon was under the sovereignty of the Turkish empire. In 1899 the Sultan Abdul-Hamid invited some German engineers to construct the Baghdad railway line and at the same time gave permission to archaeologists to carry out excavations near the village Babil, a hundred kilometers south of Baghdad.

The leader of the excavations from 26 March 1899 to 22 May 1918 was the architect Robert Koldewey on behalf of the German Oriental Society. The archaeologists had no idea of the immensity of the work ahead of them when they put up their tents under the date palms on the eastern bank of the Euphrates, where the temperature rarely dropped below 35 °C even in the shade. The Arab residents welcomed the archaeologists from the west, whose presence meant safe jobs in the area for eighteen years. There were no modern digging machines at the time, the equipment used consisting of picks, spades, shovels and wheelbarrows. What was it that researchers were looking for under the hillocks covered with brown, yellowish sand?

They were looking for the secret of the city which is believed to have been the cradle of European civilization, going back five thousand years. Its ancient Sumerian name is *Ka-Dingir*, and in Semitic-Accadian language *Bab-Ilu* meaning God's Gate or Gate of Gods. Ethnographic and archaeological finds support the supposition that it was through this gate that human culture and civilization set out towards the West: writing, arithmetic, architecture, sculpture, organization of the state, astronomy, ethical and legal rules, religious cults and ceremonies.

The interest in Babylon has been made all the more intense by the Holy Scriptures, which, from the first book of Moses to the last book of the apostle John, outlines in a tone often quite dramatic, some history of Babylon as well as the final destruction of the city. The names of places and proper names mentioned in the Hebrew text are identical with the data furnished by the Accadian cuneiform writings. The old Hebrew name of *Bab-Ilu* is Babel (BBL). After the Assyrian deportation and Babylonian exile of the Israelites (722-538 BC), the phonetic form and meaning of the word were changed: BLL pronounced with vowels gives *balel*, which means confusion or chaos (*balal* = to disperse and confuse).

A few statements by Moses' scribe shed light on the reasons for the name having this meaning:

After the Deluge the descendants of Noah's sons settled in the land of Shinar, between the Tigris and the Euphrates. As their welfare increased, they made the same mistake as their ancestors before the Deluge: they were overcome by greed and the lust for power. They spoke the same language, they had still the same vocabulary. They said to one another: Come, let us make bricks and bake them in the fire. Let us build ourselves a town and a tower with its top reaching heaven. Let us make a name for ourselves, so that we may not be scattered about the whole earth. But afterwards mankind sinned again with overweening pride and greed and its punishment was that the Lord Almighty confused their language and scattered them thence over the whole face of the earth, and the town was named Babel, therefore, because there the Lord confused the language of the whole earth (Gen 11: 4-9).

The authenticity of this description was confirmed by the first Greek historian, Herodotus, who visited Babylon in the years between 450-440 BC. Without having read the book of Moses, he called the luxurious life and overweening greed of the city a "hybris" which sooner or later was "to be punished by the gods". His writings did a good service to the archaeologists during the excavations. This is how he describes what he saw and heard:

The city consists of three and four story houses, it is criss-crossed by straight streets which are either parallel or intersect each other and cross the river. There are brazen gates at the end of each street, as many gates as streets. The external wall is the rampart of the city, inside there is another wall which is not much smaller but it is wide enough for four-horse carriages to drive on between the battlements... Standing in the centre, there is a building in either part of the city. One is the royal palace surrounded by a wall, the other one is the temple of *Zeus-Belus* [Marduk] with its huge doors of iron. At the time of my visit, I could see the quadrangular temple court each side of which measured about two stadia [about 400 meters]. In the center there is a tower built of baked bricks, the length and width of its foundation are about one stadium respectively. On top of the foundation there is another tower, and yet another tower on top of that one. There are altogether eight towers built on top of one another. Around each tower there are staircases leading towards the top and halfway in each there are benches for the visitors to take some rest. The topmost tower is furnished as a large sanctuary with an ornate bed and a gold table beside it. There is no statue in it and nobody sleeps there apart from the indigenous woman chosen from among the others by god [Marduk] himself, as I was told by the Chaldaeans, the priests of the sanctuary. They also say, although I found it hard to believe, that this god sometimes visits the sanctuary and sleeps there in that bed... In the Temple Court of Babylon there is another sanctuary with a large statue of Zeus [Marduk] in it, in a sitting posture, with a gold table [altar] and chair before it... On the festival of their god, on new year's day, the Chaldaeans burn frankincense worth 1000 talents on the altar outside the sanctuary (Herodotus, *Histories*, I. 179-183).

The city of Babylon was indeed characterized by the presence of many races and a chaos of languages. During its history of three thousand years the tower reaching heaven saw many empires being founded and destroyed one after the other: Sumerian, Accadian, Assyrian, Semitic-Chaldaean, Mede and Persian rulers succeeded one another until the whole of Babylonia was occupied and annexed to the Greek empire by Alexander the Great in 331 BC. From then on its Greek name was Mesopotamia, which means the plain between the two rivers. (**12**)

Herodotus visited Babylon during the Persian reign and could see the buildings which had been restored by the kings of the Chaldaean dynasty. The last large scale reconstruction works had been carried out by Nebuchadnezzar between 605-562 BC, which period saw the beginning of the last golden age of Babylonian astronomy and star religion. Thousands of cuneiform writings preserved intact testify to the astronomical observations, calculations and records made by the Babylonian astronomers for four hundred years. The astronomers were the most prominent members of the clergy and the priests always belonged to the ethnic group of Chaldaeans, which is why Herodotus simply called them Chaldaeans. Because of their reputation for great knowledge they survived even the Persian and Greek rulers, who called them Magi.

According to Greek and Roman writers some of the terraces of the tower, which had been preserved intact, were visible even in 20 AD, and "it was from its top that the Chaldaeans carried out their astronomical observations, carefully recording the rising and setting of the stars". (Diodorus Siculus quotes a description of *Ktêsias*, court physician to Artaxerxes, *Hist. Bibl.* II. 8).

How did the "tower reaching heaven" disappear off the face of the earth? The houses and walls built on the loose and sandy soil sank about 2 millimeters each year. The findings uncovered during the excavations revealed that the roads, foundations and walls of the city had been raised or embanked every 300 years on average. However, as a result of recurrent floods and earthquakes the rate of sinking and the amount of debris increased. At the time of the Persian-Greek war most of the houses and temples were ruined. Alexander the Great wanted to have the city rebuilt and had ten thousand people work for several months at clearing away the debris of rubble. After his early death, however, his successor Seleucus Nicator did not think it worthwhile to carry on the reconstruction and preferred to have a new capital built for himself on the bank of the Tiger, which he named Seleucia after his own name. This is how Pausanias writes about Seleucus:

> Otherwise Seleucus was a just and devout man. Namely, when he had his seat transferred to Seleucia and had the inhabitants of Babylon move there, he did not destroy the walls of the city and the Sanctuary of *Belus Marduk*. He ordered the Chaldaean priests to stay there and continue their work (Pausanias, *Histories* I. 16).

Thus Babylon had slowly become deserted with only the astronomer-priests and their families staying there and working faithfully in the temple of Marduk for another three hundred years.

In the first century the temple and the remaining part of the tower were destroyed by the Parthian Arsacids and the bricks were carried away and used by the people to build their own houses. The priestly families fled from among the ruins, which became dens of robbers and jackals. The little that was left of the sinking ruins above ground level was gradually buried under a layer of sand made thicker and thicker by desert storms. The prophecies of Isaiah and Jeremiah were literally fulfilled: the city of Babylon, which had been the political, commercial, scientific and religious center of ancient civilization for centuries turned "into an uninhabited desert for ever" (Jer 51: 29).

The old apostle John exiled to the island of Patmos by the emperor Domitian in 85 AD gave the following staggering description of how the prototype of one time Rome was destroyed:

The kings and traders who had made a fortune out of Babylon will be standing at a safe distance from fear of her agony mourning and weeping. They will say, with tears and groans: Mourn, mourn for this great city; for all the linen and purple and scarlet that you wore, for all your finery of gold and jewels and pearls; your riches are all destroyed within a single hour (Rev 18: 9-23).

English and French archaeologists started the excavations near Nineveh and Assur along the northern banks of the Tigris as early as 1843. They found the ruins of a three-story tower temple and the drawing of the six-story Babylon tower engraved on a stone tablet under the Nimrod hillock. About thirty thousand cuneiform writings were uncovered from the Nineveh library of Ashurbanipal (668-626 BC). The tablets made of baked clay being extremely resistant, the cuneiform writings engraved on them several thousand years ago are legible even today. The Sumerian and Accadian texts containing important data were deciphered by Assyrologists and were of great help to archaeologists at the Babylonian excavations.

Among the cuneiform writings uncovered at Nineveh archaeologists found the Assyrian lists of kings, which provided them with good information concerning the date and length of each king's reign, their military campaigns and the dates of constructions carried out during their reigns. Astronomical records were also used to determine the dates of major events. The eclipses of the Sun and the Moon, or the transit of the planet Venus across the front of the Sun's disk, which events are mentioned in certain cuneiform writings, made datings possible until the second millennium before Christ. (Cf. Kugler 1912, II. pp.280-307; Pannekoek 1961, pp.33-35).

Thus researchers were able to determine that the first Babylonian world empire was founded by the Amorite (Semitic) king Hammurabi between 1792 and 1750 BC. He made Babylon the seat of his empire and had a magnificent temple built there in honor of the "King of kings, the greatest everlasting Lord", whose ancient Accadian name was *Marduk*. He took over the old Assyrian divine rank as *Bel*, that is, Lord.

Hammurabi's Code of Laws contains the first Code we know of in the history of mankind. The 282 articles of its laws cover all the aspects of public, social, family, religious and moral life. Certain basic ideas of the Mosaic ten commandments originating in ancient Hebrew traditions can be traced back to it. Today this Code of Laws engraved on a 2.25 meter diorite column is to be seen in the Louvre. An artistic relief on the top of the column represents Hammurabi receiving the insignia of royalty, the ring and scepter of justice and law, from Marduk. From then on this Mightiest Lord, *Marduk Belu*, became the patron god of Babylon and his cult the official religion of the whole empire.

The priests of Marduk were astronomers. They designed the structure of the terraced tower in accordance with the system of wandering stars, and they adjusted the walls and streets of the city to the Sun's position at the vernal equinox. In their didactic poem (*Enuma elish*) written to explain the origin of the world, they describe Marduk as the maker of heaven and earth. He is the son of Sun-god and the personification of Jupiter, the brightest wandering star, who defeated the darkness of the nether world and made a universal order from chaos. Belu Marduk combined all the qualities and power of the several hundreds of earthly and heavenly gods worshipped previously. Marduk's festival was held on new year's day under the new moon of the vernal equinox, and his main feast was the summer solstice.

Robert Koldewey had been familiar with all these data, which helped him to find the Tower of Babel. His first comprehensive report on the results of the excavations was published in his book "Babylon Revived" just before the outbreak of the First World War. In its preface he says:

> We have completed about half of the work envisaged since the beginning of the excavations in Babylon, although we had 250 people working there every day in winter and summer. This is not surprising when we think of the size of the ruins and the immense dimensions of the territory once inhabited here. The usual width of the ramparts in other ancient cities is 3 to 6 meters, in Babylon, however, it is 17 to 22 meters. While at most of the ancient excavation sites the ruins are buried 3 to 7 meters under the debris, here we have to dig 12 to 24 meters deep to reach the foundations (Koldewey 1913).

In the chapters that follow the author describes the location and size of the ruins uncovered in the course of fourteen years. The length of the external wall surrounding the eastern part of the city on the bank of the Euphrates was 15 km that of the internal wall with wide canals along it on either side was 6 km. Archaeologists found the remains of 1000 battlements and watch towers on the walls. The palace of Nebupolassar with its throne room of 17 by 52 meters is situated on the bank of the river in the north western part of the city. Next to it is the ornate Ishtar Gate, the huge walls of which are decorated with 575 reliefs covered with color tiles, representing dragons and bulls. The main street of the city, the two kilometer long Procession Road, passes through the Ishtar Gate. To its west we find the 409 meter long wall of the Temple Court and inside it the Palace of the Priests. The parapets of Procession Road are decorated with reliefs of lions in mosaic colors. Another long road called Marduk Road leads to the main entrance of the Temple Court from the east (see p. 58).

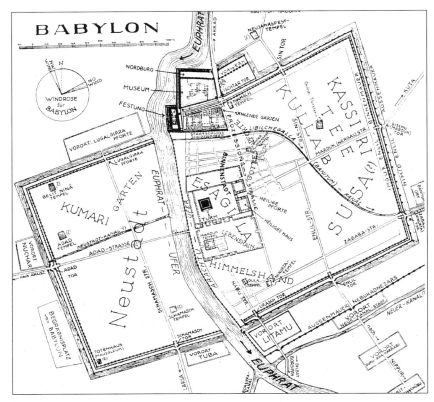

Fig. 3: Map of Babylon reconstructed on the basis of cuneiform finds after the excavations. The place where the Tower of Babel stood in the center of the city on the eastern bank of the Euphrates is marked with a black square. (Unger 1931)

Several inscriptions engraved on the bricks of the wall make it possible to determine the position of the Marduk Sanctuary and the tower. The inscriptions contain the names of the kings who again and again had the sanctuary and the tower restored over the centuries. The temple court is called *Esagila*: the house of Light. The Accadian name of the tower is *Ziggurat* and *Etemenanki*, the Column of Heaven and Earth. Written in cuneiform characters this reads *E-temen-te-an-ki*, which, according to recent linguistic interpretation means navel cord, the connection between the Earth and Heaven, that is the channel through which the Earth is fed by Heaven.

One of the inscriptions bears the name of Nebupolassar: "I was ordered by Marduk to fasten the foundation of the tower of Babil to the chest of the nether world and to raise its top to heaven". This work was subsequently carried out by his son and successor. The name of *Nabu-kudurri-uzur* (rendered into Hebrew *Nebuchadnezzar*) the last king to rebuild Babylon is engraved on several thousands of bricks. The meaning of the name is: "Let Nabu protect my borders". Nabu was the son of Marduk-Jupiter, the personification of the star of Mercury, the deity of reason, architecture and commerce.

During the excavations archaeologists found one of the documents of Nebuchadnezzar, in which the king lists the building materials he ordered for the renovation of the sanctuary and the tower: baked bricks, air dried bricks, pitch, cedar wood, bronze, silver, gold and precious stones. Then he writes: "I started to raise the top of Etemenanki so high that it should rival the heavens" (Koldewey 1913, p.192).

The Israelite priests and scribes had witnessed all this. Four cuneiform writings testify that in 597 BC Nebuchadnezzar made Judah his vassal and had Jehoiachin, the king of Jerusalem and his family brought to his palace in Babylon. Nine years later he had Jerusalem destroyed because of the revolts there and had great numbers of Judaeans as well as the treasures of the Temple carried away to Babylon (2 Kg 25: 8-15).

All this enables us to understand why the book of Moses, too, talks about "the tower of Babel reaching the heavens". However, instead of a figurative sense the priests of Marduk took this literally: to them the top of the high tower served as an excellent place from which to observe the heavens. In dry weather the air of Babylon was so dusty that the stars were hardly visible from the ground floor. Almost one hundred meters high, the top of *Etemenanki* "reaching the heavens" always emerged above the dust clouds.

In conclusion Koldewey remarks that in spite of having worked for eight months and having had 30 thousand cubic meters of earth carried away from the hill hiding the ruins of Ziggurat, they had been unable to dig out the tower. The wall surrounding the Temple Court and the adjoining chapels were uncovered before 1913. The foundations of the tower of Babel were dug up the following year. The cuneiform writings waiting to be interpreted were carefully packed away, but could not be sent to Berlin because of the war. The cases that contained them reached the Kaiser Friedrich Museum in 1926. Robert Koldewey, however, did not live to see this.

Archaeologists and architects continued the renovation of Babylon in the Berlin Museum. They found six cuneiform writings containing detailed information concerning the buildings of the city and the size of the tower. In most cases this coincided with the facts noted down by Herodotus and Ktêsias. Thus, with the help of the photographs made of the ruins uncovered on the shores of the Euphrates, scholars were able to restore Nebuchadnezzar's city and the tower temple of Marduk exactly in accordance with the original.

Great interest was aroused by an expert study entitled "The Holy City of Babylon as Described by the Babylonians" written by professor Eckhard Unger (1931). He uses the copies and translations of the original cuneiform writings as well as 57 photographs and drawings to illustrate the masterpiece of the magi, the first metropolis, whose temples, palaces and hanging gardens were ranked among the seven wonders of the world by the historians of antiquity.

The trapeziform plan of the town and the location of its streets and temples, says Unger in his study, reflect the shape of the constellations: "Babylonian astronomy and astrology that have been so famous ever since ancient times are eloquently expressed in the total aspect of the town of Babylon". The lines connecting the fixed stars of Taurus the Bull, Aries the Ram and Pisces the Fishes are clearly recognizable in it. For 4000 years before Christ the vernal equinoctial point passed through the constellations of Taurus and Aries, which were visible in the night sky of Babylon from the autumnal equinox to the winter solstice. They culminated, that is reached the highest point of their path at midnight one after the other in the last days of September, October and November.

When, after having been reconstructed several times, the city acquired its final form during the reign of Nebuchadnezzar (between 600-560 BC), the vernal equinoctial point had already entered into the sign of Aries. A cuneiform writing relating the origin of "heavenly Babylon" mentions that the Temple Court of Marduk is the "field of the Ram". Nebuchadnezzar calls himself the horn of the Ram after the brightest star of the constellation, the *Hunga*. (Today it is called Hamal, or Alpha Arietis, and it is a giant star of orange light).

The seven main temples of the inner city were dedicated to the Sun, the Moon and the representatives of the five planets known at the time: the communal festivals were held in the temples of Ishtar (Venus), Nergal (Mars), Marduk (Jupiter), Nabu (Mercury) and Ninutra (Saturn). Apart from these, there were over 700 chapels or sanctuaries that served to meet any individual religious demands. From among the 384 sacrificial altars erected at cross roads and in squares, the most important ones were: 7 altars in honor of the constellation of Pisces, 12 altars in honor of the Seven Sisters (Pleiades) shining in Taurus and 180 altars in honor of the Venus of Ishtar.

From an astronomical point of view the Temple Court was particularly important. This had an area of 450 × 550 meters and was divided into two equal parts by an inner wall with four gates. The temple of Marduk stood in the southern court, the seven-story tower *(Etemenanki)* in the northern one. According

54

to a cuneiform document, the measurements of the tower were as follows:

> The lowest tower had and area of 90 × 90 meters, its height was 33 meters. The diameters of the towers gradually decreased from the lowest to the topmost tower with the width of the terraces measuring 9 meters from the second story upwards. The height of the second tower was 18 m, the following four stories were 6 m high each. On the top of the sixth tower there was a sanctuary of an area of 21 × 24 m and a height of 15 m. Thus, counting from the foundation stone to the top, the building was exactly 90 m high, but since the Temple Court was built on a hill of the city, the topmost terrace of the tower was about 120 meters above the ground level. It was from that terrace that the Chaldaeans made their observations and calculations concerning the place and time of the rising and setting of celestial bodies.

When Nebuchadnezzar had finished building the seventh tower, he issued a document to commemorate the event: "I raised the top of Etemenanki with baked bricks and decorated it with bright blue stones (lapislazuli) and roofed over it with cedar wood covered with bronze, because this is the dwelling place of Marduk, the Lord Almighty of the gods". In this sense the sky blue top of the tower of Babel "rivalled the sky".

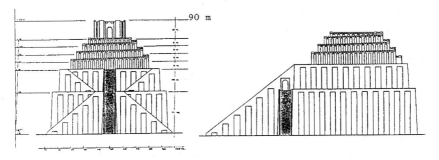

Fig. 4: The southern and the eastern side of the Tower of Babylon. The substructure of the Tower is 51 meters high, and the seventh tower on top is the Marduk-Jupiter Sanctuary. Viewed from the east, the main staircase begins at a distance of 60 meters from the substructure and ascends at an angle of 40 degrees with the ground level. Drawing by the architect Walther Bünte, one of the organisers of the excavations. (Unger 1931)

The above map shows that the location of the Temple Court and the tower deviate by 14 degrees to the southeast of the direction of the city walls and roads. This orientation was made 1500 years after the walls had been built. The first person to have the city rebuilt was the Assyrian king Esarhaddon (680-669 BC), who noted in one of his documents that "the roads of Babylon lead towards the four directions of wind." The directions of the two main winds were correlated with the rising and setting of the Sun.

At the time of the vernal equinox the Sun stands in the celestial equator and rises at the horizon exactly from the east. Later,the rising point of the Sun moves slowly towards the north until the summer solstice. 4000 years ago, at the time of the summer solstice, the azimuth of sunrise was 119° in Babylon, that is 29 degrees to the north of the eastern direction. This is the exact direction of Marduk Road, the road leading towards the northeast of the city. (The geographic azimuth is the angle along the horizon, measured eastward from the south point, to the intersection of the horizon with the vertical circle passing through a certain point.)

This is yet another proof of the fact that as long as 4000 years ago the Babylonian magi who were architects, used protractors (for angular measurement) and relied on astronomical observations to build their temples. The location of the tower rebuilt deviated by 14°30' from east to north, which meant it was exactly orientated to the point of sunrise between the vernal equinox and the summer solstice. What could have been the purpose of this?

Cuneiform writings testify that both the tower and Marduk Road served as a means of measuring time in Babylon. In a year when Babylonians observed that the point of sunrise reached the line of the northeastern road with a delay of exactly 29 days at the time of the summer solstice, they added the 13th month after the last day of that year. That was how they brought the lunar year into harmony with the solar year.

The original orientation of the Marduk Road had also a festive purpose. At the time of the summer solstice, the northern declination of the Sun was an average of 23°26' for a week and thus its culmination height was 81° in the zenith of Babylon. That was the time when Babylonians celebrated the entry of Marduk (Jupiter), the son of Sun-god into his Sanctuary. The rising Sun passed exactly along the line of Marduk Road and at noon it stood above the Tower. The sky blue Sanctuary shone in its full splendor and the Tower cast no shadow. From the direction and length of the shadow of the Tower, Babylonians were able to determine the beginning of both the seasons and the hours.

The path of Jupiter was equally significant: when it reached its largest northern declination, it culminated exactly above the tower of Marduk. (13) On the basis of such observations, Babylonians were able to determine the meridian of the city, that is, the great circle which passed through the place of the tower and the north and south poles of the Earth. When the new palaces of Nabuchadnezzar were built, they were located exactly in this orientation.

All this illustrates well the development of Babylonian astronomy, the great age of which started in the 7th century BC with the work of the Chaldaean priest-astronomers. They drew from the heritage of their Sumerian and Assyrian predecessors, but the picture book of the heavens was little by little considered by them a book of arithmetic. To calculate the dates of the equinoxes they used the 19 year lunisolar cycle. Since the time of the Seleucids, the secrets of the Chaldaean astronomers' cuneiform writings had been passed on to the peoples of the west by Greek scholars. Their basic forms of calculations are used even in our days.

The Chaldaeans were the first to divide into 360 degrees the small and large circles in which they observed the motions of the celestial bodies from sunset to sunset and from spring to spring. In accordance with their observations, they measured the length of the day by 12 double hours and that of the year by 12 months. The degrees and hours were further divided into 60 arc minutes and the minutes into 60 arc seconds. This is another proof of the meticulous care with which the Chaldaeans worked. The advantage of the sexagesimal system is that its basic number 60 is divisible by ten numbers without a remainder.

Moreover, the Chaldaeans designated also certain groupings of stars or constellations in honor of characters or animals of their mythology. They observed that the Moon and planets were always found within a narrow band of the heavens, which they called the "Belt of the Year", and they determined its width as 18 degrees. They divided it into twelve parts or signs each 30 degrees long. This system was named *Zodiakos* by the Greeks, which name originally meant a "circle of living beings". Today it is known as the "zone of the animals" (the Zodiac), because seven of the twelve constellations bear the name of an animal. Modern astronomers still make use of these constellations to indicate certain locations on the celestial sphere. (14)

Fig. 5: View of Babylon from the northwest at the time of Nebuchadnezzar. The main street called Procession Road runs from the Royal Palace through the Ishtar Gate to the Temple Court, the entrance of which is halfway along the road and leads, on the right, to the seven-story Tower. This was the luxurious city admired and cursed by the deported Israelites and also the place where the prophet Daniel lived for fifty years. (Unger 1931)

The Magi

Throughout four hundred years, from the year 141 BC on, Mesopotamia was ruled by the Parthian kings of Iran, who followed the monotheistic religion of Zoroaster (*Zarathustra*). They destroyed the temples built in honor of the deities of stars, but they kept the tower of Babylon and its surroundings because they, too, needed astronomers able to determine the calendar.

Leaving the ruins of the temples of Barsippa, Uruk and Sippar, the best astronomers moved to Babylon where they could continue their work freely for another two hundred years. Being no longer the official priests of the state, the Chaldaean magi were able to preserve their independence and astronomical and religious traditions.

Hundreds of accurately dated tables in cuneiform writing testify to the regular observations and calculations made by the Babylonian astronomers until the 354th year of the Seleucid era, that is, 42 AD. The last and only fragment dating from 75 AD only shows that the order of the Babylonian magi gradually became completely extinct in those decades.

After the Parthian occupation increasing numbers of Chaldaeans fled Mesopotamia. Some of them founded schools or sects in Syria and Greece, allowing Israelites and Greeks to join. These latter arbitrarily took up the name of magi. Those of them who were serious and talented managed to win the confidence of some high-ranking state officials, made their living by serving as court advisors to imperial governors. Others made a living out of practicing ordinary astrology, wandering from town to town and taking advantage of the credulity of simple people. Several hundreds of such false magi were expelled from Rome by the Emperor Tiberius.

In the Acts of the Apostles St. Luke relates the story of two false magi. The apostles met Simon the magician in Samaria, a Hellenistic city known as *Sebaste* at that time. He had already practiced magic arts in the town and astounded the Samaritan people. Eminent citizens and ordinary people alike had been won over to him. But when Simon saw the wonders and great miracles worked by the apostles even he himself became a believer of Christ, and he received baptism. One day he observed that the Holy Spirit was given through the imposition of hands by the apostles, and he offered them some money: "Give me the same power" he said to them. Peter severely warned him and explained that the Holy Spirit is supremely the Gift of God, and it is a grave sin to think that money could buy God's gift (Acts 8: 9-24).

The other magician was Elymas Magos. Luke called him a "false prophet". He was one of the attendants of the proconsul Sergius Paulus on the island of Cyprus. The proconsul summoned Barnabas and Paul and asked to hear the Good News, but Elymas tried to stop them so as to prevent the proconsul's conversion to the faith. Then the apostle Paul took firm measures and rebuked him:

> You impostor, you enemy of all true religion, why don't you stop twisting the straight-forward ways of the Lord? Now watch how the hand of the Lord will strike you; you will be blind, and for a time you will not see the sun (Acts 13: 4-12).

At that instant everything went dark for him, but the proconsul became a believer in Christ.

The figures of the Magi visiting Bethlehem clearly emerge against the background of these stories. They were not regarded as frauds or false prophets by Matthew, or the Apocrypha or any of the Fathers of the Church, although none of them knew their names. Anonymity was a rule to be observed by the order of real magi. They never signed their writings and never introduced themselves to anyone, because instead of seeking their personal glory they only wanted to serve the King of Heaven.

Those who wish to characterize the magi usually quote the descriptions of Herodotus, Plinius or other Greek and Roman authors, although none of their descriptions quite corresponds to the facts. Otto Neugebauer is right when saying: "Before the cuneiform writings had been deciphered, the classical sources presented but a caricature of ancient oriental culture" (Neugebauer 1975, p. 610).

Herodotus visited Mesopotamia between 465-450 BC, during the reign of the Persian king Artaxerxes I. In his writings he called the Babylonian priests Chaldaeans, although he was not very familiar with the origin of the magi or the science practiced by them. He called the members of the Meggu tribe of the Medes *magi*, probably because of the similar sounding of the two words. (Hist. I, 101).

According to linguists the word *magi* comes from the Indian *maha-guru* ("great master" in Sanskrit) and so does the Latin *magister*, which also means teacher and official. The Greek *magos* was an adjective originally used in reference to oriental sages, scholars and priests. Philosophers like Plato and Aristotle usually made a difference between the scholarly "Persian magi" and the popular "sorcerer magi".

In this respect it is interesting to examine the account Herodotus gave of the story of Cyrus (*Kyros*). Having interpreted the dreams of the Mede King Astyages, the magi predicted to him that his grandson Cyrus, the son of his daughter and the Persian Kambyses, was to bring the Medes' rule to an end and was to be the founder of the Persian world empire. So as soon as Cyrus was born, Astyages wanted to have him killed, but the magi saved the baby's life and later helped him to the throne (Herodotus, *Hist.* I. 108-128).

Thus the prophecy was fulfilled. It is known that for the Israelites who were carried away from their homeland Cyrus represented the Messiah and indeed it was Cyrus who freed them from the Babylonian captivity. Five hundred years later some magi from the east arrived in Jerusalem to pay homage to Christ, the true Messiah, who, to their knowledge, was born in Judaea and whom Herod wanted to have killed. How could they have known this? Matthew notes that "they were warned in a dream not to go back to Herod" (Mt 2:12). Consequently, these magi also knew how to interpret dreams. But who would have thought of Herodotus' account of Cyrus at that time?

Herodotus describes the habits of the Persian priests who did not build temples and did not erect statues because they did not believe in gods having human figures. They offered their sacrifices to the Sun, the Moon, fire and water from the top of mountains. No man was allowed to offer a sacrifice without the assistance of these priests, who sang about the origin of the gods during the ceremony (Herodotus, *Hist.* I. 131-140).

At this point the Greek historian shows some lack of information. He says that Aphrodite was called *Mitras* by the Persians and that the magi were allowed, with the exception of dogs, to sacrifice any animal. This proves that he must have met the priests of the sect which united the cult of the Indian Sun-god, *Mitras*, with the teaching of Zarathustra. However, these priests did not belong to the order of the Babylonian magi and did not know Aphrodite, the Greek goddess born of the waves of the sea.

Herodotus on the other hand did not know Zoroaster. He did not know that it was against the cult of Mitras of worshipping the sun and sacrificing bulls that the Iranian prophet had founded his new religion in 589 BC. According to his teachings the only and omnipotent creator of the world was *Ahura-Mazda* (Lord-Wisdom), who governed the stars with the help of good spirits or angels and did not wish to have bloody sacrifices. At the end of the "world era" he was supposed to send along the Redeemer King, who was to free mankind of the reign of *Ahriman*, the evil deity.

Zoroaster and his priests were not magi, they merely adopted this name during the age of the Seleucids. Their prophecy of the advent of the Messiah became more and more widespread in Mesopotamia. The apocryphal Arabic Gospel of the Savior's Infancy written in the 3rd century by Syrian Christians converted from the Mitras cult, refers to Zoroaster's prophecy. The writing is a skillfully compiled blend of certain Persian traditions and quotations from the gospel of Matthew,

Luke and Jacob. In the seventh chapter of the Latin translation from the sixth century entitled *Evangelium Infantiae Arabicum* we find the following description:

> And it came to pass, when the Lord Jesus was born at Bethlehem of Judaea, in the time of King Herod, behold, magi came from the east to Jerusalem, as Zaradust [Zoroaster] had predicted; and there were with them gifts, gold and frankincense and myrrh. They adored him, and presented him their gifts. Then the Lady Mary took one of the swaddling bands, and, on account of the smallness of her means, gave it to them... And in the same hour there appeared to them an angel in the form of that star which had before guided them on the journey; and they went away, following the guidance of its light, until they arrived in their own country. (Hennecke and Schneemetcher 1963).

This is the only ancient text which explicitly mentions the magi being guided by an angel "in the form of that star", which reflects the teaching of Zoroaster: the Lord governs the stars and guides good people with the help of angels. This is not in contradiction with Christian tradition and the most old Christian works of art represent the magi dressed as Persian priests and being guided to Bethlehem by an angel.

On the other hand, Berossos, a Babylonian priest of Marduk, claimed that the order of the magi was founded by the Chaldaeans. They had been the masters of arithmetic, geometry, architecture and astronomy for thousands of years and they were familiar with the hidden forces of nature. The name *Chaldaean* finally became the adjective qualifying the profession itself. Some reliable data are provided by Strabon (63 BC - 21 AD), a contemporary of Caesar Augustus. Strabon worked in Rome, Athens, Egypt and Syria writing studies of geography and ethnology. After praising the strict moral values and science of the Babylonian magi, he says:

> After the death of Alexander the Great only the local sages were allowed to stay in Babylon in a determined dwelling place. They are called Chaldaeans and are astronomers. Some of them know how to interpret the constellations of the hour of birth, but they are not recognized by the others. The Chaldaean astronomers have different schools originating in Uruk, Barsippa and other cities. They follow different methods and teach different theories concerning the same subjects. They have some excellent mathematicians among them, like for example Naburianus, Cidenas, Sudines, Seleucus and many other renowned people (Strabon, *Geographika Bibl.* XVI. 1: 5-6).

The names of the four mathematicians are also known from other sources. Seleucus, who was of Greek origin, returned from Babylon to Athens in 170 BC, and there he was a senior contemporary and perhaps even the master of Hipparchus; he was the first known astronomer to teach the rotation of the earth round its axis and the first to want to prove this.

Sudines, whose name in cuneiform writing is *Anu-se-su-idinna*, became the astronomer to the court of Attalus, king of Pergamos in 240 BC. The most famous, however, are the other two Chaldaeans, because they were the founders of the first scientific schools of astronomy. To indicate which of the two scientific methods they used, their students wrote their names on their tables of calculations. Naburianus or *Naburiannu* devised the so-called first method (System A) around 480 BC, after having precisely determined that the interval between two successive new moons was 29 days, 12 hours and 44 minutes. This is the length of a synodic month, and 235 synodic months total almost exactly 19 solar years, when the phases of the Moon are repeated on the same days of the year.

This was the calendar system used by Cidenas (*Kidinnu*) around 350 BC, when he determined the periodical changes perceived in the motions of the Moon and the planets by a series of numbers similar to the sine function. Cidenas is believed to be the author of the second and more precise method (System B) and the last ephemerides in cuneiform writing were made with his method of calculation.

These historical data enable us to picture the astronomical knowledge of the Magi, who went on a pilgrimage to Jerusalem in 7 BC. However, the passages quoted above also show that the notions people had of the magi at that time were just as confused as the ones that exist today. This circumstance makes it all the more difficult for translators to render the proper meaning of the respective expressions in the Bible.

What kind of Magi did Matthew talk of in the introduction to the Gospel? He had a profound knowledge of both the writings of the Old Testament and the Middle East of his age. The Hebrew prophets in Egypt, Israel and Babylon fought against the priests of magic for several hundreds of years. When they mentioned them, they called them different names: diviners, sorcerers and magicians, interpreters of signs and dreams, starmongers, conjurers, herbalists, healers and enchanters. Their equivalents in today's society seem to be people with paranormal abilities, palmists and graphologists, astrologers, spiritists, and in a sense also psychologists and hypnotizers. What in ancient times was but the secret trade of a few initiates, is today mostly practiced at a scientific level and is controlled by state institutions. (15)

The Hebrew prophets have always recognized and rejected the mistakes and harmful effects of magic, and this shows their spiritual maturity and strength. The law of Moses very wisely forbade the priests to use any magic arts, so that they would be free to listen to the word of the Lord Almighty and avoid recourse to human practices. The Lord alone knows the secrets of nature and the future of Man, and he will send the true Messiah who can save Man from the destructive effects of blind natural forces. (Deut 18: 10-15: "There must never be anyone among you who practices divination, who is soothsayer or sorcerer, who uses charms, consults spirits, or calls up the dead... The Lord your God will raise up for you a prophet like myself, from among yourselves; to him you must listen".)

The original form of the word *Magus* occurs only once in the Hebrew Bible, namely in the book of the prophet Jeremiah (39: 3-13); when Nebuchadnezzar had Jerusalem destroyed in 588 BC, it was in the presence of his Chief Magus, *Nergal-sharezer Rab-Mag*, "prince of Sin-Magir". The Hebrew expression *rab-mag* is rendered into English as "chief officer". In all probability he was the head of the Magian priestly cast which especially worshipped the deities of Mars (*Nergal*) and the Moon (*Sin*). Some tables in cuneiform writing refer to this event and they call the Chief Magus *Nergal-sar-uzur Sin-magiru*, who actually became king of Babylon after Nebuchadnezzar's death and ruled for four years (Kugler 1912, II. p.391). The rebel king Zedekiah was carried away and blinded together with his men. Jeremiah, however, was set free because the Babylonian magi knew and respected the Hebrew prophets. The books of Jeremiah, Ezekiel, Daniel, Ezra and Nehemiah testify to this.

In the years of exile Ezekiel, Daniel and the Israelite priests could freely practice their profession and teach their people. The Chaldaean and Persian kings were greatly impressed by their wisdom, strong faith and deep piety. Finally, they too worshipped the God of Israel as the King of Heaven, because "He is the living God, and his kingship never ends; He saves, sets free, and works signs and wonders in the heavens and on earth" (Dan 4: 34; 6: 27-28; Ezra 1: 2).

For forty years Daniel was the most confidential counselor of the Babylonian kings. He arrived in Babylon as a child, with the first group of exiled Israelites in 597 BC. Nebuchadnezzar selected a few Israelite boys of noble origin, who received a schooling of three years. They learned the language, writing and all the other sciences of the Chaldaeans so they could serve in the royal court. Daniel was the most talented among them; he had prophetic faculties: "Daniel had the gift of interpreting every kind of vision and dream" (1: 17). He received also a new name, *Bel-tsar-uzur*, which means "the Lord protects his life". (The Latin transliteration of his name is *Balthassar*, and in the new English translations *Belteshazzar*.)

Nebuchadnezzar once had a significant dream concerning the future of his nation, but he could not remember it in every detail. He summoned his magi and ordered them to tell him what he had dreamt. However, the magi declared that if he himself could not remember his dream, no magus would be able to interpret it. Their answer enraged the king and he ordered the magi to be executed. Their life was saved by the young Daniel because the king's dream and its meaning concerning the future were revealed to him by the Lord of Heaven. Daniel's prophetic faculties were then recognized by Nebuchadnezzar, who "also made him governor of the whole province and head of all the sages of Babylon" (Dan 2: 48).

These accounts are written in Aramaic in the first eight chapters of Daniel's book, while the other chapters are in Hebrew. Its editors most probably quote the original Babylonian writings, because the dialect the Chaldaeans spoke was also Aramaic. When the king saw that every prophecy of Daniel had been literally fulfilled, he conferred the rank of Supreme Magus on Daniel; he made him head of the Chaldaean magi (Dan 4: 6; 5: 11). The Aramaic expressions *rab-haretumija* or *rab-hartumi* is the equivalent of the Babylonian term: "great scholar" or "great master" (cf. *BDB*. 1977). In the Old Syriac and Greek text he is the head of the Chaldaean magi (*archônta epi magoi chaldaîoi*, Dan 5: 11; according to Theodotion).

In the Bible translations we find mostly "magicians" or "sorcerers", which can lead to wrong conceptions. These passages in the Book of Daniel are not about the Egyptian pharaoh's priests, who by magic art change their sticks into snakes or water into blood when they want to imitate Moses (Ex 7: 10-25). They are not circus magicians either, who conjure white doves out of a top hat without the public knowing how they perform their astounding tricks.

The Book of Daniel characterizes the Babylonian magi repeatedly by the same words in a positive sense as the scientists of that time: they are interpreters of signs and dreams, enchanters, soothsayers, Chaldaeans. In the Aramaic text these words are always used in the collective sense. Therefore they all denote the profession of the magi.

Traditionally the science of the Chaldaeans is astronomy and the true sage among them is one who, besides being able to calculate the position of the stars in advance, is also capable of foretelling the events of the future. A true magus is someone who not only understands symbols, graphic signs, constellations, visions and dreams, but can interpret their meaning concerning the future as well.

Among the Babylonian sages it is only the prophet Daniel who has the power to do all this, because "he is a man in whom lives the spirit of God Most Holy" (Dan 4: 5; 5: 11). That was why he became head of the magi. Besides being familiar with their science, he could determine the date of future events. He was considered the greatest magus in the whole empire. He is the only Hebrew prophet whose memory was honored by an ornate sepulcher, which can be seen among the ruins of Shusha even today. (The winter palace of the Persian kings was in the town of Shusha southeast of Babylon, and that was where the Israelite Mardokeus became one of the most important men of King Xerxes. His story is related in the Book of Esther.)

Daniel refers to a direct divine revelation when he gives the number of years to come until the advent of the Messiah and the destruction of Jerusalem. However, a seal will be set on his prophecy: "You must keep the vision secret, for there are still many days to go", that is, he is made to write it in a form which, until the prophecies are fulfilled, is understood only by the initiates. Calculating from the date of the royal order for the return of the exiles and the rebuilding of Jerusalem, "seventy weeks are decreed for your people and your city for anointing the Holy of Holies" and "seven weeks for the coming of the anointed Prince", the Messiah, "and after the sixty-two weeks the city and the sanctuary will be destroyed by a Prince who will come" (Dan 8: 26; 9: 24-26).

Here the "weeks" are weeks of years; one week means seven years, thus we have $(70 \times 7) + (7 \times 7) = 490 + 49 = 539$ years. If this interpretation is correct, the 539 years give precisely the year when the Messiah (Christ) was to be born, calculated from the first year of the Persian King Cyrus. The first year of his reign began in the month Nisan (March) 538 BC, and in the same year he proclaimed that the Temple in Jerusalem shall be rebuilt. (The edict of Cyrus is quoted in the Book of Ezra 1: 2; 6: 3).

Christ refers to Daniel's prophecies several times. With his advent, he claims, they were partially fulfilled and everything else will be fulfilled in future from the destruction of Jerusalem to the world's end (Mt 24: 1-36; Lk 21: 5-38). In the year 70 of our era, as a matter of fact 77 years after the birth of Christ, the Roman army led by Titus destroyed the city of Jerusalem and with it the Temple (Josephus, *Bellum Iud.* IV. 3).

The Babylonian magi, already including some Israelites at the time, must have carefully preserved this prophecy of their master. They were probably able to interpret the dates of the prophet much better than we can today, and with the help of those dates they could calculate the date of the Messiah's advent to Jerusalem. We know from rabbinic traditions that Daniel himself made astronomical observations and calculations, because it was required of all those who served the Chaldaean and Persian kings. Although his prophecies are definitely not linked to his astronomical activity, his dates correspond to certain astronomical periods found in some Babylonian cuneiform tables. (**16**)

Ezekiel, the other great prophet among the exiled Judaeans, had no personal contact with the Babylonian priests, but he was familiar with their science and used their calendar. He made use of the Chaldaeans' geometry to determine the huge size of the temple of the future, and he gave the exact place and time of his visions, i.e. between the years 593-571 BC. He did not give any dates to denote the beginning the era of the Messiah, but repeatedly declared he was to come soon, as "the good Shepherd for all his people and Prince of peace for ever", who was to be the founder of his eternal kingdom in Jerusalem (Ezek 37: 21-28).

This prophecy was taken literally by the faithful Israelites, both those who had returned to their country and those who stayed in Mesopotamia. Since they were unable to conceal the source of their national pride and hope before the Gentiles, the news of the prince awaited in Jerusalem quickly spread among the peoples living under Persian and Parthian rule. The Gentiles also expected the advent of a liberating king who was to bring about peace among the nations.

A striking feature of Ezekiel's prophecies is that the four cardinal constellations play a symbolic role in the advent of the Messiah and the establishment of his Kingdom. They appear in his visions as "four living beings" which move in great circles between heaven and earth "where the spirit urges them". Their faces look like human faces, "and all four have a lion's face to the right, and all four have an eagle's face". Over their wings is a sort of vault, gleaming like crystal, and above the vault high up on a throne sits a being that looks like a man surrounded by a bright rainbow (Ezek 1: 4-28).

The prophet always emphasizes that these figures are only analogies and reflected images (*mareoth* in Hebrew), suggesting the glory or light of the Lord Almighty: "It was something that looked like the glory of the Lord [He-who-is]. I looked [thus], and I prostrated myself". These are the words with which the prophet concludes his first revelation. It is very important that he never confounds the images and reality itself, he always takes good care to distinguish appearance from invisible reality. In this way he warns people against superstition and idolatry.

In this description of Ezekiel we can trace some images of the Babylonian memorials and certain expressions found in cuneiform writings, but the significance and purpose of the vision are inconsistent with mythological ideas. The entrances of Assyrian-Babylonian palaces and temples were guarded by statues of lions on the right and winged bulls with human faces on the left. The border stones and city gates were decorated with the constellations of the Lion, Bull, Water Bearer, Scorpion and Eagle, and in the inscriptions they feature as gods. The prophet, however, sees and shows us that they are not gods; they simply look like living creatures, because it is the Lord's spirit that sets them in motion and controls them. The stars are the creations and servants of Israel's God, the sole omnipotent Lord, and they silently preach his glory with their light and movement.

This revelation saved what was left of Israel from idolatry and from being absorbed by a multitude of foreign peoples. The revelations of the prophet, however, were so characteristic of Babylon that they inevitably aroused the interest of some magi, who wanted to be informed about the future from the motions of the stars. Ezekiel's vision started with the prophet contemplating the heavens, but later it went so far beyond the bounds of physical space and time that Ezekiel's contemporaries were unable to grasp the deepest meaning of the revelation. It was only after the same revelation was even more clearly repeated in the Book of Revelations of the apostle John that the followers of Christ began to realize what it meant. (17)

This was also the case with Balaam's vision. The prophecy of the star of Jacob was known centuries before Ezekiel and Daniel both in Mesopotamia and Israel, but it was interpreted in different ways. This is the prophecy of an Assyrian-Babylonian magus, not a Hebrew prophet. The story is described in detail in the fourth book of Moses (Num 22-24).

By that time the first Israelite settlers had reached the eastern bank of the Jordan and had set up their camp on the plateau of Moab. The Moabite king, having seen the victories they won over the neighboring peoples, dreaded their presence. He sent messengers to summon Balaam and asked him to curse Israel. He said to him: "We may then be able to defeat them and drive them out of the country. For this I know: the man you bless is blessed, the man you curse is accursed" (Num 22: 6).

Balaam came from the village of Petor (*Pitru*) on the northeastern bank of the Euphrates. Archaeologists found the name of the village on the monument of Shalmaneser II, and the benedictions and maledictions of the magi can be found in many of the Assyrian cuneiform texts.

In the Book of Moses Balaam is characterized as a true magus who is aware of the name and will of the Lord Almighty. In vain do the Moabites promise him gold and silver, they cannot bribe him. While watching the camp of the Israelites from the neighboring hills, Balaam speaks of the tribe of Jacob in terms of the highest praise, calling them the chosen and blessed people of the Lord:

The oracle of Balaam, the man with far-seeing eyes, who hears the word of God...: I see him, but not in the present, I behold him, but not close at hand: a star from Jacob takes the leadership, a scepter arises from Israel (Num 24: 17).

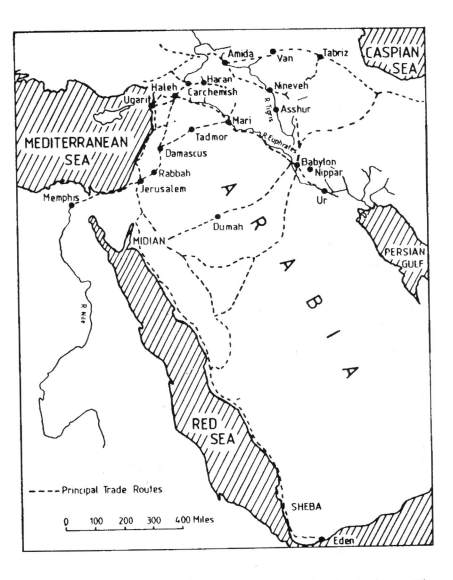

Fig. 6: Map of Mesopotamia and Arabia at the time of the birth of Jesus. The principal caravan road between Babylon and Jerusalem ran through the cities of Mari, Tadmor, Damascus and Rabbah.

This new English translation is a paraphrase of the rising star of Jacob in the Hebrew original. In the ancient East the star signified the deified king. Many scribes of the Old Covenant after the Exile referred

Balaam's prophecy to the Davidic dynasty from which the Messiah was to come, the anointed King. The early Church Fathers saw the sign of Christ in the "star of Jacob". On the one hand they interpreted it figuratively, as the Messiah himself, and on the other hand in a concrete sense, as a star in heaven. The Septuagint renders Balaam's words as follows: "A star rises from Jacob and a man [or a leader] from Israel." This version was used by the early Fathers. St. Justin Martyr in the 2nd century was the first to put down the following view:

> It was Moses himself who told us that he [Christ] was to be born like a star from the kin of Abraham: A star rises from Jacob and a leader from Israel. Another passage also says: Rising [Anatolê] is his name [Zech 3: 8]. And when the star appeared in the sky at the time of his birth, as it says in the Memorandum of the Apostles, the magi of Arabia realized what had happened and came to pay homage to him (Justin Martyr, *Dialogus cum Tryphone* 106: 4).

The description Origen gives of this old Christian tradition is even clearer. The magi visiting Bethlehem, he says, were not wandering Chaldaeans but learned priests. The star they observed must have been one of the rare celestial phenomena which, according to Greek astronomers, usually point to a happy event. However, none of them was able to foretell this one. Balaam alone had predicted the rising of the star signifying the arrival of a king from Israel. "And when the magi saw the sign given by God in heaven, they wanted to see him too who was announced by that sign. We believe they knew about Balaam's prophecy" (Origen, *Contra Celsum* I. 58-60).

In a later speech Origen definitely proclaims:

> Although it was Moses who had introduced Balaam's prophecies into the Sacred Books, the inhabitants of Mesopotamia had a lot more reason to preserve them, since they held Balaam in great esteem. In addition, they are believed to be Balaam's disciples as far as magic is concerned. Traditionally, it is to him that the eastern countries trace back the magi, who were supposed to know the words of all his prophecies, including this one: A star rises from Jacob and a man from Israel. The Magi had this text. When Jesus was born, they recognized the star and realized that the prophecy had been fulfilled (Origen, *Homilia in Num.* 24: 13-17).

St. Jerome, too, mentions that the Magi of Matthew were the successors of Balaam, as heirs to his trade and prophecy. (*Comment. in Matth.* I. 2). The most distinguished Fathers agreed with this view. However, the question arises: What is the origin of this tradition? Where does it come from? And what is its significance? It is remarkable that neither Matthew nor the Greek apocrypha refer to Balaam.

St. Luke relates that at the time of the Judaean persecutions a great many followers of Christ fled to Syria. The first religious communities were formed in Damascus and Antioch and it was there that they were first called Christians (Acts 9-11). Recent findings testify that it was there that the first Christians had a direct contact with some magi who considered themselves the priests of the Persian Zoroaster. Many of them became Christians, and they identified Balaam with the Iranian prophet. The "Arabic Gospel of the Savior's Infancy" explicitly refers to Zoroaster's prophecy.

The Apostles who had been to Syria must have noticed this error. Furthermore, they disapproved of Balaam, since it was his advice the Moabites followed when they invited the Israelites to take part in their sacrificial feasts, which induced them to be unfaithful and finally cost twenty-four thousand Israelites their lives. (Num 25: 1-9; 31: 16; 2 Pet 2: 15; Rev 2: 14)

This may be one reason why Matthew does not quote Balaam's prophecy. Nevertheless, the Syrian traditions and the comments of the eastern Church Fathers are significant to us because they testify to the following facts, which are also suggested by Matthew's text: (1) the magi visiting Bethlehem were astronomers and priests; (2) they were familiar with and believed in the prophecies of the Messiah awaited in Judaea; (3) they watched and recognized the heavenly signs indicating the birth of the Messiah; (4) they came to Jerusalem from the direction of Persia through the Arabian Desert and Damascus.

Why do the Church Fathers of the first centuries talk about Persia as the homeland of the Magi? It seems obvious that what they have in mind is not Iran, which is farther to the east, but Mesopotamia (Iraq today). The Arabian Desert lies between Babylon and Jerusalem and the busiest caravan route to Jerusalem leads through Mari, Tadmor (Palmyra) and Damascus.

The most authentic facts were collected by the Syrian born St. John Chrysostom (350-407 AD) in Antioch, the very scene of the original tradition. First he also claimed that the Magi arrived in Judaea from the north, through Damascus. Later he gave a more accurate definition of where their country was:

At the time the peoples of Egypt and Babylon suffered more from aggressive violence than the rest of the world. Christ, however, wanted to make them realize that he would save their lives and give the world hope for renewal, if they were ready to convert to the Christian faith. So he sent the Magi back to Babylon and he himself went to Egypt with his mother...It follows that those Magi, having hastily returned home, must have heralded the good news in Babylon (Chrysostom, *Comment. in Matth*. VI. 2; VIII. 2-4).

The old Christian writers never claimed that Matthew's Magi were Persian. On the other hand, they were right when they called their country Persia, because the Arsacids reigning at the time of Jesus were of Persian origin and from 226 to 651 AD Mesopotamia was again ruled by the Persian dynasty of Sassanides.

This explains why throughout ancient Christian art the Magi were represented in Persian clothing. The first such paintings were probably made in Syria in the 2nd century and, in the course of the following three hundred years they served as models for the reliefs, mosaics and frescoes to be seen even today in the Roman catacombs, medieval churches and a great number of museums. The oldest works of art are significant not only for the theologian but for the historian, since they testify to the original tradition in the most authentic way. They never represent angels, only the three Magi with their gifts in their hands, as they approach with long steps the infant Jesus sitting in his mother's lap. The first of the Magi usually points at the star above the heads of the mother and child.

Their gifts are liturgical objects characteristic of the ones used in the temple of Babylon and probably originating from its treasury. Writing about the Chaldaeans, Herodotus mentions that they usually sold part of the sacrificial donations received from the people and kept some of the more valuable objects in the treasury of the temple. The rich offered expensive scents, frankincense and myrrh, as well as gold vessels and censers or incense boats. The priests of Babylon "burned frankincense worth a thousand talents on new year's day in honor of their god" (Herodotus, *Hist*. I. 183).

According to all indications the Magi visiting Bethlehem were the priests of the Babylonian Marduk sanctuary, which accounts for their knowledge of astronomy too. From among the Christian works of art dating from the 3rd century the most popular ones were those representing the three Magi in the presence of the prophet Daniel. If we compare them to the Stone Tablet of Sippar the similarity of composition is apparent: the stone tablet in cuneiform writing also represents three magi approaching the King of Heaven with three stars above his head. The ancient Christian artists could never have seen this tablet, so the similarity can only be explained by historical and psychological correlations (see Fig. 35: p. 231).

A magnificent mosaic similar to the one described above decorated the façade of the church built in Bethlehem over the nativity cave by the emperor Constantine the Great in 326 AD. It was the mosaic that saved the church in 614 AD when Palestine was occupied by the

Fig. 7: The Magi from Babylon. This relief is exhibited as the "Sancto Dogmatico No.104" in the Lateran Museum (Rome). Its earlier version from the 3rd century is preserved in the Vatican Museum (No. 310-320). On this relief we can see Ezekiel prophesying the resurrection of the dead in Babylon. In his left hand he has a scroll, the sign of the prophets. Behind him stands the young Daniel. In his right hand Ezekiel holds the tree of life, with which he resurrects the dead: "They come to life again and stand up on their feet, an immense army" (Ezek 37: 10). The Magi (with their camels in the background) come from the direction where Ezekiel and Daniel stand, i.e. from Babylon. The first of the Magi holds a gold diadem (*aurum coronarium*) in his left hand. He points at the six-pointed star which is both the sign of the conjunction and the monogram of Jesus Christ (the letter I joined to the letter X). The second Magus brings a basketful of frankincense, and the third one some myrrh. According to St. Ireneus (*Adv. Haer.* 3: 9), by offering the gold diadem, the Magi recognize the sovereignty of Jesus, and the frankincense expresses their reverence; myrrh is offered to him as the Savior who has come into the world to give his life for mortal mankind.

Persians, who destroyed the Christian churches. The bishops of the Council of Jerusalem (836 AD) noted:

> "The Persians, having destroyed the towns of Syria and arriving in Bethlehem, saw there, to their great surprise, the picture of the Magi. Out of respect to their forefathers they showed their goodwill by sparing the church. That is why it still stands there intact today." (Cf. Mazzoleni 1985).

Can we take it for certain that the magi were all Gentiles? As a matter of fact, the idea that the three Magi of East represented Gentile nations became widespread only in the 8th century, following the appearance of writings of Bede the Venerable. Let us come back to the account of the apostle Matthew. Why is it that he fails to mention the prophecy of Balaam or that of Isaiah or the Psalm, according to which the kings of Arabia and foreign princes were to come to Jerusalem with valuable gifts to pay homage to the Messiah? The early Fathers had every reason and right to link these to the visit of the Magi to

Fig. 8: Most reliefs representing Daniel the Magus ornament the sarcophagi (stone coffins) of ancient Christian cemeteries. One of them is to be seen on the tomb of Pope Clement IX, the others are in the *Museo Pio Cristiano* of the Vatican Museum. This manner of representing Daniel was very popular, because it was in Babylon that he had prophesied the date of the Messiah's coming. Once, however, Daniel was falsely accused and, deprived of his clothes, he was thrown into the den of hungry lions. The animals did not touch him, which proved his innocence and magic power. Therefore the king decreed that in his empire all shall worship the God of Daniel (Dan 6: 27). In accordance with this story the central figure of these reliefs is the prophet Daniel standing among the lions, with his hands raised in prayer. Again, from the direction where Daniel is, the Magi come from the East, viz. from Babylon.

Jerusalem, but it cannot be proved that the writer of the Gospel was inspired by these prophecies. He was very much aware of the fact that the Magi were neither kings nor pagan princes, nor did they come from Arabia. He also knew that even though the Magi were familiar with the Assyrian Balaam's prophecy, they had nothing to do with him.

The original texts provide no decisive evidence of the assumption that these Magi from the East were all of Gentile origin. There are certain references which rather seem to suggest that there were some Israelites among them. They may have been the descendants of those who did not return to Judaea after the Babylonian exile. Texts of the Old Testament and Mesopotamian finds testify that these Israelites had mastered the science of the Magi, some of them held important state offices, others fell victim to certain delusions and astrology, but they always remained conscious of their race and had faith in the God of their fathers.

It seems most likely that one of the Magi of Matthew was of Judaean origin and it cannot be excluded that all of them were related to an exiled tribe of Israel. This is shown by their faith in Hebrew prophecies promising the advent of the Messiah, and by the fact that they could make themselves understood in Jerusalem and Bethlehem without the help of any interpreters. Also, on arriving there they were definitely looking for a king of the Judaeans and wanted to pay homage to him, which no Gentiles would have done.

74

The three traditional names of the Magi first occurred in Syrian sources: *Karsudas, Hior and Bazantor*, which are most probably symbolic names dating from a later period, because their original names were not known. In the 5th century these names developed into *Caspar, Melchior* and *Balthassar* in the Aramaic and Greek dialects. Balthassar is the Babylonian name of the prophet Daniel, and Melchior is distinctly a Hebrew name: *Melekh-ior* ("king of light"), which is suggestive of Jupiter, the star of the kings. Caspar may be the abbreviated form of the Persian *Gathasphar*, which in turn contains the name of Saturn. In any case, it seems that at least one of the three Magi, the one called Melchior, was considered to be of Hebrew origin by some old Christian traditions.

And finally we come to the last question, which might as well have been the first one: Why does Matthew call the visitors from the East simply "Magi"? He might have called them Chaldaeans or astrologers or magicians, since he was well familiar with these characteristic terms and the people they referred to. However, the Magi in question obviously did not belong to any of these groups. Their rank in the Syrian text is *meguse*, that is, master. At the same time their characteristics are given clearly and unambiguously. They are aware of the significance of the star and the dream, they are looking for the king born in Judaea, they have complete faith in Micheas' prophecy about Bethlehem where they do find the infant Jesus, they have no doubt about Jesus being the king they are seeking, they pay homage to him with gifts and then they do not return to Herod to betray him for money. These characteristics describe scholarly, religious, wise and honest people. There is no hint of false magi or magicians here.

Consequently, in order to avoid any false associations with the modern usage of the word, it is best to translate Matthew's Magi as "Sages of the East". On the other hand, the word is rendered as "astrologers" in some recent Bible translations. This seems unacceptable as it is obviously contrary to Matthew's intention.

The Fathers of the Church stress that the redeeming force and divine wisdom of Christ put an end to every practice of magic and to the misconception that man's fate is determined by the stars. In this respect they are no doubt right. However, as noted by Raymond Brown, a member of the Pontifical Biblical Commission:

> My own opinion is that such references reflect a Christian use of Matthew in an apologetic against magic rather than a true exegesis of Matthew. There is not the slightest hint of false practice in Matthew's description of the Magi: they are wholly admirable. They represent the best of pagan lore and religious perceptivity which has come to seek Jesus through revelation in nature (R.E. Brown 1977).

Fig. 9: Base relief from the 3rd century: The Magi in Bethlehem. The first Magus points at the three stars above the head of Jesus and his mother. Behind the throne stands Joseph, the guardian of the Holy Family. These reliefs bear witness to the early Christian tradition concerning the star of Bethlehem. (*Museo Pio Cristiano*, Rome; with permission of the Vatican Museum.)

But surely this revelation in nature begins with the observation and consideration of the heavens and the stars.

From Babylon to Bethlehem

Despite the upheavals of many centuries, the ruins of Babylon still remain. They help us to corroborate historical data, even if we cannot explain everything. Today the ruins of Babylon are linked to Bethlehem with concrete roads. The highway from Baghdad crosses the Syrian desert almost in a straight line. At a fork in the road a sign indicates the way to Jerusalem. By car we can make the 870 km long journey in ten hours.

Two thousand years ago the shortest caravan way was about 1200 km long leading through Mari, Tadmor and Damascus, and then in the Jordan basin to Judaea. At that time instead of automobiles the travelers used camels, horses and donkeys, and the journey was as tiring as it was dangerous. The best means for transport of persons and goods were camels, because they were able to endure the desert without water for weeks (see Fig. 6. p. 69).

From the Book of Ezra we know the story of the exiles who returned from Babylon to Jerusalem. The journey of the first group took seven months. This was because they were burdened with a great deal of goods and were so many in number, 45,000 people altogether. By order of King Cyrus, they received back 5,400 vessels of gold and silver which Nebuchadnezar had carried away from Jerusalem, and they drove 8,136 domestic animals, among them 6,720 donkeys and 435 camels (Ezra 1: 7 - 2: 67).

Later on, Ezra migrated from Babylon to Jerusalem with 1,500 people. During the journey they took rest periods of three days and they arrived home within four months in the hottest period of the year, from 8 April to 4 August (Ezra 7: 8). They needed pasture and water for the animals. They must, therefore, have circled the desert and followed the western bank of the Euphrates till Haleh or Petor, from where they took the usual route to Damascus. The courier and commercial caravans usually consisted of six or seven members and they traveled faster on the route through Mari and Damascus. According to some ancient records, a loaded camel could cover 25 or 30 kilometers a day. Thus the journey of a caravan from Babylon to Jerusalem took around 48 days.

On the basis of Babylonian customs we can assume that the Magi of Matthew took the usual route of the commercial caravans. When did they start and when did they arrive at Bethlehem? This is what we would like to learn with the help of the records of Matthew and of the new Babylonian finds. We accept the assumptions that were made in the previous chapter: (1) Jesus was born in Bethlehem in the period of the first census in the year 7 BC, as this is supported by the record of St. Luke and the Memorandum of Augustus; (2) the celestial phenomenon mentioned by the Magi in Matthew's text must have been the conjunction of Jupiter and Saturn, which was observable for seven months, and their apparent standstill or stationary points in that year; (3) so, the Magi went to Bethlehem in the year 7 BC sometime during those seven months, when these phenomena were observable.

The possibility of this was demonstrated by the grammatical and linguistic analysis of the original text. The following historical and astronomical reasonings will prove the probability of these statements. We claim that the Magi probably arrived in Bethlehem on November 11 or 12 in the year 7 BC. (I use the plural "we" because I am thinking of the astronomers and researchers with whom I worked for years and who agree on this matter. Some of them are mentioned above. We do not talk of a subjective probability which only would derive from personal interests and conceptions without objective basis. We state as probable the things that are closer to reality than others, because there is stronger evidence supporting them. Those who find other reasons which seem to be as acceptable as ours, from other points of view, can choose as they wish. The decisive question is to what extent one can understand and evaluate the facts.)

The primitive observations of the stars became a mathematical science in the fourth and third century BC, when the Chaldaean astronomers managed to determine the synodic period of the five planets. The synodic period of a planet is the time in which the oppositions and conjunctions, i.e. the same positions relative to the Sun, repeat themselves. Knowledge of the periods in which the same phases of the planets repeat themselves is the first stage of scientific astronomy. The observed periodicity of the celestial phenomena enabled the Chaldaeans to predict the motions of the planets with considerable accuracy.

The most important cuneiform Chaldaean Tables were found in the underground archives of the Babylonian temple. Unfortunately, the ancient terracotta tablets arrived damaged or broken into fragments to the European museums. Otto Neugebauer tells in his last work that from the 60,000 fragments there are only 300 restored and deciphered. These can be divided into three main groups: (1) tables of predicted positions or ephemerides in the modern sense of the word, i.e. day-by-day positions of the Sun, the Moon and the planets; (2) astronomical almanacs which are yearly lists of lunar and planetary phenomena, eclipses, solstices and equinoxes; (3) diaries which concern astronomical and historical events in chronological order, month by month in a given year (Neugebauer 1975).

The ephemerides give the positions of the planets calculated for several decades in advance. For all the successive years, the day and the ecliptic longitude of each planet are given in zodiacal signs, degrees and minutes. These planetary tables deal with the outstanding phenomena in five sections: heliacal or morning rising (conjunction with the Sun), first station or eastern turning point, evening rising (opposition to the Sun), second station or western turning point, heliacal setting. Thus these tables indicate also the period of alternation of retrograde or westward motion, and direct or eastward motion of the planets along the ecliptic. (See: Fig. 13. p. 87).

The Chaldaeans set up an ephemeris for each planet. From these planetary tables they compiled a star almanac for each year, indicating the dates of the phenomena which were observable in certain zodiacal signs. These almanacs served for practical observations and therefore they omitted lists of the degrees of longitude for the planetary positions. The skilled astronomer could calculate the angular distances or aspects between the planets making use of these almanacs.

The greatest part of the preserved cuneiform ephemerides contain the positions of Jupiter and Saturn. The phases of Jupiter were usually computed for 71 years which are equal to six revolutions. They knew and used also the great period of Jupiter which lasts 427 years, that is

36 complete revolutions, when the planet's positions relative to the stars return to the same degree of longitude. The motions and positions of Saturn were computed for 88 years which is equal to the time of three revolutions. Finally, they recognized that 72 Jupiter revolutions = 29 Saturn revolutions = 854 years for the common great period of the two planets, when they meet within the same zodiacal sign (see below: p. 257).

Such data were found in some cuneiform ephemerides only up to 30 BC. A complete table of Jupiter computed for 71 years gives the data from 131 to 60 BC (Neugebauer 1955, 344, No. 611). However, many almanac fragments prove that there existed ephemerides which gave the ecliptic longitudes and phases of the Moon and planets up to 30 AD.

Concerning our subject, the most important almanac is the one which lists the celestial phenomena for the year 305 of the Babylonian Seleucid era, that is, for the year 7/6 BC. It is specially remarkable that precisely this cuneiform almanac is preserved in four copies on different tablets or fragments. The first copy, a tablet of Sippar was found by J. Schaumberger in the Museum of Berlin, and he presented it in the periodical *Biblica* (Schaumberger 1925). His results were supported by the text of the Babylonian almanac found in the Museum of London. This was evaluated and presented by K. Ferrari d'Occhieppo in his books about the Star of Bethlehem (Ferrari d'Occhieppo 1965, 1977, 1978, 1991). This almanac was prepared in the decades before Christ, probably between 30 and 20 BC, on the basis of the ephemerides computed at that time.

In the Babylonian Star Almanac are listed the dates of the following astronomical phenomena which occurred from 4 April 7 BC to 18 April 6 BC: the ingress of the planets in certain zodiacal signs, their rising and setting, the new moons and full moons, the equinoxes and solstices, a solar eclipse on 28 April, the evening setting of Sirius on 15 May, and its morning rising on 28 July, the rising of the Seven Sisters (Pleiades) on 10 November at sunset. We also find the days of the most significant phases of the two giant planets, Jupiter and Saturn, which moved for seven months together in the constellation of Pisces. These data are of special interest to us and, therefore, we have translated them into English (see the Table below: p. 81).

On the front side of the Babylonian Almanac are given the data from 2 April to 20 November 7 BC, and on the reverse side to 18 April 6 BC. The dimensions of the tablet are 12 by 20 centimeters with a thickness of about 4 centimeters. Some professionals have made handwritten copies of each tablet, because it is difficult to read the cuneiform signs on the photographs. (The hand copies were published by A.J. Sachs, 1955. The Babylonian Almanac is to be found in the British Museum under Reg.Nr.BM 35429, and its copy has Sachs

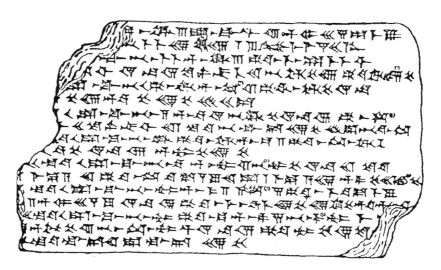

Fig. 10: The front side of the Babylonian Star Almanac (Sachs 1955, Nr.1195, BM 35429)

Nr.1195; the museum registration number and copy number of the other three tablets are: BM 34614 = Sachs 1193; 34659 = Sachs 1194; and the Almanac of Sippar: Berlin, VAT 290-1836 = Sachs 1196.)

The Chaldaean astronomical tables and almanacs are of special interest for the history of science. These cuneiform writings show that in the years around Christ's birth there were still active astronomers in Babylon and that they made correct calculations as well as predictions using the method of Cidenas. Moreover, the fact that there are four surviving versions of the same almanac for the year 7 BC is proof that the Chaldaeans considered the astronomical phenomena expected in that year to be specially important, both from the astronomical and the historical point of view.

From the astronomical point of view the motion of the two giant planets was going to be a very rare and interesting event: for seven months, from 24 May to the end of December, they moved together in the constellation of Pisces along the ecliptic (i.e. in the plane of the Earth's orbit); for four months, from 20 July to 20 November, they moved westwards, close to each other (in common retrograde motion); on 15 September in the evening they appeared simultaneously on the horizon, when they were in opposition (180°) to the Sun and thus they were the brightest among the stars (since at the time of opposition the planets reflect the greatest fraction of incident sunlight); their common evening rising occurred immediately before the autumnal equinox (when every place on the Earth receives 12 hours of daylight and 12 hours of night); and finally, between 12 and 19 November they came together to an apparent standstill in the western stationary points of their paths, and then moving eastwards again they separated quickly.

The astronomers who lived in Mesopotamia in 7 BC had never seen such a phenomenon before. However, according to the cuneiform tables, they knew the 20 years average period of the single Jupiter-Saturn conjunctions in different signs as well as the 140 years average period of their triple conjunctions in the same signs of the Zodiac. But these phenomena lasted only for some few days and were not observable each time. (Of course, these planets are not visible when they rise just after the Sun and set just before the Sun.)

Dates of the positions of Jupiter and Saturn as given in the Babylonian Almanac for the years 304/305 of Seleucid era and converted into dates of the Gregorian Calendar

DATE	JUPITER	SATURN
8 BC	PISCES	PISCES
15 March	morning rising	not visible
7 BC	PISCES	PISCES
4 April	direct motion	morning rising
20 July	eastern stationary	direct motion
27 July	retrograde motion	eastern stationary
29 July	retrograde	retrograde motion
15 September	evening rising	evening rising
25 September	retrograde motion	retrograde
12 November	western stationary	retrograde
13 November	western stationary	western stationary
6 BC	ARIES	PISCES
11 February	ingress Aries	direct motion
27 February	direct motion	evening setting
21 March	evening setting	direct motion
18 April	direct motion	morning rising

The Magi travelling to Jerusalem might have used a copy of the above mentioned almanac. In any case, they knew that the common motion of the two planets would be observable for three months in that year. And in the three months September, October and November the weather conditions were usually favorable there in the area between the Euphrates and the Jordan. The cloudless sky was a good opportunity for the traveling astronomers. When they arrived in Jerusalem, they stated two times that they had observed the star at the

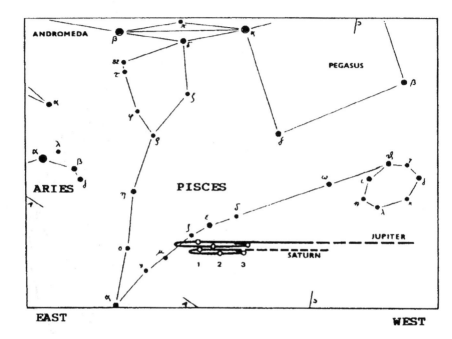

EAST   WEST

Fig.

11: This star map shows the path of Jupiter and Saturn through the constellation of Pisces during the triple conjunction of 7 BC. The dotted line indicates the intervals from the 1st of January until the days of the morning rising of the two planets; until 15th March (Jupiter) and 4th April (Saturn). The continous lines indicate their paths with the regressive loops, until 20th December, 7 BC. From April on their direct motion becomes slower and slower until their eastern turning points, 20 and 27 July, where their position seems to be unchanged for around ten days. Thereafter they move backwards, in retrograde motion, for three months, until their western turning points on 12 and 29 November respectively; then they recommence the direct motion from right to left. (Drawing by Herman Mucke, in the book of Ferrari d'Occhieppo 1977.) The three small rings indicate the following dates:

    1. 27/28 May, the first exact conjunction (within 1°);
    2. 15 September, the last common evening rising (1°1');
    3. 12/13 November, the western stationary point.

82

time of its evening rising. According to their almanac it was on 15th September that this occurred. Consequently, it must have been in their own country, in Babylon, that they had observed the evening rising of that star, and a few days later they would start out for Jerusalem. Therefore, if we reckon with the usual journey time of a Babylonian

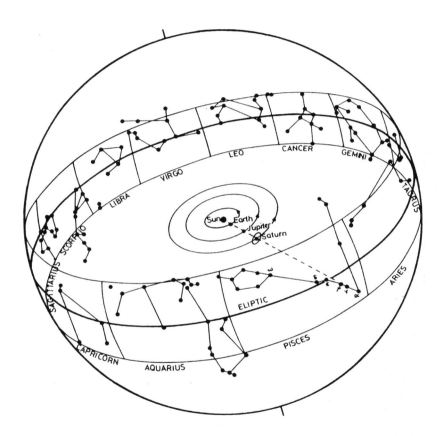

Fig. 12: The conjunction of Jupiter and Saturn against the background of the ecliptic plane. Looking from Earth, at sunset on 15 September 7 BC, the two planets appeared to be close together on the same ecliptic longitude in the constellation of Pisces, when they were in opposition to the Sun in Virgo. (Hughes 1979)

caravan, we can assume that it was the first week of November when the Magi arrived in Judaea.

This assumption seems to be supported by the statement of Matthew that, when the magi, traveling on the road from Jerusalem to Bethlehem, saw the star, "they rejoiced with exceeding great joy" (Mt 2:10). What was then the real cause for their great joy? Certainly not the view of the star again, since it was visible from April till December. But the second stationary points of Jupiter and Saturn was predicted in their almanac, and these would occur on 12 and 13 November. It could be only the observation of this phenomenon that made the Magi rejoice. If so, they arrived in Bethlehem on some day between 10 and 14 November. This assumption is supported also by the sequence of the astronomical events.

In the years around Christ's birth the 51 meter high substructure of the Babylonian tower was still in a good state of preservation. It was from this high platform that the astronomers observed and measured the time and place of the rising and setting of the planets. The aim of their observations must have been to ascertain the reliability of the old star almanac, in which they had found predicted data. What could they have observed in the year 7 BC?

On 15 March at dawn Jupiter was observable only for a few minutes when the stars of the zodiacal signs had already disappeared in the sunshine. From 20 July on, after its first stationary point Jupiter was rising shortly before midnight and Saturn followed it 15 minutes later. Henceforth they were rising some minutes earlier each night while their position shifted westwards, that is their retrograde motion began. Between 1 and 15 September the two planets were visible close to each other every night from evening till morning among the fixed stars in the western branch of Pisces.

The most important date of the Babylonian almanac was the 21st day of the 6th Babylonian month (*Ululu 21*) or 15 September. On that day the angular distance of the two planets relative to the Sun was exactly 180 degrees, thus they had maximum brightness and rose simultaneously at sunset. This was their last observable evening rising in that year. September 15 was also the day of the traditional autumn festival of Marduk-Jupiter, the heavenly Protector of Babylon. At that time the followers of Zarathustra had certainly substituted Marduk with *Ahura-Mazda*, the Lord of Wisdom, and the Magi, who were preparing to go to Jerusalem, must have celebrated the day together with the others (Zarathustrians), regardless of whether they believed or not in the prophecies of Zarathustra. This was perhaps the reason why they left Babylon after the 15th of September.

In the following weeks, when the Magi were on the way toward Damascus, the two planets were rising earlier each day before sunset.

84

In October the heliacal setting of Jupiter was still visible at dawn, but this was not interesting for the Magi; it was not even recorded in their almanac. The next important dates indicated the second standstill of Jupiter and Saturn at their western stationary points, November 12th and 13th. On these days the phenomenon would be observable from evening till midnight. Therefore, we can safely assume that the Magi strove to arrive in Jerusalem by that time. One of them probably had already been there beforehand. Thus they could have been aware that Jerusalem was situated 700 meters higher than the tower of Babylon, and that from there they could better observe the celestial phenomena.

Fig. 13 below helps us to explain these phenomena. The star maps show the actual paths of Jupiter and Saturn through the constellation of Pisces during the triple conjunction. The figures under the star map represent the retrograde motion and the apparent stationary points. An observable triple conjunction and retrograde motion of the superior planets occur when they are at opposition to the Sun and in perigee, i.e., closest to the Earth, while the Sun moves 60 degrees away from the line of opposition. From 15 September to 13 November 7 BC, the Sun proceeded 60 degrees in longitude (from 22° Virgo to 21° Scorpio), while Jupiter and Saturn were retrograde, i.e. they moved westward from 24° to 20° of Pisces. At the same time, the angular distance between the two planets changed only 20 arc minutes, which was not perceptible to the naked eye. In view of the Magi, these last sixty days were the most important period of the great conjunction.

According to recent calculations the three exact conjunctions of Jupiter and Saturn occurred on 27th May, 6th October and 1st December. However, these dates are not given in the Babylonian star almanac, and the three conjunctions are not even mentioned in cuneiform writings explicitly. The importance of this phenomenon is nevertheless implicitly given in the dates of the stationary points of Jupiter and Saturn.

Since the Babylonian astronomers believed that the Earth was at the center of the Universe, the retrograde motions and the stationary points of the superior planets were some very mysterious omens for them. They had not known the dynamical explanation of these phenomena, but they saw in them a certain purpose of the Lord of the Heavens. Later, the Greek astronomers, Hipparchus and Ptolemy for example, constructed a very complicated system of eccentric circles and epicycles to reproduce the observable regressive loops of the planets. Finally the heliocentric theory gave a correct explanation of this phenomenon. The basis for the figures 12 and 13 was first proposed by Copernicus in his work about the revolutions of the planets around the Sun (*De revolutionibus orbium coelestium*, 1543).

The retrograde displacement and apparent standstill of a superior planet, as Jupiter and Saturn, are perspective effects caused by the changing velocities and positions of both the planet and the Earth. Seen from the Earth, these phenomena are only perceptible against the background of the more distant stars. Therefore, the Babylonian astronomers determined the motions and positions of the planets relative to the fixed stars of the constellations in which they were observable.

Jupiter moves for one year, Saturn for 2.5 years in a zodiacal sign of 30 degrees, while the Sun (actually the Earth) goes through 12 signs, i.e. 360 degrees per year. Thus the Earth every year overtakes these slower moving planets, and in this way their apparent retrograde motions and stations occur. The motions of Jupiter and Saturn are represented below in the ecliptic coordinate system, showing their longitudes and latitudes from February 7 to May 6. The two planets are in an exact conjunction when they come together in the same ecliptic longitude. However, they can never be seen as one star, because their latitudes and declinations (angular distances from the celestial equator) are usually different.

In Fig. 13 the points on the orbit of the Earth and of the Jupiter show the position of the two celestial bodies relative to the Sun. Seeing and measuring from the Earth, we can observe that when the Sun is 90 degrees away from the superior planet, then Jupiter is in a direct motion, i.e. eastwards, and its stationary point usually occurs at an angular distance of 120 degrees. After 6-7 days, its retrograde motion begins, and it is greatest during the opposition (180°), when the three celestial bodies are on the same line and the Earth moves between the Sun and Jupiter. When the Earth departs 60° from the line of the opposition, the motion of the planet is again direct (eastwards).

Finally, we have still to understand the statement: "the star stood above [the place] where the child was" (Mt 2: 9). That is to say, it must have appeared to the Magi that the star radiated its light down over Bethlehem. Was it a natural phenomenon? Or perhaps a supernatural vision?

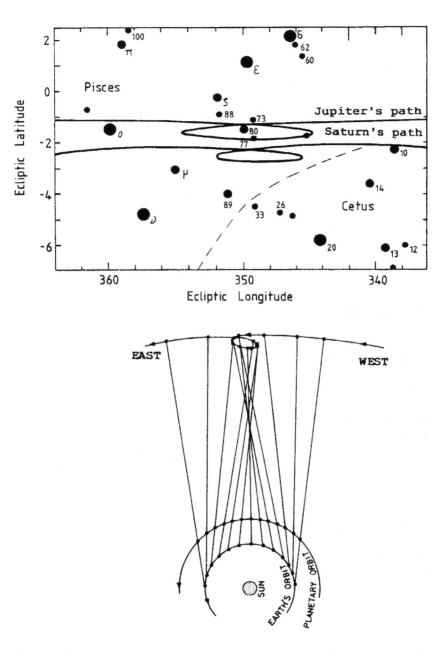

Fig. 13: The path and the retrograde motion of Jupiter and Saturn against the background of the stars of Pisces, in the ecliptic coordinate system. The lower diagram shows the method by which the regressive loops are formed. (Hughes 1979)

The Light over Bethlehem

It was on 12th and 13th November of 7 BC that the Magi were expecting the fulfillment of the predicted astronomical event, the simultaneous standstill of Jupiter and Saturn. The results of modern calculations are slightly different from those dates, but for the observation of the phenomenon the dates of the Babylonian almanac were indeed the most suitable.

The standstill of Jupiter began on November 11th and it continued till 18th, while Saturn stood apparently still from 19th to 29th November. However, between the two dates, 11th and 19th November, the mutual position of the two planets changed only five arc minutes, which was not perceptible with the naked eye. The waning crescent moon rose at about 9 o'clock on the evenings of November 12th and 13th, and thus the Moon did not dim the brillance of the zodiacal light which was visible above the southwestern horizon, just in the direction of the Magi's route, from Jerusalem to Bethlehem.

The conjunction was specially spectacular on the evening of 12th November, when it occurred near the apex of the zodiacal light cone. Saturn was standing slightly to the left of the brighter Jupiter, which was exactly on the axis of the light cone. It appeared that the light from these two planets radiated directly onto the hills of Bethlehem. The faint lens shaped glow in the night sky is actually reflected sunlight. A large cosmic dust cloud is concentrated in the plan of the ecliptic, and those small particles reflect enough sunlight to produce the faint illumination of the sky, after sunset along the zodiac. Between the equator and the latitude 32° N, this zodiacal light can be observed every night and is very conspicuous, because there the ecliptic is more perpendicular to the horizon. Even in the more northern latitudes it is visible to a certain extent, in the areas where the illumination from artificial lights does not dim the southwestern skies.

Because of the atmospheric refraction of the sunlight, the sky does not immediately darken when the Sun sets. The Sun must be 18° below the horizon for the so-called twilight to be absent. In the geographic latitude of Bethlehem this astronomical twilight disappeared at 6.45 p.m. On the evening of 12th November, the sky was quite dark at a quarter to seven. From 7 o'clock to 9 o'clock the altitude or angular height of the two great planets in the apex of the zodiacal light was 50 degrees from the horizon, and they were visible until midnight.

The axis of the light cone is an arc of the ecliptic (the dotted line in the middle, see Fig. 14). Its angle of inclination, relative to the horizon, moved only 11° within two hours, it grew from 48°15' to 59°54', while the star Alpha Pegasus descended from 62°06' to 44°36', which means that the arc of Alpha Gamma took a turn of 41°15' clockwise. This

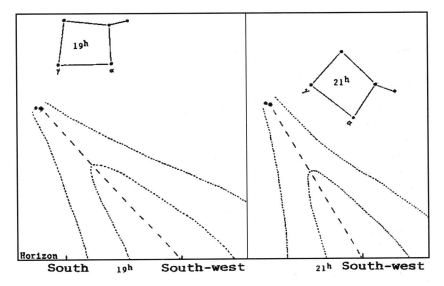

Fig. 14: The position of the zodiacal light over Bethlehem between 7 and 9 p.m. on 12 November 7 BC. (Ferrari d'Occhieppo 1991)

illustrates that the altitude of the two wandering stars did not change perceptibly relative to the movement of the Square of Pegasus. During that time, the axis of the light cone was pointing for four hours towards the same point of the southwest horizon, when the phenomenon was observed from the north, or from the way leading to Bethlehem. Besides it is worth noting that a bright planet can truly be said to be pointing the way, when it is due South, close to the zenith above the observer's head.

The Babylonian astronomers must have observed the zodiacal light every night, but they did not know about its origin. According their mythology they could have imagined it as the glory of *Ea*, the lord of the southern abysses, who was the father of Marduk. However, they never recorded it in their star almanacs, because the zodiacal light was not even visible when they observed the rising and setting of the planets, right before sunrise or right after sunset.

We can assume that the Magi arriving in Jerusalem had not expected that the two wandering stars would stand in the apex of the zodiacal light. It might have taken them by surprise when they saw Jupiter exactly on the axis of this light cone, which was pointing towards Bethlehem. Matthew certainly related this phenomenon as the Magi had seen it, and as many others could have seen it on that night, when they were looking towards Bethlehem from the mount of Jerusalem. His statement is, therefore very significant from an astronomical point of view: "the star which they had seen in its evening rising went ahead of them, while, in its course it stopped up above [in the direction] where the child was" (Mt 2:9). This was an appropriate description of the planet's apparent standstill, i.e. its western stationary point.

It was Jupiter which played the leading part in this event, because it was the brightest object in the sky at that time. In the Babylonian almanac the 12th of November was given as the date of the western stationary point of Jupiter, and the whole phenomenon was best observed on that evening. From all these considerations we may draw the following conclusion: It was probably on the evening of the 12th of November (give or take one day) that the Magi arrived in Bethlehem, in the year 7 BC. This claim is supported by chronological and astronomical calculations.

Matthew's laconic report is still very meaningful. King Herod calls the visitors from the East to a secret meeting, and thereafter he sends them to Bethlehem, likewise in secret. By reasons of this context, we may suppose that this happens on 12 November. At that time everyone else in the city knows that the Magi are looking for the Messiah: "When King Herod heard this he was perturbed, and so was the whole of Jerusalem" (Mt 2:3). Therefore, Herod must have let them go to Bethlehem late in the afternoon, so that they would not draw attention to themselves.

Now let us try to accompany the Magi on the way. Bethlehem is situated 8 kilometers south of Jerusalem, in the same geographical longitude (35°10'). The road also runs straight southwards; it only bends slightly to the west after five kilometers, then it bends again towards the southeast. At first, the road leads steeply down to the valley, where we continue through a flat landscape for half an hour, then the road leads upwards again. The time is around 5 p.m., twilight is coming. In half an hour the Sun is down, and Jupiter appears about 30° high over the southeastern horizon.

As we approach to the hills of Bethlehem it is growing dark, and we can see a fainter light glimmering close to Jupiter. We recognize that it is Saturn. Now, we may be about 2 kilometers from the houses of the ancient settlement, when the twinkling stars of Pegasus and Pisces appear over the lower hills in the southeast. In the meantime, the zodiacal light is also getting more and more intense, and it gives the impression that it is coming from the resplendent Jupiter towards the southwestern hill. We proceed in that direction. We consider this phenomenon as the sign of the "one born king" whom we are looking for. But would someone show us the house where he is to be found?

It is around seven o'clock when we reach the first house, which is built of rubble. The inhabitant of this house may be an old shepherd who has heard the message of the angels and knows the dwelling place

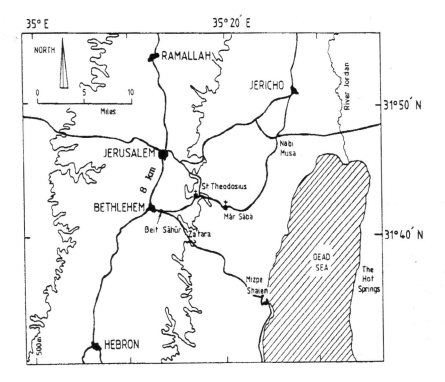

Fig. 15: This map shows the geographic position of Bethlehem and its surrounding district. The road from Jerusalem to Bethlehem runs directly southwards, the distance is 8 km, about a two hour walk. About one km from Bethlehem is Beit Sahur, the fields of the shepherds who watched their flocks through the night when Christ was born (Lk 2: 8). The possible return route of the Magi was past Beit Sahur, Mar Saba, and Nabi Musa to the ford across the Jordan.

of the Holy Family. Thus he can understand the question of the Magi and guides them to the Messiah. And the Magi "rejoice with exceeding great joy" (Mt 2: 10) when they see the most brillant star for hours together, staying in the sky over the place to which they go. This is still the same royal star which they have observed in its evening rising in their homeland!

It is very possible that the Magi used their acute intuitive powers to find the house where the Holy Family was living. However, the most natural assumption is that one of the shepherds helped them in Bethlehem. This description of the journey formulated in the present tense may sound like a pious reflection, but it has a sound basis in reality if we view the events according to Matthew's account. He was surely convinced of the events as he reported them, even if he could not explain the phenomenon.

Were then is the miraculous to be found in this event? Not in the retrograde motion and standstill of the two wandering stars, because all this was precisely predicted and can be determined by subsequent calculations as well. It is the peculiar coincidence of all the events, i.e. the birth of Christ, the astronomical predictions, the research of the Magi and their journey to Bethlehem, which shows a higher providence which could not be predicted nor subsequently explained by human reason. An unexpected and marvelous concurrence for the Magi must have been that the light below the two planets radiated over Bethlehem, punctually at the time of their arrival. Finally, it was marvelous that they found there the one for whom they were looking.

Today, the majority of the astronomers dealing with this subject agree that the zodiacal light might have played an important part in the phenomenon of the Bethlehem star. It was K. Ferrari d'Occhieppo, professor of astronomy at the University of Vienna, who discovered the importance of the zodiacal light regarding the descriptions of Matthew. He does not assert that the zodiacal light was necessary as a final guide for the Magi. But he says that it must have been "an impressive concurrence during the apparent standstill of the two planets over Bethlehem, in the year 7 BC" (Ferrari d'Occhieppo 1991). This can help us to correctly interpret the statement that the Magi saw the star halting over Bethlehem.

Ferrari d'Occhieppo (1991) notes that there are some readers who doubt his conclusion, because they have never had an opportunity to observe the stationary Jupiter-Saturn conjunction within the zodiacal light. He therefore briefly relates that once he himself had observed the same phenomenon, which corroborated his assumption.

From 4 August 1940 to 20 February 1941, there occurred a triple Jupiter-Saturn conjunction in the constellation of Aries the Ram. In January 1941, after the western stationary point, the two planets were in direct motion again. On the 20th of January, the author was on night duty in Lower Brittany, France, when he observed the brilliant Jupiter high within the zodiacal light and Saturn to the left of it, two weeks before the exact conjunction. In the background of the zodiacal light he could see well the contours of the houses two kilometers away westwards. This observation reminded him of Matthew's account of the Magi, and he thought that they could have seen the same phenomenon over Bethlehem. Twenty years later he carried out the necessary calculations for the same phenomenon relative to the geographical position and local time of Bethlehem. He found that in the year 7 BC the stationary Jupiter-Saturn conjunction had occurred within the apex of the zodiacal light cone on 12 and 13 November, and this was much more conspicuous that the same event in 1941.

Let us return to the question of the miracle. How could the Magi from the East find the Messiah king? How could they recognize him in the person of a young child born in a poor settlement? Maybe from the observed positions of the stars and by their traditional symbolical interpretation? But this would not be enough, because it could only show a possibility. Were they familiar with the predictions of the prophets? Not even this could be enough, because the prophecies gave them hope only. Even our most precise calculations and plans are uncertain until they are realized. The uncertainty of the Magi is hidden in their question: "Where is he...?"

It is a real wonder that, in spite of Herod's wickedness and slyness, they could find and recognize him for whom they were looking. This surpassed human science and power, and this can be called a divine miracle. "A man's heart plans out his way, but it is the Lord who makes his steps secure" (Prov 16: 9). From this wise statement of Solomon originates the proverb: "Man proposes, God disposes".

On their way to Jerusalem, the Magi had surely been informed about Herod's cruelties. They must have heard that in the same year Herod had his two sons and their soldiers killed, because they threatened his power. In the same year, he also arrested 6000 scribes and Pharisees, because these refused the oath of fealty to the emperor. Josephus Flavius writes that many of these scribes had talked of the expected Messiah and Herod, therefore, had put them to death. (*Ant.Iud.* XVII. 2-4)

The Wise Men were aware of Herod's spite, when he said to them: "when you have found him, let me know, so that I too may go and do him homage" (Mt 2: 8). In the end, "they returned to their country by another way", avoiding Jerusalem.

Nevertheless, it seems that their meeting with Herod was the direct cause for the massacre of the Innocents (Mt 2: 16). But independent of their visit, the message of the Messiah's birth had been spread. Both the shepherds and Simeon and Anna "spoke of him to all who looked forward to the deliverance of Jerusalem" (Lk 2: 17-38).

Matthew does not blame the Magi for the death of the children in Bethlehem, rather he presents them as the means of Divine Providence. He draws attention to the rich gifts, gold, frankincense and myrrh, which they gave Jesus' parents to help them in their flight into Egypt.

What part did the stars play in the Divine Providence? This is still a difficult question for us: What relation could the Magi find between the position of the stars and the birth of Christ? How could they see the possibility that he was born in Judaea, when they had observed the evening rising of the two great planets in their own country?

This question raises great difficulties for us, because the natural sciences are always looking for causal relationships. However, the sequence of events in time does not always imply a necessary causality. Matthew is speaking about the simultaneity of two events: a certain celestial phenomenon and the birth of Christ occurring at the same time. This professes the harmony of creation and salvation, because Christ is "the Lord of Heaven and Earth". St. Augustine has explained this question by the following statement:

"Now we [as opposed to the Manicheans] set the birth of no man under the fatal rule of the stars, so that we can loose from any bond of necessity the free choice of his will, by which he lives well or ill, for the sake of the just judgment of God. How much less then, do we think that the temporal incarnation of the eternal Lord and Creator of the Universe is in any way under the influence of the stars! So that star, which the Magi saw when Christ was born according to the flesh was not a lord governing his nativity but a servant bearing witness to it; it did not subject him to its power but in its service pointed the way to him" (Augustine, *Contra Faustum Manichaeum*, II. 5).

In Antioch at the same time (309 AD) St. John Chrysostom speaks of this question. He admits that he can explain neither the nature of the star nor the behaviour of the Magi from an exclusively human point of view. Agreeing with the ancient beliefs, he says, that according to his opinion, it was not only the star which lead the Magi, but also a divine inspiration, because only this can explain their faith and obedience, their courage and wisdom. Thereafter he continues as follows:

"Who are those Magi? And what urged them to undertake the long journey? If you wish, then let us begin with the thing that the enemies of the truth say. What do they say? They claim that the account of Matthew about the rising of the star and the birth of Christ corroborates the principles of astrology. But if Jesus had been born according to the principles of astrology, then why has he abrogated all illusions of magic and belief in the power of fate? And how could those Magi have known from the position of the stars that that child was the King of Judaeans? In reality he was not even a king of an earthly country, as he himself told to Pilate: My kingdom is not of this world. It belongs not even to the art of the astrologers to know from the stars those who were going to be born. They only state that they can predict what is going to happen with a new-born human, after having observed the stars at the time of his birth. But those Magi were not standing there near the mother [Mary], when she gave birth to her child and wrapped him in swaddling clothes. They did not know the hour of Jesus' birth and they did not try to predict his future life from the motions of the stars. It is most surprising, however, that after they had observed the

Fig. 16: The apparent standstill of Jupiter and Saturn together with the zodiacal light, at 9 on 12 November 7 BC. To the right of the two planets, the stars of Pegasus and Pisces are visible above the hills of Bethlehem. The Magi might have seen this phenomenon when they were on the way from Jerusalem to Bethlehem. (Photograph by H. Mucke at the Urania Planetarium of Vienna. Courtesy of K. Ferrari d'Occhieppo)

star for a long time in their own country, they went to Bethlehem to visit him who was born there. What kind of thought could have prompted them to go on that dangerous journey? What ever reward could they expect for the endeavor that they came from a so distant country to pay the one born king homage? Even if they thought that he might one day be the king of their own country, this would not be a sufficient reason..." (Chrysostom, *Comment.in Matth*. VI. 1-2).

An Epoch-Making Constellation

The Fathers of the Church knew neither the cuneiform writings uncovered by archaeologists nor the astronomical data which are at our disposal today. Had they been familiar with them, they would have found it easier to understand both the human aspects of the Magi's behavior and the nature of the star. To us, nevertheless, Chrysostom's discourse is highly informative: it clearly testifies that the Magi described by Matthew had come from Babylon, and also that they were no ordinary astrologers since they did not cast a birth horoscope for Jesus.

Besides mathematical astronomy, symbolic astrology was a major science in Babylon. It would be erroneous to call it mere superstition; symbolic astrology was rather a kind of intuitive understanding of nature. Its adherents found that certain constellations and historical events were correlated in a way that subsequent observations repeatedly seemed to justify.

Throughout the centuries celestial phenomena were carefully observed and recorded. Instead of the causes underlying the phenomena, Babylonian astronomers usually sought to find out their purpose, what their meaning might be in respect to the country's history. That was what the reports they submitted to the king were about. If the astronomers happened to be wrong, they always sincerely admitted their mistake.

According to Chaldaean symbolic astrology, each planet and every sign of the Zodiac had a particular significance indicated by its figure, brightness and motion. However, these qualities were in each case modified by the changing configuration of the planets and the Moon with respect to the Sun and to one another. Just as the signs of the Zodiac formed special groupings according to their geometrical relationships, the planets, when similarly positioned, were said to be in *trine* or *quatrile* aspect (120 or 90 degrees apart), either in conjunction or in opposition.

Furthermore, the political, social and economic situation played an important part in deductions concerning the future. Actually, to make their predictions the Chaldaean magi did not rely on a single planetary configuration, but the general effect of the historical and astronomical picture of that time. They found the indications for a new epoch by a reasonable combination of all the historical, cultural and celestial phenomena of their own days. By this method they were able to recognize the epoch-making constellations, which could repeat themselves centuries later.

The treatises written after Kepler have placed too much emphasis on the triple conjunction of Saturn and Jupiter, as if it were the only sign of Jesus's birth. In the Babylonian star almanac there is no separate indication of the date of the three conjunctions, nor is it implied by Matthew's text. Consequently, it was not the one sign considered to be crucial.

The statement of the Magi in Jerusalem (Mt 2: 2): "We saw his star in its rising", implies a combination of all the current astronomical events. The "star", determined here by the possessive "his", refers obviously to the whole constellation, which traditionally served to herald the epoch of the Messiah. The Magi visiting Jerusalem at the time were unlikely to be people living in seclusion, involved in nothing but the contemplation of the stars. They were just as aware of the historical events of their age as of the celestial phenomena. What kind of considerations could prompt them to look for the one born king in Judaea, one who would become the true king of a new era, as they believed it? Their conclusions could have been reached as a result and under the influence of the following: (1) the formation of a new world empire under Roman sovereignty; (2) the Hebrew prophecies about the coming of a Savior King, the Messiah, awaited in Judaea; (3) the Babylonian cuneiform writings predicting the celestial sign of the birth of the "Great King"; (4) the extraordinary conjunction of Jupiter and Saturn in 7 BC, and the shift of the point of vernal equinox into the constellation of Pisces.

It was during the decades preceding the birth of Christ that the Roman Empire stretching from the Atlantic Ocean to Mesopotamia became strong and powerful. In that period all people had some presentiment of the dawn of a new era. The age of the Roman Empire began in 27 BC with Octavianus, the victorious emperor receiving the title of Caesar Augustus from the Senate. From then on this became the name of the monarchs in the new world empire. The peculiar position of the stars under which this event took place was very well known to the magi: the conjunction of Jupiter and Saturn occurred exactly over the royal star of the Lion (Regulus, or *Stella regina Leonis* according to Plinius) and was joined by the Moon and Mars. That was the time when Herod, vassal of Rome had his royal castle built in Jerusalem and had the Antonia Castle added to the northern wall of the Temple court in honor of the Roman emperor.

Twenty years later, in 7 BC, during the appearance of the great conjunction, a huge monument was erected by the Egyptian magi in honor of the Emperor Augustus on the island of Philea on the Nile. Its inscription said that Augustus was the embodiment of Jupiter as the Lord of the world. The first general census and assessment of property took place in the same year in Syria and Judaea, where the terror of Herod was at its height. The new state organization of Augustus guaranteed a relative peace, but the military dictatorship and the severe taxation weighed heavily on the oppressed peoples. The prophecies of the Messiah became more and more widespread across the borders of Judaea.

The Babylonian magi, who kept regularly in touch with the Chaldaean astronomers in Damascus, were most probably well informed about the situation. Moreover, it can be taken for certain that, as some of them were Israelites, they knew the prophecies of Daniel and Ezekiel. This point was sufficiently discussed in the previous section. In one of his writings Origen definitely states that the magi remembered Balaam's prophecy of "the rising star of Jacob". According to Chrysostom they were also guided by divine inspiration thanks to the Hebrew prophets, who predicted the future during the years of the Babylonian exile. Without knowing these prophecies the Magi could hardly have resolved to travel to the land of Judah.

The cuneiform writings the Magi had found in the old archives of the Marduk temple may have contributed to their decision to travel. From the remaining fragments it is possible to reconstruct the most important data the Magi had at their disposal beside the above mentioned star almanac. These cuneiform writings dated back to centuries before, but the Magi may have relied on them to interpret celestial signs. (Cf. Kugler 1912, II. pp. 85-86 and 554-562; Pannekoek 1961, pp.39-45.) These Babylonian traditions tell that Jupiter (*Kakkabu pizu* = Glistening star) is the Lord of the heavens and the sign of the King of kings. Those men born at the time of its rising or when it is at its highest point in the middle of the sky (*Nibiru*, i.e., on the meridian) are said to become generous and righteous rulers. Saturn (*Kaiwanu* = Persistent) is the "Sun of the night", the star of the western countries, especially the star of Syria (Judaea), and its evening rising is said to be a sign that there will be wise and powerful rulers. These two huge planets are particularly significant in the constellation of the two branched Pisces (the Fishes) which is associated with the end and the beginning, death and the new life. Its western branch stretches over Judaea while Mesopotamia is situated under its eastern branch. (In the center of Babylon there were seven sacrificial altars erected in honor of Pisces.)

The following quotations taken from cuneiform writings illustrate how certain magi interpreted the motions of the royal star of Jupiter:

Fig. 17: View of Babylon, seen from the west side of the river restored after the excavations. (Unger 1931)

When the star of Marduk [Jupiter] appears as a morning star in the sky, at the beginning of the year, there will be abundant harvest in that year... When Jupiter follows the way of the Sun [eastward among the fixed stars], Babylon will live in prosperity and the power of the king will increase. When it passes towards the West [retrograde], the country will know peace and security ... When that... [conjunction?] occurs, a great king will appear in the West, there will be justice, peace and friendship in every country because he will bring happiness to every people... (Cf. Pannekoek 1961).

Unfortunately we do not know exactly which astronomical phenomenon this last sentence refers to because the relevant part of the text was damaged, but in the light of what has been said above we can assume that it was the Jupiter-Saturn conjunction awaited in the constellation of Pisces. These may have been some of the considerations that prompted the Magi to go to Jerusalem. Eventually they had to rely on their own observations, as they said it themselves: "We saw his star in its evening rising."

According to the traditions of the first century the star over Bethlehem was of a particularly large size and shone so brightly that it obscured the surrounding stars (Protoevangelium of James, Ignatius, Clement, Justin). Although this was not written by astronomers, it need not be regarded as an overstatement made in expectation of a miracle. Neither is it a poetic image nor a symbolic interpretation. The statement actually corresponds to the facts, especially as far as Jupiter is concerned. This is demonstrated by the following:

In 7 BC from September to December Jupiter and Saturn were at perigee, i.e. closest to the Earth, and they were at opposition (to the Sun) at the time of their evening rising. Thus their visible discs were the largest possible with maximum brightness. At opposition Jupiter is about 375 million kilometers closer to the Earth than at the time of its morning rising. It is then 500 times brighter than the surrounding stars. The brightness of Saturn depends also on the inclination of the plane of its ring system to our line of sight (see Fig. 18).

The ring system of Saturn consists of three concentric rings and a myriad of small particles orbiting the planet in a thin disk shaped layer in the plane of its equator. The entire ring is 270,000 kilometers across and 3 kilometers thick. It is inclined 27 degrees to the plane of the planet's orbit and this again forms an angle of 2.5 degrees to the plane of the Earth's orbit. Therefore, twice during a revolution period of 30 years the plane of the rings sweeps across the Earth's orbit, and then the ring system becomes invisible, because it is edge on to our line of sight. Every 15th year the rings of Saturn present their northern and southern faces alternately to the Earth, and the planet appears extremely bright, because its rings reflect to us two times as much sunlight as does the planet's disc. In the year 7 BC, at the time of the evening rising of Saturn, the northern face of the ring system was visible. This widest opening of the northern face of the rings made the planet 38 times brighter than the brightest stars in the constellation of Pisces. Jupiter was 13 times brighter than Saturn. Thus they were the

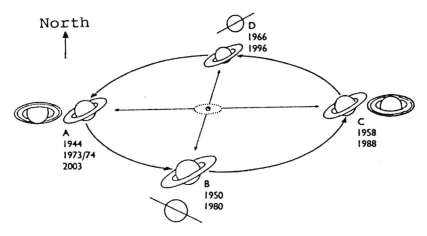

Fig. 18: Orientation of Saturn's ring system as seen from the Earth with Saturn at four different places in its orbit. Between September and November 7 BC, it was just the northern face of the ring system which was visible (C). (From Seljo 1971)

most impressive celestial objects, dimming the nearby stars at that time.

The Babylonian astronomers did not know the physical qualities of the planets. The diameter of Jupiter and Saturn is 11 times as great as the Earth's diameter, Jupiter is 318 times and Saturn 95 times more massive than the Earth. Saturn is twice as far away from the Sun as Jupiter, and so on. Data which we find listed in modern astronomical tables, but which were of no interest to the ancient astronomers. They were satisfied with what they observed with the naked eye. Their eyesight, however, must have been much better than ours and some of them were surely capable of using their intuition. They were perhaps also able to perceive even things not perceivable to the senses, which ability is called extrasensory perception by modern parapsychology. The physicist of our days can hardly enter into the world of ideas of those ancient scholars.

Matthew's Magi lived at the time of the Hellenistic culture when the stars were no longer believed to be gods who determined the fate of man. Still, they must have thought of them as living creatures or angels preaching the will of the Lord of Heaven as far as the present and the future were concerned. Could they have been wrong? But then even the prophets of the Old Testament used the expression "an army of angels" when addressing the stars:

Let the heavens praise the Lord [He-who-is]: praise him,
all his angels, all his armies! Praise him, Sun and Moon

and shining stars! Let Earth praise the Lord, at whose
command they were created; he has fixed them in their
orbit... (Ps 148; Dan 3: 57-63).

Although the inanimate celestial bodies cannot praise their creator
in intelligent words, the light of their silent existence awakes the clear
sighted and faithful man to the awareness of the Lord and is
transformed into a loud praise of God. Thus, the beginning of a new
era was recognized by some clear sighted sages two thousand years
ago. As for us today, we can say that history has proved them right.
They were also right in assuming that each new era is characterized by
the personality of a great "king" whose influence on his age is due
mainly to his inborn gifts and character, and not to his military power.

Apart from divine inspiration and intuition, man also needs
external signs to be able to make sure of the correctness of his
observations. The Magi who came to Jerusalem looking for the true
king of the new era, saw such a sign in the constellation of Pisces. The
significance of this constellation is testified by a number of ancient and
mediaeval traditions preserved in Accadian, Aramaic, Greek and Latin
writings. However, the explanations furnished by these writings are
not satisfactory. The decisive factor must have been the shift of the
vernal equinox from the sign of Aries the Ram into Pisces, the
heavenly sign of Abraham and Moses according to old Hebrew
traditions. Furthermore, at the time of the great conjunction of Jupiter
and Saturn in November, 7 BC, the stars of Pisces actually crossed the
meridian of Judaea.

Calculating with the present rate of precession (1° per 72 years), the
vernal equinox passes through each 30° sign in about 2160 years. This
period was considered a world month, after the lapse of which the
position and altitude of the stars over the horizon changed and it was
necessary to make new star maps. By comparing major events of world
history, some historians have since proved that the period of great
changes was also 2160 years. Nevertheless, this cannot be determined
very precisely, because there is a transitional period between each
cultural era which usually lasts 540 to 600 years. It is still an open
question whether there is any correlation between the precession of the
equinoxes and the world eras, though in the light of recent research
this seems most probable. (18)

Kepler remarked that the triple conjunction of Jupiter and Saturn in
7 BC marked a new world era, since by divine dispensation Christ was
born when the great conjunction was visible near the vernal equinox
between the constellations of Pisces and Aries (*Kepleri Astronomi
Opera Omnia* VII.701: *Discurs von der grossen Conjunction*). The
Chaldaean astronomers were aware of the slow westward drift of the
vernal equinox among the stars of the Zodiac, and, therefore, they

gradually reduced the number of degrees for the position of the vernal equinox in the sign of Aries from 10° to 8° and in turn from 8° to 4°. Finally, in the 2nd century BC, Hipparchus fixed the vernal equinox on Aries 0°, usually called the "First Point of Aries", where the brightest star of Pisces was to be seen in its morning rising around 22 March. The zodiacal signs were counted from this vernal equinox. Hipparchus came to the conclusion that the equinoctial points move at least one degree per century in a direction opposite to the order of the zodiacal signs. Thus the Greek astronomers reckoned with 3000 years as a world-month, that is as a precessional period of each zodiacal sign. (Cf. Neugebauer 1975, pp.598-600).

A hundred years after Hipparchus, the magi of Damascus, whose work formed part of the Hellenistic culture, used his data to make their calculations, which consequently must have been known to their Babylonian colleagues. When they observed the morning rising of Jupiter on 15 March in 7 BC, the Sun rose a few minutes later on the 20th degree of Pisces in the old Babylonian system. Their star almanac was made on the basis of that old system in which the date of the vernal equinox was 28 March, which was equivalent to 4° Aries. If then they observed the rising of the stars, they could see that the Sun rose in the border line of the two neighboring constellations: before dawn the stars of Aries and those in the upper part of the eastern branch of Pisces were still visible.

This made it clear to the Magi that for centuries onwards the season of spring blossoming would be marked by the morning rising of the stars of Pisces. The beginning of a new era was even more distinctly shown by the constellation that occurred in the evening of 15th September: the star of Heaven's king (Jupiter) rose together with Israel's star of the Sabbath (Saturn) in the very band of the vernal and autumnal equinox. They were exceedingly bright as they moved across the sky from evening to morning, and when they disappeared in the western horizon, the Sun rose with the star Spica of Virgo (Alpha Virginis). In the north this marked the time of autumn and the beginning of the harvest, in the southern hemisphere it meant springtime. The celestial sign of the great kings of the future, therefore, spanned the whole world and was addressed to the whole of mankind.

The position of the epoch-making constellation then moved towards the west. Viewed from Babylon, it shifted exactly towards Judaea. Finally, any doubt of the Magi was resolved when they saw "with exceedingly great joy" (Mt 2: 10) that the same constellation crossed the meridian of Jerusalem and Bethlehem on the night from 12 to 13 November. This proved to them that the prophecies of the awaited Messiah and his birth in Bethlehem had been fulfilled. If we take all this into consideration, we shall better understand the peculiar world of the Magi from the East, and so we can understand why

Matthew chose to relate their story. The idea of Israel and Judah being linked to Pisces and Saturn seems to have been quite obvious to those Magi. But where did this idea come from? Did it originate in traditional popular belief? Or in astronomical observations?

The Hellenic astronomers set up a classification of each country and people under the signs of the Zodiac. A detailed description of this astrogeographic system has come down to us through the works of Manilius (50 BC - 23 AD) and Ptolemy (120 AD). Manilius recorded when and how long each constellation was visible. He believed the largest geographical area, stretching from the Red Sea to the Caspian Sea and including Mesopotamia, belonged to the constellation of Pisces. However, Syria as well as Judaea lay in the border zone between Pisces and Aries (Manilius, *Astronomica* IV. 800-807).

Ptolemy looked for a physical and geometrical explanation, but the system he elaborated is so complicated that it can hardly be understood let alone verified. He assumed that each country was related to the sign in which the total eclipse of the Moon was visible. On the basis of the 120° aspects between the zodiacal signs he drew regular triangles on the northern hemisphere, and he found that the southeastern countries were situated inside the triangle of Taurus-Virgo-Capricorn; the southwestern ones inside the triangle of Cancer-Scorpio-Pisces. According to this model, Mesopotamia and Palestine were situated in the central part of Virgo and Pisces, but Ptolemy noted that "Aries was more characteristic of Syria and Judaea, because their people were brave, free of superstitions and idolatry, they were venturesome and good traders" (*Tetrabiblos* II, 3-5).

According to a cuneiform tablet, the region of the Tiger and Euphrates lay under the upper eastern branch of Pisces, whereas its western branch stretched over the Egyptian Nile. Thus in the Babylonian system Judaea was located under the southwestern stars of Pisces, that is in the central part of the constellation (Schaumberger 1943).

Were there some natural facts on which this astrogeography was founded? In any case, the constellations of the Zodiac are not visible everywhere every night. Ancient people observed where each constellation was best visible for the largest part of the year. This depended on the seasons and the geographic latitude as well as the angular diameter of every single constellation. The two largest constellations of the Zodiac are Virgo (48°) and Pisces (44°). In the latitudes of Babylon and Jerusalem (31°-32°) the stars of Pisces were visible from May to January; at a maximum altitude from September to December. The stars of Virgo were visible from February to July, with a maximum altitude in April and May.

In this respect it is worth noting that in Judaea the greatest feasts after Passover and Pentecost were held in the autumn months, when the stars of Pisces (the Fishes) stood very high in the night sky. These feasts correspond to the following dates in 7 BC: the Jewish New Year: Tishri 1 = September 25; the day of Atonement: Tishri 10 = October 5; the Feast of Tabernacles: Tishri 15 to 23 = October 10-17; the Dedication of the Temple: Chislev 1 = November 24.

Babylon was a long way geographically from Bethlehem. But the historical lapse of time from the birth of Abraham in Ur of the Chaldaeans to the day when Christ was born in Bethlehem of Judah presents us with a mathematical figure of still greater magnitude. It was one "world-month", the time it took the vernal equinox to cross the sign of Aries the Ram. And throughout its history the generations of Abraham, whether guided by true faith in God or misguided by erroneous beliefs, always venerated the stars.

The constellation of Pisces was definitely linked to the name of Moses, the first prophet and savior of Israel. According to an old Hebrew narrative Moses was born when Jupiter rose with the sign of Pisces, but since the date of his birth is unknown this cannot be verified. His name, however, refers to a fish caught out of water (in Egyptian usage Mo-Uses = Rescue; Hebrew Mosheh from the verb mashah = to draw out). When the pharaoh's daughter found the baby hidden in the reeds along the Nile and adopted him, "she named him Moses because, she said, I drew him out of the water" (Ex 2: 10).

Traditionally, Egypt lay under the sign of Pisces. The Pharaoh ordered Jacob's youngest son, Joseph, to be "the leader of his whole land". Thus the dream Joseph had had as a child was fulfilled: he had seen eleven constellations all of which were at the service of his star. Jacob's last fatherly blessing characterized him as belonging to the sign of Pisces and Virgo: "The Most High (El Shaddai) blesses you with blessings of heaven above, blessings of the deep lying below, blessings of grain and flowers" (Gen 49: 25). The "grain and flowers" were the symbols of Virgo.

According to Josephus Flavius the twelve precious stones on the breastplate of the high priest are signs of the 12 months, i.e. the zodiacal signs, and they symbolize the 12 tribes of Israel (Ant.Iud. III. 7: 5-7). As a matter of fact, the expressions which describe the sons of Israel in the blessings of Moses do indeed correspond to the signs of the Zodiac. During the wandering in the wilderness of Sinai the four main leaders of the people are characterized by the cardinal signs of the Zodiac and their camps are located in the direction of the respective constellations: "The sons of Israel are to pitch their tents all round the Tabernacle of the Testimony, every man by his own [heavenly] standard". On the east side, towards sunrise, is the standard of the camp of Judah "who is a lion cub" i.e., Leo; on the south side, the standard of the camp of Reuben, who is "uncontrolled as flood" like Aquarius; on the west side is the standard of Ephraim the "first-born of the bull" i.e., Taurus; and Dan is the leader of the northern camp "like a serpent who bites the horse on the hock and its rider falls backward", which is an allusion to the sign of Scorpion behind the horse of Sagittarius the Archer (Deut 33: 17; Gen 49: 17).

Back in the time of Moses these signs counted as quite natural comparisons, but the prophets later on often accused the people of making idols in honor of the stars. Jeroboam, the first king of Israel after Solomon, was of Ephraim's tribe and thus he had the sign of Taurus the Bull. He had two golden calves made and he said to the people: "Here are your gods, Israel, these brought you up out of the land of Egypt" (1 Kg 12: 28).

Josiah, king of Judah (640-609 BC) ordered the removal of all the cult objects that had been made for Baal (Jupiter) and Asherah (Venus): "He did away with the spurious priests who offered sacrifice to the Sun, the Moon, the Constellations and the whole array of heaven" (2 Kg 23: 5). Unlike the Babylonians, who worshipped Marduk-Jupiter, Israel venerated mainly the star of *El-Saturn*. The earliest witness of this cult was the prophet Amos (around 750 BC), who foretold the forthcoming Assyrian danger to the king of Israel and his people: "Now you must shoulder Sakkuth your king and Kaiwan your god those idols you have made for yourselves; for I mean to take you far beyond Damascus" i.e. to Assyria (Amos 5: 26). *Kaiwanu* was the Accadian name of Saturn, Aramaic *Kevan*, and Sakkuth was its idol with a "law book". (This interpretation is proper according to a fragment of the Damascus Scroll, 7:14-20, found among the Qumran finds.)

The deacon Stephen, the protomartyr of Christ, quoted Amos's words according to the Qumran interpretation. He said before the Sanhedrin of Jerusalem: "you carried the tent of Moloch on your shoulders and the star of the god Rephan" (Acts 7: 43). *Rephan* is the Greek transcription of *Kevan* = Saturn, since the letter *v*, non-existent in Greek, was substituted for by *phi* and *K* was misread for *R*. The Saturn cult of Israel was so known that it was often referred to by some of the Greek and Roman writers. Tacitus, for example, noted that the astrologers of Judaea considered Saturn the heavenly representative of Israel (*Hist.* 54: 29). In one of his famous poems Tibullus mentioned the Sabbath star of Judah, which reminded him of the good old times when Saturn ruled. In Rome Saturday was called *Saturni Dies* and a carnival was held from 17 to 25 December each year to celebrate the days of *Saturnalia*. (Tibullus, *Delia et Nemesis* 3: 18).

Western peoples must have taken over this custom from Babylon. The Hebrew "Talmud of Babylon" (156 a) is the first writing to explicitly mention Saturn being the *Sabbath-star*. Epiphanius, the Greek Church Father and Bishop of Cyprus in 367, also testifies to this tradition (*Panarion* 16, 3). How did Saturn become the star of

Sabbath? Sabbath was the seventh and last day of the week, which we still call "Saturday", because Saturn was the seventh and last star according to the ancient astrological tradition. However, there may be an even deeper reason for this.

The Israelite priests, who recorded the time of the new moon so accurately, must have observed the motions of the planets. Apart from the Babylonian *Kabbalah* the Hebrew apocrypha also testify to this (e.g., the Book of Enoch, 83:2-3). They must have noticed that Saturn or *Kevan* makes halts of seven days every four months and every seven months, namely during its apparent standstill at the east and west stationary point, respectively. By analogy it must have seemed obvious to connect the seventh day with Kevan = Saturn, for it was *sabbath*, the official day of rest, which was repeated four times every month.

Traditions like these gave birth to the idea that the great Jupiter-Saturn conjunction was the star of the Messiah. However, even if Christ was born under a conjunction like this, we think those who believed this were wrong. The conjunction of two planets in the same constellation is a phenomenon which recurs from time to time. But the birth of Christ is an event happening once, and it is independent of any recurrent astronomical phenomenon. That is why we have tried to show that instead of the great conjunction itself, it was the general effect of the historical and astronomical picture of that time in the light of a preternatural inspiration that had a decisive influence on the Magi traveling to Jerusalem.

Surprisingly, however, astronomical calculations suggest that the celestial phenomenon that occurred in 7 BC can never recur in exactly the same form. At the time of the Babylonian astronomers it was possible to reckon with a 854 year period of the triple conjunctions of Jupiter and Saturn, but it cannot be used over a very long period of time. The precession of the vernal equinox causes continuous variations in the right ascensions and declinations of the stars. Furthermore, because of the varying declinations of Jupiter and Saturn, the angular distance between them varies at the time of the conjunctions as do the phases of their apparent standstills. A synchronous retrograde motion and standstill of Jupiter and Saturn is rarer than their triple conjunction, nor is it always visible. In 848 AD, for example, the two planets come together three times in Pisces again, but far away from the vernal equinox, and they had neither simultaneous rising nor observable synchronous standstills.

If the Magi who lived in the year Christ was born knew the history of the previous centuries, they might have known that 853 years earlier the Assyrian Shalmaneser III occupied Babylon and then defeated twelve western kings, including Achab, king of Israel. The great conjunction of Jupiter and Saturn then occurred in the northwestern part of Pisces and the vernal equinox had not yet left

Aries. At the same time the prophet Elijah appeared, who was one of the greatest miracle workers before Christ. He became well known beyond the borders of Israel. Centuries later, at the time of Jesus, the scribes were awaiting his return. In Judaea it was the reign of Jehosaphat, whose virtues and victories are praised by the Book of Chronicles. His name is mentioned by Matthew in the genealogy of Jesus (Mt 1: 8; 17: 10). The Magi might have in these events seen a prototype of the future messianic constellation.

However, the ancient astronomers did not yet know that the mutual gravitation of the planets causes certain deviations of the planetary orbits, the equalization of which takes several centuries. In modern astronomy it is the theory of perturbation that deals with the solution of this problem: How can we determine and predict the motions of three or more bodies of different masses all interacting under the influence of their mutual gravitation? A single equation does not describe their orbits for all time.

In addition to the influence of mutual gravitation we have to consider the continuous proper motions of the Sun and fixed stars as well. Modern analysis of the proper motions and radial velocities of the stars around the Sun has shown that the Sun with its planets is moving at a speed of 20 km/sec toward a point near the bright star Vega in the constellation of Lyra. At the same time, all the so called fixed stars also move at a rate of 30-40 km/sec, and after some thousand years they will noticeably change their positions relative to one another. The apparent groupings which the stars seem to form i.e., the constellations, look today as they did 2000 years ago, but after 20,000 years they will have quite different figures and the form of the traditional zodiacal signs will no longer exist. Theoretically speaking the same constellation which is referred to as the "star of Bethlehem in 7 BC" would repeat itself in 25,732 AD, if the form of the zodiacal signs and the rate of the Earth's precession remained unchanged. But in actual fact this will be physically impossible, and the future history of the human race is in any case uncertain. After all is said and done, on the basis of astronomical considerations we have to say that the entire constellation of 7 BC was a unique occurrence "once for all", as was the birth of Christ. According to the teaching of the Apostles "Christ has made his appearance once and for all, now at the end of the last age, to do away with sin by sacrificing himself" (Heb 9: 26).

The Star of the Messiah

Ancient history as far back as four thousand years contains the tradition of the "Star of the Messiah". The Scriptures however avoid using this terminology as the prophets were aware how susceptible the people were to mythological misconceptions. Ordinary people in ancient times were incapable of clearly distinguishing between physical and spiritual reality. According to popular belief the eternal king of the world was the brightest star visible in the sky, which was expected to come down to Earth one day and make man immortal.

The prophets of Israel awaited the Messiah to come from a purely spiritual world. Seven hundred years before the birth of Christ they set out to preach that the Messiah would be born of a virgin in Bethlehem of Judah, and he would bring about justice, cure the sick and finally sacrifice himself to save his followers. At the end of time "he will come again in glory to judge the living and the dead and his kingdom will have no end" (cf. Is 7: 14; Dan 7: 13-14).

These prophecies were later misinterpreted by the scribes of Judah. They believed the Messiah would come down directly from heaven in human form to restore the earthly kingdom of Israel. Therefore, Jesus repeatedly asked the disciples "not to tell anyone that he was the Messiah". He called himself "the Son of Man" to express his lowly state as a man. He did so to insure that his disciples would not reinforce the false concepts or hopes which people had about the Messiah. At the same time Jesus knew that his disciples faced being executed if they revealed his real identity. In spite of this the news spread that Jesus was regarded as the Messiah. The chief priests of Jerusalem protested violently: "Yet we all know where he comes from, but when the Messiah appears no one will know where he comes from...; prophets do not come out of Galilee" (Jn 7: 27 and 52).

Finally, Jesus himself decided to face the chief priests in order to save the lives of his disciples. He agreed to undergo a legal hearing and to the claim of Caiaphas the high priest he declared openly that he was "the Messiah, the Son of God", and he remarked: "Moreover, I tell you that from this time onward you will see the Son of Man seated at the right hand of the Power and coming on the clouds of heaven" (Mt 26: 63). At this critical moment Jesus quoted the prophet Daniel and predicted his second coming, on Judgment Day at the end of the world, when everyone will see his glorified figure. Thereby he revealed himself not as an earthly Messiah of traditional expectation, but as the Lord of the prophets, and the mysterious personage of heavenly origin whom Daniel had seen in a vision. The chief priests took Jesus' statement for a grave blasphemy, and therefore they condemned him to death.

But where at this time was the star of Bethlehem, the observation of which had given a few sages an "exceedingly great joy" (Mt 2: 10)? By the time of these tragic events it had long been forgotten. Among the magi there were perhaps but a few who remarked that Jupiter and Saturn came together again at the time when Jesus of Nazareth was crucified because of the false accusation brought against him that he would be the king of Judaea. Yet this conjunction lasted only a few days and not in the sign of the Fish but among the stars of the Lion and Crab, in the sign of the Roman Empire.

The star of Bethlehem was called the "star of the Messiah" by the early Christian writers, who believed that Matthew's account was obviously connected with Balaam's prophecy. To them the star of the Magi was a natural phenomenon which, they stressed, was also a symbol of supernatural significance. This interpretation was necessary from the standpoint of apologetics at a time when most rulers and their people were fanatic worshippers of some star-god or other. Christians were regarded as foolish and faithless for adoring an "invisible god" and refusing to offer sacrifices to the gods visible in the sky and their earthly statues. From Damascus to Rome, city heights were adorned with magnificent temples raised in honor of Jupiter or *Zeus-pater*, the brightest wandering star in the sky.

St. Luke relates the experiences of Paul and Barnabas in the Greek town of Lystra. The event reflects the mentality of the times. There was a man who had never walked in his life, because his feet were crippled from birth. Paul said in a loud voice to him: "Get to your feet, stand up!" And the cripple jumped up and began to walk. When the crowd saw what Paul had done, they shouted: "These people are gods who have come down to us disguised as men!" Since Barnabas was very tall and silent they addressed him as Zeus-Jupiter. Paul was shorter of stature, and he was the principal speaker, therefore they called him Hermes-Mercury. The priests of the Temple of Jupiter brought garlanded oxen to the gates, proposing that the people should offer sacrifice in honor of Paul and Barnabas. When the two apostles heard what was happening they rushed into the crowd and shouted: "We are only human beings like you. We have come with good news to make you turn from these empty idols to the living God who made heaven and earth and all that these hold" (Acts 14: 8-16).

The Church Fathers could not provide an astronomical explanation for the extraordinary heavenly phenomenon that guided the Magi to Jerusalem. Nor was it their task to find such an explanation. Their intention was to ensure that the faithful did not attribute the powers of Christ to some influence of "mortal star deities". It was Tertullian who called Jupiter, Saturn and Mars mortal gods, when some people used these planets in an attempt to explain the birth of Christ.

The conjunction of Jupiter and Saturn being the sign of Christ's birth was no new invention. Kepler himself referred to Rabbinistic and early Christian traditions which induced him to verify by astronomical calculations the physical possibility of such a conjunction at the time of Christ's birth. Even today, by emphasizing the literary interpretation of Matthew's account, most biblicists follow the path of the early

Christian writers. Their starting point is usually Balaam's prophecy and then they turn to other Old Testament texts to interpret Matthew's intention.

Among Semitic people the star and scepter had been the signs of divine power ever since ancient times. In the hands of Assyrian-Babylonian rulers these became the insignia of royal dignity received from heaven. Ancient Mesopotamian monuments surviving from the time of Hammurabi and Abraham testify that the new kings received the star and the scepter from Marduk, that is Jupiter, the heavenly lord of justice and law. Relying on this tradition, the Greeks and Romans adopted the idea of the Savior of the world. From the 4th century BC onwards a number of coins, seals and reliefs feature the star above the head of kings with the arbitrarily assumed messianic title *Sôtêr* or *Salvator*, that is Redeemer or Savior, written beside their names.

The first and most interesting find is the diadem of Alexander the Great: the eight-pointed star of Jupiter is within the crescent Moon, and under this there are two six-pointed stars. These are the symbols of Castor and Pollux whom the Greeks held for sons of Jupiter (*Dioskoroi*). This became the emblem of victorious military leaders. (Cf. Plinius, *Nat. Hist.* 35: 93).

With the help of finds some scholars tried to prove that "the star above the head of sovereigns, quite apart from the celestial phenomenon visible in Palestine and far beyond the messianic ideas, had a symbolical meaning which was obvious to everyone in the Greek-Roman Empire." Thus they claim that Matthew simply applied the well known symbol to the child born in Bethlehem. "That was how he intended to convince them that instead of Augustus or any other Roman pretender to the throne, the true Lord of the world was Jesus, who came to create a new era" (Küchler 1989).

However, this one-sided literary interpretation creates the impression that the star was a mere symbol for Matthew, not a real celestial body. On the other hand, a one-sided astronomical explanation which ignores the profound symbolism is equally insufficient. Apparently these two views are so much opposed to each other that it seems impossible to reconcile them. Two different fractions, however, can be added if we bring them to a common denominator. And here the common denominator is precisely the entire astronomical and historical constellation of that time, the importance of which was shown previously. The symbolic interpretation of certain celestial phenomena was a result of both astronomical observation and of historical considerations.

Balaam, the Assyrian magus was a contemporary of Moses (around 1200 BC). When referring to his prophecy, we have to note that, judging from contemporary cuneiform texts, he must have meant a real star when he foresaw the rising star of Jacob-Israel. It is highly improbable that he used the word "star" in a figurative sense as we use it today to praise some famous actor or athlete. However, the original symbolical meaning of a certain celestial phenomenon remains unchanged even if it has been applied to different events and persons throughout the centuries.

Research in psychology of religion proves that the "star of Messiah", as an archetype of the divine Savior, has been created so as to form an integral part of human psyche. Along with the ancient star myths this is quite clearly recognizable in the Scriptures. For instance, Genesis reads as follows: "God created man in the image of himself, in the image of God he created him, male and female he created them" (Gen 1: 27). However, after the fall the human being lost the consciousness of the "primordial image of God". The account of the fall in the Book of Genesis uses figurative language, but affirms a primeval event that took place at the beginning of the history of man. The serpent is here used as a disguise for the mortal enemy of our human nature. But the Lord (He-who-is) says to this serpent: "I will make you enemies of each other: you and the woman, your offspring and her offspring; he will crush your head" (Gen 3: 15). This passage in Genesis is called the *Proto-Evangelium*: the first announcement of the Messianic Savior who will be born of a Woman. The Christian tradition sees this Woman in the Holy Virgin of Nazareth, the mother of Jesus.

This *Proto-Evangelium* is indeed the first prophecy of salvation, man's ultimate victory over sin and death, which is fulfilled in the person and work of Christ. The image of God is like an unconscious archetype in the fallen man's psyche, "but to all who did accept Christ he gave power to become children of God" (Jn 1: 12), that is, they can awake to a full consciousness of God's image through Christ and in him. According to this revelation man is predestined to reproduce the image of God's Son made Man, the "image of the invisible God, so that Christ shall be the eldest of many brothers". This is the genuine interpretation given by the apostles (Col 1: 15; Rom 8: 29).

In the Book of Revelation (John's *Apocalypse*, 12: 1-12) the mother of the Messianic Savior appears as "a great sign in heaven: a Woman, adorned with the Sun, standing on the Moon, and with the twelve stars on her head for a crown". Then a second sign appears in the sky, "a huge red dragon [*Draco*], the primeval serpent, and it stops in front of the Woman". We can here see an implicit allusion to the well known constellations of antiquity *Virgo* and *Draco*. The circumpolar stars of *Draco* the "huge Dragon" are never seen to set by people living in the northern hemisphere. The image of the "woman adorned with the Sun" is an excellent example of the archetypical effect and symbolic interpretation of celestial phenomena. The light of the Sun is the creative love of the Father Almighty. The changing Moon and the

112

serpent under the mother's feet are the transitory world and the fallen human nature which she has now defeated and is dominating. Her Son will govern the nations with a "scepter of iron" that is with the force of a just law. Above her head she has the crown of total victory, the twelve constellations of the path of the Sun and Moon: this is the symbol of both the chosen nations and the twelve apostles, who have recognized the Messiah in Jesus and have accepted him with faith.

The apostle Peter encourages the faithful in his last letter to follow with attention the prediction of the prophets "as a lamp for lighting a way through the dark until the dawn comes and the Morning Star rises in your minds" (2 Pt 1: 19). At the beginning of John's Apocalypse Jesus declares: "To those who prove victorious, and keep working for me until the end…,I will give them the Morning Star", and finally he presents himself saying: "I am the root of David and the bright Morning Star" (Rev 2: 28; 22: 16). The meaning of this expression is the same as that of the Greek word *Anatolê* which, in the usage of the prophets, is a name of the Messiah. In the Chaldaean tradition, the Morning Star was the symbol of resurrection and triumphant glory, a feature of Jupiter.

Even in the past few decades the origin and story of the "star of Messiah" was a subject widely researched by some scholars. They repeatedly asked the question: Where, when and why was the star of the Magi included in the Gospel? New light was shed on this question by the writings of the Essenes, or the Qumran finds, found on the northwestern coast of the Dead Sea between 1947 and 1957. The results of the research can be summarized as follows:

It was in Syria where the tradition of the star of Bethlehem became widespread and survived, especially among the Christians living in Damascus. The first preachers of the Gospel there were the Israelites converted from among the Essenes, who were devout promoters of the prophecy of Jacob's star (Nb 24: 17). They saw the fulfillment of this prophecy in the story of the star of Bethlehem. This account was very important to them, since it included the magi, who counted as the most prestigious scholars and priests of the people in the whole of Syria. Some of these magi opposed the views of the apostles while others accepted them and were baptized, but these, following the spirit of astral mythology, misinterpreted the birth of Jesus. An example of this is the case of Simon the Magus (Acts 8: 9-24). For 12 years after the first Pentecost the apostle Matthew worked in Syria and in all probability it was there that he recorded the traditions he had collected.

Under the circumstances it was both possible and appropriate for the star of Bethlehem to be included in the introduction to the Gospel as the celestial sign of Christ's birth. This was necessary to the peoples of Syria, since they were under the influence of the magi's teachings and they were more familiar than anyone else with the symbolic significance of celestial phenomena. Thus the account of the Magi visiting Bethlehem was of great help to them in accepting Jesus' teachings with faith.

In his book, entitled "The Early Christian Symbols", Jean Daniélou provides a convincing justification of the above statements. This biblicist and theologian gives a detailed analysis of the works of early Christian writers and other sources along with the Qumran finds. Furthermore, he quotes from the writings of his contemporaries, who had arrived at the same conclusion as he had. Let us have a look at the main results of this research. Balaam's prophecy of Jacob's star and the prophet Amos's statement concerning Saturn were first and most frequently quoted by the Qumran writings made by the Zadokites and Essenes returning from Mesopotamia to Judaea in the 2nd century BC. When the temple of Jerusalem was again consecrated after the victory of the Maccabees, the legitimate high priest was a descendant of Zadok. His followers were the Zadokites, the Just ones. Their name comes from the Hebrew *saddiq* (or *zadik*) which means "just" or "righteous". The Essenes (*Hassîdîm* = pious ones) allied themselves with these Zadokites in abiding by the orthodox Hebrew tradition and in waiting for the Messiah's coming. King Solomon had entrusted the legitimate priesthood to the sons of Zadok, who belonged to the priestly tribe of Levi, because they remained loyal to the service of the Sanctuary in Jerusalem. The prophet Ezekiel had also prescribed this for the service of the new Sanctuary after the Exile: "These are the sons of Zadok, those of the sons of Levi who approach the Lord to serve him" (Ez 40: 46; 44: 15).

Despite this traditional law Jonathan Maccabaeus accepted the appointment of high priest of the Jews from the hand of the Syrian king Alexander Balas (1 Mc 10: 18). This action of the Maccabees must have constituted an unforgivable sin in the eyes of the Essenes who had joined the revolt because of the Syrian attempt to replace the Zadokite priesthood. They abandoned the illegitimate Maccabaean priests and the Temple, and they built a settlement for their religious community on the Qumran plateau in the northwest corner of the Dead Sea. They lived there in a full community of property and under rigorous rules of discipline. While the Maccabaean priests used a lunar calendar of Babylonian origin, the Qumran Essenes strongly defended the traditional Hebrew solar calendar of 364 days. This was a fixed calendar, where every year and every week began on Wednesday, and the same dates fell on the same weekday every year (cf. *The Book of Jubilees*, 6:4).

There are a number of indications that John the Baptist and his disciples were in contact with the Qumran Community without, however, following their zealous habits. Many of them became the followers of Jesus and preached the Gospel. When the war in Judaea began in 68 AD, the Qumran Community had already been joined by a number of Christians. Before the Roman armies destroyed their settlement, they placed their valuable documents in stone jars, which they sealed and hid in the caves along the northwestern coast of the Dead Sea. These so-called Dead Sea Scrolls are considered to be among the most valuable archaeological finds of our century (*JBC*. 68: 67-93).

With regard to our matter one of the most important Qumran documents is the Testament of the Twelve Patriarchs, which contains the legacy and prophecy of each of Jacob's twelve sons, the Patriarchs. This was a document the Syrian fathers, Ignatius of Antioch, Justin Martyr and Ireneus, often quoted from and it was later referred to by Origen and Jerome. Jean Daniélou and his collaborators have found that the original of this Testament was written in Hebrew, and its Greek version was made by Christian Essenes in the Qumran Community, by those who were converted to Christian faith after Jesus' resurrection. Some biblicists suppose that the Greek version of the Testament was among the sources used by the writers of the Gospel.

The following statement is found in the *Testament of Levi* (18:3), the father of the chosen priestly tribe: "His star rises in heaven as the star of a king who radiates the light of knowledge." The Greek expression *Anatolei ástron autoû* has a meaning which is the same as the meaning of the statements of Balaam and Matthew about the star of the Messiah. This star is not the Messiah himself but the sign of his advent in the sky (*en ouranô*). The prophecy ends with the warning of the prophet Hosea (10:12): "It is time to go seeking the Lord until he comes to rain salvation [or righteousness] on you!"

In this text the figure of the Messiah is both king and high priest, which is indicative of Christian thinking. In the Aramaic Qumran writings the Messiah appears as two different persons: one is the king as Interpreter of Law who represents the executive power of the state, the other is the high priest as Teacher of Righteousness. His followers are the Sons of Light, who constantly do battle with the Sons of Darkness. This pair of antonyms, however, is reminiscent of the magi's teachings.

The patriarch Judah was the inheritor of the messianic promise, and in the *Testament of Judah* (24: 1) Balaam's prophecy is quoted as follows: "A star rises from Jacob and a man appears as the Sun of righteousness". The word "scepter" is here replaced by "man", which again is indicative that this was written by Christians. This was how Origen had translated Balaam's prophecy. Furthermore, Judah evokes the prophet Micah, who foretold that the Messiah would be born in Bethlehem. Finally he refers to the prophecy of Malachi (3:20): "But for you who fear my name, the Sun of righteousness will shine out with healing in its rays". And in the Gospel Jesus himself is the risen Sun of righteousness (Lk 1: 78).

The Qumran fragment of the *Damascus Scroll* (a Hebrew writing of the Essenes) is related to these chapters of the Testament. Apart from referring to Balaam, it quotes the warning of Amos concerning the star-god of Israel and gives the following explanation thereof:

> The Book of the Prophets is the foot stool of the Idol, because Israel has rejected the words of the Prophets. The star, which has come to Damascus, is the Interpreter of Law. As it is written: A Star will rise out of Jacob, and a Scepter out of Israel. The Scepter is the Leader of the Community, he is the Teacher of Righteousness, as the expected Messiah (*Damascus Scroll*, 7: 14-20).

In old Hebrew tradition the star of Law is Saturn, and righteousness is the characteristic feature of Jupiter. We may therefore assume that the quoted text of the Testament implies a symbolic interpretation of the great conjunction of the two royal stars. This assumption will be justified in the following discussions.

Finally, it was the deacon Stephen who quoted the words of Amos before the Sanhedrin, the Supreme Priestly Council in Jerusalem. He directed the charge against the high priests who had Jesus, the Just One, killed. His name, *Stephanos*, and his entire discourse show that he was a Greek-speaking Israelite and belonged to the community of the Essenes. Luke mentions several times that the Christians from Judaea fled to Syria because of the persecutions that started following Stephen's execution. Barnabas and Paul also worked there: "they were received by that Church a whole year; they instructed a large number of people, and it was at Antioch that the disciples were first called Christians (Acts 7: 43-53 and 11: 26).

The bishop Epiphanius testifies that the Zadokites possessed a settlement also in Syria, around 15 kilometers southwest of Damascus, the typical name of which was *Kocheba* i.e. Star, and a Christian Dositheus was living there. He had known John the Baptist, and later he became the teacher of Simon the Magus. It was also to this settlement that the Essenes fled during the Judaean war, and where the Nicolaitans, the followers of Balaam, came from. The latter were reprehended by Peter because "they have left the right path", probably because with Balaam as their master, they practiced astrology for considerable gain. (Epiphanius, *Panarion* 2:8, 25-30; Rev 2: 14; 2 Pt 2: 15).

On the basis of all these data Daniélou concluded that it was in Damascus that the historical character of the star of Bethlehem was preserved by the first Christians. As a matter of fact, it was the first really convincing sign that the messianic prophecies had been fulfilled and it was a particularly appropriate proof in an environment where the Gospel had to be preached among magi. It was in Damascus that the Christian Essenes met the Babylonian magi. That was why Justin and others said that the Magi came from Damascus to Jerusalem. Therefore Matthew's account of the star can, indeed, be traced back to the events related by some magi. Thus the star of Bethlehem has a real historical value.

According to Matthew, Jesus himself was already well known in Syria: "teaching in Galilee and curing all kinds of diseases and sickness among the people, his fame spread throughout Syria…, and large crowds followed him, coming from the Decapolis" (Mt 4: 23-25). Decapolis was a federation of 10 free towns, the most important of which were Damascus and Antioch.

Some scholars recently have suggested a new solution concerning the literary genre of the Gospel narratives about Jesus' birth. For instance, René Laurentin, professor at the French Catholic Institute and at Dayton University, thinks that Matthew's 2nd chapter is related to the apocalyptic literature. He also quoted from the Qumran writings, but doubted that they had been used directly for the Gospel narratives. Having compared the accounts of Matthew and Luke, he found that they "both talked of a star but from a totally different point of view". In Matthew's account the star of the Magi is a real star in the sky, heralding Christ's birth in Judaea. For Luke, on the other hand, heaven is not the sky in the physical sense of the word but the habitation of God's angels; and the rising of the star is an allegory or a narrative description of the Messiah's advent: "he has visited us as the Rising from on high (*Anatolê ex hypsous*), to give light to those who live in darkness and the shadow of death" (Lk 1: 78).

In this respect, says Laurentin, we need neither Balaam's prophecy nor any astronomical explanation to be able to interpret correctly the texts in question. We have only to remember that stars and angels have the same function in the apocalyptic literature, e.g. in the Book of Daniel and John's Apocalypse. They are two equivalent transmitters of God's messages. Likewise in the Gospel, both the stars and the angels express a relationship between man and God, showing at the same time the transcendence of God.

In antiquity, according to Laurentin, the star was "a symbol with various meanings representing, for instance, a god or a deified king, the Messiah or anybody else who was born under a lucky star, as it is still said in our days". Even today many people believe in astrology. Consequently "we need to be very careful when we want to clarify how much of the account refers to a cosmic phenomenon and how much of it is a projection of human ideas or a symbolic interpretation of the phenomenon".

The symbolic element is more obvious in Matthew's account than in that of Luke, says Laurentin. He objects, however, that one cannot come to a knowledge of the rules of interpretation used by the Magi on the basis of Matthew's writing. Still, the symbolic meaning of the star and the historical character of the account are related to each other, since at that time it was quite natural to link the earthly course of events to the motion of the stars. A believer in the Old Testament would look up at the stars as if they were the angels of God, who transmit heavenly messages for people on Earth.

Although R. Laurentin is correct in this respect, his arguments do not prove the historical validity of the account, since they furnish no explanation as to the phenomenon of the Bethlehem star. Using the old and incorrect translation, we falter when the text says "the star went before them [i.e., from north to south] until it stopped exactly over the place where the child was". Laurentin asks: *Est-ce un miracle de première grandeur?* (Is this a miracle on a grand scale?) Had these been the exact words of Matthew, we would only be able to interpret them as an allegory or as reference to an angelic apparition, like the ones found in apocalyptic literature. However, a more accurate linguistic analysis of the original text has shown that this is not the literal meaning of Matthew's account (see above: pages 18-22).

As against the many one-sided views it must be repeatedly stressed how important it is to take into account the totality of the concurrences of that time. All the historical, astronomical, cultural and psychological factors come together in the light of these concurrences. To clear up any eventual misunderstanding, let us set down the following points:

1. Matthew draws a clear distinction between the star of the Magi and the angel appearing in Joseph's dream. Here the star is exclusively the celestial sign of Christ's birth in Bethlehem, not a "symbol with various meanings". The "rules of interpretation" can be found in both the Babylonian cuneiform writings and in old Hebrew traditions. The history of ancient astronomy testifies that the symbolic interpretation of certain celestial phenomena and constellations can be traced back to the observation of simultaneous events.

2. Every astronomer knows that there is no need for an astronomical explanation when we wish to give a theological interpretation of the chapters of the Bible which deal with stars. However, astronomical calculations can help to show the historical validity of certain biblical events. By claiming that the star of Bethlehem was probably the conjunction of Jupiter and Saturn in 7 BC, we do not wish to give a new explanation of Matthew's account but merely wish to verify the historical reality

of the phenomenon. For this purpose, however, it is not enough to present the results of astronomical calculations. In following discussions we shall show that on the basis of ancient symbolic astronomy it is the Jupiter-Saturn conjunction which most fully answers to the messianic interpretation of the star of Bethlehem.

The messianic interpretation was not invented by the Magi nor by the astronomers of later times. It was in Matthew's account that the star of Bethlehem became the star of the Messiah, a concept comprising both the physical reality and the symbolic contents of the natural phenomenon. This is shown by the statement of the Magi: "Where is he who is the one born king of Judah, for we saw his star in its evening rising and have come to pay him homage". Then the scribes of Jerusalem tell them "where the Messiah was to be born" according to the prophets (Mt 2: 4). When Matthew quotes these sentences he seems to agree fully with them. He is aware that the event did take place and also knows who the Messiah is: Jesus of Nazareth, who is Messiah, not as a king of one people only but as the Son of God, Savior of the world (*Filius Dei, Salvator mundi*: Mt 26: 63; Jn 4: 42; 1 Jn 4: 14).

It is the task of theology to explain and prove this article of faith. We now merely wish to point out that we have a certain astronomical phenomenon, and that it contains symbolic elements which bear a messianic interpretation. This can be shown both by examining ancient cultural traditions and by the appropriate biblical passages.

Symbolic Interpretation of the Star

The Greek word *symbolon* means half of a broken object, and the verb *symballein* means to compare and verify. Thus half a seal may be presented to some one as a token of recognition. The two parts could then be joined together verifying the bearer's identity and the genuiness of the object itself.

According to ancient symbolic astronomy, celestial phenomena were imprints or reflections of supernatural realities. The visible order of the stars was considered the model of a proper earthly order and life. This is seen in the ancient expression: "As in heaven, so on earth". For the Chaldaean magi and the Hebrew prophets "heaven and earth" as the cosmos, was the first and greatest living symbol: a reality of two parts which complement each other perfectly in a single universe.

According to the Greek version (Septuagint) of the Hebrew Bible God extended the heavens above all the lands and waters like an enormous tent. The heavens beyond the sky are his dwelling place and from there he governs the army of stars which perform his will. In this sense he is the "Lord of the Armies". The universe is dependent on the power of this omnipotent Lord. It is he who maintains it and "his glory fills the whole world" (Is 6: 3). His heavenly habitation symbolizes his spiritual existence, that is, his transcendence beyond space and time. Like the heavens which are visible everywhere, God is present everywhere. The patriarch Jacob awakes to the consciousness of this fact by an extraordinary vision. He sees an enormous ladder, standing on the ground with its top reaching to heaven, and there are angels of God going up it and coming down. Jacob exclaims then: "Truly, this is a house of God; this is the gate of heaven!" (Gen 28: 17).

These images are neither poetic exaggerations nor childish fancies. They are symbols which originate in real visions revealing some hidden realities. *Symbolon* means also a collection or summary. In this sense the Apostle's Creed is called *Symbolum Apostolicum*, that is the summary of the Apostle's teaching as "the spiritual seal" and common characteristic of the Christians (St. Ambrose, *Exp. Symb.* 1-7).

The symbols of a truly religious life of faith illustrate the final aim of man: salvation and happiness in a personal contact with the living God. He himself will conclude an alliance with the faithful. The symbols of the Old Covenant, which the Lord Almighty had made with Abraham and Moses, were distinctive signs which marked true worship (as the anointing of kings and priests, laying on of hands, sacrifices, and above all the Passover). These were no longer solely celebrations of cosmic cycles and social gestures, but signs of God's mighty deeds for his people, as against other ancient cults which worshipped personified natural forces. The monotheistic prophets of Israel also respected the natural forces but called them to serve and praise their creator. They preached a cosmic covenant comprehending the whole world. This cosmic covenant had begun with the seventh day of creation and developed until it reached complete fulfillment in the life and work of Christ the Savior. (19)

The great symbol of this Covenant was the Temple, the "House of God" on Earth. The Lord himself had given the pattern that Moses followed in making the Tabernacle of the Covenant (Ex 25: 9). According to the Book of Wisdom the Temple built by Solomon in Jerusalem was "a copy of that sacred Tabernacle which the Lord prepared from the beginning", that is heaven, the true Temple of God. Then the everlasting Temple appears in the cosmic visions of the prophet Ezekiel and finally in the Revelations of Saint John: the Cosmos of the "New Heaven and the New Earth" (Wis 9: 8; Ps 11: 4; Rev 21: 1-3).

The prophets also observed the celestial phenomena through which they perceived divine revelation. The stars signaled to them the descendants of Abraham, the advent of the King Savior, the end of the world era and the light of eternal salvation. The influence of the celestial symbols and historical memories set the hope of the people on an epoch-making heavenly event: "You heavens! Send the Just One like dew! Oh, that you would tear the heavens open and come down!" (Is 45: 8; 63: 19f).

The sign of the messianic era and of the cosmic covenant could not have been one single star, which appeared unexpectedly in the sky. In accordance with the sense of the mystery "the rising star of Jacob" must have been a certain configuration of stars known and observed for thousands of years. Otherwise, Balaam's prophecy could not have been quoted in the book of Moses. These known stars complemented each other's role and thus symbolized the main characteristics of the awaited Messiah's person and his epoch.

The symbolic role of each star was designated by their particular names, which in turn was derived from their specific motions. The Sumerian-Accadian names of stars were taken over by the Assyrians, the Chaldaeans and the Hebrews. The symbolic designations of the heavenly phenomena were expressed in the most obvious way in the writings of the Hebrew priests. They kept the adjectives denoting religious ideas, but they omitted the names of mythological star-gods.

The idea of the covenant with God, the Creator and Savior of the world, developed among the descendants of Abraham. His ancestors in Chaldaea had worshipped the Moon and the stars. When he left his fatherland, four thousand years ago, he heard the voice of the Most High:

Look up to heaven and count the stars if you can. Such will be your descendants. Abraham believed the Lord and it was reckoned to him as righteousness. He received the promise that in his progeny all the nations will be blessed, and among this progeny will be Christ himself, the Messiah (Gen 12: 3; 15: 6; Gal 3: 16).

The counting of the stars here refers to their quality rather than quantity, that is their symbolic role in the future of Abraham's descendants. Abraham's Chaldaean ancestors associated the idea of blessing and salvation, law and justice with the two greatest wandering stars Jupiter and Saturn, because of the observable regularity and steadiness in their motions.

In Berossos' writings Abraham is described as a righteous man, famous for his observations and correct interpretations of celestial phenomena. Josephus relates that when Abraham visited Egypt (Gen 12: 10), he taught mathematics and astronomy to the priests and preached that the regular motion of the stars and the changing of seasons testified to the power of the world's heavenly Lord. (Cf. *Antiquitates Iud*. I. 8: 2; VII. 7: 5).

The original name of this distinguished man is *Aba-am-ram* (or Abram) which means "great by reason of his Father", i.e., he was of noble descent. When the Lord the Most High made a covenant with him, his name changed into *Abraham*, i.e., "father of a multitude" (Gen 17: 5). In a spiritual sense he became the father of all the people who believe in the Lord Almighty, creator of heaven and earth. Both names correspond to the ancient Sumerian name of the brightest planet: *Mulu-babba* (or "star-father"). This solemn address was even used by the Chaldaean and Persian priests. In the Accadian myth this is the star of Marduk, the restorer and maintainer of the universal order, and in this sense he is the representative of the heavenly King.

The name of this great star has the same meaning in Indo-European languages. The old Indian Sanscrit *Dyáus-pita* means Heavenly father. This expression is the source of the Greek *Dios-patér* or *Zeus-patér*. It is also the origin of the Roman Jupiter, which in today's astronomy is simply the name of the giant planet, but according to Latin etymology it means *Juris-pater* or *Justitiae-pater*: the father of Law and Righteousness.

The Sumerian-Accadian name of the other significant planet (Saturn) is *Kaiwanu* or *Kaivan*: Steadiness, Legality, Maturity. Its revolution period of 30 years indicates the minimum age for a mature man to begin working as a teacher or priest. Its Greek name has a similar meaning: *Chronos* designates the "fullness of time" known to man through the experience of autumn and harvest or old age and death. The Latin *Saturnus* has the same meaning: Fulfilled and mature in accordance with the law of time.

The symbolic interpretation of the two giant planets is clearly described in some cuneiform writings (Kugler 1912, II. pp. 77, 348, 476). When Jupiter and Saturn are in opposition to the Sun, that is, just at the time of their evening rising, they radiate the full light of their power: blessing and victory to the just king, salvation and welfare to his people. According to a Sippar inscription, Saturn is the "Sun of night", i.e., the lord of darkness, and as such it is supposed to keep guard over peace and order. Saturn represented the peoples of Syria and Judaea, but it became the star of the Assyrian kings when they conquered these countries. At the time of the great conjunctions Jupiter, the star of Babylon, defeated Saturn and took over its power (861 BC and 702 BC). According to another interpretation, the long conjunction of the two planets represented the covenant of peace between East and West.

Ptolemy (around 130 AD) drew the rules of symbolic interpretation from the Chaldaean tradition. He characterized the symbolical nature of the Jupiter-Saturn conjunction as the celestial symbol or type of righteous, wise, peaceful, generous and glorious kings. He noted also that these two planets are in a relationship with the southwestern stars of Pisces, and, therefore, their conjunction is particularly significant there (*Tetrabiblos* I. 9; III. 14).

There is another factor of even greater importance concerning the messianic symbol: the main features of the two royal planets in the Babylonian cuneiform writings are right and order, or righteousness and law (*kittu u mesâru*). And these same ideas form the axis of salvation history in the Bible from the righteous Abraham through the Law of Moses to Christ, who is the light of righteousness and declares: "I have come not to abolish the Law or the Prophets, but to complete them" (Mt 5: 17).

In the Qumran writings we find two persons whose cooperation is needed to fulfill the messianic role: the Teacher of Righteousness and the Interpreter of Law. The Zadokites explained the prophecies in this sense. They returned from Babylon to Judaea in the second century BC, and consequently they knew very well that these expressions referred to Jupiter and Saturn. The Qumran community had some astronomers who divided the calendar into 52 weeks, that is they reckoned with years of 364 days. Their records show that they made astronomical observations and used the rules of symbolic interpretation.

It was in the Babylonian exile that the Hebrew prophets began to use these expressions to describe the era of the Messiah. Isaiah predicted in accordance with the Psalms the coming of the Deliverer from the House of David. He is the eternal king of peace and justice. By justice he gives judgment for the poor, with equity he passes sentence for the oppressed; righteousness is his shield, and he will endure like the Sun and Moon (Is 11: 3-5; Ps 72). The prophet Jeremiah used the same expressions to describe the coming Redeemer (23: 5-6): "See, the days are coming, it is the Lord who speaks, when I will raise a virtuous Branch for David, who will care for law and righteousness...And this is the name he will be called: He-who-is our Righteousness."

Daniel confessed that the faithless people must suffer punishment according to divine justice: "The curse written in the Law of Moses has come pouring down on us, because we have sinned, but the coming Messiah will put an end to transgression, and he will implement everlasting righteousness" (Dan 9: 24). Comparative literary studies show that the writers of these biblical texts used the symbolic contents of the traditional messianic constellation, but in a purely spiritual sense. Thus they averted the worship of stars. Star cults could be extremely tempting to people who were not yet familiar with the nature of celestial bodies and the physical laws of their motions.

Although today everyone knows that stars are not superhuman creatures, there are many people who fall victim to the old astrological belief. Moreover, certain persons tend to believe that some distant stars are inhabited by creatures far better and far more intelligent than we are and who will soon descend from there by space ships or UFOs to save us from destroying ourselves. According to C.G. Jung "this new myth is characteristic of the age of technology" and expresses the increasing desire of mankind for the appearance of an embodied deity or the second advent of Christ.

As early as the first century a great number of distinguished personalities realized that the messianic prophecies were fulfilled in the person and work of Jesus. One of the first was Paul of Tarsus, who studied at a Greek school in his native city and later became the disciple of Gamaliel, the famous rabbi in Jerusalem (Acts 22:3). At first he was among the most cruel persecutors of Jesus's followers, but after his conversion he gave a more detailed description than anybody else of the unity of law and righteousness in the New Covenant. People in the Old Covenant were not able to implement righteousness, because their faith was adjusted to external rules and signs. Opposites were reconciled in the work of Jesus Christ. The apostle Paul contrasted the old Mosaic law with the new Christian faith:

> We acknowledge that what makes a man righteous is not obedience to the Law, but faith in Jesus... Now before we came of age we were as good as slaves to the elementary principles of this world [i.e. both the elements of the physical universe and the Mosaic Law], but when the appointed time came, God sent his Son, born of a woman, born a subject of the Law, to redeem the subjects of the Law... He has let us know the mystery of his purpose, the hidden plan he made in Christ from the beginning to act upon when the times had run their course to the end; that he would bring everything together under Christ, as Head, everything in the heavens and everything on Earth (Gal 2: 16; 4: 3; Eph 1: 9).

With these words the Apostle shows how the whole body of Creation, having been cut off from the Creator by sin, is decomposing, and how its rebirth is affected by Christ reuniting all its parts into one organism with himself as the head. In the first centuries of Christianity many would regard Paul's letters written in Greek as the new interpretation of the symbols well-known from the ancient star cult. This interpretation was made possible by the realization that the Old Testament prophecies had been fulfilled.

The 7th chapter of the Letter to the Hebrews is particularly interesting. It quotes David's psalm about Jesus' inborn royal and priestly dignity, which was recognized by Abraham in the benediction of Melchizedek. This suggests the symbolic contents of the traditional messianic constellation. The prophetic Psalm says:

> He-who-is [the Lord Almighty] said to my Lord: Sit at my right hand... Royal dignity was yours from the day you were born, royal from the womb... the Lord has sworn an oath which he never will retract; You are a priest of the order of Melchizedek, and for ever (Ps 110).

This psalm was also quoted by Jesus to the Pharisees, who professed that the Messiah was David's son (Mt 22: 44). Jesus asked them: "Then how is it that David, moved by the Spirit, calls him Lord, where he says: The Lord Almighty said to my Lord...If David can call him Lord, then how can he be his son?" They could not answer this question because they did not understand that the Messiah (Jesus himself) was a divine person, that is God Almighty in human form. The apostle gives the following explanation of this Psalm:

> You remember that Melchizedek, king of Salem, a priest of God Most High, went to meet Abraham..., and blessed him. By the interpretation of his name, he is king of righteousness and also king of Salem, that is king of peace; he has no father, mother or ancestry, and his life has no beginning or ending; he is like the Son of God, and he remains a priest for ever (Heb 7: 1-3).

Thus this mysterious high priest, Melchizedek, was the prototype of the promised Messiah, already at the time of Abraham. His name and his blessing are implicit references to the star of the Messiah or his celestial symbol. He pronounced this blessing: "Blessed be Abraham by God Most High (*El-Shaddai*), Creator of heaven and Earth" (Gen 14: 20).

The names *Melchi-Zedek* and *El-Shaddai* might have been associated with Jupiter and Saturn in the old Hebrew tradition. This claim is supported by the research paper of R..A. Rosenberg (1972). In the view of the ancient East there were always the same three astrological symbols (Jupiter, Saturn, Pisces) which signaled the time of peace, freedom and welfare as well as messianic salvation.

Besides the priests whose task it was to write the Bible, there were some secular scholars among the Israelites. Their tradition has been preserved by the book of *Kabbalah* edited originally in Babylon from where it spread later, in the course of the Middle Ages. In the texts of *Raziel Kabbalah* the Hebrew name of Jupiter is *Sedeq* (or Zedek) which means Justice. This royal star is represented by *Melkhi-Sedeq* of

Canaan, who is at the same time the priest of *El-Eljon*, the Almighty One. According to St. Jerome the original meaning of *El* is Power and Strength. Phoenician inscriptions preserved from the 15th century BC testify that in the Canaanite cult the name of Saturn was *El*, meaning a celestial Superpower. His son was *Baal* (Lord), the star of Jupiter to whom he occasionally gave over all his power. In Greek-Roman mythology the relationship of Chronos-Saturn and Zeus-Jupiter is characterized by the same features.

Although the Israelites in Canaan disapproved of the hideous idol of Baal and his immoral cult, they took over the notion of *El*, which they completed with appropriate adjectives. This word became the name of their God until the time of Moses: *El-Eljon*, the Almighty One, "who creates heaven and earth"; *El-Roi*, the Omniscient One, "who always sees me"; *El-Shaddai*, the Most High, "who has made a covenant with Abraham on the Holy Mountain" (Gen 16: 13; 17: 1). These names derive from the symbols of the ancient star worship. People did not know who that celestial "Most High Power" (*El-Shaddai*) was until He himself had revealed his proper name.

The great revelation occurred on Mount Sinai 800 years after Abraham. There was a rose bush blazing without being consumed, a symbol of the eternally Living One. He gave the following answer to Moses' question: "I am who I am. You are to say to the sons of Israel: Yahweh [He-who-is], the God of your fathers, has sent me to you. This is my name for all time...I am Yahweh" (Exod 3: 14-15 ; 6: 6).

This name expresses a personal existence and an eternally active presence. He did not come into being nor will he come into being; he is the One who is (exists) in eternal present tense. Again, there were very few people who were able to understand this revelation correctly. In Bible translations we usually find "Lord" instead of *Yahweh*. (It is worth noting that in the Hebrew Bible only the four consonants YHWH were written. The Israelites regarded this name as too sacred to be pronounced. Unfortunately, in recent Bible translations this Hebrew word is transliterated into *Yahweh,* but this transliteration does not in fact render the meaning of the Hebrew YHWH which is "He-who-is", i.e., the eternal and almighty One.)

It was 500 years after Moses that the prophets started to preach that the Lord was the Messiah himself. To fight the bewitching influence of star worship and idolatry, the Lord himself sent this message to the people suffering in the Babylonian exile: "I am Yahweh [He-who-is], there is no other Saviour but me" (Is 43:11). When Jesus appropriates this name, he is claiming to be the one incomparable savior: "If you do not believe that I am He, you will die in your sins... I tell you, before Abraham ever was, I Am" (Jn 8: 24 and 58).

126

In spite of the prophets insisting on a purely spiritual approach to the Messiah, the astrological interpretation of the messianic prophecies spread among the people and had a significant influence on rabbinic exegesis. This is illustrated by the following examples. The first great king of Judaea after the Babylonian exile was Jehonatan, whose Greek name was *Jannaios* (103-76 BC). The eight-pointed star representing the Messiah became his emblem. Josephus Flavius described the strange circumstances in which Jannaios was born (*Ant.Iud.* XIII.12). His father, Johannes Hirkanos, fought as the Syrian king's general in the war against the Parthians. In this duty his advisors were certainly some Chaldaeans, who were familiar with the significance of future constellations. In 126 BC Jupiter and Saturn were in conjunction for a long time in the western branch of Pisces, that is over Judaea. The data referring to this phenomenon are preserved on some cuneiform tablets, so the Chaldaean magi must have kept track of the events.

Jehonatan, Hirkanos's third son, was born about one year before the Jupiter-Saturn conjunction. At that time an angel appeared to his father in a dream and foretold that his youngest son had to be his successor as king and high priest in Jerusalem. The historian Josephus remarked: "Indeed, the heavens did not deceive Hirkanos". Jehonatan had the eight-pointed star engraved on his coins and in between the points of the star he had "Jehonatan the King" inscribed in Hebrew. This Babylonian representation of the Morning Star lived on in the memory of the Israelites and became for them the emblem of the messianic king.

The second and fatal Jewish war against the Romans was led by Simon Ben Kosibah in 130-135 AD. The Talmud of Jerusalem relates his story: "When the Rabbi Aqiba recognized Ben Kosibah, he proclaimed: This is the king, the Messiah!" (Tan. 4,68.d). He then changed his name to *Bar Kocheba*, which means "Star's Son". Along with the high priest Eleazar he was the "Reigning Prince of Israel" for three years. He persecuted his Christian compatriots in a most cruel way because they refused to recognize him as the Messiah. One of his letters bearing his seal with Jacob's star was found at Qumran. His silver coin represented the façade of the restored Temple with the eight-pointed star on one side and the inscription, "The first year of Israel's redemption", on the other.

It seems that Bar Kocheba's astronomers reckoned with the conjunction of Jupiter and Saturn correctly. In 134 AD the triple conjunction took place in the sign of Sagittarius, when Bar Kocheba celebrated his victory. The following year he was killed in battle and the rabbi Aqiba and the high priest Eleazar died martyrs (Eusebius, *Hist. eccl.* IV. 6: 2).

Fig. 19:   Coin of Jehonatan   Coin of King Herod   Coin of Bar Kocheba
            and Salome (103-67 BC)   the Great (37 BC)   (132 AD)

After the war of independence had been repressed, the emperor Hadrian expelled the Israelites of Judaea. He had a shrine built on Calvary in honor of *Jupiter Optimus Maximus*, whose ancient temple had been standing on the heights of the Capitol in Rome since as early as 510 BC. A strange story! One hundred years after the crucifixion and resurrection of Christ, the Roman emperor declares Jerusalem the City of Jupiter!

While the eight-pointed star represented the messianic king, mediaeval rabbinic traditions suggest that the six-pointed star was the symbol of Jacob-Israel. In the cabalistic system Jupiter was the star number six and Saturn the number seven. The six-pointed star is visible on the seal of Sidon from the 7th century BC, as well as on some ancient tombstones, coins and jewels found in Palestine. When Herod the Great became king of Judaea, he had the six-pointed star above the Roman helmet engraved on his coin. Perhaps he wanted to gain the favor of the Jews.

A remarkable find is the relief in the Synagogue of Caphernaum with two six-pointed stars on it. They look like the wheels of a carriage transporting the Sanctuary of the Covenant. However, they are not carriage wheels, but rather the celestial circles described by the prophet Ezekiel in connection with the Cherubs and the New Temple. The Synagogue of Caphernaum was built in the first century with the help of the Roman centurion living there, whose dying servant was cured by Jesus (Lk 7: 5).

The six-pointed star drawn inside a circle became the secret emblem of the early Christians in the years of persecution. It was interpreted as the monogram of Jesus Christ, looking like a compilation of the Greek initials I and X. At the same time Christian belief was hidden in the symbol of the Fish (*Pisces*). The Greek word for FISH is ICHTHYS, and the letters of this word are the initial letters of the following words: *Iesos Christos Theou Ychos Sôtêr* = Jesus Christ God's Son Savior.

128

Fig. 20: Relief from the Synagogue of Capharnaum with two six-pointed stars.

In his work entitled "Aion", Jung (1971) gives a detailed analysis of the symbolic meaning of Pisces in relation to the age of the Messiah. He illustrates his view by a great number of Old Hebrew and Christian sources. From the point of view of depth-psychology it seems that the two Fish (in the constellation of *Pisces*), moving in opposite directions, are an appropriate symbol of Christ, who unites in his own person the two opposite elements: human and divine nature, the earthly and the heavenly, the mortal and the immortal *(coniunctio oppositorum)*.

Daniélou (1961) discusses the symbol of the Fish from a theological point of view. The Fish, he says, symbolize the mystery of "death and resurrection"; a symbol of the New Man who is reborn by the sacrament of baptism and lives in the fullness of the Christian era. Christ made religion a practice of purely spiritual character in order to liberate us from the effect of visible and changing phenomena. That is why the apostle Paul warned the faithful: "Make sure that no one traps you by some empty teaching based on the principles of this world instead of on Christ." The old symbols concerning the annual festivals, New Moons and Sabbaths "were only pale reflections of what was coming: the reality in Christ" (Col 2: 8-17). The reality of the risen Christ is the first evidence that the new creation has already begun.

The apostles and the Church Fathers interpreted the water and fish in the cosmic vision of the prophet Ezekiel as baptism by Christ. Water flows out on the right side of the new Temple, and it becomes a great river, as Ezekiel has foreseen. "And fish will be very plentiful, for wherever this water goes it brings health, and life teems wherever the river flows." (Ez 47: 9) The water flowing out from the right side of the Temple is a prototype for the crucified Christ: "One of the soldiers pierced Jesus' side with a lance and there flowed out water and blood" (Jn 19: 34).

In the course of the millennia before the new age (i.e., before the advent of Christ), the constellation of *Pisces* was the twelfth and final station on the annual path of the Sun, and at the same time it was the sign for the beginning of a new spring. In this sense the sign of *Pisces* indicates the "fullness of time" and also the beginning of "a new world-year". With Christ's resurrection and ascension the final epoch of the world has begun, and the renewal of the universe is irrevocably in progress. The Prophets and the Apostles call this time the "age of the Messiah" who reveals:

> Now I am making the whole of creation new…I am the Alpha and the Omega, the First and the Last, the Beginning and the End. I will give water from the well of life free to anybody who is thirsty (Rev 21: 5-6; 22: 13).

The Rabbi Isaac Abarbanel (1497 AD), in his commentary on the book of Daniel, tried to prove the authenticity of Old Hebrew traditions by astronomical calculations. Referring to the prophets he stated that the constellation of *Pisces* was the sign of the chosen people and their salvation. That was the constellation which heralded the end of the deluge to Noah, as we read in the book of Moses: "It was in the first month and on the first of the month, that the water dried up from the earth" (Gen 8: 13). The first month Nisan was associated with Aries the Ram, whereas the month preceding Nisan was Adar, the month of *Pisces* the Fish. On the last day of Adar the Sun and Moon rose in conjunction at the last degrees of *Pisces*, that is, the spring new moon occurred just on that day. With this a new epoch started. The liberation of the people by Moses from the slavery in Egypt also took place in the month of *Pisces*. This again marked the beginning of a new epoch. That was why Moses ordered the month Nisan to be the first month of every new year.

Rabbi Abarbanel knew Ptolemy's astronomical tables and astrological rules, and making use of these he reckoned with a 20 years' period of the Jupiter-Saturn conjunctions. He supposed that every twenty years the conjunction should occur at around 118° distance from the place of the previous one, that is in a third zodiacal sign. And since $3 \times 118° = 354°$, every sixty years the two planets would come together in the same sign of the Zodiac. He called these "middle conjunctions", which usually signaled the periods of war or peace and the births of kings, in accordance with the character of the constellation.

Abarbanel tried to determine the increasing importance of these conjunctions by studying historical parallels or similar events recurring from time to time throughout centuries. Starting from the dates and records he had found in the Hebrew Bible and the Talmud, he concluded that both the era of Abraham and the eras of Moses, David and Elijah were heralded by a certain conjunction of Saturn and Jupiter. The Lord sent a great prophet or king to save his people in time of need.

For example, 240 years passed from Moses to the king David, then again 240 years from David to the prophet Elijah. Every 240 years there occurred the so-called "great conjunctions", each time in a different zodiacal sign. Nevertheless, more important were the "large conjunctions" every 960 years which indicated the time of the renewal of the Covenant: 960 years passed from Abraham to Moses. The most significant one should, however, be the "mighty conjunction" heralding the advent of the Messiah, when Saturn and Jupiter would be in conjunction for nine months in the sign of *Pisces*, and this should occur 2860 years after the birth of Moses.

Abarbanel's calculations were wrong both astronomically and historically. (Could he or would he have recognized the Messiah in Jesus of Nazareth if his calculations had been right?) His writings are nevertheless valuable regarding our subject, since they testify to a popular Hebrew tradition of the people expecting the Messiah during the centuries preceding and following the new age. Essential to this tradition was the idea that the celestial sign of the Messiah's advent in Judaea would be a conjunction of these three astronomical factors:

> *Jupiter*, as the star of justice and salvation; *Saturn*, as the star of Sabbath, of the law and fulfillment; the constellation of *Pisces*, the sign of the final times and symbol of Israel's salvation. (See: Fig. 21.)

All this proves the existence of a particular astronomical phenomenon, the symbolic contents of which correspond to the messianic interpretation. The deciphered cuneiform star almanac and astronomical calculations in turn prove that the same conjunction occurred in the year 7 BC. It follows that it can be perfectly applied to the star of Bethlehem which is mentioned in Matthew's 2nd chapter.

Instead of Greek-Roman mythology, it is this Hebrew tradition that provides the best basis to judge the historical value of Matthew's account. We have here an ancient symbol which once characterized the epoch of the Messiah. Since this symbol has been fulfilled and explained, it became a very historical sign for us. In order to understand this statement let us quote an explanation of C.G. Jung:

> The symbol is alive only so long as it is pregnant with meaning. But once its meaning has been born out of it, once that expression is

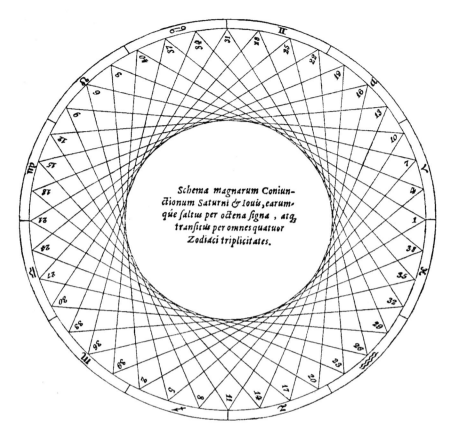

Fig.21: Diagram of the Period of the Jupiter-Saturn-Conjunctions by J.Kepler (Mysterium Cosmographicum. Praefatio. 1596)

found which formulates the thing expected even better than the hitherto accepted symbol, then the symbol possesses only an historical significance...A symbol really lives only when it is the best and highest expression for something divined but not yet known to the observer. The living symbol formulates an essential unconscious factor, and the more widespread this factor is, the more general is the effect of the symbol, for it touches a corresponding chord in every psyche. Since, for a given epoch, it is the best possible expression for what is still unknown, it must be the product of the most complex and differentiated minds of that age. But in order to have such an effect at all, it must embrace what is common to a large group of men (Jung, *Psychological Types*, 816-820).

132

Again and again there are journalists in search of sensational news, who cover recent theories which in reality have been refuted long ago. They will claim for instance, that the star of Bethlehem was one of the brightest fixed stars, or the planet Venus, or the sudden appearance of a new star or a comet, or perhaps a moon moving on a geo-stationary path for a long time. These speculations have clearly been ruled out by astronomical calculations and historical research.

Hughes (1979) discusses in detail the different assumptions concerning the phenomenon and concludes:

We have here ample justification for concluding that the Jupiter-Saturn conjunction in *Pisces* had a strong, clear astrological message. To Babylonians and Jews alike it heralded the coming of the Messiah, a man of righteousness who would save the world. The message was unambiguous and obviously impressed the Magi with the importance of the event and the necessity to journey to Jerusalem and Bethlehem. It is also clear that it was only the Jupiter-Saturn-Pisces conjunction that had this message. All other astronomical occurrences around the time of the birth of Jesus were irrelevant in the quest for the Messiah, and this alone is ample justification for ruling them out as candidates for the role of star of Bethlehem.

CHAPTER THREE

ASTRONOMY AND THE BIBLE

Astronomical Observations in the Hebrew Bible

Many researchers have been quite dazzled by the abundance of the Mesopotamian excavations. At the beginning of the 20th century they were inclined to believe that Babylonian culture had completely dominated the world of ideas to which all the ancient nations belonged. Pan-Babylonists also thought that the Hebrew Bible was an imitation of Accadian astral mythology. This conclusion has since been abrogated by the results of research in the course of which astronomers played a role perhaps even more prominent than Biblicists themselves.

Giovanni Schiaparelli, the director of the Brera Observatory in Milan, was in his time well-known for his observations of the surfaces of different planets and the discovery of the Mars canals. He rightly assumed that shooting stars and meteorites were in fact pieces of disintegrated comets. His studies devoted to the history of ancient astronomy, and published in German as well as English, caused a great sensation. In the introduction to "Astronomy in the Old Testament", one of his major writings, Schiaparelli notes:

> The astronomy in the Bible seems very primitive compared to the science of other ancient civilizations. Nevertheless, the prophets often refer to the stars and the laws of nature. The question is whether their references originate in old Hebrew traditions or in Assyrian and Chaldaean sources. This gave me the idea that it would be worthwhile to investigate how the Israeli scholars had pictured the structure of the universe; what astronomical observations they had made, how they had used them to measure and organize time. Even though astronomy was not a field where Hebrew thinking proved most original and influential, there was nevertheless nothing that could be indifferent in the life of this extraordinary people, whose history is not less important to us than that of the Greeks and the Romans (Schiaparelli 1903).

Schiaparelli studied the Old Hebrew language thoroughly and he usually began his treatises with detailed linguistic analyses. Then, with the help of astronomical calculations he went on to determine the astronomical phenomena visible in Judaea between 1000 and 400 BC, the time when the Scriptures were written. That was how he tried to decide the connection between some planets or constellations and certain words which had been ambiguously translated. He always stressed that the interpretation of the astronomical expressions used in Biblical texts should be based on Assyro-Babylonian sources.

Schiaparelli's contemporary, Edward W. Maunder, the director of the Greenwich Observatory, was in some ways the adversary of the Milanese astronomer. In his book entitled "The Astronomy of the Bible" (Maunder 1908) he proved to be a staunch defender of the originality of the Hebrew scholars and the authenticity of Biblical texts. He accepted Josephus Flavius' statement that Abraham and his people had been quite familiar with the motion and significance of the stars. Maunder believed that the Assyrians and the Accadians had drawn their astral myths from Hebrew traditions and had adjusted them to their own polytheism. The names of the most important constellations can be found in the Book of Moses, in which the ancient Hebrew tradition had preceded the Assyrian-Babylonian myths by centuries. In his preface Maunder describes his purpose in writing as follows:

Why should an astronomer write a commentary on the Bible? Because commentators as a rule are not astronomers, and, therefore, either pass over the astronomical allusions of Scripture in silence, or else annotate them in a way which, from a scientific point of view, leaves much to be desired. Astronomical allusions in the Bible, direct and indirect, are not few in number, and, in order to bring out their full significance, need to be treated astronomically. Astronomy further gives us the power of placing ourselves to some degree in the position of the patriarchs and prophets of old. Even in those early ages, when to all the nations surrounding Israel the heavenly bodies were objects for divination or idolatry, the attitude of the sacred writers toward them was perfect in its sanity and truth. Astronomy has yet a further part to play in Biblical study. The dating of the several books of the Bible, and the relation of certain heathen mythologies to the Scripture narratives of the world's earliest ages, have received much attention of late years. Literary analysis has thrown much light on these subjects, but hitherto any evidence that astronomy could give has been almost wholly neglected; although, from the nature of the case, such evidence, so far as it is available, must be most decisive and exact (Maunder 1908).

These two writings have become just as outdated today as they were up-to-date at the beginning of this century. Our tastes and styles have changed and so have the requirements of modern science, but the questions we then asked ourselves and the problems lying ahead of us remain the same. What some astronomers say in their new manuals is no exaggeration: As far as the development of science is concerned, the astronomical observations related to space research have become so important that "without any knowledge of astronomy, it has become impossible to understand modern physics" (Marik 1989). If, however, somebody were to come forward with the same requirements for the understanding of the Bible, they would be confronted with loud protests from many biblicists and theologians.

At the beginning of this century a distinguished astronomer could write about the astronomy of the Bible because his efforts were considered merely an endeavor to understand the origin of the universe and the constellations. Today, however, such writings would be unacceptable to those who bear in mind the astronomical observations and calculations made by highly developed optical and electronic equipment. Some people regard modern astrophysics as the perfection of science, the sole aim of which is to increase our knowledge and welfare; others see no more in the Bible than a writing concerned only with theological and moral teaching or perhaps ancient mythology. They will obviously be annoyed to see that in recent years the relationship of the Bible and astrophysics has been on the agenda of several scientific conferences. These conferences, however, do not seek to find astronomical explanations to the Bible as Maunder did in his time. Physicists and theologians mutually respect each other's independence and regard each other's theories as complementary.

The two astronomers mentioned above did not work in vain, for their findings are today quoted in some recent translations and interpretations of the Bible. The largest number of references to astronomical phenomena are to be found in the Books of Amos, Isaiah, Micah, Hosea and Job, prophets who lived in the 8th century BC. They invariably interpreted the phenomena from a religious point of view, that is they regarded them as the work and will of God the Creator. At the same time their references testify to their precise observations of the position of the stars and also show that they took their motion into account.

According to the Book of Wisdom that was already the case during the rule of King Solomon, after he had built the first temple (965-960 BC). The book was written in Alexandria in the first century BC in order to present the primeval Hebrew traditions in modern Greek language. Solomon praises the Lord of Wisdom as follows:

136

He it was who gave me sure knowledge of what exists, to understand the structure of the world and the actions of the elements, the beginning, end and middle of the times, the alternation of the solstices and the succession of the seasons, the cycles of the year and the position of the stars (Wis 7: 17-19).

The latter two expressions (*annorum cursus et stellarum dispositiones*) comprise the concept of astronomical calculations and perhaps the astrology of the constellations and planets as well (Schiaparelli 1925, p. 189).

However, the Old Hebrew names of the stars do not seem to have interested the translators of later centuries. Linguists and astronomers will agree that the two most frequently mentioned stars are the Pleiades, Hebrew *Kimah*, in popular terms "Seven Sisters"; and Orion, Hebrew *Kesil*, a mighty hunter in the old celestial picture book (Amos 5:8; Is 13:10; Job 9:9). Besides these two there are four other expressions which were identified with different stars in the Greek Septuagint and the Latin Vulgate. The newest translations, however, differ even from these.

The simple believer, when reading the Bible, will probably not seek to know which star is meant by the translators, because to him every star is "a creation of God". To the astronomer who understands the Hebrew text, however, the names of the stars mean a lot more. For instance, let us consider the usual translation of some verses of Job as compared with the original text (Job 9: 9 and 38: 31-35):

He has made the Bear and Orion, the Pleiades and the Mansions of the South.... The Lord said to Job: Can you fasten the harness of the Pleiades, or untie Orion's bands? Can you guide the Morning Star season by season and show the Bear with its cubs which way to go? Have you grasped the celestial laws? Could you make their writ run on the earth? Can your voice carry as far as the clouds and make the pent up waters do your bidding? Will lightning flashes come at your command?

Judging from its contents and language, this text was written in Judaea in the 5th century BC, but its author had also been to Egypt and Babylon. The central figure of the writing is the suffering Job (spelt *Ijjob* in Hebrew), who lived in the land of Uz on the border of Arabia and Edom, to the southeast of the Dead Sea. That land was the home of some pious scholars and scientists, including Job and his friends who stayed with him and kept him company when he was seriously ill. The Book of Job, one of the greatest works of world literature gives us an ample picture of the knowledge of the Hebrew scholars 2500 years ago. The lines quoted above reveal some very interesting astronomical observations. The Jerusalem Bible notes that the constellations referred to here are the ones which indicate the seasonal changes of the weather, because the preceding and following sentences mention different features of the weather such as dew, storm clouds, lightning, showers, frost, snow and ice.

The Hebrew words *Ash* and *Ajish albanejcha* (in Job 9:9 and 38:32) do not correspond to the Bears (*Ursa Major* and *Ursa Minor*, the Big and Little Dipper in popular terms) because this constellation has no cubs and its stars are visible every night, independent of the seasons. Job talks about a constellation which has cubs near it, and he depicts it as if it were guiding or leading its small ones. Consequently, it must have been a mistake to translate the Hebrew words as the Bears. The Septuagint and the Vulgate call them *Vesper*, which could not only be Venus but also Jupiter or some other bright fixed star visible in the evening sky right after sunset.

Etymological and astronomical research prove that the Hebrew *Ajish* corresponds to *Aldebaran,* the brightest star of Taurus whose cubs are the stars of the Hyades, visible to the naked eye. In the Old Syrian Bible it is called *Iljutho* which, according to the Talmud, is the head of the Bull, that is Aldebaran with the Hyades (Berachot 59,1). After having thoroughly investigated the contemporary Syrian and Arabic facts and figures, Schiaparelli finally came to the following conclusion: "The authors mentioned agree with the others in testifying that *Iljutho* (Ajish) is identical with the Aldebaran and Hyades; this identity cannot be contested any longer" (Schiaparelli 1925, p.285).

From the 8th century BC the *Pleiades*, the *Hyades* and *Orion* were the three most popular celestial indicators of the weather. Their characteristic configuration made them easy to recognize and the rising and setting of their brightest stars could be observed either at dawn or at twilight. In Job's country, in the latitude 31° North, when these three constellations were still visible before setting in the evening sky, they indicated the stormy and showery weather of spring between 4th and 24th April. On 12th April the bright evening star was *Aldebaran* (Guide) accompanying its cubs, that is the "rain stars" of the *Hyades* as they were retiring for the night. Aratos noted: "When the Pleiades rise before the Sun, the sunny weather of summer is near", and Eudoxos observed that on July 6th the full constellation of the rising Orion was visible before it disappeared in the sunlight. In the middle of October, after sunset, the family (*Kimah* = Family) of the Pleiades had already been high up in the sky when Aldebaran appeared together with its cubs, indicating the autumn rains. In November it was Orion (*Kesil* = Giant) which would rise in the evening and keep watch over Jerusalem at night. That was perhaps the reason why the ninth month (November/December) was named *Kislimu* or *Kislev*, that is the "month of the Giant".

138

The "Mansions of the South" (*Chadré théman*), mentioned after the Pleiades, refer to the stars still visible in autumn evenings on the southern horizon of Judaea. This interpretation appeared as early as the 1st century in the Aramaic Targum. According to our calculations, 2500 years ago the stars of the Celestial Ship (*Argo Navis*), the Southern Cross (*Crux*) and the *Centaur* stood 10 to 12 degrees higher; their declination today is between 45 and 65 degrees south from the celestial equator. The Celestial Ship has since then been divided into four smaller parts (*Carina, Vela, Pyxis, Puppis*). In the longitude of about 120 degrees there were five bright stars between *Canopus* (*Alfa Carinae*) and *Toliman* (*Alfa Centauri*), the two brightest stars of the southern sky. In the geographical latitude of 30° to 31° they rose in the southeast, passed through the meridian at an altitude of 8 to 18 degrees and disappeared two or three hours later in the southwest. So the arcs they drew above the southern horizon were low and narrow, in which there was nothing to be seen, compared to the broad arched path of the Pleiades in which there were countless numbers of stars glittering, "beyond all reckoning" (Job 9: 10). The precession of the equinoxes has since then resulted in such an increase of the declination of the southern stars that today they can only be seen from regions lying to the south of latitude 20°.

"Can you guide the Morning star?", is the question posed to the suffering Job, in the new translation. But in the Vulgate Version we read it as follows: "Are you the one who appoints the time for the rising of the Morning star?" The corresponding Hebrew word *Mazzaroth* or *Mazzaloth* is in plural form and it cannot mean only one star. In the Second Book of Kings (23:5) it is the twelve constellations (*duodecim signa*), according to the Vulgate. This word (*Mazzaloth*) was not translated into Greek in the Septuagint, which noted, however, that it referred to the zodiacal signs. In the Aramaic Targum it means the way of the wandering stars, which also indicates the Zodiac. (This interpretation has recently been confirmed by some biblical scholars referring to the tradition dating from the 2nd century; see Gordis 1978).

In the above quoted passage of the Book of Job it is not so much the names, but the statements referring to the stars that are important. If we interpret them correctly, in accordance with the Hebrew usage of words, we will be surprised to find how greatly they differ from the usual thinking of ancient astronomers. Even in the Middle Ages, fixed stars were believed to be affixed to the surface of the celestial sphere and revolve together with it on unchanged paths around the Earth. It was Halley who first put forward the theory concerning the proper motion of the fixed stars and changes in the shapes of the constellations. With the help of astronomical spectroscopy we have since then been able to determine the direction and velocity of the proper motion of the stars.

These phenomena in particular are made easier to grasp by Job's specific expressions: "to fasten, to untie, to bring forth, to guide, to determine everything at the right moment." Although Job realized that the regular recurrence of the rising of certain fixed stars indicated the seasonal changes of the weather, he could not explain the cause of the phenomenon.

Fig. 22: Seven visible Stars of the Pleiades at a distance of 410 light years from the Earth. A light year is the distance that light travels in one year: 9,460,000,000,000 km. The nebulae around the stars glow with the starlight reflected by their dust. (Lick Observatory Photograph).

The suffering Job finally admits his ignorance and helplessness and thereby proves that instead of human science he is guided by some superior inspiration. That is how he finds the suitable words to describe the celestial phenomena and he does not obscure "the designs of the Creator with his ignorant words" (Job 38: 2).

The Pleiades and the Hyades are the brightest open clusters in Taurus in the northern sky. The stars exist in clusters because they formed at the same time, about 80 million years ago, from a single interstellar cloud. They are moving along with a velocity of 40 to 45 km per second through the star fields. The Hyades cluster of at least 150 stars has its center 130 light years from the Sun. It is receding from us and the parallel paths of its stars appear to converge toward the brightest star in Orion, *Betelgeuse*. We may ask: What is directing the motion of the *Hyades* to that point? Or let us ask with Job: "who is leading the *Aldebaran* together with its cubs?" The stars of *Orion* however are very far away from each other and are moving in different directions. Who is untying its bands? Who is pulling its members apart?

The light of the high temperature stars of the *Pleiades* is reflected by the surrounding cosmic gas clouds and as a result 6 or 7 of its stars visible to the naked eye are adorned by a veil of nebulae. Who can "hold together its adorned members"? Who determined the gravitational force that holds together several hundreds of stars for some time? The life cycle of open clusters is relatively short, they break up in some hundred million years.

As to the "bringing forth" or the rising of constellations, who can explain the seasons and the climatic changes from the ice age to our days? Who determines the daily velocity of the Earth's rotation and the period of its revolution around the Sun? Who adjusts the inclination angle of the Earth's axis of rotation to the plane of its orbit in a way that the Sun's rays reach the surface of Earth at a different angle every three months? Do you know that the changing temperature of the four seasons is due to these facts?

The Biblicist cannot really object if the astronomer, relying on today's scientific knowledge, formulates the ancient questions addressed to Job in the above way. We may, however, find it surprising that modern physicists only wish to find out what causes these phenomena, whereas ancient scholars looked for a person behind them: who determines their courses? Who maintains their motions?

It is this vital question that the reading of the Bible addresses. There is no point in looking for astronomical explanations in it. Nevertheless, there is an astronomical writing in the Hebrew heritage, a writing which is the oldest part of the *Book of Enoch*. Archaeological finds testify that it was known as early as the 19th century BC. Originally it was a book of the Scriptures and was cited even by the apostles, but because of the deterioration of the text it was later classed as part of the Apocrypha. According to the Qumran finds or the Dead Sea Scrolls its last copy was made by the Essenes about 150 BC. Its complete text is preserved only in the Ethiopic version (an old Semitic dialect), which was later translated into Greek and Latin.

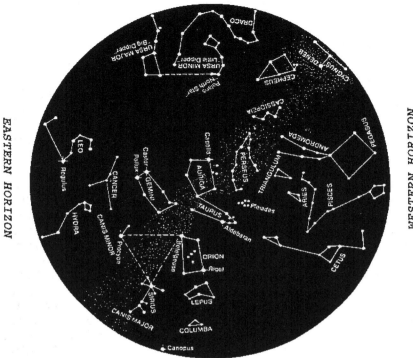

Fig. 23: The night sky in January. These stars and constellations are visible in the geographic latitudes 35° to 36° N.

Enoch *(Hannaku* = the Initiated) comes from the tribe of Seth, the third son of Adam, whom we can also find in Jesus Christ's family tree. He is believed to be the founder of Hebrew culture and science, because he always "walked with God Almighty" and was taught by angels (Gn 5:24; Lk 3:37). Ten chapters of the *Ethiopic Enoch* (72-82) contain simple astronomical observations and calculations. The following quotations show their originality, how independent they were from Babylonian and Greek astronomy:

> I have observed everything on the celestial boards. I have read and noted everything that is written upon them. I have read the book of stars which is about all the deeds of men and all the children of the body, who will be on Earth until the last generation. Then I praised

the Almighty, the glorious King of the world, because he had created all the works of the world. Uriel [an archangel] showed me twelve gates along the path of the Chariot of the Sun in heaven, from which rays burst forth. I saw twelve gates in the sky, on the border of the Earth [on the horizon], from which the Sun, the Moon, the stars and every influence of the heavens come forth in the east and west. The months accomplish the yearly turn every 364 days. Thus there are 1092 days [= 3 × 364] in three years; 1820 days in five years, 2912 days in eight years. The Moon alone gets 1062 days in three years [=3 × 354] and is 50 days late in five years...The year comes to an end in 364 days. This calculation is accurate (Enoch I: 72-73; trans. by M.A. Knibb 1978).

Otto Neugebauer tried to interpret this ancient text, but he was unable to find the meaning of all its expressions (Neugebauer 1975, pp. 467-489). Contrary to the customary interpretation of the twelve gates as zodiacal signs, he proved that the Gates of Heaven were fixed arcs of the horizon, related to the amplitude of the changes in the rising and setting of the Sun in the course of one year. The gates of the Sun were numbered from 1 to 6 starting with the rising of the Sun at the winter solstice (from the southeast) and ending with the setting of the Sun at the summer solstice (to the northwest); then they were numbered backwards from 6 to 1. "That is the law of the Sun: the great illuminator returns and rises sixty times", writes Enoch (72: 35), which means that each period of time between equinoxes and solstices lasts 60 days, that is two months of 30 days. Every third month consisted of 31 days.

The gates of the Moon were numbered starting from the new moon of the autumn solstice, when the Moon set exactly in the west at the intersection of the equator and the ecliptic. The Moon reached its largest southern and northern declination twice in an average of 30 days, so it crossed the 12 gates, that is identical points of the horizon, twice a month.

This original Hebrew calendar was completely independent of both the lunar phases and the constellations. The day of the new year on 1st Nisan was a Saturday (Sabbath) every year, and Passover began on 14th Nisan, on the sixth day, that is on Friday evening. The Qumran community or the Essenes in the 2nd century BC used this permanent calendar of 364 days. Referring to Enoch, the community claimed that "those who broke the law would cause confusion even in the succession of the seasons", consequently they had to be punished. The primeval religious calendar was replaced by the Babylonian luni-solar calendar and the Seleucid era followed. The Book of Jubilees and the Damascus Scroll both proclaimed that the 364 day year should serve as the basis of the legal calendar: 52 weeks as foreordained by the Lord. There are no records as to when the missing days of the year were recovered.

All this, however, testifies to the fact that the Hebrew scholars knew how long the tropical year was, that is how many days passed between two consecutive equinoxes. Enoch's symbolic age was 365, the measurement unit of the solar year. The Deluge started in the 600th year of Noah's life on the 17th of the second month and ended in the 601st year on the 27th of the second month, which means it lasted exactly 365 days or an entire solar year. The symbolic number suggests that a new age began with the Deluge (cf. Gen 5: 23; 7: 11; 8: 13-14).

The Bible contains a number of expressions which refer to the eclipse of the Sun or the eclipse of the Moon or remind the reader of meteors and star showers. Some expressions even suggest the aurora. Yet all this does not connect the Scripture with astronomy or theologians with astronomers. The biblical expressions which pose a serious astronomical problem to modern physicists refer to the apparent movement of the Sun and the stationary Earth.

The Heliocentric View is not against the Bible

Copernicus, Kepler and Galileo were very familiar with the Bible but initially they never really thought of connecting their discoveries with biblical knowledge. Complications set in when some over-zealous biblicists and philosophers condemned Copernicus's heliocentric theory. According to the teaching of the Bible, they argued, the Earth was stationary and was orbited by the Sun, which seemed to be an obvious empirical fact.

Nicolaus Copernicus' book "On the Revolution of the Celestial Spheres" was published in Nürnberg (Germany) in the spring of 1543. The seventy-year old canon and mathematician was lying on his death bed when on 24 May the first printed copy was shown to him. Unfortunately, he died that very day without ever being able to look through the text. Supervision over the publication of the work fell into the hands of a young Lutheran preacher, Andreas Osiander, who wrote a preface (but without signing it and without the consent of Copernicus). He says in the preface that the new heliocentric theory, as an abstract mathematical hypothesis, is merely a means to make appearances easier to explain. This statement is surely in contradiction to Copernicus' intention. He says in his dedication addressed to Pope Paul III that he is not too disturbed by those who attack him and refute his teachings with distorted biblical quotations. He considers them "people of poor judgement". He trusts that his work would be of good service to the Church.

Starting with Pythagoras several Greek philosophers assumed that the Earth was a sphere rotating daily on its axis and revolving around the Sun (e.g. Aristarchus, Seleucus). They were, however, unable to explain the apparent forward and backward motion of the planets otherwise than by epicycles. According to Ptolemy's complicated model each planet was supposed to move on the circumference of a circle, the epicycle, while the center of that circle revolved around the Earth on a second circle (deferent).

Copernicus opposed that erroneous view and showed the real possibility of a heliocentric model. He started from the simple fact that the distance covered by a moving object is the product of velocity and time. He supposed that the planets and the Earth moved around the Sun in circular orbits at constant speed. The revolution period therefore is equal to the quotient of the orbit's circumference and the planet's velocity. From this it was possible to find the radius of the orbits, that is the distance of the planets from the Sun. Thus, Copernicus described the motion of the planets around the Sun in mathematical terms, but he was not able to prove his theory by physical observations.

It was Kepler who, relying on the accurate observations of Tycho Brahe, undertook the difficult task of proving the veracity of the heliocentric theory. He was the most prominent forerunner of the new era of mathematical astronomy. Kepler discovered that the changing motion of the planets was caused by the force radiating from the Sun and decreasing proportionally to the distance. This, he thought, was the reason why the velocity of the planets changed at regular intervals and why the line joining a planet to the Sun swept over equal areas in equal intervals of time. Consequently, each planetary orbit is an ellipse with the Sun at one focus. The nearer the planet comes to the Sun, the faster it moves.

Kepler published these two new laws of celestial mechanics in his book entitled *Astronomia Nova* (1609). Ten years later, after a great number of mathematical calculations, he published the third and most important empirical law of celestial mechanics, the harmonic law : The square of the period is always proportional to the cube of the distance from the Sun. He noted in the introduction to *Harmonices Mundi:* "The whole nature of harmonies in the celestial movements does really exist, but not in the way I previously thought, but in a completely different, yet absolutely perfect manner". In other words Kepler meant that the laws had not been invented by him, he had read them directly from the Book of Nature.

He regarded his discoveries as gifts of the Lord Almighty. Physicists of modern times do not really appreciate his statements, which nevertheless demonstrate his sense of vocation and spiritual greatness.

It is worth quoting the following sentences taken from his writings (1595 - 1618):

> I wished to be a theologian. For a long time I was troubled. But look and see now how God shall be praised through my work... Since we astronomers are priests of the most high God with respect to the Book of Nature, it behooves us that we do not aim at the glory of our own spirit, but above everything else at the glory of God... For it is precisely the universe which is that Book of Nature in which God the Creator has revealed and depicted his essence and what he wills with man, in a wordless [alogos] script...The Book of Nature is highly praised in the Holy Scriptures. St. Paul reminds the heathens that in it they can contemplate God like the Sun in water or in a mirror... (Trans. by O. Pedersen 1992).

With his strong sense of vocation Kepler was the first to reveal the appropriate relationship between astronomy and the Bible. It is also to him that we owe the introduction of a successful dialogue between theologians and physicists. Before him many people believed that the heliocentric model was but a false hypothesis which contradicted the Bible. Kepler showed that the structure and order of the universe were not the inventions of the human mind, but existed independent of us and waited to be discovered. The two great books, Scripture and Nature, were the creations of the same Lord. Though written with different means and a different purpose, they were in perfect harmony. In his introduction to *Astronomia Nova*, Kepler presented a detailed and effective refutation of the false arguments held by biblicists denying the movement of the Earth. **(20)**

Galileo Galilei, the Florentine physicist, corresponded regularly with Kepler, the new astronomer of Prague. He read his books, but did not accept his views on the Bible. Galileo himself was also a firm opponent of those who, citing biblical statements, condemned the results of astronomical observations. He strove to defend both the authenticity of the Scriptures and Copernicus's heliocentric theory. He struggled to prove how these two teachings harmonized and he tried to provide convincing arguments for the motion of the Earth. However, he achieved the opposite of that for which he had striven. Instead of creating understanding and agreement between physicists and theologians, his ideas sparked off vehement disputes between them.

There is no space here for a detailed discussion of this complicated case, which can only be understood through a profound knowledge of 17th century history (see Fantoli 1996). European Christianity became divided because of the aggressive means used by the reformers. This lead to violent struggles for power by the monarchs. Millions of people died in the wars of religion that lasted several decades (1618-1648). At the same time the independence of Christian nations was threatened by Islam trying to expand and supported by an ever increasing military force. Catholics tried to carry out the resolutions of the Council of Trent in order to remedy the faults of the past. That was why they called for a unified interpretation of the Bible to be made under the guidance of the Church's Teaching Authority.

The tensions arising from the Reformation efforts also affected science, which had always influenced religious thought. It was Galileo who had to undertake the task of confronting outdated ideas and renewing scientific methods and physical theorems. Galileo, as the leading physicist of the famous Academy of the Lincei, was not the only scientist engaged in this work, but he played a major part in it. The discoveries he made with the aid of his new telescope soon became well known all over Europe, whereas Copernicus' and Kepler's writings had been known and understood by only a few mathematicians. Between 1610 and 1614 Galileo's publications caused a sensation everywhere. His discovery of the countless stars visible in the Milky Way, the four moons of Jupiter, the phases of Venus, the hilly surface of the Moon and the dark spots moving on the surface of the Sun aroused everyone's curiosity.

Although Cardinals in the Roman Curia had cautioned him against some exaggerated ideas and Pope Urban VIII himself begged him not to interfere with the interpretation of the Scriptures, he insisted all the more on the need of having a new interpretation which would agree with the heliocentric theory. Unfortunately the excessive zeal of Galileo eventually led the Church's Magisterium in 1616 to ban Copernicus's work. Galileo himself was not condemned then, as was confirmed in writing by Cardinal Bellarmine (26 May 1616). Nevertheless the books of two theologians, Didacus Stunica and Antonio Foscarini, who defended Copernicus and encouraged Galileo, were also banned. (21)

Even before the astronomers, one of the first people to present Copernicus's views that the Earth's movement does not contradict the teachings of the Bible, was the Augustinian monk and scholar *Didacus à Stunica*, called *Diego de Zuniga* in Spanish. In his comments written to the Book of Job he says:

> The passage: He who moves the Earth from its place, and its pillars are shaken (Job 9:6), shows God's great power and infinite wisdom. This passage seems to be a difficult one indeed, but it is considerably clarified by means of the opinion of the Pythagoreans, who think that the Earth moves by its own nature and that it is not otherwise possible to explain the motion of the stars which vary a great deal in their speed and slowness...In our own time

Copernicus explains the paths of the planets by means of this opinion. There is no doubt that the locations of the planets are much better and more certainly determined by this doctrine than by what is found in Ptolemy's Almagest and in the views of others. It is well known that Ptolemy was never able to explain the motion of the equinoxes or to establish an exact beginning of the year. He confesses this in his Almagest [III,2] and leaves these matters for the discovery of later astronomers who would be able to compare more observations over a longer period of time than he could (Diego de Zuniga, *Commentary on Job*, Toledo 1584, p. 205; trans. by Blackwell 1991).

The other very original and important treatise is of the Carmelite Provincial Paolo Antonio Foscarini: "Concerning the Opinion of the Pythagoreans and Copernicus..., it is shown that that opinion agrees with, and is reconciled with, the passages of Sacred Scripture and theological propositions which are commonly adduced against it" (Napoli, 6 January 1615). Foscarini compiled rules for the interpretation of the Scriptures, which help to avoid all unnecessary disputes and misunderstandings concerning astronomical terms. Those rules are opportune even today. (22)

It is indeed surprising that, instead of astronomers and physicists, the first people to study and understand the theories of Copernicus and Kepler and to reconcile them without any difficulty with the Bible were those absorbed in contemplation and prayer. (In 1822 Pope Pius VII ordered the ban on the works of Copernicus, Zuniga and Foscarini to be lifted, and in 1964 the Vatican Council II completely abolished the Index of Forbidden Books).

Kepler was right about the interpretation of the Scripture, when he pointed out that the Bible does not speak about the physical features of the Sun and the Earth. An example is the Psalm 19, where the Sun "comes out of his pavilion like a bridegroom, exulting like a hero to run his race; he has his rising on the edge of heaven, the end of his course is its furthest edge, and nothing can escape his heat." The partisans of literal interpretation considered this sentence a divine statement about the physical movement of the Sun. As a follower of the Fathers of the Church, Kepler stressed that this was merely a poetic image linking the glory of the Sun with the advent of the Messiah. Galileo, however, was trying to find an appropriate physical interpretation and maintained that the psalm must have referred to the light and heat radiation of the Sun: "therefore the radiation and the movement refer to the sunlight, not the body of the Sun" (*Opere* V. 291-305).

St. Robert Bellarmine, at that time the most powerful Cardinal of the Church's Magisterium, acknowledged the merits of Foscarini's writing, but asked both him and Galileo to be cautious and wise; to talk about hypotheses only and always to make conditional statements because, he warned, we were more likely to be able to set up an imperfect model than to solve the secret code of creation.

Modern Cosmology and the Scriptural Account of Creation

Both the proponents and the opponents of the heliocentric view believed that the eternal home of the deceased was above the visible heavens. They all wanted to go there. Their writings suggest that they were just as interested in the position of the Sun and the Earth as in the relationship between Man and God, i.e., eternal life and happiness of Man. Kepler and Galileo would today reproach us for believing neither in God nor in the Scripture. They would say: All you are thinking of is dark and cold space, you cannot picture the spiritual reality, the existence of which is eternal and beyond the material world.

While theologians might smile quietly at this reproach, physicists would protest loudly: This has nothing to do with our science! Show us the boundaries of the universe. According to our assumptions, the universe has no boundaries in space and time... Our defunct scholarly ancestors would merely reply: You will see for yourselves, when you leave for ever the boundaries of physical and earthly existence.

The reason why we are investigating the secrets of physical space and time is that we wish to find our place in it. Some of the information we possess today about the structure of the universe is in agreement with reality. As we observe with huge telescopes the phenomena that took place billions of years ago, we hope to avoid being misled by appearances. The furthest celestial body observed so far is about 10 billion light years away from us, which means that 10 billion years ago it was where we see it now; the light rays it emitted have only reached the Earth now. (The velocity of light is 300,000 km/sec).

It is the merit of eminent physicists and skillful journalists that the astrophysical description of the origin of the universe has been at the center of interest in recent years. Today nobody trusts ancient mythology. Little children as well as adults know that the Big Bang means the creation of the world. They are even more inclined to believe in it than do scientists who use this enigmatic technical term which, in fact, is a long way from the correct concept of creation. (It was Fred Hoyle, a British astronomer, who invented the term "Big Bang".)

How did the physical universe that we can observe here and now begin? Does the universe have a beginning and an end at all? How exactly did the universe assume the form we see it in today? Even in the last century there was nothing, apart from the Bible, that scientists, religious or not, could turn to for an answer to these questions.

Cosmology was the central matter in the mythology and philosophy of ancient cultures and has become one of the most important fields in today's scientific research. The theories of the origin of the universe or creation have always been linked, explicitly or implicitly, to man's innate religious and moral needs. Even today the false belief of pantheism, according to which the universe is identical with God, is extremely tempting to both scholars and the unlearned. We shall not analyze these theories in depth here, but we shall briefly outline their most important arguments and make clear their basic concepts. Then we shall show the possible link and essential difference between astrophysical cosmology and the Scriptural history of creation.

The word "cosmos" originally meant order and ornament in Greek. It was used to denote the beautiful and magnificent order of the whole of nature, the ornate order of the universe: universal order. In the Greek Septuagint the Hebrew "array of heaven", used in the Hebrew account of creation, is translated into "cosmos". "Thus heaven and earth [i.e., the complete universe or cosmos as universal order] were completed with all their array". (The Hebrew word *saba'* is rendered "cosmos" in the Greek Septuagint at Gn 2:1; Is 40:26; Dt 4:19. The same Hebrew word denotes also the "host of heaven" or "array of heaven". Cf. Murray 1992, p. 11).

The Latin interpretation of cosmos is *universum*, which means a unity in the plurality of different things. The universe is an ordered whole, a harmonious system. Philosophical cosmology observes the phenomena of nature and from them concludes that the various lifeless and living members of the universe exist in a coordinated unity ensured by one common purpose and cause.

Astrophysical cosmology studies the forces and processes which are perceptible, measurable or calculable inside atoms and in space on a very large scale. The space mapped so far with the help of huge reflecting telescopes and radio telescopes shows the same properties in every direction, that is to say it is *isotropic*. It follows, that from whichever point of space we decided to make our observations, we would perceive the same cosmic process. This means that the universe is *homogeneous*, it consists of similar elements and systems. In the large scale structures of the universe, observed from a distance of 100 million light years, the universe looks the same as we see it from the Earth. These words define the basic *Cosmological Principle* which declares that observations made in a few determined directions provide a sufficient basis to set up comprehensive models of the universe. Thermodynamics and Quantum Mechanics, Elementary Particle Physics and the General Theory of Relativity enable us to make cosmological models which correspond to the perceived phenomena and the known laws of physics. By solving field equations we can draw conclusions as to the past and future of the universe.

Those who do not know these new fields of physics very well and do not understand the language of mathematics, may try to read about these concepts in popular scientific literature, which, however, will hardly help them to arrive at a correct view of the world. In the same way we may say that those who do not know the Old Hebrew language and do not understand its symbolical expressions will not be able to fully grasp the Scriptural account of creation, not even with the aid of literal translations.

Albert Einstein published his first cosmological work based on general relativity in 1917, which suggests that the structure of the universe and even the paths of light rays are determined solely by the gravitational field. When asked to explain briefly the theory of relativity, the famous physicist said: "If you do not take my answer too seriously, but regard it in a lighter view, I can give you the following explanation: people used to believe that if all matter disappeared from the universe, only space and time would remain. According to the theory of relativity, if matter disappeared, space and time would also disappear" (Frank 1947). Einstein, however, took seriously what he said and assumed that the universe was constant and static. For that reason he introduced a cosmological constant into the field equation of general relativity, so that the solution of the equation would be in agreement with the concept of closed and static space-time. In that static model all mass, energy and radiation stood in a state of stability in the gravitational field.

Some years later, however, the Russian mathematician Alexander Friedmann showed that the gravitational field equations had several solutions according to which the size and properties of space-time were the function of time, so space-time could gradually expand or contract and oscillate. At first Einstein rejected this, but eventually had to admit that he had been wrong, because all observations justified Friedmann's calculations. This is one case which illustrates what an important role belief in certain assumptions can play in scientific research until the belief turns out to be misplaced.

It was only at the beginning of the 20th century that astronomers were able to determine accurately that the phenomena which previously had been taken for cosmic nebulae or clouds were star clusters or galaxies, far outside our Milky Way Galaxy, as for example the Small and Large Magellanic Clouds and the Andromeda Nebula. In our days it is *Extragalactic Astronomy,* the most rapidly developing branch of astronomy and the basis of cosmological research, which studies these phenomena. On the photographs taken of the northern and southern skies, the distribution of about two million galaxies have been studied. Large photographic atlases and detailed catalogues of the galaxies and clusters of galaxies were published between 1956 and 1976.

Each galaxy is a large aggregate of billions of stars, interstellar dust and gas gravitationally constrained. Concerning the origin of galaxies it has been found that one of the most striking features of the universe is the hierarchical organization of matter. Stars are often born in fairly small-sized groups, existing in galaxies, which are grouped in clusters of galaxies. The clusters of galaxies are parts of even bigger formations called superclusters. An obvious explanation of this hierarchical organization is that clouds of matter having the same mass as superclusters broke up during the fall in temperature that followed the primeval explosion. These clouds of matter consisted mainly of hydrogen and elementary particles. The hierarchical system means that groups of smaller mass are subordinated to clusters of bigger mass, because they depend on the gravitational field. The distribution of mass in space or the determination of the density of cosmic matter are of decisive importance in cosmological theories.

In 1929 with the help of the astronomical photos made at the Mount Wilson Observatory, Edwin P. Hubble calculated the distance of 18 galaxies from the luminosity of their most luminous stars. Later he counted 44,000 galaxies in one section of the northern sky. By spectroscopic measurements he verified then that the distance of galaxies from us is linearly related to their redshift, i.e., the shift of spectral lines toward longer wavelengths in the radiation received from a galaxy due to its relative motion along the line of sight. Sources receding are shifted toward the red, and this can be interpreted as a Doppler effect. When the source is receding the frequency decreases and the wavelength increases. If we interpret the wavelength shifts as velocities, we may then conclude that the universe is expanding. Regardless of were we look, distant galaxies are rushing away from us.

Hubble became the pioneer of observational cosmology. An empirical law given by him relates the velocity of recession to the distance of the source:
$v = H \times r$. The constant of proportionality, $H = v/r$, is the same for each galaxy in a given time, but it varies with evolving spacetime. At present, according to the recent measurements with the Hubble Space Telescope, the value of the Hubble constant is:

$$H = v/r = 45 \pm 9 \text{ km per second per Megaparsec}$$

(1 Megaparsec = 3.26 million light years). According to this the distance between galaxies increases considerably every 3 million years, because the rate of the expansion of space-time grows approximately 15 km/sec per one million light years. Consequently, the process of expansion began 15 or 16 billion years ago.

What could have caused the universe to expand in such a spectacular way and to continue expanding? What happened 15 billion years ago? Astrophysicists have answered even this question, but their answer is just as alarming as reassuring. Each answer leads to another question. At first it was thought that the universe was originally in a static state and started to expand at a given moment because of changes in the gravitational field. This process could last, according to the laws of thermodynamics, until the thermal death of the universe; the stars would burn out, the temperature would drop until all the atoms froze at absolute zero and the movement of elementary particles would cease. "The law that entropy always increases, the second law of thermodynamics, holds, I think, the supreme position among the laws of Nature" (Eddington 1928, p. 81).

George Lemaître, professor of physics at the University of Louvain, showed, on the other hand, that it was mathematically necessary that the initial singularity of the universe should be part of the cosmological solution of field equations. That was how the concept of the primeval atom and the theory of primeval explosion came about in 1933. Lemaître, who later became president of the Pontifical Academy of Sciences, was convinced that empirical evidence for the hypothesis of the primeval explosion could be found in cosmic radiation:

The primeval atom hypothesis is a cosmic hypothesis which pictures the present universe as a result of the radioactive disintegration of an atom. We are now going to imagine that the entire universe existed in the form of an atomic nucleus, in which all matter was unified. The initial condition must be a state of maximum concentration of energy... The purpose of any cosmogonic theory is to seek out ideally simple conditions which could have initiated the world and from which, by the play of recognized physical forces, that world, in all its complexity, may have resulted. I believe that I have shown that the hypothesis of the primeval atom satisfies the rules of the game. It does not appeal to any force which is not already known. It accounts for the actual world in all its complexity. By a single hypothesis it explains stars arranged in galaxies within an expanding universe as well as those local exceptions, the clusters of galaxies. Finally, it accounts for that mighty phenomenon, the ultrapenetrating rays. They are truly cosmic, and they testify to the primeval activity of the Cosmos. In their course through wonderfully empty space, during billions of years, they have brought us evidence of the super radioactive age. Indeed they are a sort of fossil rays which tell us what happened when the stars first appeared (Lemaître 1950, 134-162).

Some physicists rejected the theory of a primeval explosion and argued that it contravened the principle of the conservation of energy, because energy cannot be created of nothing and cannot be destroyed. They rejected the idea of an absolute beginning and believed in an ever unchanging universe. (The physicists of the Soviet system of that time, to whom dialectical materialism was compulsory, accused Lemaître of wanting merely to justify the Scriptural account of creation for the sake of the Pope. He rejected their accusations and defended the mathematical and physical validity of his theorems.)

According to the advocates of the unchanging universe, the state of the universe cannot be a function of time, because the laws of physics are always the same everywhere and billions of years ago they functioned in the same way as they do today. They developed the so-called Steady State Theory; cosmic density is constant in continually expanding space-time, because the same amount of matter is continually created which is necessary to make up for the thinning caused by the expansion. Most astrophysicists were dissatisfied with this theory because it lacked the necessary mathematical and empirical evidence. Where does matter continually come from? Is it created simultaneously in every point of the universe or only in the core of the galaxies? Does this correspond to the principle of the conservation of mass and energy?

Finally, it is the theory of Lemaître and Friedmann which has been verified by further calculations and observations. In 1965 radio astronomers discovered the cosmic background radiation, the existence of which had been predicted by Lamaître fifteen years before, as a conclusion of the Primeval Explosion Hypothesis. Radio telescopes measured a radiation at wavelengths of 0.33 to 7.35 cm which comes from all directions of space. This radiation corresponds, with small variations, to a 3 degree Kelvin blackbody radiation. (On the Kelvin temperature scale 3 °K corresponds to –270 °C). In recent years the measurements made by the satellite, Cosmic Background Radiation Explorer, confirmed the cosmological significance of this observation.

Counting backwards in time, the volume of the universe is gradually decreasing whereas the rate of density, pressure and heat is approaching the infinite. At the explosion of the primeval atom, the first act of the evolution of the universe took an unbelievably short time in an extremely small space. This *initial singularity* is the end of cosmic space-time and also the limit of scientific knowledge. Beyond it neither the laws of physics, nor general relativity, nor quantum theory hold true.

All a nuclear physicist can say is that after the primeval explosion for one billionth of a second the temperature could be beyond 1500 billion degrees in a very small space the diameter of which is ten billionth of a millimeter and in which only the smallest elementary particles can exist. Very big numbers like these create the impression of being fictitious and many people are inclined to say that the whole thing makes no sense whatsoever. Mathematicians, however, are

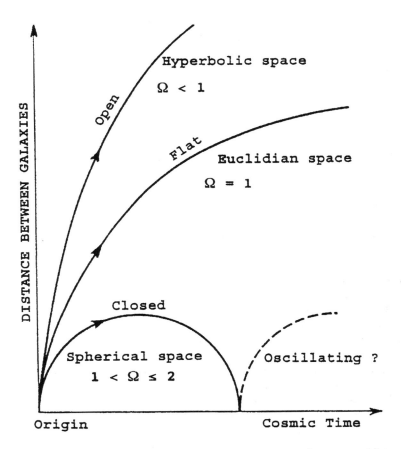

Fig. 24: Most cosmologists agree that the Lemaître-Friedmann model is the correct choice, but few of them agree on the value of the density and of the Hubble constant. The critical density of matter in the Universe is defined as $\Omega = 1$ which indicates the flat state (Euclidian geometry). If its density is greater than one, the Universe is closed spherical space, i.e., it contains enough matter and will one day collapse back on itself. If its density is less than one, it is in hyperbolic space, it contains too little matter, and gravity can never halt its present expansion. On the dividing line between these two states are the flat models in which the expansion rate is less than that of a hyperbolic space. The astrophysicists consider that the unseen mass or "dark matter" must account for 90% or more of the Universe, thus the density must be greater than the critical value.

convinced that their calculations correspond to physical reality even though they cannot explain it.

Steven Weinberg became a very popular nuclear physicist and cosmologist of Harvard University when he wrote in simple, everyday language the story of "The First Three Minutes" (1977). He begins as follows: "One hundredth of a second after the primeval explosion the temperature was merely one hundred billion degrees and at this point the continual creation and annihilation of photons, neutrons and positrons was already possible." Weinberg notes that the terms he uses here have no theological meaning. By *creation* he means the birth of a new elementary particle from the interaction of two particles, and by annihilation the process we can observe in laboratory experiments.

One second after the primeval explosion a decisive period begins in the life of the universe: the period of the hot radiation, which lasts about one million years. Three minutes after the explosion the temperature falls to one billion degrees; the protons and the neutrons combine to create the first nuclei and all the elementary particles necessary for the formation of the celestial bodies. The universe expanding as a result of the force of the explosion gradually cools until the positive protons eventually combine with the negative electrons, and hydrogen and helium atoms solidify.

For one million years it is the energy of light, i.e., the radiation of hot photons that determines the evolution of the universe. During the following billions of years, in the whirling gas clouds of enormous mass, the galaxies are formed. In the period of the formation of solid matter, gravitation gradually slows down the rate of expansion of space-time.

And here we are, building enormous observatories on a tiny planet belonging to one of the solar systems of a galaxy, and from a perspective of 15 billion earthly years we are observing this universal process. As far as the details are concerned, there are quite a few uncertainties in cosmological observations and calculations. But we can say in summary that the physical universe began with some kind of huge explosion and that it has been evolving ever since. The finite existence and expansion of the universe is proven by the following observations:

(1) The 3-degree Kelvin background radiation that can be equally measured from every direction is the energy of primeval photons remaining from the period of hot radiation; the gradual decrease of radiation energy shows the continuous evolution or expansion of the universe;

(2) This explains the fact that interstellar matter and the stars in their initial state consisted of about 75% hydrogen and 25% helium. Heavier elements are formed in the inside of stars. The Sun burns

hydrogen even today: about 655 million tons of hydrogen are burnt into 650 tons of helium and the resulting energy radiates as heat and light;

(3) The age of matter can be fairly accurately determined from the proportion of the radioactive isotopes of the elements (mainly from the percentage of the uranium isotopes, U-235 and U-238): meteorites, the oldest stones of the Earth and the stones brought back from the Moon were formed about 4500 million years ago. This corresponds well to the 5000 million (5 billion) year age of the Sun, which can be calculated from its mass and hydrogen resources;

(4) According to radioactive dating and the theory of the evolution of the stars, the age of the oldest stars observable in our Milky Way and the nearest galaxies is between 10 and 15 billion years;

(5) It inevitably follows that the currently observable universe began at least 15 billion years ago. This is proven by the cosmological redshift that can be observed in the spectra of distant galaxies, according to which the age of the universe must be between 15 and 20 billion years;

(6) finally, the continual expansion and finite character of the universe is proven by the fact that the sky at night is dark. If space-time were static and infinite, the intensity of the light radiating from the galaxies would increase in proportion to their distance from the Earth, and the night sky would be as bright as the Sun, with a temperature of 5000 degrees Celsius. This would exclude the possibility of any form of life on earth. The darkness of the night, however, proves that the distance between the galaxies radiating light is increasing, because space-time is expanding. (A good illustration of this is an inflated balloon: the more we inflate the balloon, the larger the distance between the spots on its surface.)

On the basis of all this, physicists consider it a proven fact that the cosmic space-time we are living in here and now has not existed for ever but began at a given moment. They also think that this universal process must at some future time come to an end. If there is any disagreement, it concerns the way in which the universe should come to an end:

– *in the open* models, the universe is evolving towards a state where the density and temperature of matter approach absolute zero;

– *in the closed* model the universe stops expanding at a certain point in time and starts to contract under the influence of gravitation towards a point of inconceivably high temperature and density. A recurrent explosion and evolution is theoretically possible but is practically unlikely because after the complete collapse of the universe all its matter would be concentrated in one single quantum of neutron radiation.

The discoveries of modern cosmology represent real progress, but at the same time pose new problems. Real progress, because the dominant view from the time of ancient mythology and philosophy until the 20th century was that the universe is eternal and unchanging. The Bible is the single ancient writing in which the Hebrew prophets, and later Christ and the apostles, quite distinctly teach the beginning and the end of the universe, although they intend it in a much different sense than cosmologists. For this reason many people demand that astrophysicists and theologians should engage in serious dialogue in order to overcome their old misunderstandings and conflicts. The great task today is to serve the good of the human community by providing a correct explanation of the origin and meaning of the universe. This is only possible through mutual goodwill and intelligent cooperation. (23)

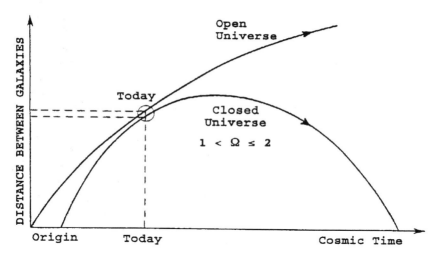

Fig. 25: The density of matter in the Universe today lies very close to the critical value, and the state of the Universe today would look much the same whether it were just open or closed. The expansion rate slows down more quickly in a closed model, i.e., the age of a closed universe is less that the age of an open universe. According to recent measurements the value of the Hubble constant is H = 45 ± 9 km/s per megaparsec which means that the expansion rate of space-time grows approximately 15 km/s per one million light years. This indicates that the process of expansion might have begun 15 or 16 billion years ago.

158

Steven Weinberg is one of the physicists who were seriously depressed because of the predictable fate of the universe. The final words of his book show this depression:

> However all these problems may be resolved, and whichever cosmological model proves correct, there is not much of comfort in any of this. It is almost irresistible for humans to believe that we have some special relation to the universe, that human life is not just a more or less farcical outcome of a chain of accidents reaching back to the first three minutes, but that we were somehow built in from the beginning... It is even harder to realize that this present universe has evolved from an unspeakably unfamiliar early condition, and faces a future extinction of endless cold or intolerable heat. The more the universe seems comprehensible, the more it also seems pointless. But if there is no solace in the fruits of our research, there is at least some consolation in the research itself. Men and women are not content to comfort themselves with tales of gods and giants, or to confine their thoughts to the daily affairs of life; they also build telescopes and satellites and accelerators, and sit at their desks for endless hours working out the meaning of the data they gather. The effort to understand the universe is one of the very few things that lifts human life a little above the level of farce, and gives it some of the grace of tragedy (Weinberg 1977).

Indeed, without the revelation of Christ the work of man and the fate of his universe remains a mere farce or tragedy. Sacred Scripture affirms the common destiny of the material world and Man: "The whole creation is eagerly waiting for God to reveal his sons". The universe itself, which is so closely related to man and which attains its destiny through him, will be perfectly re-established in Christ, and there will be "new heavens and a new earth" (Rom 8:19; Rev 21:1). Decree on the Church, *Lumen Gentium* 48. Vatican 1965.

When physicists had discovered that the Earth was not the center of the universe but a tiny planet among many others in infinite space, they believed this implied that man did not have a privileged position in it. This was the effect that Copernicus's work had for 400 years. Scientists continually professed the idea that the universe was homogeneous and everywhere the same, and the Earth had no privileged position in it. This, however, has proven to be a scientific miscalculation because it has been shown that if we observe a smaller region of the universe, we will find that each galaxy and each star in it is in a different and specific position. The development of life necessitates particularly favourable physical conditions, and such conditions are not specific or characteristic properties of the universe.

In no point of space-time investigated so far have we observed the conditions of atmosphere, water, temperature or chemical elements necessary for the development of living creatures. We do not know of any solar systems except ours. Life and the evolution of the intelligent human being are only found on the Earth. How is this possible? Every living organism as well as the human body is made up of the same elements and atoms as the celestial bodies. The human body, considering its size, is but a tiny, insignificant speck of dust in the universe, the human being is nevertheless aware of his intellectual power with which he can discover the laws of nature.

A significant event took place in 1973, when the International Astronomical Union celebrated the 500th anniversary of Copernicus's birth in Krakow. The subject of the Symposium was the confrontation of cosmological theories with observational data. At this meeting Brandon Carter, a physicist from Cambridge, United Kingdom, gave a lecture on observational cosmology, and there he initiated the following methodological principle: "All the cosmological theories have to take into account the fact that our location in the Universe is necessarily privileged to the extent of being compatible with our existence as observers." Carter has called this the *Weak Anthropic Principle*. This leads to some important conclusions, which can be empirically verified:

(1) Since man exists and is able to consciously observe the physical evolution of the universe, his location in cosmic time cannot be arbitrary, in other words it cannot be incidental that we live in this particular place in space-time-mass continuum, this place we call Earth;

(2) The presence of a certain amount of heavy elements is an essential prerequisite of the origin of life. These elements are formed inside massive stars in the course of thermonuclear fusions, which take a long time. Living creatures can not develop in a young universe, because the elements (carbon, nitrogen, oxygen etc.) necessary for organic processes have not yet been produced in it. On the other hand, a universe that is too old does not possess enough stars which produce energy, consequently it lacks the conditions allowing for the development of life.

By reason of these observations Carter formulated the *Strong Anthropic Principle* as follows: "The Universe (and hence the fundamental parameters on which it depends) must be such as to admit the creation of intelligent observers within it at some stage of its evolution." This may sound a bit awkward, but the author adds that the present universe really possesses all the properties that are "necessary for the creation of intelligent, conscious beings".

Physicists use the concept of creation as if matter itself created human life. We should take great care here not to misinterpret this basically correct methodological principle. First of all, we wish to stress that the existence of physical prerequisites is necessary, but on its own is not sufficient for the creation of human life. On the other hand we must take into account that the material world is a specific field of each branch of physics and that the existence of the human spirit and God the Creator are methodologically excluded from their domain. Thus the scientist, whose sole subject is physics, cannot talk about the human spirit or God, which does not mean that he denies their existence.

Thanks to the talent and devoted work of mathematicians and physicists, human life today is much more beautiful and much easier than it was two thousand years ago, when there were, for instance, no electrical appliances. It is, however, an even greater achievement that scientists have been able to calculate the exact value of the *natural-constants*, without which there would be no life on Earth: the velocity of light, the gravitational constant, Planck's constant, as the quotient of radiation energy and frequency, the masses of the electron and the proton, the freezing point of water and absolute zero, as the freezing point of all matter, and other constants that are determined and coordinated in an almost frighteningly exact way. Even the slightest change in the value of any of these constants would have meant that the universe would never have reached the state of evolution it is in today, there would be no Milky Way System and no Solar System and we would not exist. All these phenomena cannot be explained if we do not take account of human existence. The matter of the universe had to cool down to a determined temperature to enable the formation and existence of vegetable, animal and human life on Earth. In addition to this there is another surprising discovery, namely, that compared to the dimensions of cosmic space-time human life is very short and is only possible in a very small region of the universe.

The research method based on the anthropic principle is the reverse of the ones previously used. Its starting point is not the external physical world but our own human existence and observational experience. This fact strictly limits the range of possible cosmological models. The conditions for the existence of an intelligent personal being in an impersonal, lifeless universe can only be satisfied through a definite number of initial conditions, which can be found in the *natural-constants* mentioned above.

This clearly shows that of all sciences it is astrophysical cosmology which has reached the border line between physics and metaphysics. From that line it is possible to look into and see the domain of theology, which is basically the methodical study and interpretation of the revelations of God given in the Bible.

After a lecture on the results of modern cosmology given to the general public, the astrophysicist will almost certainly be bombarded with the following pertinent questions:

161

What is the origin of the primeval atom from which the universe started out? Where was the primeval atom, if there was no other existing physical point except the primeval atom? What sparked off the explosion? Did the atom explode by itself? Where is the expanding universe? In what direction is it expanding? Is it in an immaterial and infinite field?

If the physicist has some sense of humor, he will not let these questions upset him. He will calmly reply:

We do not ask questions that we cannot answer. It is impossible to find out with mathematical and physical methods what there is outside the space-time structure of the universe. There is nothing beyond it for us.

A clever person will respond to this in the following way:

This statement is ambiguous, because it either means that physical space-time is infinite (it is the only thing that has ever existed and will exist for ever), or that the primeval atom was produced out of nothing. Logically, both statements seem to be self-contradictory.

What will the physicist say to this? He may ascertain that unfortunately few people understand the quantum theory. The evolution of the universe is the radiation of energy from the beginning. But the radiation is not continuous, it takes place in small quantities called *quanta*, which are determined by the value of Planck's constant. The energy-quanta of light are the *photons*, which behave in the same way as material particles. Light is of dual nature: it is both an electromagnetic wave and a photon. Is there no contradiction here? The dialogue between Jean Guitton, the philosopher, and the Bogdanov brothers, physicists, illustrates well how difficult it is today to find generally acceptable and clearly unambiguous answers. The philosopher expects modern physics to uncover the order, symmetry and unity governing the universe. What is meant by "the quantum theory ending the difference between material and immaterial reality?" This is how the physicist answers:

Let's go back to the origin of the Universe. In accordance with the biblical approach we may say that in that very distant age, some fifteen to twenty billion years ago, there was symmetry... This is manifested by the existence of elementary particles, which combine to form a unity in fours, the mass of which is zero and each of which strictly resembles the other... (Guitton and Bogdanov 1991).

What strikes us in this answer is that a physicist wishes to explain something "in accordance with the biblical approach" and is obviously hinting at the scriptural account of creation.

162

What does a theologian have to say to this? He may be glad to acknowledge that all educated people today know the Bible. Furthermore he may think it fortunate that some physicists today find that certain sentences of Scripture come close to scientific facts. The question is, however, how close do certain scientific theorems come to the principles of theology? (24)

The purpose of physical theories and research is to improve the life and well being of Man in the material world. Observations and calculations in recent years have been aimed at explaining the origin and fate of the Universe. The purpose of theological research and teaching is also to help improve the life and well being of Man, though not only in this world, but also beyond it. This is made possible by a superior inspiration and revelation to which the prophets testify and the veracity of which is proved by historical facts, philosophical considerations and psychological observations. Without these nobody would give credit to the Scriptural writings. How do modern cosmological theories effect all this?

Let us quote some of the most important passages of the Bible referring to the origin and end of the Universe, so that we can compare them, in broad lines at least, to the latest results of cosmology:

In the beginning God created the heavens and earth. Now the earth was a formless void, there was darkness over the deep, and God's spirit hovered over the water. God said: Let there be light, and there was light (Gen 1:1-3)... However, a flood was rising from the earth and watering all the surface of the soil. The Lord Almighty fashioned man of dust from the soil. Then he breathed his nostrils a breath of life, and thus man became a living being (Gen 2: 6-7).

My Lord and my God, how great you are! Clothed in majesty and glory, wrapped in a robe of light! You stretch the heavens out like a tent... You made the Moon to tell the seasons, the Sun knows when to set... You turn your face away, they suffer, you stop their breath, they die and revert to dust (Ps 104: 1-2 and 19-29).

The Sun will be darkened, the Moon will lose its brightness, the stars will fall from the sky and the powers of heaven will be shaken. And then the sign of the Son of Man will appear in heaven... Heaven and earth will pass away. But as for that day and hour, nobody knows it (Mt 24: 29-36).

And then with a roar the sky will vanish, the elements will catch fire and fall apart, the earth and all that it contains will be burnt up. What we are waiting for is what he promised: the new heavens and new earth (2 Pet 3: 10-13).

Then I saw a new heaven and a new earth; the first heaven and the first earth had disappeared (Rev 21: 1).

There is no uncertainty in these sentences, their meaning emerges clearly from the dark background of the cosmological theories outlined above: although the material world will come to an end, a new and indestructible Universe will follow, because "I am making the whole of creation new" he said (Rev 21: 5). In a new authorized translation of the Bible the sentences quoted above are commented upon as follows: "Modern scientific attitude does not consider this impossible", but "there is no need to reconcile the biblical account with modern scientific thought".

What is possible and what is necessary ? This depends on how one interprets the biblical account and modern scientific theories. According to physicists it is possible that the cosmic density of matter exceeds the critical value, in which case the universe will collapse as a result of the gravitational force that holds it together, and then in the increasing heat every celestial body and element will be burnt up. The Solar System, however, will be destroyed long before this total cataclysm: the Sun will gradually use up its hydrogen reserves, it will become unstable and in the fire spreading with the great explosion it will burn its planets together with the elements.

Bibilicists will say that the prophets and Christ himself are unlikely to have referred to these present day astronomical observations, but astronomers will answer that, if that is so, they happened to have made a good guess. This is a characteristic of the prophets. Those who are guided by supreme inspiration and intuition are often unaware of the full significance of their utterances.

The task of the biblicist is to analyze and interpret the ancient texts, and the simple believer will rest content with the authority of the Scripture and the Church. Today, however, it is modern physics that basically determines the way most people see the world while at the same time they try to find the truth of the Scriptural writings. That is why Pope John Paul II states in connection with the revision of the Galileo case that his aim was legitimate and is of interest even today:

In his letter to the Grand Duchess Christina, Galileo reaffirms the truth of Scripture: Holy Scripture can never lie, provided its true meaning is understood, which is often hidden and very different from what a simple interpretation of the words seem to indicate. Galileo introduces a principle of interpretation of the sacred books that goes beyond the literal meaning but is in accord with the intention and type of exposition proper to each of them. It is necessary, as he affirms, that the wise men who explain it should bring out their true meaning (*Science*, 207/1980; 1166).

164

Galileo is right when he says that:

... both Sacred Scripture and Nature are derived from the Divine Word..., and granting that two truths can never be contrary to each other, it is the task of wise expositors to try to find the true meaning of sacred passages in accordance with natural conclusions which previously have been rendered certain and secure by manifest sensation or by necessary demonstrations (Letter to Castelli).

This task, however, is just as difficult today as it was at the time of Galileo, because there are critical limits as to producing physical evidence as well as to the interpretation of the Scripture. Physics deals only with the phenomena of the material world. The main task of theology, however, is to study and explain spiritual reality, related to religious and moral life. There is a seemingly unsurmountable gap between the two domains, because physicists and theologians either tend to regard material and spiritual reality as two opposites excluding each other (it is impossible for something to be body and spirit at the same time) or accept the objective reality of only one of them (reality is either only matter or only spirit).

The prophets clearly see the difference between spirit and matter, which, however, complement each other in the unity of full reality. It seems quite natural to them that changing and transient matter is the work of an unchanging and eternal Spiritual Being and that the material world is kept going by that omnipotent Spirit. Where is the Universe evolving and for how long? The prophets reply, in God the Creator himself and for as long as He will it. "For He is not far away from any of us, it is in Him that we live, move and exist", preaches the apostle Paul to the philosophers of Athens. They did not know that the "Unknown God" is the creator and maintainer of the whole world (Acts 17: 23-28).

The first words of the Bible indicate that matter is not eternal and the universe has not been created from time immemorial, but there is an absolute initial starting point related to which there is no past time. Since the Creator of the world is essentially eternal, we may say that the universe as an eternal idea exists in his mind; the Almighty in his eternity wants to create at a certain moment the primeval atom or that energy quantum which carries the germ of the universe. Thus it was not in space and time, but with space and time that the Almighty created "the heavens and the earth". According to Saint Augustine the "heaven and earth" created in the beginning formed the primeval material of the world, from which the words of the Lord created the planets; then He brought forth the plants and the animals from earth and water; finally He fashioned man of dust from the soil and breathed into his nostrils the breath of life. (Cf. Augustine, *Confessiones* XII. 29; *De Genesi* VII. 28).

The arrangement in seven days of the account of creation is an artistic masterpiece written in Hebrew rhythmic verse. The inspired author writes in a solemn tone befitting great events, in the style of ancient wisdom literature. The author relates what really happened, but there is no need to take each word of the account literally. The "six days" here do not correspond to 6 × 24 hours, but to the six acts of the creation. This is clear from the contents: e.g. the emergence of the continents from the sea and the formation of plants and fruit trees "on the third day" cannot have taken place in 24 hours. The Hebrew *jom* (day) can mean a longer or shorter period, according to the event described. "With the Lord, a day can mean a thousand years, and a thousand years is like a day" (Ps 90:4; 2 Pt 3:8; Gen 2:3). Biblicists are also aware of the results of cosmological, geological and paleontological research, according to which the development of the Solar System, the Earth and living beings lasted several billions of years. There is no contradiction between these and the biblical texts. (Cf. Tanquerey 1956, *Brev. Synopsis* 593-607).

The sacred authors certainly did not intend to teach geology and paleontology, but it would be wrong to believe that their account lacks any serious science. They had reached the highest level of science at that time, a science we are only beginning to understand today in the light of linguistic and archaeological research. There is no room here for a detailed explanation of the text, but it is worth noting a few interesting points.

The prophets continued writing and interpreting the account of creation. As we have seen in the Books of Ezekiel and Daniel, the numbers express actual systems, their symbolic sense goes far beyond the limits of their numerical value. The number *six* always refers to physical reality actually in process, in development and it is thus the symbol of creative activity. Consequently, accomplishment and totality are expressed by 6 + 1 = 7.

Three systems emerge from the first scriptural account of the creation: a philosophical system, a numerical system and an existential system. The philosophical system incorporates the uplifting religious thought: Man is the image of his Creator, so he should follow his example. His example is shown by the following system: "Your all powerful hand did not lack means, the hand that from formless matter created the world,... you ordered all things by measure, number and weight" (Wis 11: 17-20).

The numbering of the "days" corresponds to a definite order of creation, which, concerning the Earth, agrees with empirical evidence. God's creative activity consists of two series, each of which includes the creation of four works: the first four involve the creation of the environment necessary for higher forms of life (light, air, water and soil together with the seasons); the other four involve the creation of living creatures in order of their state of perfection (fish, winged animals, mammals and finally the human being). The layer that separates the lower and upper waters, that is the sea and the clouds, is the atmosphere of the Earth. Etymological studies show that the Hebrew word *raquia* means a thin layer, which is in agreement with the atmosphere, but following the erroneous term used in the Greek Septuagint it was translated as "solid vault" or "firmament". This is even contextually wrong. The creation of the heavens (*shamaïm*) is revealed as early as in the first sentence of the Bible.

The stars appear in the "fourth act", which can be explained by the fact that, as a result of frequent volcanic eruptions and the formation of thick clouds, the light of the celestial bodies reached the surface of the Earth only 1000 million years after the development of the Solar System. It was only then that the Sun and the Moon became visible. The first sentence of the Creator, "Let there be light!", is more interesting from the point of view of modern cosmology. The Hebrew word *ôr* means radiating light, which however is interpreted as "full daylight" in the translations. In the generally accepted cosmological theory the primeval explosion was immediately followed by the formation of the photons, the first energy quanta, so after one second that was the energy of light that played the decisive role in the formation of the atoms and later the galaxies.

The prophets discovered a constant natural law in the measure of the number six, which had been observed by the Creation from the very first moment. That was what they could see in the $4 \times 6 = 24$ hour rhythm of the Sun; the $2 \times 6 = 12$ months of the solar year; what they admired in some regular hexagonal formations, like the honeycombs of bees, snow flakes, the mountain crystals of crystalline quartz and six-petalled lilies and flowers. We may in turn find it surprising that the two *natural constants* which ensure the formation of the Solar System and our existence on Earth also maintain the function of the number six; the constant of proportionality in the attraction between two unit masses a unit distance apart, i.e., gravitational constant:

$$G = 6.66 \times 10^{-8} \text{ dyn cm}^2 \text{ g}^{-2}$$

and the constant of proportionality relating the frequency of a photon to its energy quantum, i.e., Planck's constant:

$$h = 6.63 \times 10^{-27} \text{ erg seconds.}$$

Astrophysicists certainly did not have the scriptural account of the six days of creation in mind, when they discovered that from the moment of the primeval explosion the formation of the universe could be divided into six characteristic periods: from the Planck age to the age of solid matter, in which we live. It is obvious that the theory of the primeval explosion does not refer to the creation of the universe, but only to the beginning of the observable cosmic process. The fact that English scientific language uses the word creation to denote this has given way to misunderstandings. Strictly speaking creation is a deliberate activity or an intended work. To create means to bring something into state of being from non-entity or to call something into existence from non-existence. The theological concept of creation indicates the production of the being of things out of metaphysical nothing. God Almighty is the only subject capable of communicating being, as He possesses the plenitude of being. Before the creation of the world there is no physical cause and effect. (Cf. St. Thomas Aquinas, *Summa Theol.* I.45 a.1; q. 46 a.1.)

In the language of the prophets every existing being is a creature even if they are not brought into a state of being by the word of the Lord, but are born with each other's cooperation, like for example plants growing in the soil and human beings giving birth to human beings. Their existence and development is ensured by the perpetual activity of the creative Spirit. If this Spirit ceased to be, everything would be annihilated. Creation is not only production but preservation in existence as well, the aim of which is the eternal life and happiness, in other words the salvation of man. This truth is convincingly taught and testified to by the Bible, from its first sentence to the last.

The exact time of the creation of the universe or of the primeval atom cannot be determined by mathematical and physical methods. Nor can the "day and hour" of the end of the world be calculated in advance. It would, however, be wrong to infer that the universe is eternal on the basis of the conservation of energy. The anthropic principle has perhaps brought modern cosmology one step nearer to the Scriptural account of the creation. This Scriptural account is not an abstract theory, but a philosophy based on experience. The history of the past helps us to understand the present and to come to conclusions concerning the future. The basic difference, however, remains: cosmology deals only with Man's physical existence, whereas the Bible stresses his spiritual life as well: "To exist, for this the Lord [He-who-is] created all... For God created human beings to be immortal, He made them as an image of his own nature" (Wis 1: 14; 2: 23; Gn 1: 26).

Those who have a profound knowledge of the Bible, and who understand well the language it was originally written in, will realize that it is essentially a philosophical and theological cosmology, the concepts of which comprehend our whole existence and are always true. This is also verified by the idea of cosmic covenant. (19) It is not only the Book of Genesis that describes the origin and destiny of man. The subject is clearly presented by the prophets and the Book of Wisdom, and it is finally the work and message of Christ which shows us the full meaning of creation. That is where a reassuring answer will be found by the mathematicians and physicists who do not want to stop at the limits of their science. The Creative process has not yet reached its termination, but it is continuing until the everlasting new heaven and new earth are made thanks to the regenerative power of Christ (Rev 21: 5-6).

Joshua's Long Day: the Halting of the Sun

The same day that the Lord delivered the Amorites to the Israelites Joshua declaimed: Sun, stand still over Gibeon, and, Moon, you also, over the Vale of Aijalon. And the Sun stood still, and the Moon halted till the people had vengeance on their enemies. Is it not written in the Book of the Just? The Sun stood still in the middle of the sky and delayed its setting for almost a whole day (Jos 10: 12-13).

These are the biblical sentences which sparked off the dispute about the heliocentric system, the story of which is instructive to both biblicists and astronomers even today. It shows how easily the Bible can be misunderstood by those who do not know the original Hebrew text and the meaning of the ancient terms. Today it is difficult to understand why those sentences, which had been formulated 2000 years earlier, were taken so literally in the 17th century. Kepler made every effort to prove that although apparently the Sun had stopped, in fact it was the axial rotation of the Earth that had slowed down. Galileo wanted to put forward an even more accurate explanation by suggesting that the biblical expression was literally correct, because the axial rotation of the Sun could indeed have stopped for a while and this could have caused the halting of the Earth's rotation. The description namely talks about a divine miracle.

This error made in good faith comes from the concept that whatever the Bible describes as miracle must be in contrast with the laws of nature and suspends their effect for a short time. That is why some people consider the star of the Magi as described by Matthew to be an extraordinary phenomenon, which excludes any natural explanation. On the other hand, those who do not believe in such false miracles see nothing but poetic symbols in the account. They do not realize that the prophets themselves, when describing miraculous events, often wished to emphasize the fact of synchronicity. Certain extraordinary natural phenomena occur at the time and in the place where a faithful person most needs God's help. Such experience of synchronism will convince the believer of the presence of God Almighty, even if he is familiar with the natural explanation of the phenomena.

What can today's astronomer do with Joshua's case? Considering the sentences cited above, not much. Schiaparelli, having taken these sentences from their context, came to the conclusion that the story was basically an epic depicting Joshua's deeds. The "Book of the Just" was written at the time of King David, some 200 years after Joshua, in praise of the heroes of the past. If we take the expression "halting of the Sun" literally, there can be no question of astronomical observation. Even biblicists disagree about this question. Many simply regard this chapter as literature belonging to the genre of ancient folk poetry. According to them the halting of the Sun and the Moon is simply the poetic symbol of victory. Similarly, the "Sun cannot strike you down by day, nor Moon at night" in the Book of Psalms has but a symbolic meaning (Ps 121: 6).

Others believe this view is wrong because it oversimplifies the problem. Joshua's book is about historical events and the whole event cannot be regarded as the work of poetic fantasy because of the poem cited after the victory. The poem would not have been cited if it had not been for something unusual observed in the position of the Sun and the Moon. The rare phenomenon seen on that day is repeated three times in the Hebrew text and it is not treated as a mere symbol, but as a veritable heavenly sign reminding the people of the day of victory. There is no doubt the witnesses described the event in accordance with the facts, but being unable to explain it, they regarded it as some preternatural phenomenon or divine miracle.

In order to provide an astronomically acceptable explanation, with the help of the data given in previous chapters, we shall have to establish the time and date of the event. Joshua's scribe noted that they had set up their camp in Gilgal on 10th of the first month (Nisan) and celebrated their first Passover there on the 14th. We know that Passover started on the day of the spring full moon and lasted seven days until the last quarter Moon. In that year this occurred probably towards 22nd April, because the text mentions the swelling of the Jordan at the time of the harvest. Jericho was occupied after the holidays, during which they had walked round the city every day for a week; consequently this took place in the second month of their calendar, which is May according to our calendar.

Then Joshua carried out the orders of Moses. He summoned the people and "read all the words of the Law to them". This must have happened on the day on which they commemorated the Law which they had been given on Mount Sinai. This must have occurred on the 50th day after Passover, on the 7th of the third month, i.e., around 4th June in our calendar (Jos. 4:19; 5:1; 6:15;8:34). It was then that the Amorites attacked the town of Gibeon, which was about 35 kilometers to the south of Gilgal. The Gibeonites were the allies of Joshua, so they asked him for help. Joshua and his warriors left Gilgal in the evening and marched the whole night until they reached Gibeon. The Amorites had their camp on top of the 617 meter high Beth-horon, and when they had noticed Joshua's dread army, they wanted to flee but on the western slope of the mountain "the Lord hurled huge hailstones from heaven on them, and more of them died under the hailstones than at the edge of Israel's sword" (Jos 10: 9-11).

That was when Joshua exclaimed: "Sun, stand still..!" And his scribe noted: "That was how the Lord fought for Israel". Those who can read between the lines will realize that the hail coming from the northwest did not reach Joshua's army because the soldiers had not yet left the district of Gibeon. They were still at least ten kilometers away, to the southeast of Beth-horon. Consequently, from there it must have appeared to Joshua's men that the Sun was above Gibeon in the middle of the sky, and the Moon above the valley of Aijalon.

It follows from this that the miraculous happening was mainly the sudden downpour of the heavy hail, which smashed the camp of the enemy at the right moment. In addition, there was another rare phenomenon, that of the Sun and the Moon being visible for a long time after the quick passing of the storm. This fact and the chronology of the events show that these events took place after the summer solstice, when the Sun was visible above the horizon for as long as 14 hours. According to the original text, it was not the movement of the Sun that Joshua wanted to stop in order to prolong daylight. As a matter of fact, he did not need to do that. The misunderstanding stems from the sentence which says that the Sun "delayed its setting for almost a whole day". The Hebrew text uses two words to describe the phenomenon: one is *damam*, which in the language of the prophets means the ending or ceasing of a particular activity; the other one is *amad*, which generally means to stop, or in this particular context to stay, to be delayed. (Cf. *BDB. 1977*).

According to linguists the sentence should not be interpreted as one referring to the stopping of the Sun's spatial motion. The Sun radiates heat and light. The correct interpretation of the sentence would therefore be: Joshua declaimed "Sun, cease to shine!" And the heat of the Sun ceased as it reached the zenith over Gibeon and the Moon stood over the valley of Aijalon, i.e., over the western horizon.

The "middle of the sky" in eastern languages means the meridian line or the zenith. The Sun's northern declination is the largest in summer. Over Gibeon, at latitude 32° N, the Sun has an altitude of 80 degrees at its highest point in the meridian, which means it is indeed in "the middle of the sky". The heat then, at noon, is almost unbearable. Joshua and his soldiers were tired after having marched for about eight hours at night. The hail over the enemy camp was of help at first, but later, in the midday heat they did not have the strength to pursue the enemy and capture their leaders. That was why Joshua wished the heat of the Sun would cease. And it probably ceased thanks to the thick clouds while the Sun was high in the sky, i.e., while "it was delayed".

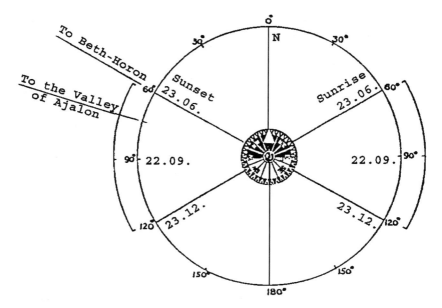

Fig. 26: The position of the rising and setting points of the Sun as seen from Gibeon, between June 23 and December 23. (Maunder 1908)

From the original meaning of the Hebrew word *damam* some astronomers have drawn the conclusion that it must have referred to the disappearance of the Sun's light, in other words to a solar eclipse. It was on this basis that they tried to determine the exact date of the Gibeon events. According to archaeological finds it was around 1200 BC that Joshua occupied Canaan. On 5th March 1223 a total eclipse of the Sun was visible in that region. A more precise analysis of the text however shows that the downpour of hail took place after the harvest, in summer; the description about the Sun and the Moon excludes the possibility of an eclipse. Joshua did not want the light of the Sun to cease.

The Moon, when still visible at noon on the western horizon, is a singular celestial phenomenon. E. Walter Maunder (1908) worked out an acceptable and detailed astronomical explanation of this phenomenon, in accordance with the analysis of the text. Joshua must have made his observation in Gibeon on or around 22nd July at noon. At that time the declination of the Sun was about 21° North. The Sun rose at 5 a.m., and set at 7 p.m.; the day being 14 hours long. The Moon must have been just before its last quarter, somewhat larger than half full, and waning. Its declination was 16° North. It had risen at 11 p.m. the previous evening, and so it shone at night for the troop marching up from Gilgal. At noon it was probably 5° above the horizon towards the west, i.e., towards the valley of Aijalon, and it was due to set in one half hour. A 90 degree position like this between the Sun and the Moon is very rarely visible, so Joshua may have taken it for a divine sign when he looked up at the sky to "speak to the Lord on that day". E.W. Maunder pointed out that instead of directly observing the position of the Sun, the Israelites had measured the time by the length of the distance covered. The sentence "the Sun delayed its setting for almost a whole day" simply states that the length of the march made between noon and sunset was equal to an ordinary march taking the whole of a day. When they victoriously returned, it seemed to them they had covered one day's distance in half a day.

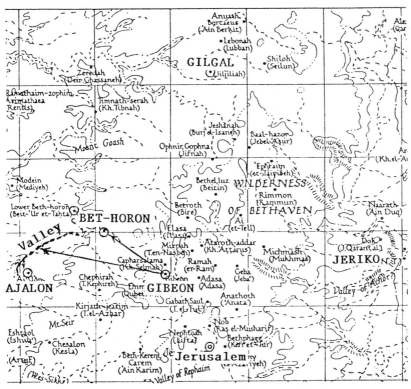

Towns in Western Palestine at the time of Joshua.

SUPPLEMENTARY
EXPLANATIONS

1. *Allegorical Interpretation*

Some exegetes and other scholars often quote the allegorical interpretation
of the star of Bethlehem by the early Church Fathers, and they often accept
it as the only literal meaning of Matthew's narrative. This old mistake
should be cleared up. The star in Matthew's 2nd chapter obviously is a
natural phenomenon, not an allegory of the Messiah. The early Christian
writers never denied the historical meaning of the Magi's account, but it
was against the contemporary superstition of astrology that they
emphasized the allegorical meaning of the star of Bethlehem.

Allegory is defined as a description of a subject under the guise of
another suggestively similar subject, or as an extension of symbolism. As
opposed to literal meaning, allegory presents something not directly
expressed. St. Thomas Aquinas made it clear that many passages of the
Scriptures have both literal and spiritual senses (*Summa Theol.* I.q.1,a.10):
the literal or historical meaning expresses the thing the words directly
speak of, and this is the point of departure for the spiritual meanings which
may be allegorical, moral, and prophetical, referring to realities beyond
time and space.

The first allegorical interpretation of the star of Bethlehem is to be
found in a letter of St. Ignatius, Bishop of Antioch in Syria. Under the reign
of Trajan, about 107 AD, he was arrested and taken to Rome. On his way
to martyrdom he wrote the following in his letter to the Ephesians:

> A star shone in heaven beyond all stars; its light was beyond description
> and its newness caused astonishment. All the other stars, with the Sun
> and the Moon, gathered in chorus around this star, but it far exceeded
> them all in its light (Ignatius of Antioch, *Ep. ad Ephesios*, 19:2).

St. Ephraem used a similar allegory in his hymn for the feast of the
Epiphany, when the public celebration of Christ's birth was still allowed in
Bethlehem and Jerusalem, about 350 AD:

> A star shone forth suddenly with preternatural light, less than the Sun
> and greater than the Sun. Less was it than the Sun in manifest light, and
> greater than the Sun in its secret might. The star of light shed its rays
> among those who were in darkness, and guided them as though they
> were blind (Ephraem, *Hymn of Epiphany*, 14-15).

Now, let us try to realize the situation of these Christian writers at the time of persecutions, so we can understand them correctly. When they mention the star, in its literal sense, it is the phenomenon visible in the sky, according to the Gospel; allegorically, however, it refers to the appearance of Christ, whose might will outshine the power of the emperor (Sun), the king (Moon), and the reigning princes (stars). By his spiritual light he will guide his people living in the darkness of ignorance. A good part of the allegorical interpretation of the early Christian writers was based on the belief that the prophets of old predicted the life and history of Christ. The psalms of David and the writings of the prophet Isaiah foretold that kings would come to the Temple of Jerusalem. They would bring gold and silver and offer gifts for the Messiah: "Above you the Lord rises and his glory appears; the nations come to your light...; everyone in Sheba will come, bringing gold and incense and singing the praise of the Lord" (Is 60:3-6; Ps 72:10-11). These statements do not refer to the Magi who came to Jerusalem. Here in its literal sense Jerusalem is the capital of Israel, but allegorically it is the Church of Christ or the heavenly city in which eternal peace and bliss will be attained. The apostle John spoke of this heavenly Jerualem in the 21st chapter of his Apocalypse, and the early Christian exegetes understood its spiritual meaning. Nevertheless, they were happy believing that those prophecies had been fulfilled by the Magi's visit to Bethlehem.

In his Gospel Matthew quotes twelve prophecies of the Old Testament to convince people that Jesus truly is Christ the Messiah. However, he does not refer to any prophecy concerning the visit of the Magi, and he does not call them kings. This fact also shows that it is an original and true account that Matthew gives in his second chapter. The Church Fathers never asserted that the Magi had been kings, rather they held them for mathematicians or astrologers. This can be proven by several quotations from their works. Here it suffices to quote Tertullian, the Roman jurist of classical education. He was 33 years old when he was baptized in 193 AD and he energetically defended the correct interpretation of the Gospel narratives against heretics. According to his view the Magi of Matthew can be considered allegorically as kings, and thus Psalm 72 can be applied to them, but the star is a real sign for them:

The Orient for the most part held the Magi for kings..., and together with the gold and frankincense Christ won also the Magi who bowed to the ground in homage to him, because they had recognized him as the divine king, on the basis of the interpretation of the star which was a sign and guidance for them (Tertullian, *Adversus Marcionem*, III.12-13).

In another writing Tertullian mentions that the Magi saw real stars, but they did not worship them:

The Magi and astrologers came from the East. It is well known that astrology formed a part of the science of the Magi. Those Magi, therefore, as interpreters of stars [*quasi stellarum interpretes*] announced the birth of Christ, and then they paid him homage... What is the meaning of this? Perhaps that from then on all the astrologers [*mathematici*] should follow the religion of the Magi? For today there is a science [*mathesis*] also about Christ, interpreting his stars, not Saturn and Mars and stars of other mortal deities. That science [*mathesis*, i.e., astrology] was permitted [by divine providence] only until the time of the Gospel, so that no one from then on, after Christ's appearance, should interpret anyone's nativity from the heavens (Tertullian, *De Idololatria*, IX.3-7).

Here Tertullian gives us an example of the allegorical mode of expression. "The stars of Christ" are the apostles interpreting his teaching.

2. Astrology and the Church Fathers

In antiquity there were very few scholars who made a clear distinction between astrology and astronomy. Even today many people confuse these two terms. Astrology deals with the traditional aspects of the zodiacal signs and with supposed influences of the configurations of the Sun, Moon, and planets on earthly events and human destiny. Astronomy, on the other hand, deals with the observation and mathematical determination of motions and positions of celestial bodies. In its origins however astronomy everywhere was linked to religion and divination, because astrological diagnoses and prognoses were not possible without astronomical calculations. Therefore, the mathematicians of antiquity were both astronomers and astrologers.

Ptolemy (*Klaudios Ptolemaios*, 100-170 AD) was the first ancient scholar who made a scientific system of the theories of previous Babylonian, Chaldaean and Greek astronomers, and he separated mathematical astronomy from symbolical astrology. In the thirteen books of the *Mathematikê Syntaxis*, known under its Arabic title *Almagest*, Ptolemy laid the mathematical foundations for geocentric astronomy for the coming 1500 years. The aim of the accurate determination of the geocentric motions and positions of the stars was, of course, the practical knowledge of future happenings on Earth. Therefore, the Almagest was followed by the other well known work entitled *Tetrabiblos*, i.e., "Four Books", about astrological prognostications. In this work Ptolemy described the traditional qualities and influences of all the celestial phenomena which were known at that time. In his preface he said that the influence of the stars was a common human experience: "This is entirely clear to everybody and needs little comment". He notes, however, that "the astrological interpretations have not the same degree of reliability as astronomical computations".

Nowadays popular astrology uses the interpretative rules of the *Tetrabiblos*, almost word for word, presuming that the configurations of the celestial bodies determine both man's destiny and all terrestrial events. This sytem and way of thinking would have been foreign to Matthew; the star of Bethlehem is a natural sign in the sky, and it has neither a physical influence on nor causal connection with the recorded events.

The writings of the Hebrew prophets have a unique part in ancient literature and culture. In a world where the common religion was the worship of deified stars, these prophets unanimously declare that the stars are no deities but creatures, and through the observation of "the grandeur and beauty of the stars we may, by analogy, recognize and praise the power of their Author" (Wis 13:2-5). In Deuteronomy Moses strictly forbade the worship of stars:

> When you raise your eyes to heaven, when you see the Sun, the Moon, the stars, all the array of heaven, do not be tempted to worship them and serve them... If there is anyone, man or woman, among you, who worships the Sun or the Moon or any of heaven's array..., you must stone that man or woman to death (Deut 4:19; 17:2-7).

The prophet Isaiah call upon the people to "lift your eyes and look: who made these stars if not he who drills them like an army, calling each one by name?" (Is 40:26). And the psalmist of King David sings a cosmic hymn of praise:

> Let the heavens praise the Lord [He-who-is], praise him, all his armies! Praise him, Sun and Moon, and shining stars! Let them all praise the name of the Lord, at whose command they were created; he has fixed them in their place (Ps 148:1-6)

The biblical conception naturally prevailed in the theology and philosophy of the early Church Fathers. They energetically condemned the "mathematicians" who would determine and predict the destiny of each individual on the basis of their birth chart or horoscope. A horoscope is a diagram of the celestial sphere showing the relative positions of the Sun, Moon, and planets at a given time. To set up a horoscope the astrologer must know the exact time and place of the client's birth. Each of the zodiacal signs was said to be associated with a definite element or temperament. The astrologers claimed that they were able to predict the future of the clients from the structure of their horoscopes.

The first great authority among the Church Fathers who condemned the horoscope mongers was St. Augustine, the bishop of Hippo Regius (395-430 AD). In his younger days he studied astronomy, and he was himself an eager follower of astrology. Later, after he became bishop, he pointed out that a knowledge of astronomy is necessary for the understanding of the Scriptures, and not only for the calendar. Then he attacked "those impostors called astrologers" who let most people believe that a man's fate is ruled by "the power of the configuration of the stars, as it is given when a man is born". Finally, St. Augustine rejected the entire popular astrology, as it was in his time, and on the basis of his own experiences he summarized the counter arguments as follows. The time of birth cannot be measured accurately enough, and the calculation of the astrologers are almost all mistaken, their predictions do not come true; two children born at same time with precisely the same birth chart, as well as twins, have quite different abilities and fates, therefore, the horoscope does not show a man's destiny; the belief in the power of the stars and in the astrological predictions weaken man's faculty of free decision and diminish the sense of responsibility; and finally a fatalistic astrology is contrary to true religion and worship, because it destroys faith in God's providence. (Cf. Augustine, *Confessiones*, IV.3; VII.6; *De Doctrina Christiana*, II.21-29; *De Civitate Dei*, V.1-7).

The Church Fathers intended to save the faithful from all superstition and idolatry, but they failed to impede the practice of astrology, because it pervaded all ancient culture. One reason for this must be that astrological belief was a manifestation of man's natural need of religion. Some scholars, both ancient and modern, assert that astral religion thus paved the way for a deeper and purer form of divine worship. In the Middle Ages, Christians knew well that the stars in the sky were neither gods nor angels, yet they believed in the influence of the celestial bodies upon earthly happenings and on man's life.

From the 13th century on the Latin translation of Ptolemy's works was current, and astrology spread rapidly throughout Europe. The observed or supposed causal connection between some celestial phenomena and terrestrial events, e.g., between the moon's phases and tides, induced medieval man to consider astronomy as the supreme science of nature. Astrology appeared as an all embracing doctrine, and it became a compulsory subject at the universities. The greatest Christian thinkers in the 13th century, Roger Bacon, Robert Grosseteste, St. Albert the Great, and St. Thomas Aquinas, cleared astrology of superstitions and accepted it into their philosophical worldview. In their theocentric system God rules all things on the Earth by means of the celestial spheres. But human beings are not completely subject to the dominion of the stars, because they have the faculty of free decision, as they are created in the image of God. Every man is responsible for his own fate and fortune. Thus they are in agreement with St. Augustine that the fortune teller astrologers are severely to be censured.

Robert Grosseteste, a member of Oxford University and Bishop of Lincoln (1234-1253 AD), accepted the use of astrology in meteorology and in medicine. He assumed some effect of the constellations on man's behavior, but he denied the possibility of determining individual fates from horoscopes. St. Thomas Aquinas (1225-1274 AD) intensively treats the questions of medieval astrology in his work entitled *Summa Theologica*. He begins with the question in which all were greatly interested: "Whether the motions of celestial bodies are cause of human acts". In his answers Thomas explains that the celestial bodies have only physical influences (like cosmic rays or corpuscular radiations in modern physics), which can not affect man's mental faculties directly, i.e., those cannot determine our choices. However, physical radiations affect the body and the organs of sense, and thus they can have some influence on our mind indirectly. *Astra inclinant, non necessitant*, i.e., astral influences can incline us, but they cannot constrain us to do something.

How is it possible that astrologers often accurately predict the time of wars and other events, the source of which is man's mind? St. Thomas answers to this question:

> Most people follow their passions, which are motions of the sensitive appetite; few men are wise enough to resist passions of this sort. Therefore, astrologers, in most cases, can make true predictions, and this especially in general; not however in particular, because nothing

can hinder any man from resisting his passions by his free choice. Hence the astrologers themselves say that the wise man is master of the stars, inasmuch as he is master of his own passions. (*Summa Theol.* I.q.115,a4; II/2,q.95,a5; *Summa contra Gentiles*, III.84-87).

This philosophically cleansed astrology was able to survive as a science among Christian scholars until the 17th century. Astrological symbolism permeated European culture so much that many works on architecture and many literary works were unintelligible without a knowledge of astrological principles. In the course of three hundred years many reigning monarchs and influential prelates consulted "mathematicians" who were both astronomers and astrologers.

During the Lutheran Reformation in Germany Philipp Melanchton published a standard Latin translation of Ptolemy's *Tetrabiblos*, and he delivered lectures on astrology at the University of Wittenberg (1540 AD). The astronomer of Pope Paul III (1534-1549 AD) was Lucas Gauricus, who had predicted the earthquake and the epidemic of the plague which raged in Rome in 1540. It was on the basis of his advice that Paul III convoked the Council of Trent in 1545. This Council forbade the use of horoscopes and astrological divination under pain of excommunication. Nevertheless, the Council Fathers distinguished between judicial and natural astrology. It was judicial astrology which was forbidden as superstition, because it would pass definite judgments on man's affairs which belonged to his personal freedom. It is important to remember that no one questioned the possibility of natural astrology which dealt with weather forecast, or prediction of storms, floods, earthquakes and other physical catastrophies. Finally, Pope Sixtus V, with reference to the resolutions of the Council of Trent, condemned the grave errors of judicial astrology (determinism, fatalism, and atheism) which denied man's freedom and God's providence, but he admitted the validity of natural astrology which dealt with natural phenomena. (*Caeli et Terrae Creator*, Rome 1586).

The leading astronomers in the 16th and 17th century, such as Tycho Brahe, Johannes Kepler, Galileo Galilei, and Isaac Newton, practiced astrology by calculating and comparing horoscopes. It was Kepler who put an end to ancient astronomy. He studied astrology as a doctrine of cosmic unity and harmony, but not as an infallible art to predict human destinies. With the publication of the three laws of heliocentric motions of the planets (1619 AD) he also established new basic principles for natural astrology. Kepler elaborated a theory of the effective configuration angles which are central angles of the arcs of the ecliptic circle, when two or more celestial bodies form an angle of 30, 45, 60, 90, 120, 135 and 180 degrees relative to one another, measured from the Earth as center. (Cf. *Harmonices Mundi*, Lib.IV. Cap. 5-6).

The *Music of the Spheres*, the ancient idea of Pythagoras, received a new interpretation by Kepler's harmonic theory. He supposed that the motions of the planets produce a certain harmony which is comparable to the harmony of musical notes, the pitch of note resembling the speed of each planet. To understand this let us recall the laws Kepler discovered concerning the planetary motions. The orbits of the planets are not perfect circles. They move around the Sun in ellipses having the Sun at one of the foci. According to the harmonic law the square of the revolution periods of a planet is in direct proportion to the cube of its mean distance from the Sun. Variations in both the planet's distance and its velocity are determined by the eccentricity of its orbit: the nearer it comes to the Sun, the faster it moves; the faster it moves, the greater the pitch of its note will be.

Kepler used the known revolution periods and eccentricities of the planets to derive the system of notes which is illustrated below. The orbit of Venus has the smallest eccentricity; its distance and its speed do not vary perceptibly, hence it emits always the same note. Mercury, on the other hand, has the largest range of notes because its orbit has the largest eccentricity.

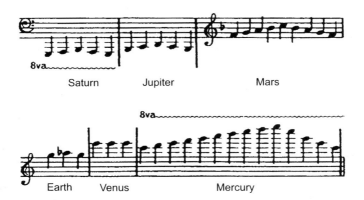

Fig.27: Notes written by Kepler, representing the music given by the revolution periods of the planets (from his *Harmonices Mundi*).

The distance between a given planet and the Sun varies because planetary orbits are elliptical. The major axis of a planet's orbit is the sum of its maximum and minimum distance from the Sun. Half of this sum, the semimajor axis, is the mean distance of a planet. Kepler reckoned the Earth's period for the unit of time (one year), and the mean distance of the Earth from the Sun for the unit of distance taken as 1.000. For example, calculated with this astronomical unit the mean distance of Mercury is 0.387, and that of the Saturn is 9.540. The values of the maximum distance (aphelion) and the minimum distance (perihelion) of each planet given by the harmonic theory and by the actual observations are compared in the following table. It is surprising how the musical notes on a properly tempered scale agree with the observed values of the aphelion and perihelion:

180

	By observations Aphelion – Perihelion distance	By harmonic theory Maximum – Minimum distance
Mercury	0.470 – 0.307	0.476 – 0.308
Venus	0.729 – 0.719	0.726 – 0.716
Earth	1.018 – 0.982	1.017 – 0.983
Mars	1.665 – 1.382	1.661 – 1.384
Jupiter	5.451 – 4.949	5.464 – 4.948
Saturn	10.052 – 8.968	10.118 – 8.994

Concerning this comparative table the British astronomer Fred Hoyle has noted that "the agreement is frighteningly good; frighteningly because the idea has no physical relevance whatever. One wonders how many modern scientists faced by a similar situation in their work would fail to be impressed by such remarkable numerical coincidences" (Hoyle 1962, p. 119).

Kepler was able to give reliable weather forecasts based on the calculated configurations of the Sun, Moon, and planets. He also set some individual horoscopes, although with the warning that astrological diagnoses and prognoses are only conjectures or suppositions, because many other factors are at work in man's life, both natural and supernatural causes: descent, nationality, social milieu, rearing, erudition, character. Moreover, there are personal gifts of divine grace with which we cannot reckon in advance (cf. *Harmonices Mundi*, Lib.IV. C.6). Kepler strove to explain and verify the validity of astrology by means of analogous musical harmonies, effective configuration angles, and gravitational or magnetic attractions between the stars and planets. He was close to the truth when he assumed that some psychical factors played an important part in the art of astrology (see below: p. 248). However, his endeavor to give a modern scientific character to ancient astrology remained fruitless.

At the end of the 17th century, after the foundation of academies of sciences, astrology was expelled from the universities, because from a natural scientific viewpoint it was completely unfounded. Nevertheless, both judicial and natural astrology continued to exert a hidden influence on political and cultural life. The pseudoscience of contemporary astrology is a widespread and lucrative job. Many hundreds of thousands of astrologers throughout the world give elaborate predictions for millions of credulous people. For example, in China, Korea, and Japan they give advice on the appropriate days for weddings and trade agreements. However, there are scholars both in Europe and in America, who are engaged in serious research on the experimental and theoretical basis of astrology. They evaluate its contributions from a psychological point of view.

Apart from this, the effect of cosmic radiations upon man's life has become the subject of various strictly scientific studies, especially with regard to astronautics and space research. Modern astrophysical and geophysical studies discovered a certain correlation between some planetary configurations and solar activity (eruptive prominences and flares), the semiregular sunspot cycles of 11 and 22 years and climatic changes. In recent astrophysical textbooks there are interesting chapters about the so called solar-terrestrial effects. Solar corpuscular radiations disturb the ionospheric layers which may disrupt the reflection of radio waves transmitted from the ground. Intense sunspot activity causes storms in the Earth's magnetic field, and geomagnetic variations affect some chemical and biological processes. The first International Symposium on Solar-Terrestrial Physics was held in 1976, and since then the proceedings of these Symposia have been published (see Fairbridge 1961, Schröder 1992, Williams 1976).

3. *Primary Source for Matthew 2: 1-12*

From the view point of literary criticism it is probable that the primary source of the account of the star of Bethlehem is an original report of the Magi. This claim is corroborated by the original mode of expression in Matthew's text, which is similar to the style of the Babylonian astronomer priests, as found in Chaldaean and Greek writings. At the same time, there are several records proving that after the ascension of Christ, the apostles had contacts with certain Magi, if not with the immediate witnesses from Bethlehem, then at least with their successors. We shall discuss this assumption in the following comments about the Magi and about the star of the Messiah. For the present, it will be enough to point to some convincing data.

The evangelist Luke writes in the Acts of the Apostles that, during the first speech of the apostle Peter on the day of Pentecost, there were present in Jerusalem also "Parthians, Medes, and people of Mesopotamia", and they all understood the language of the apostles. Some of these people from Mesopotamia might have been the Magi who were still alive, or their sons and successors. Matthew was certainly present, and his name is mentioned in the Pentecostal community of the apostles (cf. Acts 1:13; 2:8-12).

At that time, trade caravans were regularly going between Mesopotamia and Judaea and these also performed the duty of messengers, because there were many Israelite settlers living in Mesopotamia. We can safely assert that the Magi from the East who had found Jesus in Bethlehem never forgot their experiences and that they continued to follow his life. Chrysostom says, certainly based on a Syrian source: "It follows that those Magi, having hastily returned home, must have heralded the good news in Babylon" (*Comment. in Matthew* VIII. 4). They obviously told their experiences of the journey, at least to their relatives and colleagues. Some of these, or the Magi who were still alive, could have gone again to Jerusalem, decades after, and they could have met the apostles there or in Galilee.

According to the earliest tradition there were three Magi, and it is possible that one of them was still alive, 40 years after Christ's birth. When they went to Bethlehem, they had to be around 30 to 35 years old, because those who were older usually did not take on the hard caravan journey lasting for weeks. The usual camel caravans consisted of six or seven persons, including the servants and the camel-drivers. The three Magi also had such companions, who must have been younger, and they also were eye witnesses of the happenings. Clement and Eusebius recorded that the apostle Matthew had worked for 12 years in Galilee, Samaria and Syria, after the ascension of Christ, when he collected and wrote down the oral traditions about Jesus' life and teaching. Afterwards he preached the Gospel in Arabic Ethiopia and Persia, meaning *Mesopotamia* (Clement of Alexandria, *Stromata* VI.5,43; Eusebius, *Hist. Eccl.* III.24,6). Based on this information, we may assume that he somewhere could have met one of the Magi or perhaps some of their successors, who after forty years might still carefully remember the account of the visit to Bethlehem and the star. The particular style of the account of the Magi shows that Matthew might have used not only the oral tradition, but also an original written account.

St. Thomas was the other apostle who is said to have evangelized the lands between the Caspian Sea and the Persian Gulf, i.e., in the country of the Magi. The early Christian writers assert unanimously that St. Thomas went to Syria, and he was teaching in the town of Edessa for a while. Then he continued the apostolic work in southwest India, where he founded the first Christian community. From the 3rd century there is preserved an apocryphal writing, entitled "The Acts of Thomas" (*Acta Thomae*, Cod. Vaticano Greco No.1608). According to this document Thomas entered India as a carpenter, but later he was called *magus*, because he performed several miracles. He converted and baptized the Indo-Pathian king *Gadaphar*, or Gathasphar. This name is preserved as an inscription on a coin and is also found in an inscription carved into a cliff in the mountains of Kush, in West Pakistan. The Latin name *Caspar* comes from this name, and it was associated with the oldest Magi. Based on this tradition, a legend of the Middle Ages relates that the Apostle Thomas baptized the Magi who had been in Bethlehem. Regardless of this legend, it is still possible, that during his missionary journey in the East he met the Babylonian Magi and perhaps also Matthew. The "Christians of St. Thomas" along the Malabar Coast of India claim him as the apostolic founder of their church. The apostle Thomas died a martyr's death in the year 70 AD, near Madras, in West India. His church and tombstone are still venerated in Madras. (Clement of Alexandria, *Stromata* IV,9; Eusebius, *Hist. Eccl.* III.1; St. Jerome, *De vita apostolorum* 5; about the Indian Christians of St. Thomas, see L.W.Brown 1956, pp.43-64.)

4. Chaldaean Gospel

The magi at the time of birth of Jesus were Chaldaeans, if not by origin, at least by profession. So it is not just by chance that the Chaldaeans were the first among the Oriental people who in great numbers accepted Christ together with his Gospel. The Chaldaean Catholic Church today is composed of faithful living in Iraq, Iran, Syria, Lebanon, and Turkey. They are descendants of the East Syrian Christians, and are subject to the Chaldean Patriarchate of Babylon. The standard version of their Gospel, the *Peshitta* (=Popular) is preserved in fifth century manuscripts of excellent quality. It was prepared in the fourth century and spread under the Bishop Rabbula of Edessa (411-435 AD). Until the 6th century Edessa (today Urfa in southeastern Turkey) was the cultural and literary center of the Syrian

Christians. Linguistically the *Peshitta* rests on the Old Syriac version which was revised several times, but the revisions have not erased the original expressions of the older language. Recent research shows that the basis of the Old Syriac version was a second century work of Tatian, the first known writer of the Old Syrian Church and a scholar of Babylonian origin. He was a student of Justin Martyr, and from 170 AD on he worked in Antioch and Edessa. He produced a harmonistic work of the Gospels, the so-called *Diatessaron*, which is an unbroken and chronologically ordered text of the four Gospels. Translated into Latin it is called *Tetraevangelium Sacrum*, which throughout the centuries was held equivalent to the Vulgate version.

Like the Aramaic and Arabic, the Old Syriac and Chaldaean dialects belong to the Semitic family of languages. The Babylonian magi were Chaldaean speaking people, thus they did not need an interpreter in Bethlehem. Matthew, the writer of the first Aramaic Gospel, must also have understood correctly the original account of the Magi about the star. Our new translation of Matthew 2:1-9 is based on the comparison of the ancient Syriac, Greek and Latin versions. Our purpose here is to reach a better understanding of the literal sense of the sentences quoted. Up to the present none of the exegetes took pains to make such a detailed linguistic analysis of this passage, because they were not interested in its possible astronomical significance, and because it seemed to be unimportant for theological and moral teaching. For the translation we have used the critical edition of the Peshitta by The British and Foreign Bible Society (New Testament in Syriac, London 1920). Like the Hebrew and Aramaic the Syriac way of writing goes from right to left and denotes only the consonants with scripts, while the vowels are points and commas above or below the scripts. For the interpretation of the Syriac expressions we are indebted to René Lavenant, S.J., professor of Syriac grammar and patrology at the Gregorian University. (We have used the linguistic works of Payne-Smith 1981, Palacios 1954, Lampe 1961 and Bauer 1988). The text of the Latin Vulgate is important because for his translation St. Jerome, in additon to using the Greek, worked also with the ancient Aramaic version, as he mentions in his letters and commentaries (cf. *Comment.in Matthew*, Cap. 2,6,12,27; *Epistulae* 57-58).

The fact that the Prelate of the Chaldean Catholic Church is called Patriarch of Babylon might be a discrete allusion to the Babylonian Magi who found Christ in Bethlehem according to Matthew. The contacts of the Chaldeans with the Bishops of Rome, the legitimate successors of the apostle Peter, began during the period of the Crusades. From 1240 AD on their patriarchs repeatedly sent letters to the Popes, with the profession of the Catholic faith and the expression of their loyalty. The definitive union with Rome took place in the 16th century. The Chaldean bishops had chosen a highly respected priest as candidate to the patriarchate, *Yohanan Sulâqâ,* the superior of the Convent of Rabban-Hormizd, and they sent him to Rome, armed with the proper documents. On November 15, 1552 he arrived in Rome, where he was consecrated a bishop by Pope Julius III in the Basilica of St. Peter. The Pope promulgated his Bull of February 20, 1553, proclaiming Sulâqâ patriarch of Babylon. This is the official birthday of the Chaldean Catholic Church. Yohanan Sulâqâ arrived in his patriarchal residence in Mosul on 12 November,1553, where he was

Matthew 2: 1-12 in the first critical edition of the Peshitta, published in London, 1831,
in memory of the martyrdom of Patriarch Yohanan Sulaqa:
Syrorum Novi Testamenti Versio quam Peschito nuncupat, iuxta exemplare Viennense a J.A. Widmanstadio, A.D. 1555.

܀ ܒ ܀ ܩܦܠܐܘܢ

¹ ܟܕ ܕܝܢ ܐܬܝܠܕ ܝܫܘܥ ܒܒܝܬ‌ܠܚܡ ܕܝܗܘܕܐ ܒܝܘܡܝ ܗܪܘܕܣ ܡܠܟܐ: ܐܬܘ ܡܓܘܫܐ ܡܢ ܡܕܢܚܐ ܠܐܘܪܫܠܡ. ² ܘܐܡܪܝܢ ܐܝܟܘ ܡܠܟܐ ܕܝܗܘܕܝܐ ܕܐܬܝܠܕ: ܚܙܝܢ ܓܝܪ ܟܘܟܒܗ ܒܡܕܢܚܐ ܘܐܬܝܢ ܠܡܣܓܕ ܠܗ. ³ ܫܡܥ ܕܝܢ ܗܪܘܕܣ ܡܠܟܐ ܘܐܬܕܘܕ. ܘܟܠܗ ܐܘܪܫܠܡ ܥܡܗ. ⁴ ܘܟܢܫ ܟܠܗܘܢ ܪܒܝ ܟܗܢܐ ܘܣܦܪܐ ܕܥܡܐ ܘܡܫܐܠ ܗܘܐ ܠܗܘܢ ܕܐܝܟܐ ܡܬܝܠܕ ܡܫܝܚܐ. ⁵ ܗܢܘܢ ܕܝܢ ܐܡܪܘ ܒܒܝܬ ܠܚܡ ܕܝܗܘܕܐ: ܗܟܢܐ ܓܝܪ ܟܬܝܒ ܒܢܒܝܐ. ⁶ ܐܦ ܐܢܬܝ ܒܝܬ ܠܚܡ ܕܝܗܘܕܐ: ܠܐ ܗܘܝܬܝ ܒܨܝܪܐ ܒܡܠܟܐ ܕܝܗܘܕܐ: ܡܢܟܝ ܓܝܪ ܢܦܘܩ ܡܠܟܐ: ܕܗܘ ܢܪܥܝܘܗܝ ܠܥܡܝ ܐܝܣܪܐܝܠ: ⁷ ܗܝܕܝܢ ܗܪܘܕܣ ܡܛܫܝܐܝܬ ܩܪܐ ܠܡܓܘܫܐ ܘܝܠܦ ܡܢܗܘܢ ܒܐܝܢܐ ܙܒܢܐ ܐܬܚܙܝ ܠܗܘܢ ܟܘܟܒܐ. ⁸ ܘܫܕܪ ܐܢܘܢ ܠܒܝܬ ܠܚܡ ܘܐܡܪ ܠܗܘܢ. ܙܠܘ ܥܩܒܘ ܥܠ ܛܠܝܐ ܚܦܝܛܐܝܬ. ܘܡܐ ܕܐܫܟܚܬܘܢܝܗܝ ܬܘ ܚܘܐܘܢܝ ܕܐܦ ܐܢܐ ܐܙܠ ܐܣܓܘܕ ܠܗ. ⁹ ܗܢܘܢ ܕܝܢ ܟܕ ܫܡܥܘ ܡܢ ܡܠܟܐ ܐܙܠܘ. ܘܗܐ ܟܘܟܒܐ ܗܘ ܕܚܙܘ ܒܡܕܢܚܐ ܐܙܠ ܗܘܐ ܩܕܡܝܗܘܢ. ܥܕܡܐ ܕܐܬܐ ܩܡ ܠܥܠ ܡܢ ܐܝܟܐ ܕܐܝܬܘܗܝ ܛܠܝܐ. ¹⁰ ܟܕ ܕܝܢ ܚܙܐܘܗܝ ܠܟܘܟܒܐ: ܚܕܝܘ ܚܕܘܬܐ ܪܒܬܐ ܕܛܒ. ¹¹ ܘܥܠܘ ܠܒܝܬܐ ܘܚܙܐܘܗܝ ܠܛܠܝܐ ܥܡ ܡܪܝܡ ܐܡܗ. ܘܢܦܠܘ ܣܓܕܘ ܠܗ. ܘܦܬܚܘ ܣܝܡܬܗܘܢ ܘܩܪܒܘ ܠܗ ܩܘܪܒܢܐ. ܕܗܒܐ ܘܡܘܪܐ ܘܠܒܘܢܬܐ. ¹² ܘܐܬܚܙܝ ܠܗܘܢ ܒܚܠܡܐ ܕܠܐ ܢܗܦܟܘܢ ܠܘܬ ܗܪܘܕܣ. ܘܒܐܘܪܚܐ ܐܚܪܬܐ ܐܙܠܘ ܠܐܬܪܗܘܢ ܀ ¹³ ܟܕ ܕܝܢ ܐܙܠܘ:

received triumphantly by clergy and people. However, in January of 1555, by order of the Pasha of Amadya, Sulâqâ was arrested and subjected to torture for four months. Finally, because of his resistance, he was put into a sack and thrown into a lake to drown. Thus he became the first martyr of the Chaldean Catholics. (Rabban 1955) Until 1830 the residence of the

The Greek text of Matthew 2: 1-12 in the critical edition:
The Greek New Testament, Institute for NT Textual Research,
United Bible Societies, 1975

2 Τοῦ δὲ Ἰησοῦ γεννηθέντος ἐν Βηθλέεμ τῆς Ἰουδαίας ἐν ἡμέραις Ἡρῴδου τοῦ βασιλέως, ἰδοὺ μάγοι ἀπὸ ἀνατολῶν παρεγένοντο εἰς Ἱεροσόλυμα 2ᵃ λέγοντες, ᵃΠοῦ ἐστιν ὁ τεχθεὶς βασιλεὺς τῶν Ἰουδαίων; εἴδομεν γὰρ αὐτοῦ τὸν ἀστέρα ἐν τῇ ἀνατολῇ καὶ ἤλθομεν προσκυνῆσαι αὐτῷ. 3 ἀκούσας δὲ ὁ βασιλεὺς Ἡρῴδης ἐταράχθη καὶ πᾶσα Ἱεροσόλυμα μετ' αὐτοῦ, 4 καὶ συναγαγὼν πάντας τοὺς ἀρχιερεῖς καὶ γραμματεῖς τοῦ λαοῦ ἐπυνθάνετο παρ' αὐτῶν ποῦ ὁ Χριστὸς γεννᾶται. 5 οἱ δὲ εἶπαν αὐτῷ, Ἐν Βηθλέεμ τῆς Ἰουδαίας· οὕτως γὰρ γέγραπται διὰ τοῦ προφήτου·
6   Καὶ σύ, Βηθλέεμ γῆ Ἰούδα,
        οὐδαμῶς ἐλαχίστη εἶ ἐν τοῖς ἡγεμόσιν Ἰούδα·
    ἐκ σοῦ γὰρ ἐξελεύσεται ἡγούμενος,
        ὅστις ποιμανεῖ τὸν λαόν μου τὸν Ἰσραήλ.
7 Τότε Ἡρῴδης λάθρα καλέσας τοὺς μάγους ἠκρίβωσεν παρ' αὐτῶν τὸν χρόνον τοῦ φαινομένου ἀστέρος, 8 καὶ πέμψας αὐτοὺς εἰς Βηθλέεμ εἶπεν, Πορευθέντες ἐξετάσατε ἀκριβῶς περὶ τοῦ παιδίου· ἐπὰν δὲ εὕρητε ἀπαγγείλατέ μοι, ὅπως κἀγὼ ἐλθὼν προσκυνήσω αὐτῷ. 9 οἱ δὲ ἀκούσαντες τοῦ βασιλέως ἐπορεύθησαν, καὶ ἰδοὺ ὁ ἀστὴρ ὃν εἶδον ἐν τῇ ἀνατολῇ προῆγεν αὐτοὺς ἕως ἐλθὼν ἐστάθη ἐπάνω οὗ ἦν τὸ παιδίον. 10 ἰδόντες δὲ τὸν ἀστέρα ἐχάρησαν χαρὰν μεγάλην σφόδρα. 11 καὶ ἐλθόντες εἰς τὴν οἰκίαν εἶδον τὸ παιδίον μετὰ Μαρίας τῆς μητρὸς αὐτοῦ, καὶ πεσόντες προσεκύνησαν αὐτῷ, καὶ ἀνοίξαντες τοὺς θησαυροὺς αὐτῶν προσήνεγκαν αὐτῷ δῶρα, χρυσὸν καὶ λίβανον καὶ σμύρναν. 12 καὶ χρηματισθέντες κατ' ὄναρ μὴ ἀνακάμψαι πρὸς Ἡρῴδην, δι' ἄλλης ὁδοῦ ἀνεχώρησαν εἰς τὴν χώραν αὐτῶν.

Patriarchate of Babylon was in Mosul, in the second largest city of Iraq, near the ruins of Ninive. Since then it has been in Baghdad. The Chaldean Catholic Rite and Office were approved by the Patriarchate and the Pontifical Oriental Congregation: *Breviarium iuxta ritum Syrorum Orientalium id est Chaldeorum* (Baghdad and Rome 1886).

5. Israel and Judah

We can hardly understand the expositions and discussions in this book if we do not know the most important acts of the drama of the Old Covenant. Here we can give only the most general outline of the history of the Chosen People. The origins of the tribes of Israel is written down in the books of Moses. A more systematic historiography begins with the Book of Kings. On the basis of earlier records these books narrate the main events of 423 years, from 1010 to 587 BC, i.e., from King David to the destruction of Jerusalem. This is not an historiography in the ordinary sense. The authors of these books do not intend to emphasize the contest between the tribes for power, but rather they want to show the heroic struggle of some outstanding personalities for the victory of monotheism. The Books of Kings must be read as a history of salvation.

The descendants of Abraham were rightly called a "chosen people" because they had played a decisive part in the cultural history of antiquity, especially in the development of religion. Moreover, the unique charism of being God's chosen people is evidenced also from the fact that Israel's destiny was archetypical, i.e., it was a prophetic prototype both of the destiny of Jesus and of the history of the Church. We only need to recall the periodical recurrence of persecutions and the millions of martyrs.

According to biblical data Abraham was born in the city of Ur in Chaldaea which was the southeastern part of Babylonia. Abraham's birth occurred 1200 years before the construction of the Temple in Jerusalem. King Solomon began the building of the Temple around the year 960 BC, so Abraham would have been born circa 2160 BC (cf. 1 Kg 6:1f; Gen 21:5; 25:26; 47:7; Ex 12:40). The city of Ur in Chaldaea was the center of antiquity's astral religion. It contained the most ancient great *Ziggurat*, as well as five smaller temple towers built in honor of the Moon goddess and the five planet divinities. Abraham, however, was a worshipper of *El-Shaddaj*, the Most High who had created heaven and earth. He obeyed God's command to leave his country and kin, and migrated to the land of Canaan. As a reward for his obedience Abraham received the following promise from the Lord Almighty: "All the tribes of the earth shall bless themselves by you". Two thousand years later the apostles declare that this promise refers to Jesus: "All the nations will be blessed in Abraham's offspring, which is Christ" (cf. Gen 12:3; Gal 3:8-16; Acts 3:25).

This same messianic promise was reiterated for Isaac, the only legitimate son of Abraham, and again for Jacob, the youngest son of Isaac. Jacob went back to the land of his forefathers in order to marry a Hebrew woman. He remained in Mesopotamia for fourteen years and became the father of twelve sons. When he returned to Canaan with his large family, he experienced on his first night in Canaan an apparition in which he was challenged by an unknown powerful man with whom he had to wrestle the entire night. Jacob eventually overpowered his opponent who then said to him: "Your name shall no longer be Jacob, but *Israel*, because you have been strong against God [*El* or Mighty One], and you shall prevail against men". The Hebrew expression *Israel* is a compound word (*jisra* = struggle or battle plus *El* = Mighty One), and it expresses a desire: "May the Mighty One show his strength!" As a personal name, *Israel* may be interpreted as a "strong man of the Almighty". From this interpretation comes the idea of the "chosen people". Jacob's twelve sons became the ancestors or patriarchs for the people of God (Gen 28:14; 32:28; Deut 7:6; 33:1-29). In the theology of Jesus and his apostles the word *Israel* indicates the people of the New and Everlasting Covenant, the Christian community, as opposed to the "Israel according to the flesh", (1 Pet 2:9; 1 Cor 10:18; Gal 6:16).

Jacob's favorite son was Joseph. He loved him more than all his other sons, "for he was the son of his old age". Dreams as premonitions play a large part in Joseph's story, and they are excellent examples for the ancient view of life which was imbued with astrological symbols as signals of the future. The young Joseph had a dream and he told it to his father and to his eleven brothers: "The Sun, the Moon, and eleven stars were bowing down to me". But his father said to him: "What is this dream that you have dreamed? Shall I and your mother and your brothers indeed come to bow ourselves to the ground before you?" This dream of Joseph was fulfilled when the Pharaoh made him governor of Egypt. In a time of famine Jacob's whole family moved to Egypt, and Joseph saved them from death by starvation. Nevertheless, it was not Joseph, but Judah who inherited the messianic promise, because he was Jacob's most handsome and strongest son like a lion (Gen 37:9f; 41:40f; 46:6f; 49:9f).

The tribes of Israel lived in Egypt for 430 years, and in the prosperous conditions there they greatly increased in numbers. The Egyptians, envious of them, began to persecute them and condemned them to slavery. The Pharaoh Ramses II (1300-1234 BC) commanded that all male infants born of Hebrew women should be put to death immediately after birth. It was at this time that Moses was born. He was saved because his mother had hidden him in a papyrus basket in water near the shore of the Nile, and he was discovered by the Pharaoh's daughter who kept the beautiful male child and raised him as her own son (Ex 2:1-10).

Around 1240 BC Moses, by supernatural power and assistance, led the tribes of Israel out of Egyptian bondage. On the way to the Promised Land, on Mount Sinai, Moses established the Covenant between the Lord, the Almighty, and Israel's people, and he presented them with the stone tablets of the Law containing the Ten Commandments (Ex 19-24). After the people had wandered in the desert for forty years, Joshua heroically conquered the whole of the land of Canaan and divided it up among the twelve tribes. Around two hundred years after this, David of the tribe of Judah was chosen to be king and ruler over the twelve tribes, between 1010 and 970 BC: "David was thirty years old when he became king, and he reigned for forty years. He reigned in Hebron over Judah seven years and six months; then he reigned in Jerusalem over all Israel and Judah for thirty-three years" (2 Sam 5:4). He made Jerusalem a royal city, a capital of his new kingdom, and the transfer of the Ark of the Covenant gave the city a permanent religious importance. Finally, the prophecy of Nathan about the Davidic dynasty in Israel contributed to the general stability of the royal house of Judah. It was the first in the series of prophecies relating to the Davidic Messiah (2 Sam 7).

David himself chose and appointed his son Solomon "as ruler of Israel and of Judah". Under his reign from about 970 to 931 BC Israel reached its national golden age. In Judaean tradition the glory of Solomon's reign became proverbial. However, Solomon gave Israel "a too heavy burden to bear", and after his death the northern tribes were separated from the House of David. In the south, in Jerusalem the son of Solomon was king of Judah. Only the tribe of Benjamin remained loyal to him. In the north, in the districts of Galilee and Samaria, the kingdom of Israel had been established. Henceforth the political and religious schism between Israel and Judah was definitive and fateful (1 Kg 1:35f; 12:1-33).

In the 8th century BC idolatry and star worship began to spread among the people of Israel. Around the year 750 BC the prophets started to give witness to the punishment to come for the unfaithful chosen people who had abandoned the God of Abraham, Isaac and Jacob. The prophet Amos in Israel and the prophet Isaiah in Judah now predicted that the people will fall into the Babylonian captivity, but that "the Virgin's son, Imma-nu-El" (the Mighty One with Us), the Messiah to come, will bring release from captivity (Amos 5:27; Is 7:14; 8:7-10;1:23). The Assyrian king Sargon II conquered Samaria in 722 BC, and deported the people of Israel to the eastern part of Babylonia. He settled foreign colonists in their place. The new Babylonian king, Nebuchadnezzar, stormed Jerusalem 125 years after this and deported Judah's population to Babylonia. Fifty years later some of them returned to Jerusalem, but Judaea remained under Persian domination.

Judaea also came under Greek dominion as a result of the military campaign of Alexander the Great in 332 BC. Then in 63 BC the Roman occupation began. Under such conditions as these the longing of the people for the promised Messiah increased. He was seen as a powerful national king who would free Judaea from the foreign yoke. The Emperor Augustus guaranteed full religious freedom in Judaea. In the year 20 BC the building of the Temple in Jerusalem was begun and it became the largest and most preciously decorated religious site on the Earth. The practice of the Mosaic law and religion was again at its height in the time of Jesus. The lawyers, scribes and priests considered themselves to be the true sons of Abraham and they despised the inhabitants of Galilee whom they considered to be foreigners and heathens. However, as a result of the Assyrian colonization, different Semitic races intermarried with the remainder of Israel, and the "unfaithful of the people" moved from Judaea to Galilee, but all of them, nevertheless, held on to Abraham's faith and awaited the promised Messiah.

Isaiah had called this area "the Heathen District", in Hebrew *Galil Haggojim*, and from this comes the name *Galilee*. But Isaiah predicted that the Messiah to come would also bring great joy and light to these people. Matthew points to the fulfillment of this prophecy when he tells of the beginning of Jesus' public life, how he chose his apostles from among Galilean fishermen. And Jesus himself was called a Galilean (Is 9:1-3; Mt 4:14-25). The Israelites in Galilee were always more enthusiastic about the Messianic Kingdom than were the Judaeans. The Galileans considered the priests in Jerusalem to be traitors who simply served the Roman overlords. Revolutions and uprisings generally began in Galilee. This is evidenced by Josephus Flavius who was one of the leaders of the uprising that broke out in 66 AD. Later he joined the Romans, and as an eyewitness he wrote about the destruction of Jerusalem which occurred in 70 AD (cf. Josephus, Jewish War, V-VI). Twenty years later Josephus also wrote about Jesus of Galilee. He wrote with admiration for Jesus as he remembered him from his childhood:

> Now, there was about this time a wise man, Jesus, if it is lawful to call him a man, for he was a doer of wonderful works, a teacher of such men as receive the truth with pleasure. He drew over to him both many of the Jews, and many of the Gentiles. He was the Christ [Messiah]; and when Pilate, at the suggestion of the principal men amongst us, had condemned him to the cross, those who loved him at the first did not forsake him, for he appeared to them alive again the third day, as the divine prophets had foretold these and a thousand other wonderful things concerning him; and the tribe of Christians, so named from him, are not extinct at this day (Josephus, *The Antiquities of the Jews* XVIII. Ch.3:3/63-64).

Judaea and Galilee were always in opposition. Thus we have a sort of background for the Apostles blaming the Judaeans because "they put the Lord Jesus to death..., and now they have been persecuting us...; they are hindering us from preaching to the Gentiles and trying to save them". When some leading Pharisees also had recognized the true Messiah in Jesus, the chief priests reacted negatively saying, "Go into the matter and see for yourself: prophets do not come out of Galilee" (cf. 1 Thess 2:14-16; Acts 2:23; Jn 7:52). The most remarkable fact in connection with all this is that the question of the Magi about the king of the Judaeans (Mt 2:2) occurs again in the account of Jesus' passion and death when the Roman governor Pilate asks him:

> Are you the king of the Judaeans ? He replies: Mine is not a kingdom of this world. If my kingdom were of this world, my men would have fought to prevent my being surrendered to the Judaeans. But my kingdom is not of this kind. Pilate asks again: So you are a king then? [Here the adjective Judaean is omitted.] Jesus answers: It is you who say it. Yes, I am a king, I was born for this. I came into the world for this: to bear witness to the truth; and all who are on the side of truth listen to my voice.

After this Pilate wanted to release Jesus and declared for the accusers: "I find no case against him". Matthew remarks: "Pilate knew it was out of jealousy that they had handed him over" (Jn 18:33-40; Mt 27:18).

The apostle John was an eyewitness at Jesus' trial, and his account is, therefore, the most detailed. In chapters 18 and 19 of his Gospel he uses the expression "King of the Judaeans" seven times. He shows us that it was not out of disdain for Jesus, but rather to embarrass those who accused him, that Pilate ordered the false accusation to be attached to the cross in Hebrew, Greek and Latin:

The adjective "Nazarenus" is here synonymous with "Galilean", as opposed to Judaean which means "of Jerusalem" or from Judaea. (Since Martin Luther first translated the word *Iudaei* as "the Jew", this has come down to us in all subsequent translations. This has, in my opinion, contributed to the spread of anti-Semitism throughout the world down through the centuries. The fact is that the Apostles in speaking of "Judaeans" were describing the inhabitants of Judaea, as opposed to Galileans of the North.)

We must draw two important conclusions from these events.

(1) Before his self-sacrificing death on a cross, Jesus himself answers the question put by the Magi in Jerusalem forty years before: "Where is he who is born to be king of the Judaeans?". Jesus' answer before the Roman governor in Jerusalem shows his clear consciousness of being a king from his birth, i.e., eternal king, not for Judaea but for the entire world. This is in accordance with the prediction of the messianic Psalm 110: "Royal dignity was yours from the day you were born, royal from the womb, from the dawn of your earliest days.";

(2) The other important conclusion from these events is the fact that it was not Israel or the Jewish people which was reproved when Jesus and the apostles accused the Judaeans. They blamed only those Pharisees and chief priests of Jerusalem who appropriated the privileges of Judah to themselves and forced Jesus' crucifixion by the Roman authority.

The bishops of the Second Vatican Council state in the Decree on Non-Christian Religions that although some of the Hebrews desired the death of Jesus and were the cause of many sufferings for the Apostles, neither all Hebrews at that time, nor Hebrews today can be charged with the crimes committed during Jesus' passion:

> As holy Scripture testifies, Jerusalem did not recognize the time of her visitation (Lk 19:44), nor did the Jews in large number accept the Gospel; indeed, not a few opposed the spreading of it (Rom 11:28)... True, authorities of the Jews and those who followed their lead pressed for the death of Christ (Jn 19: 6); still what happened in His passion cannot be blamed upon all the Jews then living, without distinction, nor upon the Jews of today (Declaration on the Relationship of the Church to Non-Christian Religions, *Nostra aetate* 4. Vatican 1965).

6. *Ancient Astronomical Expressions*

In antiquity the best known astronomical phenomena were some conspicuous phases of the planetary motions, as for example the first visible heliacal rising of a planet, when it rises shortly before sunrise, and the acronichal rising, when it rises in the east as the Sun sets in the west, and the stationary point or apparent standstill of a planet. In the centuries before Christ, the dates of these phenomena were usually recorded in the Babylonian and Greek astronomical tables and star almanacs. Such phenomena are referred to in Matthew's Gospel, whether explicitly or implicitly. However, he does not use the technical terms of contemporary astronomy, but the expressions of everyday language. These expressions are to be found in the writings of Aratus and Geminus which were available also in Hebrew at that time.

Aratus of Tarsus (310-245 BC) was the court-poet of Antiochus Sôtêr in Syria. His contemporary Berossos, a Babylonian priest-astronomer, founded a Greek astronomical school at the isle Koos, and in 280 BC he dedicated his comprehensive work *Babyloniaka* to Antiochus Sôtêr. This work of Beressos was the first which transmitted the Chaldaean cultural values to the western world. Ten years later, under the influence of the *Babyloniaka* of Berossos, Aratus wrote his best known work about celestial phenomena. This popular didactic poem is an excellent introduction to the astronomical theories of Eudoxus. People learned his verses by heart as a practical guidance to the heavens, for instance, how the different constellations signaled the time of the feasts and the seasons. The first sentences of Aratus invite the readers to praise the Lord of Heaven and Earth:

> Let us begin with the Most High [Dios], whose help we invoke incessantly. The Most High is present in every place where people live and are, he permeates the sea and the coasts, and everybody will return to him, for we are all his offspring... Be praised, O Most Marvelous Father, and your wonderful first-born, heaven, real consolation for all men! (Zannoni 1948; Aratus, *Phenomena*, I.1-6).

Here it is significant that Aratus does not use the mythological name of *Theós* or *Zeus* but the most ancient Indo-European name of god *Dios*, originally *Dyâus* which means the *Most High*, an attribute of the Heavenly God, who always and everywhere is present. The observation of the rising stars suggests for Aratus the idea of the immortality of men: after earthly life the wise and virtuous men shall shine like the stars in heaven for ever.

The apostle Paul, born in Tarsus, quotes a sentence of his townsman Aratus in his sermon to the Greek philosophers in Athens:

The Lord of heaven and Earth is not far from any of us, since it is in him that we live, and move, and exist, as indeed some of your own writers have said: We are all his offspring [*Thoû gàr kaí génos esmén*] (Acts 17: 24-28).

Paul also used the comparison of the stars to explain the resurrection from the dead:

> The Sun has its brightness [or glory], the Moon a different brightness, and the stars differ from each other in brightness. So is it with the resurrection of the dead: it [the human body] is sown in dishonor, and it is raised in glory; it is sown a physical body, it is raised a spiritual body (1 Cor 15: 40-45).

Greek philosophers thought of the higher conscious soul (the *nous*) escaping from the body, to survive immortally. According to the Apostle's teaching immortality involves a resurrection of the human body effected by the risen Christ who is the "heavenly man and life-giving Spirit". After death the human body is no longer physical but spiritual (*sôma pneumatikôn*), the glory or brightness of which will be proportional to the moral maturity of the person.

Geminus (70 BC - 40 AD) summarized the contemporary knowledge of elementary astronomy. In his work entitled "Introduction to the Celestial Phenomena" (*Eisagogé eis tá phainoména*) Geminus describes the development of astronomy from the Chaldaeans to Hipparchus, but without any mathematical details. At the beginning of the Christian era this work was translated into Latin and Arabic, and at the same time Gerson Ben Salomo translated it into Aramaic with the title *Shaâr Hashamaîm*. The Greek text and a German translation with Latin commentaries has been published by Manitius (1974).

The explanation of the astronomical expressions which we meet in Matthew's second chapter are to be found in Geminus' work:

> The Pythagoreans still thought that the Sun, and the Moon, and the five wandering stars [*planetés astéres*] moved uniformly in regular orbits. They were not able to imagine such an irregularity of the divine and everlasting celestial bodies that these now move faster, and then more slowly, and that from time to time they come to a standstill (*Gemini Elementa* I.19-20).

Here the standstill of the planets is expressed by the Attic verb *hestêkénai*, originating from the same root (ste- or sta-) as *estáthê* in Matthew (2:9), which is the indicative historical past (passive aorist) of the transitive verb *histánai*, i.e., to stop. Geminus mentions that the planets periodically revert their forward motion and become retrograde, and he describes also their stationary points:

> The planets either precede [*proêgountai*] the fixed stars, or remain behind them [*hypoleípontai*], or at other times they stay with the same fixed stars, when they are called stationary.... For every planet has its own sphere of motion, and thus they are periodically in the forward motion [*eis tá proêgoúmena* = in the progressing], then they move in the reverse direction, and then they stand still [*stéridzousin*] for a while (*Gemini Elementa* XII.1).

The Attic verb *proêgountai* is a classic form of *proêgéomai*, to precede and go ahead, and it means that a planet precedes the fixed stars, i.e., rises before them, and moves ahead of them. So it is possible that Matthew's expression *ho astér proêgen autoús*, according to its primary source, refers to this phenomenon: the observed wandering star in its retrograde course preceded the fixed stars, not the Magi. This interpretation is supported by the fact that also in Matthew's version after the statement "the star preceded them", immediately follows the expression of the standstill: "it preceded them while in its course it stopped". This is the same phenomenon which is described by the sentences of Geminus quoted above. Some exegetes have indeed interpreted the passive aorist indicative *estáthê* as standstill (cf. Rienecker 1950).

The other important information which Geminus gives us is about the heliacal and acronichal rising of the planets. The ancient Greek astronomical expressions are listed in Manitius (1974, 293-363). The general term for the rising of stars is the verb *anatéllein* (to rise, to ascend). This verb usually denotes the acronichal rising, or in everyday usage the evening rising, i.e., when a planet rises as the Sun sets, and remains in the sky all night, being due south about midnight. The heliacal rising of a planet is the first time that it can be observed in the morning before sunrise. This is usually denoted with the verbs *epitéllein* and *phaínetai* (to come up and to appear or shine forth). These terms illustrate the brief appearance of a planet, when its light soon vanishes in the light of the dawn sky. Concerning these terms, Geminus states that:

> People often confuse the two expressions, but there is a great difference between evening risings [*anatolês*] and morning appearances [*epitolês*] of the stars. We call it evening rising when a star ascends over the horizon immediately before or after sunset, as stated above. However, the form of the early appearances depends on the position of the Sun... when a planet rises simultaneously with the Sun, it is invisible, but the following days it rises earlier and earlier before the Sun, and this is called an early visible appearance [*heôn phainoménên epitolên*] (*Gemini Elementa* XIII.1-10).

These statements of Geminus are very important for our subject, because they show that the term *tê anatolê* in Matthew's text refers to the evening rising of the star, whilst the expression *khrónon phainoménou astéros* refers to its first early visible appearance (Mt 2: 2 and 7).

It is fitting here to mention those outstanding scholars who investigated ancient Mesopotamian astronomy and made its methods available and intelligible for us. Our real knowledge of Babylonian astronomical science is founded on the work of three Jesuit scholars, the Assyriologist, Johan Strassmaier, and the astronomers, Joseph Epping and Franz Kugler. Strassmaier worked in the British Museum from 1878 to 1897. His task was to bring order into the colossal amount of Mesopotamian cuneiform tablets. During this work he found many astronomical texts which were incomprehensible to him. He therefore sought the help of Epping (cf. Strassmaier and Epping 1889) and Kugler, professors of mathematics and astronomy. They had translated into German and explained the cuneiform texts which were dated from 425 to 8 BC, from the temples of Babylon, Sippar, and Uruk. The results of this research have been collected and edited by Kugler (1907-1935).

These works mark the pioneering period in the deciphering of Babylonian astronomy. It was the American professor, Otto Neugebauer, who continued this research, and in 1955 he dedicated his work on "Astronomical Cuneiform Texts" (Neugebauer 1955) to the memory of the aforenamed three scholars. He completed their material by deciphering 300 new cuneiform tablets, each one rebuilt from several fragments. Twenty years later Neugebauer published his comprehensive work on "A History of Ancient Mathematical Astronomy" (Neugebauer 1975). In these books is to be found the analysis of the texts of Aratus, Geminus, and

Hipparchus, together with their Babylonian sources. The Greek Glossary of Neugebauer (1975, 1206 ff) gives the most important Accadic-Babylonian ideograms and their equivalents in Greek. For example, the cuneiform ideogram for the acronichal rising of a planet is *ana mea ina kur* i.e., "opposition in rising" (viz., when a planet is on the opposite side of the Earth to the Sun); its equivalent in Greek is *en tê anatolê*, the same expression which is used by the Magi in Matthew's account (cf. Neugebauer 1975, pp.295, 399).

We must also mention two professors, Konradin Ferrari d'Occhieppo of the Astronomical Institute at the University of Vienna and David Hughes at the University of Sheffield, who have made important contributions to the work of the astronomical explanation of the star of Bethlehem. In their books (Ferrari d'Occhieppo 1977, 1991; Hughes 1979) they have given conclusive proofs for the planetary conjunction hypothesis, but their statements are not quite convincing for all biblicists, because they have not solved the exegetical problem of Matthew's narrative. In Chapter One of the present book the literal sense of Matthew's text is given with a new and complete linguistic analysis and interpretation which may contribute to the solution of this problem. Ferrari d'Occhieppo (1965) has reconstructed the ancient method of calculation with which the Babylonian astronomers had found the time for the common evening rising and the western stationary points of Jupiter and Saturn in the year 305 of the Seleucid era, i.e., 7 to 6 BC. He has stated that:

> The competence of the astronomer in this matter cannot be denied with the objection that the evangelist intended to relate a miraculous event which excludes all scientific judgments. In my opinion it is the task of the astronomer being well versed also in history to judge whether Matthew's account excludes the scientific explanation, or makes it likely, or even demands it. I think that the known principle *miracula non sunt multiplicanda* can be applied also in this case, that is to say we must not seek miracles where a natural explanation obviously is possible (Ferrari d'Occhieppo 1977, Preface).

7. Literary and Historical Criticism

The debate about the star of Bethlehem, which began four centuries ago in scholarly circles and still continues in the journals of our day, throws light on the difference between natural scientific and theological ways of thinking. Theologians and astronomers often misunderstand each other because of their different methods and presuppositions.

Astronomers and historians wish to know what really happened, and they take as their starting point the literal sense of an account. The question for an astronomer reading Matthew's account is the following: What exactly was the star of Bethlehem? Was it an actual physical object? Does Matthew record a real astronomical observation? In any case, scientific objectivity demands that the text in question shall be taken word for word, in its literal sense. Thus for the astronomer there are only two right ways: either we ascertain that the record is sufficient for a scientific explanation and we accept it in its entirety, or it is insufficient and so the recorded phenomenon is inexplicable by known scientific laws. Of course, this judgment is only possible on the basis of a correct literal translation of the original text. Unfortunately, the literal sense of Matthew's account is obscure or dubious in the more common translations, and these versions are insufficient for a scientific explanation of the nature of the star. The basis for our astronomical investigation is a thorough linguistic analysis of the original Greek text of Matthew (see above: pp. 12-22).

Although theologians generally presuppose a literal interpretation of Matthew's text, they seem at the same time to be undecided as to its literary form and the event itself seems by a sort of dichotomy, to be unimportant for them. Rather they wish to know the intention of the evangelist, and they are looking only for the theological meaning of the narrative. However, both the intention of the author and the historical value of the narrative are to be judged on the basis of the literary form. (Cf. Decree of the Second Vatican Council *On Divine Revelation*, III.12).

In what literary form is Matthew's narrative written? Is it a short story, legend, or fiction? Or is it a Scriptural interpretation which was called *midrash* by the rabbis of old? Such questions are current; and those who do not know the proper definition of the literary genres may easily come to a wrong conclusion. Modern literary criticism seeks to ascertain the literary genre of single biblical writings, and it studies the content of the Gospel under the aspect of language, composition, and origin. After the literary analysis follows the investigation of the circumstances of the author, the thoughts and the views he shared with contemporaries. Historical criticism attempts to determine the value of the sacred writings as historical documents, both as to teaching and as to the facts. This method seeks to reconstruct the writer's life, ideas, and milieu through the use of auxiliary sciences like archaeology, ethnography, and philology. To these sources must be reckoned also astrology, as the proper science of that time (which however was not the same as the horoscopy of our days).

The majority of the critics consider the account of Matthew as a record of historical events. There are some scholars who regard it as a *midrash*, but there is no agreement whether midrash, in the Bible, is a literary genre of its own, or merely an incidental technique of composition. Matthew's writing has the title *Euangélion*, i.e., the Good News of salvation which had been promised by God and realized in Jesus Christ. At that time there were no newspapers or journals, and we may say that the authors of the Gospel performed the duty of journalists writing articles and reports on the events they had seen and heard.

The renowned biblical scholar, Addison G. Wright enumerates 14 different definitions of midrash which biblical scholars have used in the last decades (Wright 1967). He states that the *midrash* in the rabbinic usage is Scriptural interpretation, especially interpretation of the legislative portions of Moses' books. In this sense midrash cannot be in the Gospel. After a very detailed and accurate analysis of the rabbinical literature, Wright comes to the following conclusion:

> As the name of a literary genre, the word midrash designates a composition which seeks to make a text of Scripture from the past

understandable, useful and relevant for the religious needs of a later generation. Midrashim exist in three forms: exegetical, homiletic and narrative, and they are accomplished in two ways: explicitly (some homiletic comments are assembled at the side of the biblical text) and implicitly (the interpretative material is worked into the text by means of a paraphrase) (Wright 1967).

Finally, Wright puts the question: Can the early chapters of St. Matthew and St. Luke about Jesus' birth be called midrash? And will this help to explain their message? Some scholars classified the narrative of Matthew as midrash "because it contains elements apparently legendary and because of the construction of five episodes on five texts with the referral of Old Testament Scripture to Jesus in whom they are fulfilled". However, the fundamental question is: Do the narratives under discussion actualize biblical texts? The texts of the Old Testament which Matthew quotes are simply applied to a new situation:

They seem to be used not to direct attention to Old Testament material so that it might be explained but to explain the person of Jesus. Hence, in fact, Matthew's narrative does not seem to be midrash... Perhaps the best classification of our material is simply *infancy narrative*, for these chapters seem to have been written in the tradition of infancy stories, biblical and extra-biblical, sharing with them many of their motifs. The Jewish stories of biblical figures were of composite genre, midrashic infancy stories, because they were at the same time embellishments on the biblical text. The New Testament stories are not midrashic (Wright 1967).

The explanation of the star of Bethlehem in terms of midrash is unacceptable both for astronomers and for historians. As David Hughes has noted:

The midrash argument is in some ways the hardest one to answer, for it disposes of the whole problem of the star as a phenomenon and rules out a natural as well as a supernatural explanation. The star becomes merely a literary device (Hughes 1979).

Some authors thought that the whole idea of the star was a literary invention to give fulfillment to Balaam's prophecy in Numbers 24:17 and in this way to convince the Hebrew audience that Jesus was the true Messiah. Hughes claims:

Such a view cannot be right. If Matthew had invented the story of the birth of Jesus, he would surely have made it much more coherent and plausible. In particular, there is no reason why he should have made do with a very ordinary star or, in view of all the Old Testament prophecies, why he should have omitted any mention of the phrase "that it should be fulfilled" when discussing the star (Hughes 1979, p.196).

Astronomers know and accept the results of literary and historical criticism. However, the different methodologies still present difficulties. A recent paper by the theologian Kim Paffenroth is particularly interesting concerning this problem. In this paper, published as a response to the work of David Hughes, Paffenroth says:

> The explanation that an interpreter, including Hughes, opts for tells us more about the interpreter than about the Star, because it tells us what a given interpreter views as an acceptable explanation of scripture, or as an acceptable explanation of nature and God's relation to it (Paffenroth 1993).

Eventually Paffenroth presents his own explanation:

> The story of the Star of Bethlehem is a Midrash. It is not history, it is not science, it is story. By saying this, I mean neither to affirm nor to deny the possibility, or even the probability, that a historical fact lies behind the narrative. I merely suggest that such a fact, if it existed, does not cast much light on Matthew's purpose in relating this story. Hughes's work does show that the triple conjunction of Jupiter and Saturn in the year 7 BC is the most likely candidate for the fact that may lie behind Matthew's story of the Star of Bethlehem, but to claim anything more than this is unwarranted (Paffenroth 1993).

Unfortunately, astronomers and theologians have neither interest nor time enough to study the thorough astronomical and historical works of Hughes and Ferrari d'Occhieppo. We hear much from astronomers and also non-professionals proposing new and erroneous theories in the name of science. There is no general agreement among scholars on what the star of Bethlehem has really been, and this creates more confusion than understanding. Paffenroth is right when he states that "a methodology that produces one or two explanations for a given question each year must strike anyone as a less than helpful way to approach the question". Nevertheless, his criticism on the astronomer's methodology is very problematic as it appears from the following statements:

> Hughes's book is truly astonishing in its thoroughness, and will most likely go down in history as the definitive astronomical work on the Star of Bethlehem. However, in its methodology and presuppositions about what constitutes truth, it is ultimately flawed. For Hughes and so many others, to call something a story is equivalent to calling it a figment of imagination and therefore not the truth. This is not the necessary definition of story…Hughes and everyone else, astronomer, historian, or theologian, must come to realize that history is not the sole or even the best conveyer of truth… Matthew is trying to tell us something by writing a story, and therefore our question should not be: What really happened?. Such a question is not in the author's mind and deflects our attention from what is really important. Rather our question should be: What is the significance or meaning of what is recorded? Matthew's

goal is the same as the Gospel tradition previous to him, to proclaim the good news of Jesus Christ (Mk 1:1), and therefore the appropriate question is: How do the infancy narratives convey the good news of salvation? (Paffenroth 1993).

It was necessary to quote these statements because these show the view of some theologians and their methodology in finding an explanation for the infancy narratives and for the Star of Bethlehem. May we still ask them: Do you know the history and methodology of astronomy? Why do you think that the star as an actual heavenly body could not be in Matthew's mind in relating the Messiah's birth? Does the star not belong to the whole event, what really happened? Neither natural scientists nor literary critics can accept the midrash hypothesis because it is self-contradictory. The supposition that Matthew's narrative is a midrashic story seems to contradict the result of modern literary criticism, and precludes even the possibility of historical and astronomical explanations of the Star.

Léon-Dufour (1963) says that the content of the infancy narratives also belongs to the apostolic tradition. In agreement with many biblical scholars he states that the cause of the erroneous judgment of Matthew's account was an exaggerated historical criticism. He takes the midrash hypothesis for the result of a superficial methodology which exaggerated the importance of Old Testament elements. The literary analysis of the original text shows that Matthew did not use the midrashic method of conveying truth through bare story. The visit of the Magi in Bethlehem and the star they observed are preserved in several other sources from the first centuries. Besides the Protovangelium of James there are five Apocryphal Infancy Gospels which claim to contain supplementary information in regard to the circumstances of Jesus' birth and childhood.

The Apocryphal Gospels have not been accepted into the Church's official canon. They differ from the canonical writings by the excess of the miraculous element in their stories and by the esoteric aspect of their teachings. Their value consists in the evidence they offer for the first movements of Christian thinking. The canonical writings are those which belong to the list of sacred books the Church officially declared to be inspired by the Holy Spirit and to contain a rule of faith and morals.

Our astronomical explanation, the planetary conjunction hypothesis, does not divert attention from the theological meaning of Matthew's narrative, but corroborates it in accordance with the author's intention. Indeed, in the first century there were Christians like Matthew who had known the messianic significance of the conjunction of Jupiter and Saturn in Pisces. David Hughes has in his book collected considerable material to show this fact, and the present work supplements it with further arguments. We have to distinguish between an objective scientific methodology and a subjective arbitrary method. To explain certain phenomena we can use one of two entirely dissimilar approaches. One is to make up an explanation out of imagination or intuition. This is the source of all myths, legends and science fiction. The other approach is the scientific method: we make observations, and with the controlled data at hand we formulate hypotheses to explain the phenomena. Then we subject such hypotheses to critical tests to ascertain their validity.

Modern experts of different disciplines seek to harmonize and unify their knowledge. George V.Coyne, S.J. director of the Vatican Observatory defines this tendency as follows:

> The supposition is that there is a universal basis for our understanding and, since that basis cannot be self-contradictory, the understanding we have from one discipline should complement that which we have from all other disciplines. One is most faithful to one's own discipline, be it the natural sciences, the social sciences, philosophy, literature, theology, etc., if one accepts this universal basis. This means in practice that, while remaining faithful to the strict truth criteria of one's own discipline, we are open to accept the truth value of the conclusions of other disciplines. And this acceptance must not only be passive, in the sense that we do not deny those conclusions, but also active,in the sense that we integrate those conclusions into the conclusions derived from one's own proper discipline... The attempt to resolve the differences will bring us to a richer unified understanding (Coyne 1999).

8. *Myth and Tradition*

Grundmann in his commentary on Matthew (Grundmann 1968) refers to the exegetes who traced the narrative about Jesus' birth back to ancient myths and legends. Some of them took it for an imitation of the legend of the birth of Moses, as it was narrated by Josephus Flavius (*Ant. Iud.* II. 9, 2). These assumptions have been refuted both by biblicists and by scholars in the history of literature. The Gospel of Matthew surely had been written before the fall of Jerusalem (70 AD), and Josephus wrote his work 20 years later in Rome. Matthew did not know about the ancient myths, and astrological predictions could not have prompted him to write a legend about the birth of Christ.

The evangelists sealed their works with their own blood. The apostle Peter shortly before his crucifixion (29 June 67 AD) wrote the following sentence in the name of all the apostles: "For we did not follow cleverly devised myths when we made known to you the power and coming of our Lord Jesus Christ, but we were eyewitnesses of his majesty." The apostles John and Paul also condemned the myths, as in opposition to the "sound teaching" (2 Pet 1:16; 1 Tim 1:4; 2 Tim 4:4; 1 Jn 1:1).

There are Babylonian and Greek myths which have certain similarities with some of the Scriptural narratives. It was during the 19th century that those myths more and more became widespread in Westeuropean literary circles. Some scholars of the history of religion attempted to prove that the Bible also belonged to the mythology of antiquity, and that it was not an infallible work inspired by God. As a reaction to this antireligious criticism, fundamentalist conservatism defended the word for word inspiration of the Biblical texts. Fundamentalist exegetes opposed the scientific study of the Scriptures and sought to defend nearly every sentence of the Bible in what they took to be its obvious sense. They failed to recognize the distinction between various literary forms within the historical books of the Bible.

At the beginning of the 20th century, biblicists sought new methods of exegesis to overcome both the extreme modernist and the fundamentalist view. They agreed that the Bible contained divine revelations expressed by words and images generally known at that time. The prophets and evangelists had used the mythical language and imagery in a serious effort to express in words an intuition of transcendent reality. The Fathers of the Church explained the deeper meaning which was hidden in the scriptural images and parables. As the prophets had cleansed the ancient writings of mythological elements, likewise the Fathers defended the real person and life of Christ against mythological beliefs, and they never doubted the historical authenticity of the gospel narratives.

Those who forsook this patristic tradition and believed that the Gospel was a new version of the ancient Greek myths, were happy to read the new critical analyses of Rudolf Bultmann (1948, 1958). Bultmann intended to overcome the difficulty of communicating the Christian message in the 20th century, in a world where faith was no longer easy. With his demythologizing interpretation Bultmann became one of the most influential exegetes in the history of biblical studies, even though many disagree with his conclusions. According to Bultmann, the Gospel is characterized by a mythological eschatology. In the language of traditional theology eschatology is the doctrine of the last things, i.e., the imminent end of the world, the final judgment and also the beginning of eternal bliss in the Kingdom of God. These conceptions are mythological, says Bultmann, and were current among the Greeks, too. However, the Greek philosophers did not agree with Christian eschatology of cosmic events at the end of time. They found the imminent power of the gods in destiny (Bultmann 1958).

The earliest Christian community expected the Kingdom of God to come in the immediate future, but their hope was not fulfilled. The same world still exists and history continues. In his scientific worldview modern man does not believe that the course of nature and of history can be interrupted by supernatural powers or by any intervention of God. Modern man finds the mythological worldview in the Gospel incredible. Bultmann suggested the following solution:

> We must ask whether the eschatological preaching and the mythological sayings as a whole contain a still deeper meaning which is concealed under the cover of mythology. If that is so, let us abandon the mythological conceptions precisely because we want to retain their deeper meaning. This method of interpretation of the New Testament which tries to recover the deeper meaning behind the mythological conceptions I call demythologizing, an unsatisfactory word, to be sure. Its aim is not to eliminate the mythological statements but to interpret them (Bultmann 1958, p.18).

With a profoundly pastoral desire to make the saving message of Christ available to modern man, Bultmann urged an historical sense of reality and an existentialist analysis in exegesis. In other words his purpose was to illuminate the real understanding of human life contained in the teaching of Christ. One example for this interpretion is St. John's "realized eschatology", i.e., his emphasis on eternal life here and now, not in some distant future. Eschatological teaching shows the present time in the light of the future; the world of nature and history in which we live and make our plans is a temporal and transitory world, ultimately empty in face of eternity. Modern man seems to be unable to understand these conceptions.

However, it is possible that Biblical eschatology will gain force again, says Bultmann in his later reflection on this problem:

> It will gain force not in its old mythological form but in the terrifying vision that modern natural science, especially nuclear physics, may bring about the destruction of our Earth through the abuse of high technology. When we ponder this possibility, we can feel the terror and the anxiety which were evoked by the eschatological preaching of the imminent end of the world. To be sure, that preaching was developed in conceptions which are no longer intelligible today, but they do express the knowledge of the finiteness of the world, and of the end which is imminent to us all because we all are beings of this finite world. This is the insight to which as a rule we turn a blind eye, but which may be brought to light by modern technology (Bultmann 1958, p.25).

The biblicists agree that the Gospel must be interpreted with an "historical sense of reality" and with regard to the "existential wants of modern man". Disagreement with Bultmann has not been directed against the basic need to "demythologize" or reinterpret some of the mythical imagery of the Gospel, but against Bultmann's judgment on what is unacceptable imagery or myth. For instance, miracles and the resurrection from the dead, which for Bultmann were no longer meaningful for modern man, remain very meaningful in the judgment of other scholars.

As Cardinal Joseph Ratzinger said at a recent meeting on exegetical problems: "the great achievement of Bultmann was that he definitely pointed out the need for a correct method of interpretation of Scripture, but unfortunately, he was too devoted to some assumptions which greatly reduced the value of his solution". He denied the connection between the Old and New Testament as well as between the original message of Christ and the preaching of the evangelists. He exaggerated the difference between the Israelite and Greek traditions, and between the teaching of Jesus of Nazareth and those of the first Christian communities. Here he assigned most of the material in these teachings to the creative imagination of the early Christian communities.

The one-sided historical and existentialist analysis breaks the Bible up into unconnected parts, it separates spiritual and material reality, and it also separates the creature from its Creator. Regarding these problems, Cardinal Ratzinger quoted the decree of the Vatican Council II on the scientific method of literary and historical criticism (*Constitution on Divine Revelation* III). Correct exegesis always takes into consideration the following factors: (1) age of the single books, and the cultural and social circumstances of the biblical author; (2) intention of the author by determining the literary form he has employed (history or story, prophecy or apocalyptic, parable or apologue, epic or lyric poetry, etc.); (3) accurate translation of the original text, with expressions suitable for modern language; (4) theological interpretation of the original text, based on the intrinsic unity of the Scriptures. (Ratzinger 1989).

What does the "absolute unity of the Scriptures" mean? The text of the Bible was written over a period of centuries by different authors, in Hebrew, Aramaic and Greek. Yet in spite of these circumstances, we find an inherent connection between the single writings, because the authors are lead by the same spirit. A common purpose assures the material unity of the different writings, the essence of which is the history of the creation and salvation of the world. Keeping this in mind we can correctly understand the scriptural accounts. But to take a passage out of its context and interpret it on its own, can easily lead to a mistaken conclusion. For example, the narrative of the Magi of Matthew taken as a passage from its biblical context seems to be a merely mythological story. But if we consider it in close connection with the whole of Scripture, we can clearly see its significance in salvation history: after the birth of the Messiah, even the men of science observing the stars recognized the good news of salvation which concerns both all mankind and the whole of the created cosmos.

What is the relation between the Gospel and mythology? The visit of the Magi in Bethlehem gives the answer: the life and teaching of Christ is the realization and interpretation of all the myths. The history of religion and depth-psychological research show that the ancient myths express psychic realities which are independent of the literary form. The symbols and metaphors change with time, but the deepest ideals and desires of the human psyche are the same today as they were thousands of years ago. The hidden elements of ancient myths reflect some truth about the relation between Man and God, but it is expressed in a vague and confusing mode, because the ancient people were hardly conscious of it. It is only the Christian Gospel that makes people realize that "God so loved the world that he gave his only Son, that whoever believes in him should not perish but have eternal life" (Jn 3:16).

The brightest thinkers of the first Christian centuries could well have said that the Gospel became the end of myth, because all the mythological anticipations and aspirations were fulfilled by the historical person and work of Christ. Reborn in the sacrament of baptism we are protected from the forces which are active in our psyche, because we consciously choose the Kingdom of Christ, as a deliverance from the subconscious mythological gods. This is shown in the introduction of the Gospel by the account of the Magi from the East, who found the Savior King and were delivered from the darkness of star-worship because they had believed in the prophets.

Scholars of the psychology of religion also investigate the narratives of the Bible from the view point of mythological language, because the similarity of the phraseology in both is obvious. According to the latest document of the Pontifical Biblical Commission, psychological considerations can complement the method of historical criticism. There are many cases which show the possibility of collaboration between exegetes and psychologists. This is instanced, for example, when they look for the sense of ancient sacrificial ceremonies, or for the meaning of metaphorical language, or of the symbolical significance of some miracles, or when they try to discover the deeper roots of the drama in apocalyptic visions. (Cf. *The Interpretation of Bible in the Church,* I. 15 April 1993). As to psychological research, the most important discovery of Jung is the collective unconscious with its archetypes. For instance, the figure of a king of divine power, who defeats the evil one and saves his people, is the projection of an archetype living in the collective unconscious sphere of the human psyche. This can explain the similarity of certain mythological and biblical expressions which have a common psychological origin. According to Jung:

> The unconscious is a psychological borderline concept, which covers all psychic contents or processes which are not conscious, i.e., not related to the *ego* in any perceptible way. We can distinguish a personal unconscious, comprising all the aquisitions of personal life, everything forgotten, repressed, thought, felt. But, in addition to these contents, there are other contents which do not originate in personal aquisitions but in the inherited possibility of psychic functioning in general. These are the mythological associations, the motifs and images which can spring up anew anytime anywhere, independently of historical tradition or migration. I call these contents the collective unconscious, the sphere of the psyche which is common to all mankind (Jung 1971, *Psychological Types,* p.483, Definitions 56).

The concept of the subconscious was formerly used to include the preconscious (what can be recalled by effort) and the personal unconscious. Jung demonstrates with many examples that the depth-psychological nature of humankind has not changed under the influence of the modern scientific worldview. In the dreams and imaginations of the people of our time, in their novels and works of art, the same archetypes play the principle roles as in the ancient myths. We can find the modern forms of these archetypes in science fiction novels. For example, there are some superhuman beings represented by means of modern physics and technology, who travel to Earth from other planets by flying saucers or UFOs, in order to save mankind; or there are some earthly scientists traveling by a large missile in space, until they find a wonderful new planet where they land and live in peace for ever.

These archetypical wish-dreams have been realized by the lifework of Christ, not as unconscious projections, but as historical facts. The Gospel narratives are no mythological borrowings. They reveal such living realities which meet the deepest claims of the human psyche. The psychologist may call these *mythical realities,* but in the language of theology these are the mysteries of Christ: the incarnation, birth, sacrifice by crucifixion, resurrection and ascension of Christ, are real historical events proved by the writings of trustworthy eye-witnesses. However,these events still remain mysteries, because they surpass our capacity to understand. In any case we can understand that these historical mysteries are not contrary to the requirements of human reason, and that they even are appropriate and necessary for our general well being. We need to know about these truths regarding our eternal salvation.

The biblicists admit that depth-psychology can give considerable help for the interpretation of certain passages of Scripture, but the revelations given in the Gospel can not be traced back only to the archetypes of the collective unconscious of mankind. A more definite answer based on the history of religion is given by Eliade, a modern authority in this field. He explains that the myth has no historical value, because it never refers to a definite time and place, and when it relates to a historical person, it still ends up as a legend or a folk-story. Contrary to this, the Christian Gospel relates to real historical places and times, to the years of the Emperors Augustus and Tiberius in Rome, and the years of Herod and Pilate in Judaea, which were hallowed by the presence of Christ. In conclusion Eliade states that:

> Christianity leads to a theology of history, and not only to a philosophy, because the incarnation of God in the historical person of Jesus Christ transcends the limits of earthly existence; its aim is the eternal salvation of mankind. Rationalistic historicism is a by-product [Abfallsprodukt] of Christianity; it attaches a decisive importance to the historical event, which is an idea of Christian origin, but it considers the event in itself only, precluding the possibility that the event can have a supernatural world-saving meaning (Eliade 1957, II.a).

9. Kepler's New Star

John Kepler was adjunct astronomer to Tycho Brahe for two years, and after Brahe's death, in 1601 AD, he was appointed Imperial Mathematician and Astronomer to the Holy Roman Emperor Rudolph, King of Bohemia and Hungary. It was late at night on 17 December, 1603 AD, when Kepler from the tower of the imperial castle in Prague observed the first conjunction of Jupiter and Saturn. He determined the positions and motions of the two planets in the constellation of Sagittarius, and found that they would approach each other twice again in the course of the next seven months. His further calculations showed that the planet Mars would join Saturn and then Jupiter in September 1604 AD. On 9 October 1604 AD Kepler discovered a very unusual astronomical phenomenon: a point as bright as Jupiter appeared in the sky three degrees to the west of Mars and Jupiter, and four degrees to the east of Saturn. Some people thought it was only a ball of luminous vapor in the Earth's atmosphere. But Kepler knew that it was a remote "New Star", because he had already read the book of Tycho Brahe entitled De Nova Stella. Brahe observed and described one of the greatest "New Stars" in the constellation of Cassiopeia, which was visible from November 1572 until May 1574. He called it Nova, which literally means "New". Today we know that such novae are old stars which suddenly emit an outburst of light, and they remain bright for a few weeks or months and then gradually fade.

This same type of phenomenon occurred again in October 1604 AD among the stars of the constellation of Serpentarius (Ophiuchus in modern star catalogues). Kepler observed it for a year and wrote down his observations in a book entitled De Stella Nova in Pede Serpentarii, i.e., "About a New Star at the Foot of the Serpent Holder". And just because this nova outburst occurred immediately after the conjunction of the three

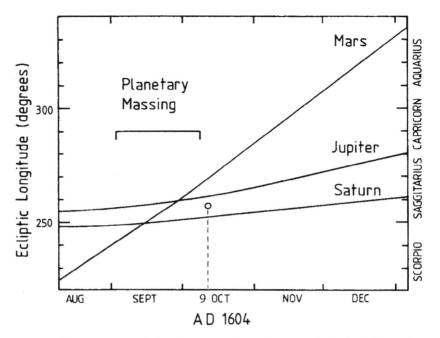

Fig. 28: The massing of the three superior planets and Kepler's New Star on 9 October 1604 AD. (Hughes 1979)

superior planets, Kepler supposed a causal connection between the two phenomena considering the "New Star" as an effect of that "fiery triplet".

This astronomical phenomenon reminded Kepler of Matthew's account. Might not the star of Bethlehem be a phenomenon like this one which occurred in 1604 AD? From the observed conjunctions he calculated backward in time to check up if a similar phenomenon had occurred around the year of Christ's birth. His calculations proved that a conjunction of Jupiter and Saturn occurred three times in the year 7 BC, and Mars joined them in February 6 BC. Thus he supposed that this "fiery triplet" may have caused a "New Star" which was visible in the sky over Judaea also in 6 BC, and that this Nova may have signaled the birth of Christ.

However, it was a problem for Kepler that this astronomical event was six years before the birth of Christ, and he had no evidence to think that there was a miscalculation of the beginning of the Christian era. All the more did he rejoice when he received the work of Laurentius Suslyga about the year of the birth and death of Jesus: *Theoremata de anno ortus ac mortis Domini.* The Polish scholar was the first who demonstrated with historical evidence that it was at least four years before our era that Christ came into the world when king Herod was still alive. As to this discovery Kepler wrote the following in the preface of his book dedicated to Emperor Rudolph:

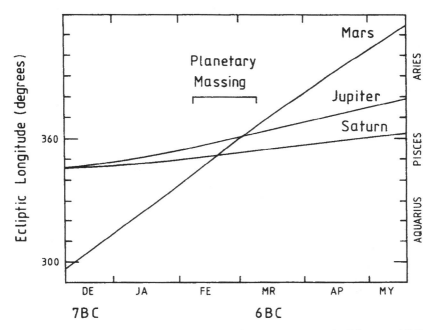

Fig. 29: The conjunction of Mars, Saturn and Jupiter in Pisces in February 6 BC. (Hughes 1979)

Taking great pleasure in the argument of this treatise [of Suslyga] I went on to think that I should accommodate it to my treatise about the New Star of the Serpent Holder. For if the statement of the author is true, as it is in my opinion, that we must add four years to the current Christian epoch to determine the accurate time of Christ, Jesus was born a year or two years after the great conjunction of the three superior planets... Therefore, the star which led the Magi to the manger of Christ may be compared to our new star... It is not so much the importance of my own matter but rather some peculiar purpose that urges me to accept and repeat the theorem of Laurentius Suslyga: I wish that as many people as possible shall recognize its truth. For I am afraid it will be ignored or neglected especially because the new book of the author emphasizes the question of chronology, and only a few people are adept at this discipline; moreover, because there are some great scholars whose opinions weigh against the author..., it is not without reason that I have proposed to contribute to a more general recognition of Suslyga's theorem also by very careful astronomical arguments (Kepler, *De Stella Nova*, pp.5-6).

As to the two astronomical phenomena, the "fiery triplet" of Mars, Jupiter, and Saturn in 1604 AD was indeed similar to that which had occurred in 6 BC, but there was not any nova outburst visible in Judaea in

6 BC. Nevertheless, it was this astronomical observation that induced Kepler to investigate the historical documents which he had found at the Imperial Library of Prague, and to write his original chronological treatise.

Who were those "great scholars" whose opinions would impede the recognition of Suslyga's truth? Kepler mentions two of his contemporaries and turns against them because "they add only one or two years to the Christian epoch". The first was Joseph Scaliger in Netherlands (1540-1609 AD) who was acknowledged as the founder of mathematical chronology. The other was the historian Cardinal Cesare Baronius in Rome (1538-1607 AD) who had written a universal history of the Church from Christ's birth until 1198 AD (*Annales Ecclesiastici Libri XII*). It was typical at that time that scholarly circles with reference to those authorities rejected all new assumptions and results. Theologians disregarded Kepler's work, but they could not refute his statements about the mistake in calculating the years after Christ's birth.

Kepler worked seven years on this chronological problem, and published his assumptions and results in three books: *De Jesu Christi Servatoris Vero Anno Natalitio*, Frankfurt 1606; *Teutscher Bericht vom Geburtsjahr Jesu Christi*, Strassburg 1613; *De Vero Anno quo Aeternus Patri Filius humanam naturam assumpsit*, Frankfurt 1614. Kepler's florid baroque style poses a difficulty for the reading of his works. Another difficulty is that he dates the events with Julian years, counted from the year of the Julian reform of the calendar (46 BC), and he does not convert these into the dates of our calendar. He merely says that "the incorrectly determined Christian era begins with the first day of January of the forty-sixth Julian year". To understand this we must know the history of the calendar. The old Roman calendar was dated from the founding of the City of Rome, *ab urbe condita* (AUC), introduced by Varro with the epoch 21 April of the first year of the Roman Republic, and ratified by Julius Caesar in the year 708 AUC. The first year of the Roman Republic was placed by Dionysius Exiguus in 753 BC. Thus 708 AUC equals 46 BC, and the forty-sixth Julian year equals 754 AUC, i.e., the first year of the Christian era, or 1 AD according to the computation of Dionysius. In this way Kepler supposes that the first census and then the massacre of the Innocents (who were two years old or under) in Bethlehem may have been accomplished in the fortieth Julian year, i.e.,in 6 BC, because he takes it for proven that King Herod died on 3 April in the forty-second Julian year, i.e., in 4 BC.

We have to acknowledge that the Imperial Astronomer sincerely sought the truth and did very good work, although by means of the available data at that time he could not arrive at more accurate results.

Modern spectroscopic measurements show that Tycho's star (B Cassiopeiae, 1572) as well as Kepler's star (SN Ophiuchi, 1604) are supernovae inside our Galaxy. In contrast to an ordinary nova a supernova means a gigantic stellar explosion in which the star's luminosity increases hundreds of millions of times its former brightness, and most of the star's substance is blown off, leaving behind an extremely dense core and an expanding gaseous nebula ejected by the star. The remnants of the supernovae of Tycho and Kepler were found and photographed with the 200 inch Hale telescope on Palomar Mountain in California in 1950. Both are registered in the catalogue of the cosmic radio sources.

Fig. 30: The picture on the title page of Kepler's book shows his sense of humor: a hen scratching about the dung hill seeks grain for her little chickens. This may well mean that "One who searches always finds".

Twenty years ago some astronomers began again to propound and advocate the nova hypothesis concerning the star of Bethlehem. They assumed that the star of Bethlehem was the nova of 5 BC which was recorded in the Chinese Annals, and that Kepler perhaps thought the conjunction of the three superior planets in 6 BC caused this nova of 5 BC. As to this assumption we must remark the following: (1) Kepler knew nothing of the ancient Chinese records, and never mentioned a nova in the year 5 BC; (2) as David Hughes has shown, there is not sufficient evidence available to enable us to decide whether the star *Huihsing* recorded in the Chinese Annals in 5 BC was a nova or a comet. According to the catalogue of *Hsi-Tsê-tsung* it was a "sweeping star" or "sparkling star" in the constellation Aquila; and according to the catalogue of *Ho Pen Yoke* it was a comet in Capricornus, both visible for 70 days; (3) the Magi in Matthew's narrative observed the "star" in its evening rising, and when it "halted in its course", and they interpreted it definitely as the sign for the birth of the awaited Messiah king. In contrast to this "star" a nova, or a comet does not stop in its course, and they were never interpreted as celestial symbols for the birth of kings.

On this subject we follow the opinion of Hughes:

The complete lack of astrological significance of the star *Huihsing* in 5 BC, its single appearance, and close proximity to Herod's death make it impossible to consider it as the star of Bethlehem (Hughes 1979, p.157).

10. *Date of Jesus' Resurrection*

The date of the passion and resurrection of Jesus of Nazareth is confirmed by the entire apostolic tradition as well as by astronomical calculation. But before going on with this, it is necessary to say something about the Hebrew Calendar. From the 5th century BC until the 4th century AD, the priests of Jerusalem used the Babylonian luni-solar calendar based on the lunar synodic month, the average length of which was 29 days 12 hours 44 minutes. This is the time from one new moon to the next following. The calendar year was composed of six hollow months (29 days) and six full months (30 days), totaling 354 days. This lunar year was 11 days shorter than the solar tropical year of 365 days, the period of revolution of the Earth around the Sun with respect to the vernal equinox. In order to adjust the lunar year to the seasons, each third year or so an extra month of 30 days was inserted into the calendar after the 12th month. The date of the vernal equinox fell then again on one of the days of the first spring month, *Nisan*.

The first day of every month was determined by direct observation of the new light of the moon, i.e., the first visibility of the waxing crescent. On the 29th or 30th day of each month two priests observed the moon in Jerusalem, and when they saw its first crescent phase, they announced it to the Sanhedrin, the Supreme Priest Council. The chief priest ordered then that they should blow the trumpets to signal for the people the beginning of the new month, as it is written in the Psalm (81:3-4): "Blow the trumpet at the new moon, and at the full moon, on our feast day, for it is a statute for Israel." According to the Jerusalem Temple Calendar the first day of every lunar month was a feast day. The two greatest feasts, Passover and Tabernacles, began at full moon on the 14/15th day of the first month *Nisan* (March/April) in memory of the liberation from Egypt, and on the 14/15th day of the seventh month *Tishri* (September/October) in memory of the period in the desert. Both feasts lasted seven days.

The week comprising seven consecutive days denoted by serial numbers is of very ancient Hebrew origin. The name of the seventh day of the week is *sabbath*, which is connected with a root meaning "to desist, to stop work". The *Sabbath* is a weekly day of rest dedicated to the Lord who "rested on the seventh day of creation". But while it does homage to God, it also benefits man (cf. Gen 2:2; Ex 20: 8-11; 23:12; Mt 12:1-8). In lunar calendars the day began usually at sunset (about 6 p.m.). The people of Jerusalem, however, reckoned the hours of the day from sunrise (about six o'clock a.m.). They could estimate the hour of the day observing the altitude of the Sun and the length of the shadow. The preparation day for the feast began always at sunset, about 6 p.m. as provided by law.

The authors of the Gospel and the apostles relate when and how Jesus of Nazareth died on the cross. Pilate condemned him to death on "the Passover Preparation Day, at about the sixth hour", i.e., about noon, says the apostle John (19:14), and Matthew remarks that "from the sixth hour there was darkness over all the land until the ninth hour, and about the ninth hour,Jesus crying out in a loud voice yielded his spirit" (Mt 27:45-50). That is to say, Jesus died between 2 and 3 o'clock in the afternoon on a Friday. The Apostles state unanimously that Jesus rose again on the third day after his crucifixion, and it was after the sabbath, towards dawn on the first day of the week, i.e., it occurred by Sunday morning, according to our calendar (Mt 27:1; Jn 20:1). Which year was it? In that year the feast of Unleavened Bread began on a sabbath (Saturday), which, according to the Law, must have been the 15th day of Nisan; thus the preparation must have begun on Friday, the 14th day of Nisan. In the course of this day the Passover supper was made ready, and everything necessary prepared so that the feast could be celebrated without violating the rest prescribed by the Law.

It was a moonlit night of spring when the Lord through Moses brought his people out of Egypt, and then he ordered that the month of *Abib* must be the first month of their year, and on the 14th day of this month they must slaughter the lambs; then for seven days they must eat unleavened bread. The month of *Abib* in Canaan was the month of young ears of corn, and this was called *Nisan* after the Exile.(Cf. Ex 12:1,6,15; Lev 23:5f; Deut 16:1f). In those countries between 30° and 33° geographic latitudes the barley bore ripe ears already at the end of March or at the beginning of April, and it could be gathered. Thus, when the ears began to ripen, the priests were able to recognize the approach of the first month of spring. Also the lambs were born at the end of March or the beginning of April, and according to the statute the Passover lamb for sacrifice must have been "a male one year old". The Jerusalem Talmud tells that the priests checked and adjusted their calendar by observing this rhythm of nature: when they saw that the ears were still unripe and the lambs delayed, they inserted a thirteenth month in order to keep their year in step with the year of the seasons.

From an astronomical point of view one of the most important chapters of the Old Testament is the one which prescribes the observation of the new moon of spring and the full moon next following upon it. These phenomena occur namely when the Sun crosses the celestial equator passing from south to north, and the Moon is in conjunction with the Sun and 14 days after in opposition to it. Now by means of the data found in the Scriptures we can determine the chronological order of the events in the last years of Jesus' earthly life. It was a moonlit night, under the vernal full moon on the 16th of Nisan, between Saturday and Sunday, when the crucified Jesus rose again and came out of the tomb. In which year did it occurr? According to the most probable chronology, Jesus had begun his public ministry in the 29th year of our era, and then he appeared in person on three Passover feasts in Jerusalem. His condemnation and crucifixion took place on the Preparation Day of his fourth Passover in Jerusalem, under Caiaphas the high priest and Pilate the Roman governor. These two officials responsible for Jesus' death held their positions until 36 AD. Between 29 and 36 AD there were only two years, viz. 30 and 33 AD, in which the Passover full moon of the 14th of Nisan fell on a Friday.

The following table shows the data of the vernal new moon and full moon in 30 and 33 AD calculated for the local mean time of Jerusalem. The geographical longitude of Jerusalem is 35°10′ east of Greenwich meridian, which measured in time units corresponds to 2 hours 20 minutes 40 seconds. Thus the local time in Jerusalem is Greenwich Mean Time plus 2h 20m 40s. The Earth rotates to the east at a constant rate of 1° every 4 minutes, thus it takes 24 hours for the Earth to turn through 360° to complete a solar day. Because the direction of the Earth's rotation is to the east, places to the east of us must always have a time more advanced than ours. In general, the difference in the local time of any two places on Earth is equal to their difference in longitude, if longitude is measured in time units. True local noon in Greenwich is the time of the day when the Sun crosses the Greenwich meridian. The Sun crosses the meridian of Jerusalem about 2 hours 21 minutes earlier than the meridian of Greenwich. Therefore, to get the true local time of Jerusalem, 2h 21m must be added to the local mean solar time of the Greenwich meridian.

Year	30 AD	33 AD
new moon	March 22, 20^h30^m	March 19, 13^h21^m
sunset	March 23, 18^h15^m	March 20, 18^h15^m
moon's altitude	March 23, 18^h15^m $9°10'$	March 20, 18^h15^m $10°30'$
new crescent	March 23, 18^h15^m	March 20, 17^h00^m
Nisan 1	March 25, Saturday	March 21, Saturday
full moon	April 6, 22^h24^m	April 3, 17^h35^m
Nisan 14 Nisan 15 Nisan 16	April 7, Friday April 8, Saturday April 9, Sunday	April 3, Friday April 4, Saturday April 5, Sunday

The date given for the new crescent is the time of its possible visibility. The new crescent is usually visible about 20 hours after the astronomical time of the new moon (the exact conjunction of the Sun and Moon), when the Moon's altitude is greater than 10° and its angular distance from the Sun is greater than 5°. On 23 March 30 AD at sunset, the position of the Moon had hardly reached the limit of visibility, and it is very questionable whether the priests of Jerusalem could observe the new light of the crescent. If in the year 30 AD the new crescent was observed in the evening of March 24th, and if March 25th (Nisan 1) fell on a Saturday, then Nisan 14 (April 7th) fell on a Friday. But this remains quite uncertain.

A comparative analysis of the available data shows that the Passover of 33 AD is the most probable time as to Jesus' passion and resurrection, both in historical and in astronomical respect. On the 30th of the month Adar, i.e., 20 March 33 AD, the new crescent was observable already before sunset, when the moon's altitude was still 14 degrees over the southwestern horizon. The visibility was especially good from the western wall of the Temple of Jerusalem, about 750 meters above sea level.

In the year 33 AD the first day of Nisan was Saturday, March 21, and the fourteenth day of Nisan was Friday, April 3 in our calendar. On this Friday, the exact full moon occurred in the hours when the crucifixion took place in Jerusalem. Consequently, the date of Jesus' resurrection must have been the 5th of April 33 AD, towards dawn on Sunday (Mt 28:1).

Based on earlier suppositions some scholars held the year 30 AD more probable for Jesus' passion. They referred to Clement of Alexandria (*Stromata* I.21; 145,2; 146,3) who in the 2nd century recorded the opinion that it was after one year of public ministry that Jesus was condemned to death, in the 16th year of Emperor Tiberius. Other scholars thought that St. Luke reckoned the 15 years until the appearance of John the Baptist from 765 AUC, i.e., from 27 AD, because the old Caesar Augustus had in that year appointed Tiberius to *Collega Imperii* in Syria. Some tried to confirm this opinion with a misinterpreted phrase of John's Gospel (2: 20), saying that the Temple was 46 years old when Jesus at first came into collision with the Scribes of Jerusalem. According to Josephus Flavius the reconstruction work of the Temple began in 20 BC and, adding 46 years, we get 26 or 27 AD for the beginning of Jesus' public ministry.

However, John does not say that the Temple was 46 years old at that time, but that "it has taken forty-six years to build this temple". We do not know exactly when the reconstruction of the Temple began. Furthermore, the evangelist Luke was a Roman citizen, and he certainly used the Roman method of calculating the year of the reign of Tiberius who succeeded Augustus on 19 August 767 AUC, i.e., 14 AD. His 15th year, therefore, was from 19 August 28 AD to 18 August 29 AD. Luke's records in the Acts of the Apostles and Paul's statements in his letter to the Galatians allow us to conclude that the martyrdom of the Deacon Stephen and then the conversion of Paul occurred in autumn of 34 or in spring of 35 AD, about one and a half years after Christ's ascension. (Cf. Acts 7:55-8:2; 11:27-30; 12:25; 15:2; Gal 1:12-18; 2:1-9. The Council of Jerusalem was held in 48/49 AD, fourteen years after Paul's conversion).

The narratives in the four gospels and the apostolic tradition prove that Jesus' public ministry lasted at least three complete years. It was three times that he appeared in the Temple of Jerusalem during the feasts of Passover, when his sermons and his acts more and more enraged the Scribes and Pharisees; because Jesus pointed out to them their wickedness, drove out the dealers from the Temple, and cured sick persons on the day of Sabbath "in defiance of the Law". In the Church a custom was established that each fiftieth year counted from 33 AD be kept as a Jubilee or Holy Year. On 2 April 1933, the last Sunday of Lent, Pope Pius XI ordered a Holy Year to commemorate the 1900th anniversary of Christ's redeeming passion and resurrection. As a preparation for the Jubilee the professors of the Pontifical Biblical Institute together with the astronomers of the Vatican Observatory undertook a comprehensive research work in order to settle the dispute about the two possible dates for Jesus' passion. They found definitively for 33 AD, and their results has been published in a book written in Latin, *Chronologia Vitae Christi* (cf. Holzmeister 1933).

The majority of the historians and chronologists seem today to agree with this conclusion. Corbishley has clearly summarized the historical evidence, and in his chronological table he holds the following dates to be most probable (Corbishley 1975, 706-708):

> BC 8/7 - First Census in Judaea and Jesus' birth
> 6 - Flight into Egypt and massacre of the Innocents
> 4/3 - Return to Nazareth
> AD 28 - in autumn, or in spring of 29, John the Babtist
> 29 - Baptism of Jesus and beginning of his public ministry
> 30 - His first public Passover in Jerusalem (7 April)
> 31 - His second Passover in Jerusalem (25 April)
> 32 - His third Passover in Jerusalem (14 April)
> 33 - His passion and resurrection (3-5 April)
> 34 - in autumn, or in spring of 35, martyrdom of Stephen and conversion of Paul

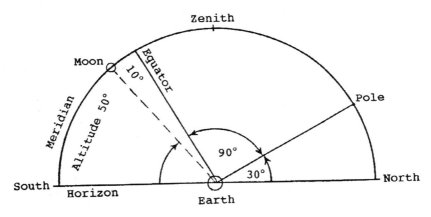

Fig. 31: With the aid of this figure it is easy to calculate the altitude of the Moon on the Meridian, for example, in the latitude 30° N. The latitude of a place equals the altitude of the celestial pole at that place. The altitude of the Moon: H = 180° – (90° + d + l) where l is the latitude, and d is the declination of the Moon.

11. *Chronology of Dionysius Exiguus*

In Encyclopedia and in textbooks we often find the statement that the Christian era, established by the Roman abbot, Dionysius Exiguus, in the 6th century, is the result of an erroneous calculation. However, in order to form a correct opinion of Dionysius' work, we have to know his mathematical method as well as the historical background of his liturgical calendar. Dionysius mentions some incorrect methods of computation which caused disagreement in the first centuries about the date of Easter. This is the reason he was commissioned to present and explain the correct method of determining the date of Easter. In his writing on the Paschal Rules, Dionysius presents his own example of how to calculate the number of the years after the Incarnation of Our Lord. He assumes that Jesus was 33 years and 3 months old when he was crucified (*Argumenta* I and XV). He expresses his intention clearly in his letter to the bishops Boniface and Bonus, written in 526 AD. In this letter he points out that he is well versed in the various chronologies, and that he intends to adapt the civil time reckoning to the Church's liturgical calendar, so that Easter shall be celebrated uniformly on the same day throughout the Church.

The Roman Emperors persecuted the Christians for a period of three hundred years. The last cruel persecutor was Diocletian who had tens of thousands of Christians put to death and their libraries burned. Therefore, Diocletian's era was called the Era of the Martyrs, reckoned from 29 August 1037 AUC (i.e., from 284 AD). Cyril of Alexandria computed his last Paschal Table up to Easter of the 247th year of the era of Diocletian. According to Dionysius this year was 531 AD. It was the Emperor Constantine the Great who put an end to the persecution of Christians by his Edict of Tolerance in 313 AD. Twelve years later, when he became monarch of the entire Roman Empire, he ordered the convocation of the first Ecumenical Council of the Christians in Nicaea, in which 318 bishops from the west and from the east participated. They adopted the Paschal rule which is valid up to the present: Easter Day every year falls on the first Sunday after the fourteenth day of the Moon that occurs on or immediately after the vernal equinox.

The Nicene Council gave the Alexandrian Church the task of reckoning the dates of Easter with the help of the Metonic 19-year cycle. This cycle of lunations was used as the basis of the luni-solar calendar and of the Easter canons of the bishops of Alexandria: Athanasius, Theophilus and Cyril; 235 synodic months, each with 29 days 12 hours 44 minutes, total almost exactly 19 solar years. However, calculating in lunar years we arrive at $12 \times 19 = 228$ synodic months, and the remainder is 7, i.e., it is 7 months and 4 days less than a solar year. Therefore, a complete Metonic cycle has 12 years with 12 synodic months (354 days) and 7 years with 13 synodic months (384 days). Thus in each 235th month the moon phases will be repeated on the same day of the year.

Dionysius has explained all this in detail in his letter to the bishops who asked him to calculate the dates for Easter Sunday in advance for five 19-years cycle, i.e., 95 years. He wrote the following explanation to the Patriarch Petronius:

We shall begin with the fifth 19-year cycle calculated by Cyril, because there are still six years left of this last cycle. Afterwards we will present computations of the five other cycles according to the norm of the same Bishop, or more correctly, in accordance with the rule laid down by the Nicene Synod. Bishop Cyril began his first cycle with the 153rd year of the era of Diocletian, and he ended his last cycle at the 247th year after the same tyrant. But we will not link the memory of this ungodly persecutor to our new cycles. We choose rather to designate time from the Incarnation of Our Lord Jesus Christ, because both the origin of the redemption of mankind and the source of our hope, namely, the Passion of our Redeemer, shall in this way be more manifest... We draw our readers' attention to the fact that this 95-year period does not retain the desired accuracy in all points, when recommenced after one cycle is terminated. The continuous succession of the years of Christ is preserved, and with the help of the fixed rules, we can determine the indictions per fifteen years, as well as the annual lunar adjections, which the Greeks called epacts; that is, the eleven days which shall be added each year to the age of the Moon. The day of *Luna 14 paschalis* will fall on the same date [April 5] in the first year of each 19-year cycle. But the number of weekdays which are left, Easter Sunday, and the age of the Moon on this Sunday, do not occur with the same regularity again... When Lord Almighty decreed that the children of Israel should celebrate this holy feast in memory of the liberation from Egypt..., the legislator Moses reminded the people: Observe the month of young ears of corn, that is the first month of spring, and celebrate the Passover of the Lord your God, because it was in this month that the Lord brought you out of Egypt by night... The 318 Bishops of the Council investigated the tradition of Moses in greater detail, and this is described by Eusebius in the seventh book of his Ecclesiastical Histories. They came to the conclusion that it was the new crescent moon, from and including 8 March up to and including 5 April, which should decide the beginning of the first month. We must, therefore, carefully investigate the days from and including 21 March up to and including 18 April to find *Luna 14 paschalis*. But that does not always occur at the same time during the revolution of the Sun, and we must therefore reckon with a definite number of days after the vernal equinox [21 March] (Dionysius, *Epistola prima,* AD 525).

The first and last day of the year on which Easter Sunday can fall are March 22 and April 25. This old text of Dionysius is strikingly accurate astronomically. He talks consistently about "Luna 14" as being the 14th day after the new moon. But in the tenth century writers began to talk about the "Paschal Full Moon" as being the 14th day of the lunation. This led to some errors. In fact, the 14th day of the Moon is not always full moon. In the course of 365 days the full moon falls only three or four times on the 14th day after the astronomical new moon; but the astronomical full moon generally is Luna 15. And twice per year the full moon occurs on the 16th day after new moon. In Dionysius' Paschal Table for 95 years we find that *Luna 14 paschalis* coincides with full moon forty-five times, while fifty times it falls on the day immediately before the astronomical full moon.

Dionysius reckoned the day from sunrise, which occurs at about 6 a.m. on the days near the vernal equinox. This fact explains some differences between his dates and our modern astronomical dates which are reckoned from midnight Greenwich Mean Time (GMT). For example, the astronomical new moon in 555 AD fell on 9 March at $0^h 39^m$, and full moon on 24 March at $2^h 53^m$ GMT, i.e., Luna 14 occurred on 23 March at $2^h 50^m$ GMT. In the Table of Dionysius we read *Luna 14 paschalis xi.kal.april.*, which is 22 March, because he reckoned the time of the day from 6 a.m. local time in Rome, where a sundial had been used.

How has Dionysius calculated the number of the years after the Incarnation of Our Lord? He gives the following example in the "First Argument on the Years of Christ":

If you want to know how many years have passed since the Incarnation of our Lord Jesus Christ, you must reckon fifteen times 34, which is 510. To this you always add twelve regular years, which makes 522. Then you must also add the indiction figure of the year you require [viz., of the year which you wish to convert]. Now under the Consul Probus Junior it is the third year of indiction, and you will get 525. This is now the number of years reckoned from Our Lord's Incarnation (Dionysius 525 AD, *Argumenta Paschalia* I).

Whereas the complicated and uncertain historical chronologies are confusing, this mathematical formula of Dionysius is clear and easy to use. The only problem in this formula is the expression "indiction", which seems to be the key to the correct conclusion. An indiction cycle was a tax period of 15 years. In the Roman Empire there was a census in every 15th year, and the tax year began on 1st September. Because the indiction cycles were not numbered, one must always use the indiction figure for a stipulated year in combination with another system, usually with the Consul dating. The Roman Consuls took over office on 1st January, and the civil year was reckoned from that day. Consul dating together with the indiction figures were officially introduced by the Emperor Constantine the Great in 1065 AUC (312 AD). From this year on there are tables giving the indiction figures for each year. Although Dionysius does not mention it explicitly, it is obvious that he has used these indiction tables together with the consular dates to convert the Roman years into years of Christ.

The indiction figure of a year AUC is found as the remainder when the date of year is divided by 15. If the remainder is zero (0), the indiction is 15. The first Roman year that Dionysius has converted into "the year of Christ" has indiction 3 under Consul Probus Junior. This is 1278 AUC under the Emperor Theoderic; 1278/15 = 85, and the remainder is 3. According to Dionysius the Christian era began on 25 March 753 AUC. This year also has the indiction 3, and 12 years remain of the complete cycle.

Thus we can understand why Dionysius uses the figures 15, 34 and 12 in his first paschal rule (Argument I). Together with the Bishops of the Church he is well aware of the fact that 500 years have past since the birth of Christ, and this time interval constitutes at least 34 full indiction cycles. But 15 times 34 equals 510, and to this we must add the 12 regular years which remain after our starting point (753 AUC with indiction 3). In this way we arrive at the date 522 which coincides with a Roman year (1275 AUC) with indiction 15. Adding the indiction figure of the stipulated year AUC, for example 3, of the year of Consul Probus, we get 525 AD for 1278 AUC. Therefore, in Dionysious' Paschal Tables, in the second column the indiction figures of the Roman years AUC follow immediately the years of Christ AD. Thus Dionysius begins the 95-year period with *"The Year of Our Lord Jesus Christ 532, Indiction 10, Epact 0, Concurrent Days 4, Moon Cycle 17, Luna 14 Paschalis 5 April, Easter Sunday 11 April on Luna 20"* (See Fig. 32, p. 218). From the year 532 on, each fourth year is marked with **B**, which means Bissextile or leap year (366 days).

CYCLUS DECEMNOVENNALIS DIONYSII.

Incipit cyclus decemnovennalis, quem Græci Enneacaidecaeterida vocant, constitutus a sanctis Patribus, in quo quartas decimas paschales omni tempore sine ulla reperies falsitate; tantum memineris annis singulis, qui cyclus lunæ et qui decemnovennalis existat. In præsenti namque tertia indictio est, consulatu Probi junioris, tertius decimus circulus decemnovennalis, decimus lunaris est ª.

ANNI DIOCLETIANI.	QUÆ SINT INDICTIONES.	EPACTÆ, ID EST ADJECTIONES LUNÆ.	CONCURRENTES DIES.	QUOTUS SIT LUNÆ CIRCULUS.	QUÆ SIT LUNA XIIII PASCHALIS.	DIES DOMINICÆ FESTIVITATIS.	QUOTA SIT LUNA IPSIUS DIEI DOMINICI.
CCXXVIIII	vi	nulla	i	xvii	non. april.	vii id. april.	xvi
CCXXX	vii	xi	ii	xviii	viii kal. april.	iii kal. april.	xviiii
CCXXXi	viii	xxii	iii	xviiii	id. april.	xiii kal. mai.	xx
CCXXXii	viiii	liii	v	i	iiii non. april.	iii non. april.	xv
CCXXXiii	x	xiiii	vi	ii	xi kal. april.	vi kal. april.	xvii
CCXXXiiii	xi	xxv	vii	iii	iiii id. april.	xvii kal. mai.	xviiii
CCXXXV	xii	vi	i	iiii	iii kal. april.	ii kal. april.	xv
CCXXXVi	xiii	xvii	iii	v	xiiii kal. mai.	xiii kal. april.	xv ogd.
CCXXXVii	xiiii	xxviii	iiii	vi	vii id. april.	iii id. april.	xvii
CCXXXViii	xv	viiii	v	vii	vi kal. april.	iii non. april.	xxi
CCXXXViiii	i	xx	vi	viii	xvii kal. mai.	xvi kal. mai.	xv
CCXL	ii	i	i	viiii	ii non. april.	vii id. april.	xvii
CCXLi ᵇ	iii	xii	ii	x	ix kal. april.	iii kal. april.	xx
CCXLii ᶜ	iiii	liii	iii	xi	ii id. april.	xiii kal. mai.	xxi
CCXLiii	v	iiii	iiii	xii	kal. april.	ii non. april.	xvii
CCXLiiii	vi	vi	vi	xiii	xii kal. april.	vii kal. april.	xviiii
CCXLV	vii	vii	vii	xiiii	v id april.	xvii kal. mai.	xx
CCXLVi	viii	i	i	xv	iiii kal. april.	ii kal. april.	xvi
CCXLVii	viiii	ii	ii	xvi	xv kal. mai.	xii kal. mai.	xvii hend.

ANNI DOMINI NOSTRI JESU CHRISTI.	QUÆ SINT INDICTIONES.	EPACTÆ, ID EST ADJECTIONES LUNÆ.	CONCURRENTES DIES.	QUOTUS SIT LUNÆ CIRCULUS.	QUÆ SIT LUNA XIIII PASCHALIS.	DIES DOMINICÆ FESTIVITATIS.	QUOTA SIT LUNA IPSIUS DIEI DOMINICI.
B DXXXii	x	nulla	iiii	xvii	non. april.	iii id. april.	xx
DXXXiii ª	xi	xi	v	xviii	viii kal. april.	vi kal. april.	xvi
DXXXiiii	xii	xxii	vi	xviiii	id. april.	xvi kal. mai.	xvii
DXXXV	xiii	liii	vii	i	iii non. april.	vi id. april.	xx
B DXXXVi	xiiii	xiiii	ii	ii	xi kal. april.	x kal. april.	xv
DXXXVii	xv	xxv	iii	iii	iiii id. april.	ii id. april.	xvi
DXXXViii	i	vi	iiii	iiii	iii kal. april.	ii non. april.	xviiii
DXXXViiii	ii	xvii	v	v	xiiii kal. mai.	viii kal. mai.	xx ogd.
B DXL	iii	xxviii	vii	vi	vii id. april.	vi id. april.	xv
DXLi	iiii	viiii	i	vii	vi kal. april.	ii kal. april.	xviii
DXLii	v	xx	ii	viii	xvii kal. mai.	xii kal. mai.	xviiii
DXLiii	vi	i	iii	viiii	ii non april.	non. april.	xv
B DXLiiii	vii	xii	v	x	viiii kal. april.	vi kal. april.	xvii
DXLV	viii	xxiii	vi	xi	ii id. april.	xvi kal. mai.	xviii
DXLVi	viiii	iiii	vii	xii	kal. april.	vi id. april.	xxi
DXLVii	x	xv	i	xiii	xii kal. april.	viiii kal. april	xvii
B DXLViii	xi	xxvi	iii	xiiii	v id. april.	ii id. april.	xvii
DXLViiii	xii	vii	iiii	xv	iiii kal. april.	ii non. april.	xx
DL	xiii	xviii	v	xvi	xv kal. mai.	viii kal. mai.	xxi hend.

B DCViii	xi	nulla	i	xvii	non. april.	vii id. april.	xvi
DCViiii	xii	xi	ii	xviii	viii kal. april.	iii kal. april.	xviiii
DCX	xiii	xxii	iii	xviiii	id. april.	xiii kal. mai.	xx
DCXi	xiiii	iii	iv	i	iiii non. april.	ii non. april.	xvi
B DCXii	xv	xiiii	vi	ii	xi kal. april.	vii kal. april.	xviii
DCXiii	i	xxv	vii	iii	iiii id. april.	xvii kal. mai.	xviiii
DCXiiii	ii	vi	i	iiii	iii kal. april.	ii kal. april.	xv
DCXV	iii	xvii	ii	v	xiiii kal. mai.	xii kal. mai.	xvi ogd.
B DCXVi	iiii	xxviii	iiii	vi	vii id. april.	iii id. april.	xviii
DCXVii	v	viiii	v	vii	vi kal. april.	iii non. april.	xxi
DCXViii	vi	xx	vi	viii	xvii kal. mai.	xvi kal. april.	xv
DCXViiii	vii	i	vii	viiii	ii non april.	vi id. april.	xviii
B DCXX	viii	xii	i	x	viiii kal. april.	iii kal. april.	xx
DCXXi	viiii	xxii	iii	xi	ii id. april.	xiii kal. mai.	xxi
DCXXii	x	iiii	iiii	xii	kal. april.	ii non. april.	xvii
DCXXiii	xi	xv	v	xiii	xii kal. april.	vi kal. april.	xx
B DCXXiiii	xii	xxvi	vii	xiiii	v id. april.	xvii kal. mai.	xvii
DCXXV	xiii	vii	i	xv	iiii kal april.	ii kal. april.	xvi
DCXXVi	xiiii	xviii	ii	xvi	xv kal. mai.	xii kal. mai.	xvii hend.

Fig. 32: Cyril's last computed cycle (above), and Dionysius' Pascal Tables for 532-550 AD and 608-626 AD (from Migne, *Patrologia Latina*, lxvii, cols 493-8).

218

Concerning the beginning of the Christian era, Clement of Alexandria suggested that it was most sensible to reckon 30 years back from the 15th year of Tiberius' reign, according to the statement of St. Luke that Jesus was about thirty in that year (cf. *Stromata* I. 21,§145). Therefore, Dionysius also took this year (783 AUC) as the starting point: 783 - 30 = 753, and because he wrote his letter in 1278 AUC, he arrived at 1278 - 753 = 525 as the number of years of Christ. This primary way of calculation in Dionysius' work is confirmed by his first Paschal Rule which can be expressed by the following formula:

$$X = 15 \times n + 12 + i$$

in order to find the number of years, X, of the era AD from the indiction i. The solution of this equation requires that we know both the indiction figure i of present Roman year and the number *n* of completed 15-year cycles since the year X(i) = 12.

Flavius Magnus Cassiodorus, the esteemed statesman and historian, after his conversion succeeded Dionysius Exiguus as Abbot of Rome. He showed the practical application of Dionysius' formula with the following example: How many years passed from the Incarnation of Christ to 1315 AUC with indiction i = 10 and n = 36, during the reign of Emperor Justinian? Substituting these figures for i and n in the above equation we get X = 562 AD. In that year Cassiodorus wrote his work on the *Cumputus Paschalis* summing up the Paschal Rules in ten clear points. (Cf. Migne, *Patrologia Latina*, lxix, cols.1249-50).

Chronological conversion tables

In the following tables only those years are listed which relate to our subject. The years of the different eras have different initial dates and different number of days. We have to reckon with these differences in converting dates of different eras into dates of the Christian era.

Seleucid Era	Augustus Era	Roman Era AUC	Christian Era	Astro-nomical
304	22	746	8 BC	-7
305	23	747	7	-6
306	24	748	6	-5
307	25	749	5	-4
308	26	750	4	-3
309	27	751	3	-2
310	28	752	2	-1
311	29	753	1 BC	0
312	30	754	1 AD	+1
313	31	755	2	+2

The Months of the 305th year of the Seleucid Era
converted into the Months of the Julian Calendar

Seleucid Era 305		AUC 747/748 BC 7/6	
1. Nisanu	1	April	2
2. Ajaru	1	May	1
3. Simanu	1	May	31
4. Duzu	1	June	29
5. Abu	1	July	29
6. Ululu	1	August	27
7. Tashritu	1	September	26
8. Arahsamna	1	October	25
9. Kislimu	1	November	24
10. Tebetu	1	December	23
11. Shabatu	1	January	22
12. Adaru	1	February	20
13. Ve-Adaru	1	March	22

The Seleucid Era in Mesopotamia begins on 3rd April 443 AUC = 311 BC. Seleucus I Nicator adopted the Babylonian luni-solar calendar with 12 months of 29 or 30 days and with a supplementary month to round out the year of the seasons every third year. The Greek ruler retained the spring New Year's Day, 1st Nisan, which was 3rd April in the Julian calendar in 311 BC. The first Seleucid year was a regular lunar year of 354 days. The 305th Seleucid year was a lunar leap year of 384 days from 2 April 747 AUC = 7 BC to 21 April 748 AUC = 6 BC. Nine months of this Seleucid year fell in 7 BC.

The Augustus Era is based on Alexandrian years of 365 days and begins on 29 August 724 AUC. Thus Augustus' 23rd year is reckoned from 29 August 746 AUC = 8 BC to 28 August 747 AUC= 7 BC. Eight months of Augustus' 23rd year, from January to September fell in 7 BC.

The Roman Republican Era is reckoned from 1 January 753 BC in the Julian Calendar. The old calendar of the Roman Republic was a lunar calendar with 12 or 13 synodic months. After the calendar reform in 46 BC, the lunar synodic month was abandoned as a basic unit in the calendar, and it was instead based on the solar year, whose length had been determined to be 365 days 6 hours. However, after four years, these 6 hours add up to 24, and so every fourth year was a leap year with 366 days, the extra day being added to February.

The Christian Era established by the Abbot Dionysius Exiguus as the Era of the Incarnation of Our Lord begins on 25 March of the Roman year 753 AUC, and this year is denoted as 1 BC, i.e., "before Christ". The Fathers of the Church adopted the Julian Calendar, and, therefore, the years of the Christian Era are reckoned from the civil New Year's Day, 1st January 754 AUC which is 1 AD. This historical method of numbering the years mathematically speaking is wrong, because it leaves out the year zero (0) which is between 1 BC and 1 AD. (The omission of the year zero cannot

220

be blamed on Dionysius, because he has never used his chronology to date events before the birth of Christ. The dating of events before the Christian Era was made with the Roman or Macedonian years. It was in the 18th century that the reckoning with the years "before Christ" became the custom in modern historical chronologies.)

Astronomical time reckoning (in accordance with the motions of the Earth and Moon) begins with zero in the natural sequence of numbers. The reader is surely familiar with the geometric representation of real numbers by means of points on a straight line. A point is selected to represent 0 and another, to the right of 0, to represent +1, to the left of 0, to represent -1. This choice determines the scale. Mathematically speaking the date of birth begins with the zero year. Astronomers measure the time from zero (0) both in positive direction after the event (AD), and in negative direction before the event (BC). If we reckon the days from 00 hour 1st January of the year 0 (1 BC) to 24.00 hours 31 December, the first year of the Christian Era begins on 1st January 1 AD, because Jesus is then one year old. However, in dating events which occurred before the birth of Christ, we must subtract one year from the years of the Christian Era in order to arrive at an accurate date. Thus the year 2 BC is denoted as -1, 7 BC is -6, and so on.

12. *Mesopotamia*

Art historians speak of the Sumerian, Assyrian and Babylonian works of art excavated by archaeologists under the general heading of the art of Mesopotamia. Throughout centuries many believers placed the Garden of Eden here, because according to the Book of Moses the creation of man had taken place in this land, which is watered by the rivers of Tigris and Euphrates (Gen 2: 8-14). In the field of modern research Mesopotamia is important because of the early civilization which it nurtured, one of the original sources of our Western civilization.

Today this ancient land belongs to the territory of Iraq. In recent years its new rulers have drawn the world's attention again towards Babylon. It is worth at least looking over its stormy history. In the sixth century BC, many Israelites living in the Babylonian captivity in Mesopotamia expected the Anointed Deliverer, the Messiah, to be a new king of Persia. One of their anonymous prophets, a "Second Isaiah" had foretold that Cyrus (*Kyros*) of Persia would be an "Anointed of the Lord", he would came to power over Babylon, and he would liberate the exiles (Is 45: 1-6).

The last Chaldaean king in Babylon was Nabonidus (556-539 BC), the son of Nebuchandnezzar. He had taken good care of his ancestors' heritage, but because of his weak health, he left his son Belshazzar to govern. But Belshazzar preferred festive banquets to the affairs of state. Daniel had predicted for him that because of his pride and negligence he would fall into the hands of the Medes and Persians (Dan 5:27). In the third year of Nabonidus' reign Cyrus conquered the enormous Median empire lying northeast of Babylon. He was the son of the Persian king and a Median princess. After he had defeated Croesus, the King of Lydia, well known for his gold mines and treasures, and the ally of Nabonidus, Cyrus had an open way to the Tower of Babel. He posed a threat to Babylon and became a symbol of hope to the exiles. Finally, in 539 BC he took over the capital intact from Nabonidus, after defeating his army at the river Tigris. He proved indeed to be a deliverer for the nations which had been subjugated by the Babylonian kings.

Cyrus began to rule by giving each of the nations autonomy and freedom of religion. He provided fair compensation for all those who had been exploited by the Babylonian rulers. His religious tolerance is well known from the so-called Cyrus Cylinder Seal, on which the following can be read:

> When I entered Babylon with peace and I settled the residence of my reign in the palace, Marduk, the mighty lord, gave me the hearts of the Babylonians, while I took care of his worship. When my powerful army entered, the inhabitants of Sumer and Akkad had nothing to fear. I have liberated the people of Babylon from the yoke, and I have rebuilt their houses...I am Cyrus, the King of Babylon, Sumer, Akkad and of all the four regions of the world (Pritchard 1969).

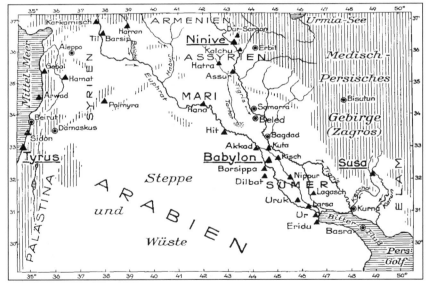

Fig. 33: Map of Mesopotamia (Unger 1931)

In 538 BC Cyrus issued a decree allowing the exiles to return to Jerusalem. The book of Ezra quotes this edict as follows:

> Thus says Cyrus the King of Persia: The Lord, the God of heaven, has given me all the kingdoms of the earth, and he has charged me to build him a house at Jerusalem. Whoever is among you of all his people, may

his God be with him, and let him go up to Jerusalem, and rebuild the Temple of the Lord (Ezra 1: 2-4).

According to Ezra the majority of the Israelites remained in Mesopotamia, but more than fifty thousand from among the younger generations returned home. During the two hundred years of the Persian domination the people of Judah lived in poverty, but they enjoyed limited political autonomy and complete religious liberty, growing slowly in number. Daniel in his prophetic visions had already seen "the fourth beast, which should crush the whole Earth with its iron teeth and its ten horns" (Dan 7:19-24; 8:5). This prophecy was a reference to Alexander the Great and the ten Seleucid kings who followed him.

Greek unity had been achieved by Philip II, King of Macedonia, Alexander's father. After he had been assassinated in 336 BC, Alexander demonstrated his ability by consolidating the kingdom. He was appointed General (*Hegemon*) of the army by the Council of the Greek League. They declared war on Persia to avenge the sacrileges of Xerxes against the temples of the Greeks. Alexander defeated the last Persian king, Darius III, occupied the Persian city states, set fire to Xerxes' palace at Persepolis, and was crowned King of Persia in 331 BC. He founded Alexandria at the Western mouth of the river Nile, the storied city which for seven centuries became the capital of Greek, Hebrew, and Christian culture. His campaign into India extended the borders of his empire to the lower Indus. In 323 he returned to his palace in Babylon, weakened and sick, where he died on June 13th in the same year.

Alexander the Great was convinced of the superiority of Greek culture and wished it to be the basis of unity among the nations he ruled. He recognized the qualities of the Persians and wanted to make them partners with the Greeks in his empire. Greek artists and philosophers made themselves familiar with the culture of Mesopotamian people. Thus Hellenistic art and literature was born from the joining of Mesopotamian and Greek cuture. This was the most important result of the endeavors of Alexander the Great. The Hellenistic period extended from 312 BC, from the beginning of the Seleucid era, to 31 BC, with the victory of the Roman Augustus at Actium. The Seleucid rulers founded Greek towns everywhere in their empire, and Mesopotamia was for another 150 years under Greek dominion.

In 141 BC the Parthian tribe of Iran won its independence, and the Persians became again the rulers of Mesopotamia up to 637 AD. In that year the Mesopotamian people fell into the hands of the Arabic tribes united by the Islamic religion. The Arabic word *Al-Islam* means the community of the Surrenderers. Its believers call themselves *Muslims*, those "who have surrendered" (to Allah). Islam was established by *Mohammed Ibn Abdallah* in Medina, on the Eastern coast of the Red Sea, as a religion and state, between 622 and 632 AD. It was said that the major influence on Mohammed must have been Jewish and Christian, and that those traditions were transformed by him into a system conformable to the Arabian psyche. Mohammed asserted that he was the bearer of a *Koran*, i.e., "Recitation", which he had received from the Angel Gabriel. He firmly insisted on the belief that this *Koran* was the final revelation of what Allah, "the God of Abraham, Ishmael, Isaac, and Jacob, and Jesus" wished to say to mankind (Koran 2:132).

The Muslims considered Ishmael,the expelled son of Abraham, as their forefather (Gen 16:15; 21:9-14). They wanted to reconquer the homeland of Abraham and declared war on the Persians. After they had occupied Mesopotamia, they began to attack and pursue the Israelites and Christians who would not accept their teaching. The successor of Mohammed received the Arabic title *Khalifah*, and his first successor was the Caliph of Baghdad, high priest and head of state in his one person. This early Islamic state received the name *Iraq el Arabi*. During the following six centuries the "Land between the Rivers" was still fertile and densely populated. Its fall began with the Mongol invasions of *Hulagu* in 1258 AD, and the end came in 1393, when Timurlenk totally destroyed Baghdad and plundered the towns. These invasions resulted in such destruction and loss of population that the irrigation system no longer could be repaired and maintained. The cuneiform records show that the Sumerian and Babylonian rulers had constructed a large and intricate system of canals in Lower Mesopotamia. This was needed both to ensure a sufficient supply of water for irrigation and to protect the country from devastating floods.

In 1534 the soldiers of Suleiman II occupied Iraq, and they reconstructed Baghdad. Mesopotamia belonged to the Empire of the Turkish Sultans until 1917. During the First World War the British army invaded Iraq and in 1917 they occupied Baghdad. Robert Koldewey and his collaborators could hear the remote cannon shots of the British artillery, when they excavated the foundation of the Tower of Babel (Koldewey 1913). Fortunately, their friend R. Campbell Thompson, the Assyriologist of the British Museum, was among the British army officers. Thus the German engineers could continue their work freely. This was also the time when Thompson discovered among the Babylonian finds the seal cylinder of Nabonidus, from the text of which he learnt that Nabonidus had "rebuilt the old tower temple of Ur-Nammu with burnt bricks and asphalt, to look like its form as it was in ancient times". Ten years later, Sir C. Leonard Woolley found the town of Ur under the hills on the Western banks of the Euphrates, 250 kilometers southeast of Babylon. The oldest pattern of the Tower of Babel was discovered here, and it had been built 4200 years ago by the Sumerian king *Ur-Nammu* in honor of the godess of the Moon. The basic area of this Ziggurat was 100 × 60 meters, and its height was 24 meters. It consisted of three superimposed platforms, each smaller than the one below. At its top there was a small garden which contained the godess' private sanctuary. This Ziggurat of Ur-Nammu was surrounded by five smaller temples, constructed in honor of the five star gods, represented by the five planets. The gold, silver and marble jewels, vessels, and instruments, which were excavated from under the ruins of the two story houses and the tombs of kings, show the remnants of an extremely developed culture. These 5500 year old finds are considered to be the crown of the Mesopotamian excavations (Woolley 1954).

Iraq has been an independent state since 1932, and, as a mandate of Great Britain, admitted to the League of Nations. In 1948 Iraq became a founding member of the League of Arab States: Iraq, Jordan, Persia (Iran), Pakistan. The last ten years of the monarchy (1948-1958) of king Faisal II were peaceful. New projects were undertaken in rebuilding of the irrigation system and communications, all financed from the oil revenues. However, opposition to the regime was increasing, and in 1958 a military coup took place in Baghdad. King Faisal, the last ally of Great Britain, was murdered, and the Iraqi Republic proclaimed. The new government requested the economic and military assistance of the Soviet Union. The "Revived Babylon" became one of the international centers of terrorism. We still remember the tragical events of the last couple of years. Instead of the sky high tower, the new Nebuchadnezzar had a seven story underground Ziggurat constructed, and he felt safe in its depth, while his ballistic missiles were trained on Israel and on the Western Allied Forces. In 1991, from 20th of January to 20th of March, millions could watch on TV the horrors of the Iraqi-Kuwait war, from the Persian Golf to Baghdad. It seemed as if the dream of Nebuchadnezzar had been fulfilled again, as the prophet Daniel interpreted it:

> I saw a tree in the midst of the earth, and its height was great. The tree grew and its top reached to heaven, and it was visible to the end of the whole earth... And a watcher [Cherub], came down from heaven, he cried aloud and said thus: Hew down the tree and cut off its branches, but leave the stump of its roots in the earth, bound with a band of iron and bronze... (Dan 4: 10-15).

13. *Marduk - Zeus - Jupiter*

The three names, Marduk, Zeus, and Jupiter, in the ancient mythologies all imply the same idea of a divine king who is always wise and righteous, creates a universal order and saves the people from destruction. This idea is probably as old as mankind itself. According to modern depth psychological research, it is an archetype of the savior of the world, which has from the collective unconscious of man been projected into the figures of the Babylonian Marduk, the Greek Zeus, and the Roman Jupiter. The common symbols of their power were the thunderbolt, scepter and eagle. Their divine qualities were equally associated with the brightest planet, the Sumerian-Accadic name of which was *Mulu-babbar*, i.e., Glistening Star (or Star Father), and which in modern astronomy retains the Latin name Jupiter. (Cf. Paulus 1928).

Herodotus and the Greek historiographers have without difficulty identified Marduk with Zeus. Marduk's six meter high gold statue in the Babylonian temple was very similar to the statue of Zeus in the Olympian temple, made of gold and ivory by Phaidias in the fifth century BC. Like Marduk who defeated the monsters of Tiamat, Zeus defeated the Titans and cast them into the depths of Tartaros. Thus he became the supreme god of the Greek Pantheon. In Rome Jupiter was always honored as the supreme lord of justice and moral order. On the Capitoline in Rome the temple of *Jupiter Optimus Maximus* was inaugurated in 509 BC. The anniversary of this temple fell on the Ides of September and was followed by the Roman Games.

225

The cult of Marduk is the most ancient and original form of the astral religions. According to a cuneiform writing it was in the 18th century BC that Hammurabi attached the title *Belu* i.e., Lord, to Marduk, who henceforth became god of the gods over the twelve sanctuaries in the new Babylonian empire. The exaltation of Marduk is related in the Babylonian creation myth which is called *Enuma elish* after the initial Accadic words of the story: "When on high the heavens were still unnamed, beneath the Earth bore not a name: The primeval ocean was their producer...". This story is based on Sumerian traditions. Marduk's Sumerian name is *Amar-Ud* which signifies "Son of the Rising Sun". Its Semitic transliteration is *Ni-marud* or, in Hebrew, "Nimrod who was the first potentate on earth. He was a mighty hunter in the eyes of the Lord. First to be included in his empire were Babel, Erech [*Uruk*] and Accad. From this country came Assur, the builder of Nineveh" (Gen 10: 8-11).

The seven cuneiform tablets of the *Enuma elish* were found in Nineveh under the ruins of the palace of Sennacherib and Assurbanipal, who were kings from 704 to 626 BC. This is the oldest preserved text of the Marduk epic, and Assyriologists assume that it was written about 700 BC. The actual account was discovered by George Smith (1876). Since then new texts have been discovered and new editions published. Regarding our subject the fifth tablet of *Enuma elish* contains important information about the development of astronomy at that time. The following statements mark a new epoch in the history of astronomy:

> He [Marduk] constructed stations for the great gods; he fixed their images as constellations [of the Zodiac]. He ordained the year, and he divided it into sections; for each [...] of the twelve months he fixed three stars.. After he had determined the seasons by the images he founded the station of Nibiru [Jupiter on the meridian] to determine their bounds, that none might go astray. He set the way of Enlil and Ea on the sky [North and South]; on both sides of the sky he made gates [East and West]...He bade the Moon come forth and entrusted night to her, he made her to measure time: at the beginning of the month, rising over the land, thy shining horns shall measure six days; on the seventh day let half thy crown appear, at full moon thou shalt face the Sun....... (Trans. by Speiser 1969).

The text goes on with still more detailed orders for the phases of the Moon and planets. This chapter of the Marduk epic gives evidence that in the scientific and religious view of the Chaldaeans it was Jupiter which played a leading part by the regular recurrence of its aspects and stationary points. Their observations indicated that, besides the motion of the Moon, the Law of Jupiter was to be taken as a major regulator of the behavior of the physical world. This assumption directed the course of Chaldaean astronomy for centuries.

The point of the vernal equinox reached the sign of Aries the Ram about 2000 BC, but it was around 800 BC that the Sun for the first time rose immediately after *Hamal*, the brightest star of the Ram (*Alpha Arietis*). At that time the priest astronomers of Marduk became aware of the fact that a thousand year old tradition did not agree with their observations, because on the spring New Year's Day the Sun did not rise with the Bull, but with the Ram. Therefore, the sign of *Aries* was then adopted as the first sign or leader of the zodiac. According to the foregoing extract from the 5th tablet of *Enuma elish* Marduk-Jupiter determines the stations or domiciles of the great gods: of the Sun, Moon and five planets. This means that each of these has its own zodiacal sign where it dominates by its maximum intensity, as for example the Sun dominates in Leo, Venus dominates in Taurus, Jupiter in Pisces. In the second line Marduk gives to each constellation a special image or design. Here it is a question of the celestial zone of the stars where the motion and position of the Sun, Moon and planets is always observable and determinable. However, this was a difficult task, because the constellations of the zodiac were unequal in size and irregular in shape. Therefore, based on the rhythm of Jupiter the Chaldaeans divided the zodiac into 12 equal sections,i.e., they put the zodiacal constellations of different longitudes into twelve signs, each with 30 degrees of longitude.In this way it was easier to determine the position of the Moon or a planet given their ecliptic longitude, i.e., the distance from the point of the vernal equinox, as measured along the Sun's apparent path during the year.

In the fourth line of the foregoing text we read that "three stars are fixed for (each quarter of) the twelve months". This statement has a double meaning. The first is that each of the four seasons have three months, i.e., each of them is determined by three successive zodiacal signs. The second meaning of the statement is that each sign is divided into three equal parts of 10 degrees along the ecliptic (cf. Maunder 1908, p.247). The sixth and seventh statement of the text indicate that both the division of the zodiac into $12 \times 30°$ sections, and the division of each sign into $3 \times 10°$ parts has been determined by the motion of Jupiter. *Nibiru* is the special Accadic name of the planet Jupiter when it is on the meridian. The Chaldaeans observed that the Moon passes through all the constellations in a month (i.e., 360 degrees in 30 days), whilst the Sun moves through 360 degrees in a year (365 days). However, the constellations are very unequal in ecliptic longitude. It is only the planet Jupiter which moves 30 degrees in a year and passes through the zodiacal constellations in 12 years. In this way Marduk, as the deity of the planet Jupiter, determines the boundaries of the zodiacal signs.

The same giant planet marks out the third part of each sign, because at stated intervals Jupiter is stationary; during one-third of each year (four months) Jupiter appears *retrograde*, moving from east to west among the stars, and its retrograde motion covers each time ten degrees within the same sign. In the 8th statement *Enlil* (Height) means North, and *Ea* (Depth) means South. When Jupiter is on the meridian, at the highest point of its path, it indicates the direction of South and North. In the course of 6 years both the declination and the culmination of Jupiter changes 47 degrees. Each 12th year it reaches the maximum northern declination of $23°30'$ and culminates above Babylon at a height of $81°$. Six year later, however, its culmination height is only $34°$ above the horizon. Thus in six years the Chaldaean astronomers measured an arc of $47°$ along the meridian circle. To the left of this line was the north-eastern gate, and to the right of it was the south-western gate of Babylon.

The seal of the Babylonian temple of the 9th century BC illustrates the astronomical character of the original Marduk epic. Here he is still adorned with the Assyrian regalia as a war god. He holds the bow in his left hand. In his right hand is the scepter with a ring; this is a measuring rod the length of which is one cubit (45 cm). Note that the print of the seal is a mirror image, where the right hand looks like the left hand. (Cf. Unger 1931, p.210).

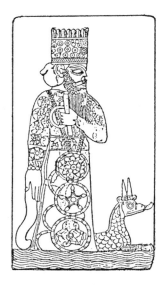

Fig. 34: Babylonian Temple Seal. Marduk's figure emerges from the heavenly ocean. At his foot lies the Sumerian dragon which he has defeated; it was the sign of the winter solstice. His garment is decorated with the symbols of the star gods. On his belt is depicted the Zodiac, and on its front the images of the Bull and the Ram are discernible, indicating the spring and the beginning of the year. Under his belt, the three rings indicate the division of the heavens into the domiciles of the three high deities *Ea, Anu and Enlil* who play the leading role in the exaltation of Marduk. Moreover, in the first ring (at the bottom) the figures of three Bulls form an equilateral triangle; this is the sign of the spring equinox. The five-pointed star in the second ring is a symbol of *Nabu* (Prophet), and its five points represent the five planets around the Sun. The regular pentagon was an essential component of the Assyro-Babylonian architecture. In the old Semitic tradition, the number five was a symbol for Law. The Hebrews called the books of Moses "the five-fifths of the Law", and the Greeks used the corresponding term *Pentateuchos*. In the third ring there is an eight pointed star, a symbol of Jupiter, within a twelve pointed star, the Sun.

In the 9th century BC the Chaldaeans founded an astronomical school at Sippar, 40 kms north of Babylon. Archaeologists found there a rare stone tablet which represents the four main feasts of Marduk: the two solstices and the two equinoxes. The cuneiform text on this tablet relates the story of the temple of *Shamash* the Sun. It was destroyed by the Assyrians, but at a later time Nabu-aplu-iddina, the King of Babylon, the elect of Marduk, ordered the restoration of the Sun temple (885-852 BC). "The great lord

Marduk with a righteous scepter had invested him to undertake the rule of the peoples", and during his reign "a model of Shamash's image, his figure and his insignia were found on the western bank of the Euphrates", as related on the Tablet (Col. III. 7-25). From this old model the missing statue of Shamash was then restored. He is represented on the sculptured relief at the head of the Tablet. The scene shows that the model may originally have been Marduk's figure. As a matter of fact, from the time of Hammurabi, Marduk-Jupiter, as the Sun's son in the religious cult overtook the authority of Shamash.

Nabopolassar, the Chaldaean king of Babylon (625-605 BC) had two clay impressions of the sculptured relief made, and he placed them together with the tablet in an earthenware receptacle. Thus he intended to protect the tablet from injury and preserve it for the future rulers. This shows that the structure of the tablet was of very great importance for the Chaldaeans.

The scene represents Shamash in the same form as Marduk was seen in the Babylonian sanctuary: in a sitting posture and with a gold table or altar before him (cf. Herodotus, I. 182). The ringed rod in his right hand is a measuring rod (one cubit) and also a protractor to measure angles. Behind his throne from the heavenly ocean rises the Sea Serpent (*Hydra*). At that time its 75 visible stars lay along the celestial equator in a longitude of around 120 degrees, between the Lion and the Scorpion, thus indicating the period from the summer solstice to the autumnal equinox. The new moon with the Sun and Venus under the Serpent's head was a symbol for the equinoxes. The inscription above them reads: "The Moon, Sun and Venus are over the heavenly ocean and announce to the year gods what they are to expect. " This may well mean that this phenomenon shows for the priests whether the year will be of 12 or 13 months. At the top of the "Pillar of Heaven and Earth" (*Etemenanki*) sits *Nabu*, son of Marduk. His temple *Esida*, the "Shrine of dusk" was in Borsippa. Twice a year, on the feasts of the equinoxes Nabu visited his father Marduk at *Esagila*, the "Shrine of light". The priests transported his image to Babylon and put it on the top of the pillar. An inscription declares: "At the appearance of Nabu both the heavenly and the earthly gods rejoice because he heralds the rise of the Sun." (Cf. Unger 1931, p.207; Kugler 1912, II. p.78).

The solar disk is exactly located in the geometrical center of the upper rectangle of the Tablet, which shows that at the time of the equinoxes the Sun stands in the celestial equator and rises at the horizon exactly from the east. But at the summersolstice it rises from the north-east and at the winter-solstice from the south-east. For this reason, to show the position of the sunrises relative to the east, the altar of the Sun is movable; it rolls on wheels and is supported by ropes held by Nabu. Thus the priest, who holds the foot of the altar, can move it forward and back according to the changing position of the sunrise.

This Tablet of Sippar is of great importance for the history of art and geometry. As to the geometrical structure, its most important part is the scene sculptured in low relief. It gives evidence of the fact that the construction of the *Golden Section* was already known and used by the Chaldaeans 600 years before Euclid. The Greek mathematician Euclid, around 320 BC, is generally assumed to be the first to construct the so called Golden Rectangle which is said to be very aesthetical because of the perfect geometrical ratio of its sides. That the Chaldaeans, centuries before Euclid, also were aware of this mathematical construction and proportion has, as far as I know, not been previously known.

The Golden Section is found by dividing a line at a point such that the greater segment (x) is to the whole line (a) as the smaller segment (a - x) is to the greater (x).

Thus we have the proportion $\frac{x}{a} = \frac{a-x}{x}$

This same equation can be written $x^2 = a^2 - ax$ or $x^2 + ax - a^2 = 0$

and its solution is $x = \frac{a(\sqrt{5}-1)}{2} = 0.618034a$

where the ratio x/a = 0.618 is a constant or fixed quantity. Substituting the measurements of the breadth (a = 178 mm) and length (b = 288 mm) of the Tablet in this equation we see that its sides are accurately in this ratio a/b = 178/288 = 0.618, and thus it is a *Golden Rectangle*.

The Golden Section determines the internal structure of the Tablet which is both horizontally and vertically divided according to the same ratio. Its upper part is divided by the central line of the Pillar such that also the rectangle produced by the greater and smaller segments has its breadth and length in this ratio:

d/c = (a-x)/x = 68/110 = 0.618, and thus the figure of Marduk sits in a Golden Rectangle, as in his sanctuary, the name of which is *E-babbar*, the "Glistening Shrine".

Moreover, in the upper part of the Tablet all the figures are symmetrically ordered within a regular pentagon whose sides have the length of the greater segment *x* of the breadth *a*, and its diagonals (= a) intersect each other according to the ratio of the Golden Section. This is the five-pointed star of *Nabu*, the personification of Mercury, who sits uppermost within the pentagon. The inscription above the solar disk reads: "Image of Shamash, the great Lord, who dwells in E-babbar which is in Sippar". Thus the head of the Tablet is the third Golden Rectangle:

c/a = 110/178 = 0.618, and there are seven Golden Sections on it.

Marduk's Babylonian temple was called the "house of light". From high Olympus Zeus revealed himself to men as pleasant daylight. Jupiter was invoked as "god of heavenly light". The mythological composition on the tablet of Sippar is an excellent symbolical expression of man's innate longing for eternal life. But in actual history, Christ is "the rising Sun visiting us, to give light to those who live in darkness and the shadow of death" (Lk 1: 79). The sculptured relief on the upper part of the tablet is a prototype of the early Christian reliefs which represent the three Magi before the throne of Christ in Bethlehem.

Fig. 35: The Stone Tablet of Sippar. It is a new discovery that the Stone Tablet of Sippar is a perfect composition of three Golden Rectangles; the Golden Section was already used by the Chaldaeans 600 years before Euclid. The tablet measures 178 mm in breadth, and 288 mm in height. As to the geometrical structure, its most important part is the scene sculptured in low relief. The edges of the tablet are bevelled, but its measurements have the following ratios: a/b = c/a = d/c = 0.618. (Diagram by Gustav Teres, S.J. The Tablet No. 91000, Copyright: The British Museum)

14. *Mesopotamian Constellations and the Signs*

On modern maps of the heavens we recognize 88 constellations, 45 of which were probably designed by Assyrian and Chaldaean astronomers around 5000 years ago. This assumption is corroborated by historical and astronomical evidence. The old Mesopotamian plan was adopted in the Hellenic era by the Greeks who renamed some of the figures after the characters and heroes of their mythology. Ptolemy's list from 137 AD enumerates 48 configurations of bright stars beginning with the 12 zodiacal signs, followed by 21 northern and 15 southern constellations. The other forty constellations have been framed after the invention of the telescope, mainly in the 18th century. Definite boundaries of constellations were unknown in antiquity. For the purpose of astrometry the constellations are now definite divisions of the heavens. By a decision of the International Astronomical Union in 1928 boundaries between the constellations were established in the equatorial coordinate system as east-west lines of constant declination and north-south segments of hour circles perpendicular to the celestial equator.

How was it possible to come to a knowledge of where and when the ancient constellations were designed ? Assyro-Babylonian boundary stones from the 12th century BC, as well as Chaldaean cuneiform tablets with star almanacs, tell us that 45 constellations were then known in the same forms as we now ascribe to them. However, the designation of the constellations must be much older than those archaeological finds. The earliest complete description of the ancient constellations is preserved in the didactic poem of Aratus (The Phenomena, about 270 BC). This work gives an excellent summary of the astronomy of Eudoxus (408-355 BC) who without more ado adopted the Babylonian system. Four hundred years later Hipparchus commented on some statements in this work. He pointed out that stars given in some old constellations were no longer there, and in other cases it was necessary to add bright stars visible to him but omitted by Eudoxus. Comparing his observations with the old data Hipparchus found that the ecliptic longitudes of the stars had increased by one degree of arc per hundred years. These observations led him to the first mathematical definition of the precession of the equinoxes.

The figure below illustrates the effect of precession on the position of a star (x). The ecliptic is a great circle defining a plane that intersects the plane of the celestial equator at an angle of 23°27'. The two points of intersection are the First Point of Aries and Libra, respectively the point of the vernal equinox and the autumnal equinox. According to modern measurements the equinoctial points move from east to west along the ecliptic at a rate of 50.26 seconds of arc per year. But the longitude of a star is counted from west to east (from 0° to 360°). Therefore, during 72 years the precession causes an increase of 1°00'18" in the longitude of the star (x), and at the same time the declination of that star as well as its altitude above the horizon are altered. During 25,788 years the celestial pole (P) describes a circle of 23°27' radius around the ecliptic pole (EP).Thus some bright stars which were visible just above the horizon, for example, in 1900, would be below the horizon in 2000.

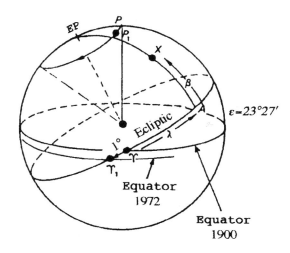

Fig. 36: Effect of Precession. The position of the stars and constellations on the Sphere of Eudoxus (mentioned in the poem of Aratus) is correct for a north celestial pole position between 3200 BC and 2600 BC, seen from the geographical latitudes between 34° and 37° North. The stars whose southern declinations were greater than -55°, were not mapped out by the ancient astronomers because they never saw them, those stars never rose above their horizon. This fact leads us to the conclusion that the ancient constellations were framed by a group of astronomers living in the latitudes 35° and 36° N, around 2800 BC. Hipparchus himself did his observations at Rhodes at 36° north latitude, which is the same as the latitude of Nineveh and Assur.

Using the known average rate of the precession of the Earth's axis (5025 arc seconds per 100 years) we can design some star maps for the time 2800 BC, and for north latitudes 35°-36°. At that time, the three largest constellations, Draco, Hydra, and Serpens, were of great astronomical importance. These were certainly designed in order to facilitate the orientation on the heavens. We recognize that the north pole of the equator was then marked by *Thuban*, the brightest star of Draco the Dragon (see below: p. 273). The Dragon never set, and it linked together the pole of the ecliptic and the pole of the equator. Hydra the Sea Serpent covered around one-third of the equatorial belt, and it linked together the constellations of the summer solstice (Leo) and of the autumnal equinox (Scorpio). The Serpent was carried by the Serpent-holder (Ophiuchus) in such a way that it climbed up and reached the zenith with its head. On the 3500 year old Mesopotamian boundary stones we recognize the symbols of the solstices and the equinoxes: the new moon appears between the Sun (right) and Venus or Jupiter (left) below the head of the Sea Serpent, rising together with the Lion (summer), or with the Scorpion (autumn), or with the Water-bearer (winter), or with the Bull (spring).

Fig. 37: An Assyrian Boundary Stone of 1100 BC. The middle section of this monument represents the zodiac; above and below it are represented the eight largest terrace temples of the following cities: Babylon, Borsippa (with the turtle), Sippar, Nineveh, Assur, Nippur, Uruk, and Ur. These boundary stones were sacred objects, and their usual inscription read as follows: "Belu, Anu, Ea, Ninib, and Gula, all the gods whose signs are to be seen on this stone and whose names we invoke, will afflict with dreadful curses those who destroy or remove this their monument". (It is perhaps owing to this threat that there are still thirty such Mesopotamian monuments preserved in the European Museums).

In his essay on "Genesis and the Constellations" Maunder (1908) states that "the constellations evidently were designed long before the earliest books of the Old Testament received their present form. But the first nine chapters of Genesis give the history of the world before any date that we can assign to the constellations, and are clearly derived from very early traditions". Look at the fifteen constellations which are represented on the maps below. In the years between 2700 and 3000 BC these stars were seen during the nights of winter and spring crossing the local meridians of Mesopotamian cities. When we compare the symbolism of these constellations with the scriptural narratives of Genesis, we find several similarities between them. There are many allusions to the Assyro-Babylonian idea that the stars are the silent "writing of the heavens". The prophets, speaking of the heavens as the creation of the Lord Almighty, used symbols and expressions found also in Babylonian mythology.

According to the account of Moses the Serpent caused the fall of the first human couple. But immediately after that fall the Lord Almighty promised salvation from the serpent's power. He said to the Serpent, "I will make you enemies of each other: you and the woman, your offspring and her offspring. He will crush your head and you will strike his heel". In the figures of the summer solstice and the autumnal equinox, the Woman as the constellation Virgo (Virgin) is to be seen above the Sea Serpent, between the Lion and the Serpent-holder. The Serpent-holder crushes the Scorpion's head, whilst the Scorpion's sting strikes his heel. (Cf. Gen 3:15f; 49:9; Rev 5:5; the Lion of Judah has triumphed over the primeval Serpent). According to the messianic interpretation of this passage of Genesis the Woman is the mother of Christ, in the actual historical sense. Christ says in John 3:15: "The Son of Man must be lifted up as Moses lifted up the serpent in the desert; so that everyone who believes in him may receive eternal life". This is an allusion to the ascension of Christ, which will show that Jesus really came from heaven. If man would be saved he must turn his eyes to Christ "lifted up" on the cross, as the symbol of his "lifting up" in the ascension.

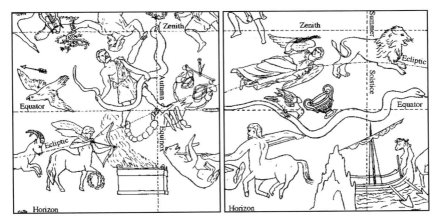

Fig. 38. Midnight constellation. The constellations which were seen in Mesopotamia, around 2700 BC, during the nights of winter (Leo, Virgo) and spring (Libra, Scorpio, Sagittarius). (Maunder 1908)

After the fall of man, "the Lord expelled him from the garden of Eden, and in front of Eden he posted the Cherubs to guard the way to the tree of life". The word "Cherubs" is the Hebrew form of the Accadic *Karibu*, the half-human and half-animal creatures which guarded the approaches to the temples and palaces. These cherubs were the symbols of the four cardinal constellations. They appear also in the vision of the prophet Ezekiel as well as in the Book of Revelation by John: the Bull, the Lion, the Man or Angel (as Aquarius), and the Scorpion transformed into an Eagle (Gen 3:24; Ezek 1:10; Rev 4:6).

At that time the constellations were so designed that the Sun at the spring equinox was in the middle of Taurus the Bull; at the summer solstice in the middle of Leo the Lion; at the winter solstice in the middle of Aquarius the Man bearing the waterpot. The fourth cardinal point, the Sun at the autumnal equinox, was assigned to the foot of the Serpent-holder on the Scorpion's head; but Aquila, the Flying Eagle, is placed above this point to show the metamorphosis of the Scorpion by the Savior's power.

The largest of the ancient constellations was the Ship resting on the southern horizon. This was *Argo Navis,* or the Argonauts' ship in Ptolemy's star list, but on the modern star maps it is divided into four smaller parts with the names Carina the Keel, Puppis the Stern, Pyxis the Compass, and Vela the Sail of the Ship. In the ancient constellation the Ship is placed on a mountain. A mighty figure (represented as a Centaur) appears to have just left the Ship and offers an animal on an Altar. In Genesis (8:5-9:13) we read about the Flood and the Ark of Noah; when the Ark came to rest on the mountain of Ararat, Noah sent out a raven which "flew back and forth until the waters dried up from the earth". In the ancient figure the raven could only alight on the Sea Serpent. And when "the surface of the ground was dry", Noah went down from the mountain, "he built an altar for the Lord, and from the clean animals he offered burnt offerings on the altar". The Lord said then to him: "I set my bow in the clouds and it shall be a sign of the Covenant between me and the Earth". This rainbow is represented by the Archer's bow in a spiral arm of the Milky Way as the cloud of smoke from the Altar (see Fig. 38).

Moreover, it has been supposed that the great stellar giant, Orion, is the representative of "Nimrod, the mighty hunter before the Lord", the founder of the Babylonian kingdom (Gen 10:9). He has been identified by some Assyriologists with Marduk, the primeval tutelary deity of Babylon. The bright stars of Orion were seen immediately below the horns of Taurus, during the nights of autumn in 2700 BC. In the meantime, the Earth's axis precessed 66°, and so today Orion and Taurus are the most conspicuous constellations of winter, visible from December until March. In general, because of precession the midnight constellations of spring in 2700 BC are today to be seen during the nights of summer; the midnight constellations of winter in 2700 BC are visible during the nights of spring.

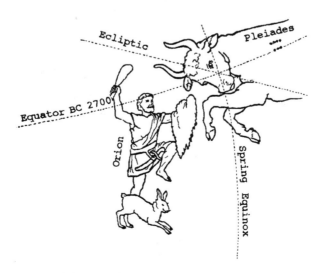

Fig.39: Orion and the vernal equinox in Taurus, 2700 BC

Edward Walter Maunder states that twenty-two of the ancient Mesopotamian constellations appear to have a close connection with some of the events recorded in the first ten chapters of Genesis as having taken place in the earliest ages of the world's history. But the constellation figures only deal with a very few isolated events in the Hebrew Bible. "The points in common with the Genesis narrative are indeed striking, but the points of independence are no less striking. The majority of the constellation figures do not appear to refer to any incidents in Genesis; the majority of the incidents in Genesis narrative find no record in the sky" (Maunder 1908, p.168).

Today the signs are not constellations in the original sense of the word. Each of the zodiacal signs has the name of the constellation it contained 2500 yeras ago, when the signs were introduced. In the meantime, the constellations are shifted by precession of the equinoxes; the celestial point of the spring equinox moved 30 degrees westward among the stars of the zodiac, and the signs also slid westward away from the respective constellations, because the signs are counted from the vernal equinox, i.e., from 0° Aries to 360°, independent from the constellations. When the ancient astronomers said, for example, "Jupiter entered Pisces on March 15", it meant that the planet Jupiter had the ecliptic longitude 330°. Thus, in our epoch, when the Sun arrives on March 21 at the vernal equinox it is then in the constellation of Pisces, and will not enter the constellation Aries.

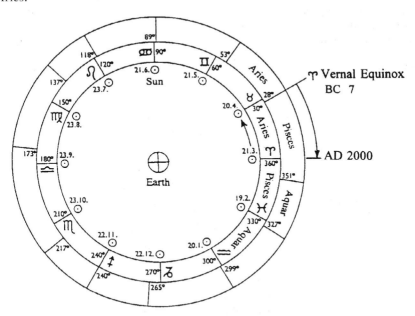

Fig. 40: The internal circle shows the 30° sections of the zodiacal signs and the dates of the Sun's position at the first degree of each sign. The external circle shows the actual longitudes and positions of the constellations with respect to the vernal equinox in 7 BC and 2000 AD.

237

15. *Magic, Religion and Science*

In ancient times the Magi were both priests and scientists. The three terms, magic, religion, science, were then still equivalent, but nowadays they have been sharply divided by modern theories. It is now said that magic is contrary to science, and science is contrary to religion. But would not some golden middle way be the best solution? In recent decades there has been an attempt on the part of research into the psychology and history of religion to find a common denominator. Researchers have been all the more encouraged to do so now that certain practices of magic have recently been gaining ground and have become widely popular.

What explanation is there for magic being linked to scientific knowledge and religious practices? Even today the clearest description and explanation of this problem is found in the books of the Bible. The importance of the question is illustrated by the story of the Magi from the East who were guided by their religious belief in their search for the Messiah King, and who also made use of their scientific knowledge to find him. Our age is characterized by a scientific view of the world and Christian culture. Whichever point of view we adopt, we consider magic outdated and reject it as misbelief and superstition. Nevertheless, an ever increasing number of books dealing with the secret science of antiquity is being published in our days. Instead of speaking about superstition they try to explain the efficiency of magic by some known and unknown laws of nature. Although neither scientists nor the Church accept their pseudoscientific arguments, there are many scientists both the Academy of Sciences and the Church refuse their pseudoscientific arguments, there are many people who believe in astrology, dream-reading, palmistry, spiritism, in charms that bring good luck and in the healing power of precious stones and noble metals, crystal pyramids, magic rings, divining rods, and so on.

Could all of this really be mere superstition or just some misplaced belief, which attributes a supernatural force to these things ? According to moral teaching anyone who attributes to something a force that was not given to it by God, commits the sin of superstition. But who knows what forces are hidden in certain creatures, forces we have not yet been able to find and assess? The rotation of the Earth had also been considered a false assumption until scientists managed to prove the fact by empirical evidence and accurate calculations. Who would have thought that it was the invisible atomic nucleus that possessed immense energy until the assumption was proven by the explosion and devastating effect of the first atom bomb ? "It is hard to say how much of old superstition is science and how much of today's science is misbelief" is an often quoted statement by Maximilian Hell. This may have sounded very wise two hundred years ago, when the Hungarian Jesuit was professor of astronomy at the University of Vienna. His witty remark, however, warns us even today to be wary about both superstition and science as long as we have no decisive evidence.

Scientific results require diligent research, and every science has its specific methods. The natural sciences use the following methods: repeated observations, experiments, measurements, calculations, the determination of results, the expression of regularities by mathematical formulas and finally the systematizing of the proved facts. Magic in this sense cannot be

238

called a science; it is only intuitive knowledge, which relies on intuition to reveal the interactions of certain natural forces. In the Hellenic age magic, combined with Chaldaean astronomy and the method of Greek natural philosophy, started to evolve into a more scientific system though even at that stage it lacked any solid scientific basis and remained the secret trade of the initiated. The biblical Book of Wisdom (17:7) refers to it very aptly as "magic arts" (*magichê technê*); it interprets the experienced interactions on the basis of uncertain and arbitrary rules, but it is unable to verify them by laws of nature. An example of this is Ptolemy's Tetrabiblos on the traditional rules of astrological predictions.

The only common feature of ancient magic and modern science is the endeavor of man to discover the laws of nature and put them to his own use.Their methods in achieving this, however, are essentially different. Magic resorts to belief and rites, science on the other hand resorts to reason and calculations. Nevertheless, these two ways do not exclude each other. People always feel that their lives and welfare depend on the action of invisible forces, which are favorable on the one hand and dangerous on the other. As long as people are unfamiliar with the origin and nature of these forces, they tend to identify them with spiritual powers or gods. This belief leads to superstitions and rites, which can be called religious practices but are in no way the same as religion. Magic has no uniformly formulated religious theses, no common creed, no organized confessions.

Man, when faced with some unknown force, is even today inclined to attribute them to ghosts, in which case, no doubt, he must be superstitious. Children are scared when they hear the wind blowing the door at night, and they think the ghosts are knocking at the door. When they look up at the sky and see clouds in all the colors of the rainbow, they think of angels. It is very instructive to read Isaac Newton's writings on how he discovered the three laws of dynamics. He describes the first physical experiments he carried out when he was a child. When there was strong wind, he would jump as long as he could against the wind and also in the direction it was blowing, and then he would measure the length of his jump in both directions. That was how he tried to determine his own physical strength compared to that of the wind, in which even he had felt some spiritual force at that time. That experiment was a long way from Newton's epochal work, *Mathematical Principles of Natural Philosophy*, which he published at the age of 44. That was perhaps the first book which truly put physical forces at man's service and in which, by the formula of universal gravitation, the secret of the motion of celestial bodies was also revealed. Unlike all the practical rules of magic, Newton's 2nd law seems amazingly simple: the net force on a body is equal to the product of its mass and its acceleration ($F = m.a$). Likewise, the amount of the gravity, the attracting force between two masses, can be calculated from the change which it produces in the velocity and path of moving bodies.

The story of optics is just as exciting. Newton was once standing by the window of his room whose thick sheet glass had a semicircular crack in it. He was observing the sunlight streaming in and suddenly, noticing some brightly colored rings around it, he exclaimed in surprise: *spectre!* The English word derives from the Latin *spectrum* and means ghost or phantom. Newton did not reveal whether he had meant a phantom or ghost at the time or whether he was just joking. In any case he had a closer look at the window pane and he came to the conclusion that the colored rings were produced by the sunlight passing through the crack. In his first study devoted to this phenomenon he referred to the biblical rainbow, which had been a divine sign to future ages after the Deluge. But Newton continued his observations and started systematic experiments. He studied the nature of sunlight with the help of prisms, lenses and mirrors and finally stated that the colors were hidden in light. That was how he devised the basic laws of optics in the phenomena of refraction, dispersion and reflection of light. The word *spectrum* is still used in Optics, but nobody thinks of ghost or divine sign when hearing it. When a beam of light passes obliquely from air into glass its direction is altered. Because the amount of the change in direction increases progressively with decrease in wavelength of the light, from red to violet, the beam is dispersed by refraction into a spectrum. Thus the rainbow is produced when sunlight is dispersed by raindrops. The formation of a spectrum can be observed by passing the light through a glass prism.

Newton devoted his whole life to the research of force and light. He regarded them as divine signs or mysteries even when he knew exactly which laws governed them. Newton was just as honest as he was intelligent and he had the courage to declare that the ultimate source of any force or light was the superior intellect which had determined the harmonic order of the laws of nature.

The solid foundations of modern science were laid in the 17th century by four men of genius: Kepler, Galileo, Leibnitz and Newton. When Newton remarked: "It is because I am standing on the shoulders of giants that I can see further than others", he had Kepler and Galileo in mind. On reading their writings today, many people are amazed to find how their world concept reflected a perfect harmony of human intellect and Christian faith, natural science and divine revelation. What has all this got to do with magic? The 17th century could well be called the age of redeemed magic, had it not witnessed the devastating wars of religion followed by the bourgeois revolutions. After the Enlightenment human thinking sank into the dark depths of extreme rationalism and materialism, where only human intellect and inanimate matter were worshipped.

How far have we come since then? Gurus and yogis from India come to Europe and America, where they are welcomed by many as the wise magi of the east who preach the practices of self-redemption. Are they not right to warn the people of the West that by having abandoned Christ and having transformed the sciences into destructive black magic they have lost their souls? We are all familiar with the terrible history of the past decades, which has seen the explosion of the atomic bomb, the failure of some nuclear reactors and an increasing radioactive pollution. In view of this we have every right to expect responsible scientists to learn from history and have more faith in the redemptive force of Christian love than in magic practices that promise self-redemption.

The Christian view of the world and scientific progress have convinced people that natural forces are neither gods nor superhuman spirits. This led some people blinded by superficial knowledge to the conclusion that there are no spirits of higher order and we do not need God either, because science will explain and conquer all the invisible forces. Have they forgotten that the uncertainty of our earthly existence can be relieved by neither the most advanced science nor high technology? The progress of science can make man's life easier, but it will never provide full health or immortality.

Many people refuse to take into account the fact that it was Christian teaching and religion that liberated mankind from the worship of natural forces. Thus, objective research and the development of technology were first rendered possible by Christian culture. The seventeenth century geniuses mentioned above revealed openly that it was the Scriptures that had inspired them. Modern man, however, is always tempted to regard both scientific progress and Christian redemption only as man's self redemption. Thus he can easily fall victim to conceit and presumption, which, according to analytical psychologists is a possession by an unconscious power complex. Ancient primitive magic is characterized by this very possession. The term *power-complex* denotes "the whole complex of ideas and strivings which seek to subordinate all other influences to the *ego* or to my own will" (Jung, *Psychological Types*, 782).

There is no place within the framework of this book to discuss in detail the very timely problem mentioned above, i.e., that many today have begun to believe in the old magical arts. We shall merely try to outline its most important features. Thus perhaps it will be easier to understand how closely the role of the Magi in Matthew's Gospel is related to the basic message of the whole Scripture and what far reaching conclusions can be drawn from it even today.

The role of magic in cultural history can be summed up in the following points. The practices of magic in ancient times include some that are useful and right and others that are harmful and wrong, but man's innate desire and wish to have real knowledge and religion, freedom and redemption are present in all of them. This process continues in an increasingly conscious and clear form in the Middle Ages (e.g. alchemy, astrology, Christian asceticism-mysticism). In more recent times certain professions and rules of magic greatly contributed to the development of relevant sciences (e.g. astronomy, physics, biology). In contemporary history, especially from the middle of the 19th century, a part of the knowledge and practices of magic are transformed into systematized sciences (e.g. chemistry, pharmacology, psychology), whereas another part forms even today the subject of scientific research (e.g. cosmology, cosmic geophysics, parapsychology).

In the following, two themes will be discussed: the relationship between magic and religious practice, and the relationship between magic and scientific knowledge. The relationship between magic and religious practice are best illustrated by the Bible: by the attitude of the prophets, and later by the attitude of Christ and his apostles to contemporary practices of magic. The relationship between magic and scientific knowledge or the influence of magic on modern scientific research is shown mainly by the development of astronomy and psychology.

In detail, Moses and his prophets made a distinction between real and false magic. Unlike Egyptian magicians, Moses was Israel's true *Magus*, i.e., its Prophet and Teacher. He forbade everything that led to the worship of idols, but he made use of what he felt represented true religious values. Writing, reading, mathematics, music and singing originally belonged to good magic, which constituted the secret knowledge of the prophets among the mostly illiterate people. Laws were introduced not because of their arbitrary lust for power but because they wanted to safeguard the purity of monotheism on the one hand, and the physical and spiritual health of the Chosen People on the other. It was for this purpose that they banned the cult of stars and natural forces, the sacrifice of children, the worship of the statues of gods, the conjuring of spirits and of the dead, witchcraft and bewitching either with drugs or incantation, prediction from external signs or in entrancement, which state was induced by vegetable drugs (*pharmakeia*). All this is false magic because it is contrary to the true knowledge and worship of God. God identifies himself for Moses as an eternal and omnipotent being: "I am Who is". Christ teaches: "God is spirit, and those who worship him, must worship in spirit and truth" (Ex 3:14; Jn 4:24).

However, the prophets determined the days of the movable feasts on the basis of the Moon's phases; they called on the stars to praise the Lord; they believed in the impact of benediction and malediction psalms; they offered fragrant incense and food sacrifices as an expression of their gratitude, and their most important propitiatory rite performed to get rid of vice was to sprinkle the people with the blood of sacrificial animals. Moses and the prophets resorted not only to human faith and spiritual force. They put the false magi to shame by the force of a greater Spirit: "They prophesied by the Spirit of Christ which was active in them" (1 Pet 1:11).

The time of the birth of Christ was indicated to the wise Magi by stars. The fact that the Magi studied and followed the stars was not a negative event in the mind of Christ. During his crucifixion the Sun grew dark from 12 noon until 3 in the afternoon. His resurrection and ascent from the closed grave of rock took place at full moon in spring. And when he reappeared the Sun and the Moon were dimmed by the brightness of his transfigured human body. He is the Lord of the forces of nature "in heaven and on earth". With his miracles he proves the presence and mercy of the Almighty who speaks to the people through him. (Cf. Mt 24:28-31; 28:18).

Jesus's self-sacrificing love put an end to the bloody sacrifices once and for all. Instead of the magic rites performed by human schemes, he administered sacraments having divine force. Through all his words and deeds, he convinced people of the supremacy of the spirit over body and matter. This spirit, however, is not only human spirit but the Holy Spirit, creator of the world, who is radiated by Christ into his sacraments and the hearts of his followers. Those who truly accept him can conquer all the forces of nature. His faithful apostles and priests testified to this, and not only in those days; they have done so in the past centuries and in our days, as well.

The apostle Paul's words on the weakness of magic practices and the futility of the Old Covenant's sacrifices are clear and convincing. He very aptly uses the term mental minority ("before we came of age") to describe the religion of antiquity, in contrast to full maturity "with the fullness of Christ". The 9th and 10th chapters of the letter addressed to the Hebrews describe magic rites as vague prototypes of real religion; as "the service of a model or a reflection of the heavenly realities" (cf. Gal 4:3; Eph 4:13; Heb 8:5; 10:1f). The Acts of the Apostles contains exciting writings on the failure of certain false magi. When the apostles preached, they were guided by faith coupled with goodwill and common sense; that was how they worked wonders in Christ's name alone, without any witchcraft or magic practices. When the people realized that they were capable of healing the sick and raising the dead, "a number of them who had practiced magic collected their books and made a bonfire of them in public; the value of these was calculated to be fifty thousand silver pieces" (Acts 19:19).

The Church's Magisterium warns the faithful against divination and magic by the following words in the new edition of the Catechism:

> God can reveal the future to his prophets or to other saints. Still, a sound Christian attitude consists in putting oneself confidently into the hands of Providence for whatever concerns the future, and giving up all unhealthy curiosity about it. . . All forms of divination are to be rejected. Consulting horoscopes, astrology, palm reading, interpretation of omens and lots, the phenomena of clairvoyance, and recourse to mediums all conceal a desire for power over time, history and, in the last analysis, other human beings. They contradict the honor, respect and loving fear that we owe to God alone. . . All practices of magic or sorcery, by which one attempts to tame occult powers, so as to place them at one's service and have a supernatural power over others are gravely contrary to the virtue of religion. Spiritism often implies divination or magical practices; the Church for her part warns the faithful against it (CCC 1992, 2115-2117).

The falsity and insufficiency of magic comes from the fact that it forms a wrong concept of both human and divine reality. It cannot differentiate between the purely spiritual Creator and spiritual and material creatures and forces. Magic is dangerous because the magician believes in evil forces, which he wants to use to the detriment of others. He seeks only his own power and glory and so wants to put both people and God to his own service. Christ, on the other hand, guides people towards true knowledge and worship of God. He shows them that *there are no evil forces, only forces used in an evil way*. Everything depends on how we make use of physical forces and our spiritual abilities; in an intelligent, moderate and fair way, or in a selfishly immoderate and unfair way, without taking account of either God or man. The achievements of modern science and technology are very useful for aquiring knowledge and establishing social well being, but blind selfishness and the lust for power turns them into a kind of black magic.

This is the danger the Apostle Paul is hinting at when he quotes the Book of Wisdom to the Romans referring to those who are aware of God and yet refuse to honor him: "For what can be known of God is perfectly plain to them, since God made it plain to them: ever since the creation of the world, the invisible existence of God and his everlasting power have been clearly seen by the mind's understanding of created things" (Rom 1:19-20). A hundred years earlier the author of the Book of Wisdom had felt sorry for those:

> ... who are unaware of God, and who, from good things seen, have not been able to discover Him who is, or, by studying the works, have not

recognized the Artificer. Fire, however, or wind, or the swift air, the sphere of the stars, impetuous water, heaven's lamps, are what they have held to be the gods who govern the world. If they have been impressed by their power and energy, let them deduce from these how much mightier is he that has formed them. Small blame, however, attaches to them, for perhaps they go astray only in their search for God and their eagerness to find him; familiar with his works, they investigate them and fall victim to appearances, seeing so much beauty. But even so, they have no excuse: if they are capable of acquiring enough knowledge to be able to investigate the world, how have they been so slow to find its Master? (Wis 13:1-9).

To this two-thousand year old question the psychologist would today say: the reason for this may be that their conscious minds were possessed by their unconscious lust for power and greed. So no matter how great their science, they are unable to make use of their mental powers of knowledge and judgment, or they did not want to use it for that purpose at all, because they are afraid of its consequences.

We will now examine the relationship between magic and scientific knowledge. There are a number of historical facts which show what a significant role magic played in scientific research. The magi seriously attempted to observe the interactions, which they perceived between certain natural phenomena and physiological processes, without at first looking for a rational explanation of these interactions. They were content with mythological beliefs, which were in accordance with the desires of the people. They thought that the respective configurations and motions of the Sun, Moon, and planets conveyed the will of gods and determined the course of things on Earth. It was actually this belief that induced them to make more accurate observations and calculations. The magi started to use mathematical formulas in order to be able to better verify the results of their observations. Their primary aim was to make more accurate calendars, measurements of time and weather forecasts and to put all this to the service of the state and society.

This practice formed part of the profession of the Babylonian magi, and originally it was a kind of natural astrology. That profession subsequently led to the formation of mathematical astronomy and its modern counterpart, astrophysics. The latter deals with the internal structure and the radiation of stars and planets. Astronomical textbooks usually mention the merit of ancient astrology:

The science of astronomy owes a great debt to astrology, because its practice required a detailed knowledge of the motions of the celestial bodies... Astronomers from the time of antiquity to the time of Galileo devoted most of their energy to constructing models or schemes that would allow the accurate calculation of the planetary positions at arbitrary times in the future. Both Tycho Brahe and Kepler prepared horoscopes as part of their duties. Had they not been employed to do so, the development of the laws of planetary motion, and ultimately our modern technology, would certainly not have come when it did (Abell 1969, p.11).

244

There were some magi who claimed to have recognized the hidden spiritual forces by observing the sky and declared that they were able to control them with the help of the stars. They believed that whatever event takes place in the world, it happens at the right moment. As to the right moment, they were able to calculate it from the position of the Moon and the planets. Sometimes they achieved amazing results, when for example they interpreted dreams and their predictions came true. They managed to cure certain illnesses by using the so called transmission of energy, magnetic slumber (enchantment), by certain precious stones and medicinal herbs. The Egyptian-Greek and Aramean magic papyrus scrolls testify to all this, and Pliny also lists several examples of their achievements (Pliny, *Hist. Nat.* 20-28, 220). These methods of healing practices as well as in order to counterbalance them, Greek philosophers worked out the theory of causality and the rules of logical thinking (induction, deduction). Perhaps the most famous achievement among them is Aristotle's philosophy, an important part of which is the nature of the psyche and epistemology, devoted to man's faculty of judgment and the method of correct cognition. Every scientific work applies the rules of logic and criticism to explain and to prove statements. The aforementioned methods of healing practices and interpretation of dreams form part of medical and psychological research today. As early as the 12th century the Benedictine Abbess, St. Hildegard, having thoroughly investigated the properties of precious stones and medicinal herbs, gave an accurate description of their effect and use. She is thought to be the founder of German pharmacology. (Hildegard Gesellschaft 1982).

Enchantment was a typical craft of the magi. It was the activity the people most often requested from them and for which they paid them. The magus would look intently at his patient and would chant or sing in a rhythmic voice the words of the magic song (*epôdos*). This would induce a sleeplike state in the patient, enabling him or her to adopt unconsciously the good or bad suggestions. Such psychical energy transfer must have had a very soothing and healing effect, but they must have also been dangerous, because they often led to derangement or crime. For that reason they were prohibited not only by the prophets, but later also by the laws of the state.

The methods of suggestion and hypnosis have derived from the ancient practice of enchantment, but only in the 20th century were their merits proven by scientifically verifiable experiments. It took decades of research and disputes before the practice of medical hypnosis was officially accepted. Innumerable cases prove how successfully it can be applied for the treatment of physical and mental illnesses where other methods have failed. The treatment by hypnosis, however, has its specific difficulties and dangers, which is why very few physicians resort to it. We have seen many cases of how harmful hypnosis can be in uninitiated hands, a reason why many people are averse to it even today.

The art of the interpretation of dreams has evolved into the so called psychoanalysis introduced by the Viennese neurologist, Sigmund Freud, because the dubious method of hypnosis did not seem to make any sense to him. Instead of predictions, however, Freud used the analysis of dreams to cure nervous and mental disorders. Today, the interpretation of the dreams emerging from the subconscious psyche is a special field of analytical psychology. The correct method of interpreting dreams was developed by the Swiss psychiatrist, Carl Gustav Jung. He determined the distinctive features of significant and insignificant dreams. Then, through a great number of cases he proved that significant dreams testify not only to the repressed memories of the past or psychic injuries suffered in childhood, but express the difficulties arising from a person's present psychical state and at the same time indicate the way to a right solution. The most important dreams, however, are the ones that reflect the healthy desires and ideas present in the realm of the unconscious psyche. Bringing them to the consciousness of the individual is very important in the formation of the mature personality. In this respect dreams indicate man's inner future too, because it is every person's innermost desire to fully evolve their personality.

It is from this point of view that Jung explains the Biblical stories in which dreams appear as divine revelations or directions. For the prophets the interpretation of dreams belonged to magic and as such they did not deal with them, but they believed in the divine origin of significant dreams. Religious people of the Old Covenant were able to interpret their own dreams, because they had a much more refined sense in this area than today's irreligious city dwellers.

The analysis of dreams has also revealed that dreams can sometimes show precisely distant events taking place in the present or events which are to take place in the future. When one's physical senses and conscious faculties are asleep, the latent psychic faculties hidden in the unconscious sometimes wake up and become active. Some people experience the activity of these telepathic faculties even in a waking state, while others are apparently even capable of using them at will. In magazines and television programs we can sometimes see persons who can read thoughts of others or read writings in a sealed envelope, who talk about future events, can move distant objects without touching them, can bend metal objects and are capable of curing illnesses by the imposition of hands. In the past only the initiated magi were supposed to possess such extraordinary powers, but in our days parapsychology deals with their study. The first Parapsychological Research Institute was founded in America at Duke University by J.B. Rhine in 1934. In the 1950s the methodical study of paranormal phenomena was introduced at several European universities. Professor Hans Bender was the director of research at the Parapsychological Institute of Freiburg for thirty years and the results of his observations were published in scholarly works. Those who nowadays wish to know more about this subject, will find plenty of reliable literature devoted to it.

Research in this field has been delayed by two circumstances. Scientists denounced the extraordinary phenomena as mere imagination or considered them delusive trickery of the kind any skillful magician could produce. Spiritists on the other hand insisted on the intervention of ghosts. The primary task of psychologists was therefore to verify, both from a quantitative and a qualitative point of view, whether such phenomena really existed. They made repeated experiments and measurements to investigate the state of mind and performance of the so called mediums, individuals with different paranormal faculties. Their findings excluded the possibility of imagination or fraud, so they were able to determine the special features and origin of the extraordinary phenomena.

These phenomena are called paranormal, because they occur beside (*para*) or on the border of a persons's usual faculties and experiences. The mediums are usually unable to control their own faculties, often they do not realize that the source of the extraordinary phenomena is in themselves and they tend to mistake those for external forces, e.g. for the activity of ghosts. The most common manifestations of extrasensory perception are telepathy (the remote understanding of the thoughts of others), clairvoyance (the faculty to perceive or see clearly remote events) and precognition (the faculty to foresee something in advance of its occurrence). Their source is human intuition which, however, does not function all the time and the results of which are not always reliable. So far, all attempts to lay down the rules of the functioning of telepathic faculties, rules that anybody might learn, have failed. The human mind and nervous system do not work in the same way as a radio transmitter and receptor. The paranormal performances cannot be explained by transmission of electromagnetic waves because the mediums can exercise these powers even when they are shut up in a room insulated from all electromagnetic radiations.

A more mysterious symptom is that of *psychokinesis*, when certain individuals can move objects without directly touching them or can change the shape of metal objects without exerting any physical force. This usually any physical force. On the basis of observations at the Parapsychological Institutes researchers suppose that the psychophysical energy, but they cannot suggest an exact explanation of it. The measuring instruments did not show any electromagnetic effects.

Yes, we always refer to the measuring instruments. As long as our electronic devices function well, we easily forget that they are, after all,the products of the human mind. Remotely controlled machines, radio, television, telephone, and telefax are all the projections or implementations of the unconscious powers of human psyche, with the help of the known laws of nature. In any case, the achievements of modern electronic engineering materialize the dreams of the old magi.

Finally, it is worth noting that in our days analytical psychology considers also astrology as a paranormal phenomenon which has become a subject of its research program. This will make it easier to understand why it was regarded as magic by Babylonian priests, the prophets and the first Christian writers. How is it possible that astrological diagnoses and prognoses often come true? Is it perhaps the work of spirits? Or is it really the position and influence of the stars which determine man's character traits and future events? Both assumptions have been proven wrong.

In recent years astrophysicists and astrologers have been engaged in an increasingly intense dispute, which nevertheless has remained fruitless. Did they fail to notice that they were putting forward their arguments in two basically different philosophical systems ? Astrological theory holds that the physical and psychical traits as well as the future prospects of the individual are determined at the moment of birth by the mutual aspects of the Sun, the Moon, and the planets according to their position in the zodiacal signs. Today's astrologers who seek scientific recognition want to prove this theory by making use of what modern geophysics and astrophysics have discovered about cosmic radiation and its effects on physical and biological processes. In the character studies and forecasts they write they use some of the well known terms of psychology and present their work as the new science of cosmopsychology and cosmobiology. Scientists vehemently protest, because all this disagrees with scientifically provable facts. Their counter arguments are briefly as follows: Astrologers still count in the old geocentric system and take no account of the precession of the equinoxes and when, for example, they give the position of the Sun in the sign of Aries, it is in fact in the constellation of Pisces. As far as cosmic radiation is concerned, neither the Moon, nor the planets nor the constellations emit such radiations. Most of these radiations are emitted by the Sun into the electromagnetic field and atmosphere of the Earth, where they sometimes cause sudden changes, which, however, are unpredictable. So far we have been unable to quantitatively or qualitatively determine the biological effects of cosmic radiation. The effect of the gravitational attraction of the Sun and Moon can be observed in the tidal variation of waters and in certain physiological processes which are connected with it. Nevertheless, by no means does this prove the theses of astrology, which are totally unfounded both from the physical and the biological point of view.

These arguments do not in the least affect the advocates of cosmopsychology, who, for their part, deny believing in the physical effect of the stars. According to them the phenomena that we face here are astral effects originating in the subconscious depths of the human mind, not in constellations or the mutual aspects of planets. The same forces and laws are functioning in a human being's psychophysical nature as in the universe, although in a different way and to a different extent. Thus the heavens or the position and motion of the planets at any moment reflect the psychophysical state of a human being. It is on this basis that a persons characteristic features can be gathered from his or her birth chart. There is no fatalistic determination, because it does not exclude man's faculty of free decision and choice, as a free agent. However, from a scientific point of view this explanation is equally insufficient.

On the basis of their comparative experiments, H. Bender and C.G. Jung stated that a large per cent of the astrological analyses of character are in accordance with the results of psychological examinations. This congruence, however, can only be explained by the *Principle of Synchronicity*, not by the causal effect of the stars. There can be a certain analogy between physical and psychical events, i.e., a coincidence without causal relation. It seems that every psychic state is in an obvious analogous relation with the physical circumstances, for example, certain constellations or climatic changes, which occur at the same time. This presupposes that both states have a common source which is neither physical, nor psychical, but a neutral third. It is a logical necessity that such a third agency is a reality outside usual space-time, so it cannot be determined by conventional methods. (Cf. Jung 1971, *Synchronicity. An Acausal Connecting Principle*).

The principle of synchronicity is the most probable explanation of paranormal phenomena. Anybody or anything that comes into being at a moment of time having a certain characteristic (such as summer or winter etc.) will possess the natural attributes determined by that particular time, claimed Jung who illustrated this statement with several examples. It is possible that in some people the examination of the constellation of birth awakens a paranormal faculty which to some extent is capable of describing the personality traits and habitual modes of response of an individual.

16. *Dates in the Vision of Daniel*

The dates in the Bible are in most cases symbolic or are rough estimates. The dates of the reigns of different kings and the dates of certain events can, however, be taken literally as long as they can be verified from other sources. The Book of Maccabees dates its accounts from 137 to 177 of the Seleucid era (175-135 BC). Its description of the time of Antiochus Epiphanes IV verifies the relevant prophecies of Daniel. The only prophets who, when talking about future events, gave dates as well, were Jeremiah and Daniel. History has partly proved these dates accurate. But besides their numerical accuracy, they have a deep symbolic meaning, however, "the key which would help explain them is lost for us, and it is difficult to find it again". (Cf. Léon-Dufour 1970, 1155-59).

Many astronomers and mathematicians have since tried to find that key, and some even believed that they had found it. The results, however, are disputable. Our calculations may be right, but, if the starting point is unfounded, they may lead to false conclusions. It is not by way of astronomical observations and calculations that the prophet finds the dates, but with the help of direct inspiration and his intuitive faculty.

Daniel's prophecies foretold not only the near future but the age of the Messiah as well. Thus only Christ's person, his teaching and his history have given us a complete and reliable explanation of these prophecies. With all his words and deeds Jesus proves that it is about him and his age that the prophets talked. He is the Son of Man, whom Daniel saw and foretold. In the Gospel of Matthew, Jesus calls himself the Son of Man twenty-nine times. Finally, Christ appears again in the Book of Revelation of the Apostle John and he breaks the seven seals of the scroll of the future, thus continuing his revelations given to Daniel. (Cf. Mt 24:18-30; Rev 5:1-5).

The proverb, "history repeats itself", comes from common experience of man experience. The preacher of the Old Testament said: "What was, will be again; what has been done, will be done again, and there is nothing new under the Sun" (Eccles 1:9). Man's attitude to life in antiquity is governed by the idea of eternal return inspired by the order of nature. Phenomena like the sunrises, the full moons and the seasons recur at alternating intervals, but they occur regularly and show the time of the annual holidays. To some extent, the chronology of historical events also corresponds to a certain cosmic rhythm. In some cases the inspired prophets clearly saw this relation. The principle of synchronicity mentioned above can help us to understand this: the features of recurring cosmic periods, historical events and prophetic visions are qualitatively analogous, because there is a reasonable inherent synchronicity between them without any causal relation. Their common source can therefore only be a reality beyond space and time. So past, present and future often merge in the prophets' visions which, for this reason, are applicable in any age.

In the course of the centuries before Christ, the prophecies about the Messiah were linked to personalities, which to some extent lived up to people's expectations. Such a Messiah was seen in King David who, a thousand years before Christ, freed his people from the enemy and peacefully united the twelve tribes of Israel. The Persian King Cyrus was also proclaimed Messiah, because he had liberated God's people after seventy years of Babylonian captivity and provided for the rebuilding of the Temple of Jerusalem. In the course of later persecutions the people impatiently awaited the advent of the promised King and an increasing number of Israelite leaders took up the name of Messiah. The last one among them was *Bar-Kochba*, the "Son of Star", between 132-135 AD. These leaders were all heroes, who fought for liberty, but they either misinterpreted the prophets, or were proclaimed Messiah by the people.

Many people misunderstand the prophets even today. What the prophets preach is not the recurrence of the eternal return, which makes no sense in itself. The regular recurrence of the spring full moon and spring resurgence can only be interpreted as the natural symbol of the resurrection of the dead. In prophetical visions the seasonal recurrence of individual events is not a closed cycle, as if the whole process should occur on the same plane. The recurring events are similar, but not the same, because they progress gradually towards a determined final end. In the visions of the prophets, the course of historical time is illustrated by a spiral line which, starting from one point progresses in gradually expanding and later contracting circles, until it finally stops at the peak. The starting and final points coincide in the eternal spirit. This is symbolized by the cross on the spire of the church tower or by the star in the vault of a sanctuary, like the North Star in the sky.

The development of human awareness and culture, the evolution of the individual and society progress together with the rhythm of historical and cosmic time. The ultimate aim of all this is "the full maturity with the fullness of Christ", i.e., full and eternal health (salvation) in the world of a "new heaven and new earth" (Eph 4:13; Is 65:17; Rev 21:1). The risen Christ says: "I am the Alpha and the Omega, the First and the Last, the Beginning and the End... I am the sprig from the root of David and the bright star of the morning" (Rev 22:13 and 16).

To understand these revelations, we must refer to the history of numbers. The ancient Hebrews and Greeks used their alphabet numerically, having no independent numeral system. All numbers were denoted by letters, and each word had its own particular number. The Hebrew alphabet consists of twenty-two consonants: Alef = 1 and the last one, Tau = 400. The Greek alphabet consists of twenty-four letters: Alpha=1, and the last one, Omega = 800.

According to the conception of the ancient East the name of a human being expresses its particular nature, defined by the numerical value of the letters. For example, the Hebrew word *adam* (adm =1+4+40 = 45) is derived from *adamah* (admh = (1+4+40+5 = 50) which signifies earth or soil. According to Moses' narrative, this formula is a perfect symbol of the way the Lord God created a human being: he fashioned a body of dust from the soil, then breathed into its nostrils a breath of life, "and thus *adam* became a living being". This collective noun was to become the proper name of the first man. The apostle Paul goes farther with his explanation: "The first man, Adam, being from the earth, is earthly by nature [subject to death]; but the second man, the last Adam [Jesus] is from heaven; he has become a life giving spirit" (Gen 2:7; 1 Cor 15:45-48). Expressed by the age old mystical numbers the earthly life of Adam is symbolized by 44; and the eternal life of Jesus by 888, beyond the physical world $(J+\hat{E}+S+O+U+S = 10+8+200+70+400+200 = 888$, written with Greek letters).

The numbers four and forty show the wholeness of human nature in the totality of the physical world. Moreover, the number four includes the number three. Through creation and incarnation the Creator of the world appears as three persons. This trinity is reflected in nature in various forms, from the structure of atoms through three-dimensional bodies to the three personal pronouns. According to the revelation of Christ, the Holy Trinity One God is "the Father and the Son and the Holy Spirit" (Mt 28:19). The second divine Person "by the power of the Holy Spirit became incarnate from the Virgin Mary, and was made man" (Nicene Creed): he is the only Son of God the Father (Jn 1:14). The Holy Trinity is visible in the person of Jesus Christ. Divine essence (3) and human nature (4) are in complete unity in him. The number seven (3+4) in this sense symbolizes the Word incarnate (7); it is in general the measure of fulfillment and fullness in the present order of Creation. The practice of associating a name with its number carried on into the New Testament. An example of this is the number of the beast in the Book of Revelation: "it is the number of a man, the number 666" (Rev 13:18).

The promise of the Messiah was made to the family of King David. The numerical value of his name is D+V+D = 4+6+4 = 14 (= 7+7). Jesus of Nazareth was believed to be the descendant of King David. Therefore, Matthew lists three times fourteen generations (or 6×7) from Abraham to Christ, wanting thus to express that Jesus is the Divine Messiah, it is in him that every prophecy is fulfilled. Eight (8) symbolizes the resurrected and glorified Christ who promises the eight beatitudes to his flock in eternity (Mt 5:3-10). Its symbol is the eight-pointed morning star.

The symbolic meaning of the numbers is in harmony with their historical importance. The three basic one digit numbers (3,4,7) really determine the rhythm of cosmic time, our calendar systems, and historical periods, too. The numbers referring to the future are to be found in chapters 7-12 of the Book of Daniel. Here the prophet is writing in the first person singular. There are twelve different numbers in his visions: 3.5, 7, 49, 62, 70, 434, 490, 1260, 1290, 1335, 2300. Seven numbers among them are exactly divisible by 3.5, and their greatest common divisor is 7. The common divisor of the last four numbers is 5, the symbol of the law and the prophets.

In the first year of the reign of Darius (522 BC) Daniel was studying the prophecy of Jeremiah and found that "seventy years were to pass before the successive devastations of Jerusalem would come to an end" (Dn 9:2; Jer 25:11). Jeremiah mentioned this when Nebuchadnezzar attacked Jerusalem and made its king his vassal in 605 BC. Seventy years had passed since then, and a part of the exiles returned to Jerusalem, but the Temple was still in ruins. Since Daniel foresaw the further persecutions threatening his people, he, penitent and fasting, begged for the grace of God and for information about the future. Then he received the revelation of the seventy weeks of years:

Seventy weeks [70×7 = 490 years] are decreed for your people and your holy city, for putting an end to transgressions..., for introducing everlasting righteousness, for fulfilling the vision and prophecy, and for anointing the Holy of Holies [the Messiah and his Sanctuary]. Know this, then, and understand: From the time there went out this message: Return and rebuild Jerusalem to the coming of an anointed Prince [Messiah], seven weeks and sixty-two weeks [7×7 = 49 and 62×7 = 483 years] with squares and ramparts restored and rebuilt, and after the sixty-two weeks an Anointed One put to death,...,city and sanctuary ruined by a prince who is to come, he will strike a firm alliance with many people for the space of a week [7 years]; and for the space of one half-week [3.5 years] he will put a stop to sacrifice and oblation, and on the wing of the Temple will be the appalling abomination [idols of Zeus or Jupiter] until the end, until the doom assigned to the devastator (Dn 9: 24-27, according to the translation by St. Jerome).

When could the message to rebuild Jerusalem have been pronounced ? On the basis of the Scriptures and traditions, there are four possibilities, and the periods predicted by Daniel's numbers are to be found in each. In the Hebrew text, the numbers are not separated from each other. They are written in a manner that makes it possible to add them by pairs and to interpret them one by one. Remarkably, the prophet does not write simple dates, but products of multiplication without any definite measure of time. It follows that he has recurring periods in mind, the unit of measure of which is not the usual earthly day.

Seven years passed between the prophecy of Jeremiah and the exile (605-598 BC) and seventy years between the same prophecy and the return of the first groups (605-535 BC). Cyrus issued the decree to rebuild Jerusalem in 538 BC, forty-nine years after the destruction of the Temple. However, the inhabitants of Samaria and Judaea hindered the work of the newly returned people, so Darius gave new and strict orders to rebuild the Temple (522 BC). From that point in time, the new Temple was built up in seven years; the sanctuary was opened on 1 April 515 BC, seventy years after its destruction (Ezra 6:1-15).

In 458 BC Artaxerxes gave special authorization to the priest Ezra to

252

restore the Laws of Moses and the religious ritual. This decree was announced by Ezra in Jerusalem in the same year, and this event played a decisive role in the spiritual revival of Israel (Ezra 7:12). For centuries the prophecies of Daniel were kept hidden by the priests of Jerusalem. It was between 167-164 BC, during the Maccabean war of independence, that the time for the publishing of the book seemed most appropriate. By then it had become obvious that the prophecies had been fulfilled: after the fall of the Chaldaean, Persian and Greek Empires, the time of "the cunning and conspiring persecutor" had come. Judaea was occupied by Antiochus IV who banned the practice of the Mosaic religious rituals. The idol of Zeus-Jupiter was erected in the Temple and sacrifices were offered to it. This was appalling abomination in the eyes of the orthodox Israelites, many of whom were executed, while many others lost their faith and formed alliance with the tyrant.

In 171 BC, 434 years after the prophecy of Jeremiah, the high priest Onias, an Anointed Prince, was murdered. The bloodiest persecutions started in 167 and lasted three and a half years ("the space of one half-week"). All this had been prophesied by Daniel, who had, at the same time, preached the coming of the divine Messiah and the ultimate triumph of justice. His book gave strength to the people and their priests during the persecutions. In their interpretation the prophecy referred only to their age and they believed that the "Anointed One put to death" was Onias. The Book of Maccabees gives a detailed account of this (1 Mac 1:10-3:27; 2 Mac 3:1-4:35).

The liberating war of the Maccabean brothers was successful. Judas, Jonathan and Simon succeeded each other as high priests and rulers of Israel and were later recognized by Rome. Judaea's priest princes stemmed from their family tree until 37 BC, the time of Herod the Great. (From 37 BC on exactly 77 years passed until the crucifixion of Christ.) When the time of the crucifixion of Jesus had become known, the fathers of the Church tried to explain how the dates in the Book of Daniel corresponded to Christ's era. In most cases, the date of Artaxerxes's decree was considered the beginning of two important periods:

483–457 = 26 and 490–457 = 33 AD. It was in the middle of these seven last years, in 29 AD, that Jesus began his public ministry, when the priests of Jerusalem had already formed an alliance with the Roman authorities.

In terms of the Roman calendar, the decree of Artaxerxes was dated in 296 AUC and if we add the "seven weeks of years", we get 296+490 = 786 AUC, the 18th year of Tiberius, when Jesus died on the cross and "on the third day he rose again". This proved the victory of everlasting justice and the beginning of the Messianic age. The author of the Book of Chronicles, however, regarded the first year of Cyrus as the starting point (2 Chr 36:22), and this year was also used by the rabbis to count Daniel's years until the Messianic age. Remarkably, it was in the decades preceding and following the birth of Christ that the expectations of the Messiah were the strongest among the scribes of Israel.

Now that we know the date of Jesus' birth, a simple calculation will prove that the number of years that passed from the first year of Cyrus and his decree to the birth of Christ was indeed 490+49 = 539. The age of the redemption of mankind started with the forty years that passed between the birth and resurrection of Jesus. At any rate, we can establish that within a period of 80 years the prophet's prediction of the beginning of the Christian era was correct, whichever liberating decree we regard as the beginning of the "seventy weeks of years". There are exactly 80 years between the decree of Cyrus and that of Artaxerxes. According to today's biblicists, Daniel's dates are symbols of historic significance. The prophet's intention was probably to indicate the chronology of the events without precisely determining their exact date. His prophecies point to three periods of similar character:

> The war of independence and the 140 year reign of the Maccabees prepare the age of the Messiah [Christ]; the difficult period of the New Sanctuary [the Church] begins after the death of the Messiah; at the end of the times the everlasting justice in the Kingdom of Christ will appear in its full light. In the meantime, the Church of Christ will struggle against all the enemies of both God and man, and after a series of victories it will achieve the definitive triumph. (Cf. Corbishley 1975, *New Catholic Commentary*, 507f).

Taking into consideration this general interpretation of texts, we can now proceed to explain the symbolic meanings of the numbers. While doing so, we shall come across possibilities and connections that we may find surprising and interesting. Daniel is most likely to have written his numbers in the sexagesimal notation, which provides the key to the symbolic interpretation. The Babylonians, namely, used the sexagesimal numeral system, the advantage of which is that its basic number sixty (60) is divisible by ten real numbers without remainder. In this system it is also possible to write integers instead of fractions. The conversion tables used by the Babylonians for converting multiplications and divisions are well known. Sexagesimally written numbers are for example:

0'1=60; 0'2=60/30; 0'3=60/20; 0'4=60/15 and so on, whereas
1'0=60; 2'0=120; 3'0=180; 1'10=1×60+10=70;
2'20=2×60+20=140 and so on, where the multiplicator of the number denoted by the apostrophe is always 60 and the number standing after it must always be added to the product of multiplication.

In this notation the three most important numbers of Daniel can be expressed as follows:

434 = 7×60+14 = 7'14 (the self sacrificing death of the Messiah)
483 = 8×60 + 3 = 8'3 (the resurrection and ascension of the Messiah)
490 = 8×60 + 10 = 8'10 (the triumph of the Church of Christ in eternity)

In this form the symbolic value and interrelation of the special numbers mentioned above is clearly visible. Daniel's numbers are the elements of an increasing arithmetical series, where the constant difference is seven. This shows not only the progress of time, but also the qualitative development of the events until the fulfillment of the prophecy.

According to the Hebrew text, the Messiah is killed after the "sixty-two weeks". The sexagesimal formula of this is 7'14 = 7'7+7, where we can recognize the divine Person incarnate (7), who is "the sprig from the root of David" (whose name is D+V+D = 4+6+4 = 14 = 7+7). The seventh and last word of Christ on the cross was: "It is accomplished!". With the self-sacrificing death of Jesus all the prophecies were fulfilled. The next number symbol is: 8'3 = 1'0+7'3; this refers to the rebuilding of the Temple, which is to be eternal. The Son of God (7) is to rise on the third day and is to enter into the everlasting glory of the Holy Trinity (8). The rebuilding was interpreted as an allegory of the resurrection even by Christ. When Jesus drove the trades people and the money changers out of the Temple, the Pharisees asked him: "What sign can you show us to justify what you have done?" Jesus answered: "Destroy this sanctuary, and in three days I will raise it up!" The apostle John remarked: "But Jesus was speaking of the sanctuary that was his body, and when he rose from the dead, his disciples remembered that he had said this, and they believed the Scripture and the words he had said" (Jn 2:14-22).

Finally, the full number 8'10 = 490 refers to the second advent of Christ, when cosmic time stops and the everlasting celebration of triumph is achieved. The prophet gives the following explanation: then transgression will end, the time of everlasting justice and of the Holy of Holies will come. This *Sanctus Sanctorum* is Christ himself together with the community of his saints. The number eight (8) is the sign of everlasting time, i.e., eternity. Ten as the main quotient of sixty and the sum of the first four numbers is the number of full measure: 60/6 = 1+2+3+4 = 10. So 8'10 is the symbol of the everlasting triumph of the Christian Church, i.e., the community of the saints in the glory of the resurrection.

In Daniel's visions there are four larger numbers, which seem related neither to each another, nor to the aforenamed Messianic products of multiplication. Written, however, in the sexagesimal notation, their relationship and significance is obvious: 1260 = 7'0+14'0 = (70×60)+(14×60) and 1290 = 7'0+14'30 is analogous with the symbolic meaning of 7'14, extended to the community of Christ, i.e., to the history of the Church. Many thousands of Christian martyrs sacrificed their lives, thus conquering people for the Kingdom of Christ. That is the reason why the prophet says: "Blessed is he who stands firm and attains the 1335 days" and "2300 evenings and mornings will pass until the restoration of the Sanctuary". In the sexagesimal notation 1335 = 8'0+14'15 and 2300 = 8'0+30'20 corresponds to the meaning of 8'3 and 8'10, i.e., the eternal glory of the resurrection.

In the last great vision the Messiah, Christ himself, gives this interpretation of the numbers mentioned above , when he appears before the prophet; his figure dressed in white, towering over the river Euphrates, his hands lifted to the heavens as he preaches resurrection: "the virtuous will shine like the stars for all eternity!" Jesus quotes these words several times (Dan 12:2-12; Mt 13:43). However complicated the symbolic interpretation of these numbers and their relationship may seem, it is worth dealing with them. Those who still misunderstand Daniel's numbers and bear only calendar time in mind, have lost confidence in prophesying and do not believe in the Messiah. (Thus the editor of the Babylonian Talmud, for example, made the following disappointing remark in the 2nd century AD: "The Messiah has not come because transgression has not ended and there is neither justice nor peace on earth.") Others, as for instance, Seventh Day Adventists and Jehovah's Witnesses, run into other extremes and keep prophesying new dates for the end of the world and the advent of the Messiah. When, however, Christ himself refers to Daniel's prophecy, he warns his disciples: "Take care, lest somebody should mislead you, because many false prophets will come using my name and saying, I am the Messiah. Do not believe it... Nobody can foretell that day and hour" (Mt 24:4-36).

Some famous medieval Rabbis tried to determine the date of the Messiah's advent by astrological methods. They based their predictions on the traditional belief that Abraham, Moses and David had been born under the conjunction of Jupiter and Saturn, which was also the celestial sign of the Messiah. *Abram Ibn-Ezra* (also known as Avenazre) concluded that in the 5225th year of the Hebrew era (1464 AD), 2859 years after the birth of Moses, Jupiter and Saturn would again be in conjunction in the sign of *Pisces* and then the Messiah would descend from heaven. As a matter of fact such a conjunction was observed in that year, although not in the sign of *Pisces*, but apart from the Jewish community being driven out of Spain, and many of them perished while fleeing, no other significant event was recorded.

Isaac Abarbanel (also known as Abravanel), who was believed to be the last great scribe of the Old Testament, wanted to make more accurate calculations. His three volume work is a detailed study of the Scriptural texts concerning the Messiah and the old Hebrew traditions (Abarbanel 1497). His notes on Daniel's prophecy are particularly interesting. He links the numbers of the prophet to the major periods of the Jupiter-Saturn-conjunction. According to his calculations the threefold conjunction of the two celestial bodies occurred in 5264 of the Hebrew era (1503 AD) in the sign of *Pisces*, and that was the year in which he expected the advent of the Messiah. He was in turn wrong in this respect, but his writings contain important historical data. The development of this astronomical tradition among the Jewish scribes was probably due to Chaldaean influence. The cuneiform writings deciphered in recent years prove that in the 6th century BC, in the age of the prophet Daniel, the astronomers of Babylon were familiar with the periods of Jupiter and Saturn. Daniel's dates correspond to these very periods. Is it perhaps only accidental ?

According to the text quoted above of the Babylonian myth, (*Enuma elish*) it was Jupiter that determined the circle of the year by its regular motion, dividing the zodiac into sections, each 30 degrees wide: it progresses 30 degrees per year and draws a full circle in 12 years. Its counterpart, Saturn, progresses 12 degrees per year and draws a complete circle in 30 years. This observation played an important role in the product $12 \times 30 = 360$ becoming the unit of measurement of astronomical calculations, both in degrees of longitude and in days. The lunar years of the Babylonian calendar consisted alternately of 12 and 13 lunar months, which was not in accordance with the periods of Jupiter and Saturn. The arithmetical and geometrical mean of the lunar year (354.36 days) and the solar year (365.24 days) is 360. Accurate calculations were made possible by this system of measurement, on the basis of which the great periods of the planets were determined. The great periods correspond to the time intervals in which each planet returns to the same point of the zodiac after a certain number of revolutions.

By comparing the observational facts of several centuries, Chaldaean astronomers had calculated that the apparent standstill, rising, and setting of Jupiter recur in the same place, compared to the fixed stars, every 427 years with 36 complete revolutions. From this it was possible to determine its average time of revolution: 427/36 = 11.86 years = 11 years and 315 days (approximately 12 years). The Chaldaeans considered the great period of Jupiter a constant point of reference, and they determined the revolution time of the other planets by comparing them with that of Jupiter. In the case of Saturn, exactly 15 more years are needed for its phases to recur in the same place: the great period of Saturn is 427+15 = 442 years, which corresponds to 15 revolutions. The period of its revolution is therefore 442/15 = 29.46 years (= 29 years and 168 days).

It follows that the great period of Jupiter is half a Saturn period smaller, which difference is equalized by double the amount, and thus the two planets are to be found in the same phase:

2 × (15-1/2) = 29 Saturn revolutions = 72 Jupiter revolutions;

2 × (442–15) = 854 years, the great period of the Jupiter-Saturn conjunctions.

(The mathematical explanation of the Chaldaean tables can be found in Pannekoek 1961, 55-75 and Ferrari d'Occhieppo 1991, 109-132.)

How do Daniel's numbers correspond to these periods? The symbolic relation is obvious in the sexagesimal notation: the sign of fulfillment is 7'7 (= 427), as the full measure of time of Jupiter's return, and 14'14 (= 854) is the numerical double of King David's name and as such the sign of the return of the Messiah, an analogy with the great period of the Jupiter-Saturn conjunction.

According to Daniel the symbolic number of the Messiah's self-sacrifice is 434 = 427+7 : the sum of the great period of Jupiter and a quarter of a Saturn period, which consists of 21 conjunctions. Originally the Hebrew years of jubilee were also determined by the period of Jupiter. The jubilee lasted from the tenth day of the seventh month of every 49th year to the tenth day of the seventh month of the 50th year (Lev 25:8). Fifty lunar years (= 600 lunar months = 48.4 solar years) had to pass until the beginning of the next jubilee, and this is equal to four full revolutions of Jupiter. Similarly, the "seventy weeks of years" indicates the final Messianic jubilee = 490 years = 442+48 years, and this is the sum of the great Saturn period and four revolutions of Jupiter.

The most significant number of Daniel is 1260. In the Book of Revelation it characterizes the transitional state of the Christian Church on earth, but not its time expressed in years. In the original text that number is expressed as follows: *one time and two times and half a time*; the Hebrew word *et* and the Greek *kairos* do not mean years, but specifically determined periods. This shows that the prophet used the astronomical measure in his calculations:

$$1260 = 360 + (2 \times 360) + 360/2.$$

Everybody in Babylon knew that 360 indicated neither a lunar year nor a solar year but the measurement of the heavenly circle, the zodiac, which was determined by the periods of Jupiter and Saturn.

17. Cosmic Vision of Ezekiel

The Israelites, who had been carried off from their homeland, lost trust in the God of their fathers. The power and magnificent culture of Babylon inspired by the cult of the stars seemed very tempting to them. Could it be that history and the destiny of man were after all ruled by the stars? The only reassuring answer to this question came from the prophets. It was in the years of exile in a foreign land that they received the most important divine revelations. It was there that they first saw the figure of the long awaited Messiah. They understood him to be the Lord of Heaven and Earth. They were convinced that he was everywhere present with his faithful, his existence was not tied to the Temple of Jerusalem. He had allowed the Temple to be destroyed because it had become the seat of idolatry, and because the priests were unjust and oppressed the poor (Ezek 8:16-18).

The people found the cosmic allegories of Ezekiel more impressive and easier to understand than the numbers of the learned Daniel. The Lord of the Heavens pointed to the revolution of the stars and revealed that on his return in the body of a human being to Jerusalem, he would restore its sanctuary and a new era would begin: "I shall make a covenant of peace with them, an eternal covenant with them... And the nations will learn that I am the Lord [He who is]" (Ezek 37:26-28).

The prophet begins the account by giving the place and time of his first vision. It came to pass in the land of the Chaldaeans, on the bank of the river Chebar, in the fifth year of exile of King Jehoiachin, on the fifth day of the fourth month. This is converted into our calendar system as 20 July 593 BC. The Chebar canal, which had its source north of Babylon in the river Euphrates, flowed to the southeast as far as Nippur, where it turned back to the big river. It was in this triangle bordered by waters that the Israelites were settled. As they had no synagogue, they performed their morning and evening prayers on the bank of the river; they needed water to fulfill the compulsory rite of purification. When praying they usually turned towards the East, with open arms, their eyes lifted to the sky.

In the Gospel there are several references to Jesus lifting his eyes upwards to heaven and saying: "Father, I thank you for hearing my prayer" (Jn 11:41; 17:1). Today, in the age of nuclear physics and space research, many might assume that in ancient times people, unaware of the structure of the universe, fell victim to some kind of delusion. We know today that the celestial bodies are located in a vast space, where even light is absorbed by black holes. It would, however, be a grave error for any of us to believe that the prophets, on turning to the Most High, stared into empty space. They could feel and accept what for us is hard to grasp, namely that the Creator of the world surpasses everything, and everything is imbued with his spiritual force. Our optical instruments do not show this.

What did Ezekiel see when, his eyes lifted to the sky, he was praying in the early morning silence? He says: "The heavens opened and I saw visions from God". With this he testifies that his visions began when he was observing the heavens and the stars. He was standing on the bank of the Chebar facing to the east. In this position he became aware of big clouds and a whirlwind looming up in the north, surrounded by a bright light similar to a burning fire. Finally the firmament began to shine, like crystal. This description reminds us of the colors of the morning sky, as seen from the position of Ezekiel. At the end of July, about an hour before dawn, the Sun's position is 6 degrees below the northeastern horizon and a cloud approaching from north is painted fiery red by its rays.

Ezekiel then tells us that the heavens opened, and this is followed by the description of four humanlike beings:

> As to the appearance of their faces, all four had a human face, and a lion's face to the right, and all four had a bull's face to the left, and all four had an eagle's face. Their wings were spread upwards, each had one pair touching its neighbour's, and the other pair covering its body. And each one moved straight forward; they went where the spirit urged them, they did not turn as they moved (Ezek 1:4-12).

A possible interpretation of this is that the figures were standing facing each other and moved in a regular circle. The human face is mentioned as being the first and if we look in that direction, the lion's face is opposite, the bull's face is to the left and the eagle's face to the right. It can be no accident that the prophet compares the celestial figures to the cardinal constellations, which are the signs of the seasons and which happen to be passing across the sky during the vision.

Ezekiel must have been watching that night, at least at the time of the fourth watch of the night between 3 and 6 in the morning, and the fascinating sight of the summer sky made him sensitive to divine visions. On summer nights, from midnight to dawn, the stars of the Eagle (*Aquila*), the human faced Water Bearer (*Aquarius*), the Fish (*Pisces*) and the Bull (*Taurus*) passed across the meridian of Babylon one after the other. 2600 years ago the brilliant star Soaring Eagle (*Altair*) culminated at midnight over the Chebar, and to its left, i.e., in the east, shone the Seven Sisters (*Pleiades*) of the Bull. Then in the morning twilight it was the red eye of the Bull (*Aldebaran*) that shone at its culmination point, and *Regulus*, the royal offspring of the Lion rose at the same time as the Eagle set on the western horizon.

In the Babylonian Calendars the early rising of one fixed star was

generally connected with the culmination of another star, as for example the rising of Pleiades
in the following text:

> When you put the pole of your observation on the first day of the month of Ajaru [May] at dawn, before sunrise, facing south, west is to your right and east is to your left, then the Heart of the Swan is in front of you in the middle of the sky, and on the left you can see the Seven Sisters [Pleiades] of the Bull (Pannekoek 1961, p.50)

In the summer and autumn months people found their bearings with the help of the Eagle, because from the end of May to the end of December its brilliant star *Altair* passed high across the sky of Mesopotamia and could be seen from sunset to dawn for about twelve hours. The Eagle soaring above the Scorpion and the Serpent, as the celestial sign of strength and power, played an important part in ancient mythology. Although the constellation of the autumnal equinox was the Scorpion, it was replaced by the Eagle. Both constellations are in the northeastern band of the Milky Way, but the Eagle is 45 degrees higher than the Scorpion. When the latter disappears, its place is taken by the Eagle which can afterwards be seen for a long time. This observation underlies the ancient myth that the Scorpion, fallen into the nether world, stings itself with its hind sting, turns into an eagle and flies up in the sky again.

In ancient oriental myth the scorpion and the serpent are the most insidious enemies of man, they are the cause of every vice, illness and death. These negative features, in the form of bad inclinations, are present also in human nature, but those who overcome them will be free like the eagle. Such allegories can be found in the Bible as well. Ezekiel's enemies are mocking him when they say "there are scorpions under you", but he is lifted by the spirit high up into the air between the sky and the earth, and like the eagle he alights on a very high mountain. The "large eagle with huge wings and a wide span" is a symbol for a mighty king, because he is the one who executes the just sentences (Ezek 2:6; 17:3; 40:2).

The prophet Isaiah preaches that "those who hope in the Lord renew their strength, they put out wings like eagles" (Is 40:2). The "woman adorned with the Sun, the mother of the male child was given a huge pair of eagle's wings to fly away from the serpent" (Rev 12:14). Christ says to his disciples: "I have given you power to tread underfoot serpents and scorpions; nothing shall ever hurt you" (Lk 10:19). Thus the motion of the autumnal Scorpion and Eagle, which can be seen in the upper branch of the Milky Way, became an allegory for resolving contradictions. The road followed by the believer leads from depth to height, from darkness to light and from death to life.

Ezekiel's vision is repeated "in the sixth year of the exile, on the fifth day of the sixth month", i.e., in 592 BC, on the night from 15th to 16th September (Ezek 8:1). At that time of year the stars of the constellation Pisces the Fishes pass through the meridian of Babylon at midnight. Early in the morning the "eyes" of the Bull and the Lion are still shining in the southeastern sky, while the human faced Water Bearer is looking back at them from the west, and the Eagle spreads its wings above the northwestern horizon. In the tenth chapter Ezekiel depicts the order and position of the signs accordingly: Bull, Man, Lion, Eagle. This description of the vision is more precise here than in the first chapter:

> I looked, and there were four wheels beside the winged creatures, one wheel beside each winged creature... In appearance all four looked alike, as though each wheel had another wheel inside it..., and I was now certain that these were cherubs (Ezek 10:9-21).

The cherubs of the Bible do not at all have the characteristics of the Assyrian statues of god, and it is quite certain that their form was not adopted from the Babylonian cult by the Hebrews. Owing to the Semitic linguistic relationships, the name is the same (Cherub = *Karibu* = Guard), but otherwise the appearance and role of the Assyrian and Hebrew cherubs are quite different. In the Assyrian cult they had animal bodies and human faces and were initially the guards of the royal palace; later, they symbolized the political power of certain kings. On the other hand, the Hebrew cherubs originally had human bodies and, as heavenly creatures, always proclaimed the presence of the Creator of the world and executed his will.

In Moses' tabernacle as in Solomon's temple there stood already two golden cherubs with wings of angels, but their faces are not determined (Ex 25:18; 1 Kg 6:23). Their outspread wings are the symbols of the sky. Between them, above their wings, is the throne of the Lord, under them the Ark of the Covenant. These five-meter gilt statues were taken by Nebuchadnezzar to Babylon after the destruction of the Temple of Jerusalem (587 BC). So the Chaldaeans may have learnt the worship of the angelic cherubs from the Israelites, and the Israelites in the Exile may have better understood their significance.

It was Ezekiel who first gave a detailed description of the appearance of the cherubs and of their role in the history of redemption. His vision seems extremely complicated and the Hebrew expressions he uses are difficult to translate accurately. In this respect his contemporaries may have had an easier job than we do today. They looked up at the sky while praying, which made the allegories referring to the constellations easier to understand. For us it would perhaps be easier to grasp the meaning of the prophet's words, if we regarded them as part of the system of constellations. The illustration below corresponds exactly to Ezekiel's description (see Fig. 41).

In his second vision the prophet mentions one living creature who appears in four different forms: "This was the creature I had seen beside the river Chebar, and I knew that they were cherubs. Each had four faces and four wings and what seemed to be human hands under their wings" (Ezek 10:21). To see four faces of only one living creature is possible, if it from time to time turns to show us some of its other sides. The Hebrew word (*panim*) itself does not mean faces, but sides turned towards us. Originally it was a term used in architecture and meant façade, a building seen from the front. Since here it refers to living creatures, it is naturally translated as faces. However, the prophet speaks of a spiritual building which is the house of the Lord Almighty. Its cosmic dimensions are described in detail in the last chapters of Ezekiel's book.

The allegory based on the observation of the heavens is obvious: the four cherubs are moving around the throne of the Lord; the circle or "wheel" of one is turning inside the circle of the other one; they are moving from east to west, then they leave the Temple of Jerusalem in the east and finally return from the east with the "glory of the Lord". They move as the constellations in rising and setting. Their whole figure and all their wings are "full of eyes inside and outside", which are like shining stars.

The throne of the Lord is the sign of his might and majesty "in heaven" (Ps 11:4; Mt 5:34). The wings and wheels (with shining eyes) express rays and lines of force. The rays of the rising Sun, for example, appear to be huge wings in the sky when they penetrate through the morning clouds. This illustrates the speed and field of motion. The cherubs carry the glory of the Lord on their wings. The word "glory" is a poor translation of the Hebrew *kabod*, which means something heavy. The heavier a thing is, the greater the force it exerts. In the language of the prophets *kabod* is the radiation of divine power and light. It means that the presence of God becomes manifest to man as a perceivable radiation of light or impulse of power. Glory in this sense means much more than fame and recognition attained by great deeds. In the Messianic prophecies it is the word that qualifies the Lord, the King Savior himself.

Thus the "being that looked like a man" among the cherubs can only be the coming Messiah himself, who radiates his light and power through four sources toward each cardinal point. Christ quotes Ezekiel several times: "You will see heaven laid open..., and you will see the Son of Man seated at the right hand of the Power and coming on the clouds of heaven" (Jn 1:51; Mt 24:30; 26:64). The twelve apostles preach through four evangelists that Jesus Christ "is the radiant light of God's glory, sustaining the Universe by his powerful command" (Heb 1:3). The vision of Ezekiel is the revelation of this spiritual and physical Universe, which contains the mystery of the Holy Trinity and the Incarnation of the Divine Word. The prophet was not fully aware of this, which is shown by the way he struggles to express himself while describing his vision.

When Ezekiel wanted to use a single word to characterize the whole vision, he heard in the vision that "the wheels were called Galgal" (10:13). The root of the Hebrew word, *gal*, expresses a wave and oscillatory motion; its double form means whirlwind or whirlpool in other Scriptural texts. St. Jerome used the Latin *volubiles* (volubles or rotaries) to translate it. This, however, does not exactly correspond to the phenomenon described. Modern translations, like the Greek *Septuagint*, kept the original Hebrew term *galgal*, and they remark that "the word's meaning is uncertain, possibly chariot".

Notwithstanding, the phenomenon is very precisely detailed in the original text, and if we read it attentively, we may be able to solve the mystery of *galgal*. We remember that Ezekiel was then in Babylonia, in the homeland of number symbolism. Thus we may conclude that instead of the grammatical meaning of the word, he had the numerical value of its letters

262

in mind: GLGL = 3333. This is all the more probable, because the whole vision is characterized by this numerical ratio (4 x 3 = 12), as is shown in the Book of Revelation by St. John. "There were four wheels beside the cherubs, one wheel beside each; in appearance all four looked alike, as though each wheel had another wheel inside it", says the prophet.

In a superficial interpretation of this passage the "four wheels" would be explained as the Chariot of the Lord pulled by the cherubs. However, wheels rotating inside one another cannot be interpreted as a four-wheeled chariot. Ezekiel himself says that the cherubs carry the glory of the Lord on their wings. When four wheels are rotating inside one another, each one is rotating around its diameter as well. This requires that the wheels have a common central point, so we cannot talk about physical axes. The natural motion of a wheel around a fixed axis is called rotary motion. It is characterized by each point of the wheel moving on a circular path and the centers of the circles coinciding in one straight line (axis of rotation). If, at the same time, the wheel is rotating around its diameter, it forms a spherical surface.

Such a complex spatial motion can only be perceived in the visible sphere of the heavens, where instead of wheels made of solid material, it is the orbits of the celestial bodies that rotate. Of course, these are apparent motions as seen from Earth. The prophet's description is fully objective, because he constantly stresses that: "It appeared as if..." His description is in accordance with the rudiments of modern astronomy. We may say that Ezekiel far surpassed his contemporary scholars. The fact that he had no intention of teaching astronomy and was not aware of this significant aspect of his vision proves the very fact that he acquired the knowledge through divine visions, not human calculations. In his vision Ezekiel can see the "wheels" in motion progressing in four directions, without turning back (Ezek 10:11). Hence each "wheel" seems to perform three different kinds of movement: rotary motion, diagonal rotation, and revolution (motion in a circular path).

So if the "wheels" are called *galgal*, the numerical value of the consonants GLGL = 3333 characterizes the three sorts of their motions. According to the rules of ancient algebra, this formula has three possible solutions: 4×3=12, is the number of the inner structure of the universe and of the geometrical elements of architecture (square and triangle in a circle divided into 12 equal sections, or the 12 signs of the Zodiac each 30 degrees long); G=3 and L=30, therefore GL+GL=3×30+3×30=180, i.e., the measurement of half a revolution in degrees (a semicircle), which in terms of time is 12 hours (e.g. from sunrise to sunset at the equinoxes). With a simple addition we obtain the symbolic number 66 = 3+30+3+30, which could refer to the precession of the Earth, since the Earth is rotating on an axis which is inclined at an angle of 66 degrees to the ecliptic plane.

However it may be, we can assume that the prophet took his allegories from the observed motions of the constellations which were known in Babylon. Let us suppose that the "wheels" correspond to the four cardinal signs of the Zodiac, the axis of rotation of which is the line joining the celestial poles. For an observer at 32° north latitude the stars on the "wheels" seem to turn daily from east to west around this axis (which is the axis of the Earth's rotation projected on the sky). The diagonal rotation is visualized by the changing height or altitude of the stars on vertical circles which pass through the zenith and intersect the horizon. The horizon system was the most obvious frame of reference for the ancient astronomers. The number of degrees along the horizon or the azimuth of a star was measured from the south point to the vertical circle of the same star.

Fig. 41: Vision of the prophet Ezekiel about the four Cherubs, illustrated as the four cardinal signs of the Zodiac. This is a symbol of the new Christocentric Universe. The lines represent the wings of the Cherubs; "Each has two wings that touches, and two wings that cover his body" (Ez 1:11). Thus these wing lines form a quadrangle and four triangles, and in the center we see the Greek monogram of Christ. (Drawing by Teres)

The revolution is perceptible by the annual period of the constellations (which is an effect of the earth's revolution around the sun). The four cardinal signs, which are always opposite one another, indicate the four cardinal points, when they pass across the meridian at night during each of the four seasons. *Leo* the Lion dominates the southern sky in spring; *Scorpius* the Scorpion in summer; *Aquarius* the Water Bearer is associated with the autumn skies; *Taurus* the Bull crosses the local meridian on winter nights. The formula of four times three different spatial motions shows that the prophet is contemplating the cosmic unity of physical and spiritual existence. When he prophesies the reconstruction of the Temple of Jerusalem, he identifies this New Cosmos with the House of the Lord Almighty. That is why biblicists emphasize that the vision of Ezekiel is eschatological, i.e., concerned with eternal existence beyond physical space and time. Since the dimensions of the new Temple surpass every earthly dimension it has never been possible to build it. (Ezek 41:5-43:17).

The mystery of the future New City is described by Ezekiel in his last sentence: "The total perimeter is eighteen thousand cubits. And the name of the city in future must be Yahweh is there". The Hebrew expression *Yahweh-sham* means that the Almighty and Eternal God fills the universe, and his faithful are permanently aware of his presence. This is expressed by the apostle Paul in the following way: "so that God may be all in all" (Ezek 48:35; 1 Cor 15:28).

The perimeter of the New City is a hundred times as long as GL+GL; $100 \times 1800 = 18,000$, which indicates an immaterial dimension, the transcendent number of the universe, that cannot be determined by an algebraic calculation. This is the symbol of unmeasurability. No matter which unit of measure we use, because only the proportions count here. The same vision returns in the Revelations of apostle John, but this time in the redeemed Universe, after "the Lion of the tribe of Judah has triumphed". The names of the four living creatures are unchanged, but the Lion stands in the first place, and each creature has only one face. Instead of silently carrying the glory of God, they loudly preach: "Holy, holy, holy is the Lord, the Almighty, he was and he is and he is to come" (Rev 4:8; 5:5).

The last vision of St. John verifies and explains Ezekiel's formula. The numerical values are higher after the fulfillment, but the proportions are the same. The New City is built in a square, its length, height and width are equal: 12,000 units. Its perimeter therefore is $4 \times 12,000 = 48,000$ units, which is the dimension of the "new Heaven and new Earth". It does not have a separate Temple, because the whole of it is the living Sanctuary of Christ. The heavenly "living creatures" have become archangels, the "wheels" of the constellations do not turn any more, and the Sun never sets. That is why instead of the number 18, which means spiritual revival, we have here 48, which is perfection: $6 \times 8 = 48$ symbolizes the Mysterious Body of Christ, i.e., His Church, in its earthly and heavenly reality at the same time (Rev 21:1-25; 1 Cor 12:12; Eph 1:23; Paul includes in his concept of the Body the entire Cosmos as unified under the Lord Christ).

The figure below illustrates the visions of the prophet Ezekiel and apostle John with the symbols of visionary geometry. The crystal cube of the renewed cosmos is seen inside the transparent sphere of the transfigured world, and inside is the everlasting tetrahedron, which in itself is invisible, but perceivable after the revelation of Christ as the symbol of the Holy Trinity. The darkness surrounding the light sphere is the part of reality which is beyond our consciousness and unfathomable by human reason. Its allegory is the world beyond the visible sky: "The heavens opened": said Ezekiel, but he described the phenomena of the other world in the symbolic language of geometry.

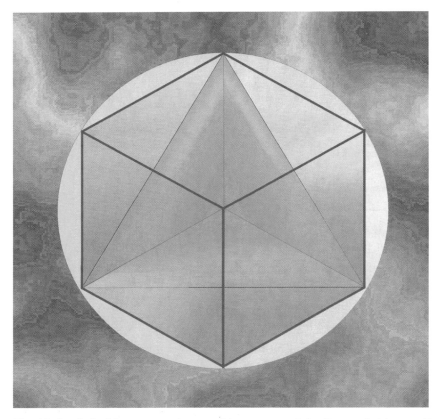

Fig. 42: Symbol of the transcendence and immanence of the Creator Spirit as well as the connection of the spiritual and material reality in the new Universe. (Drawing by Teres)

The cube (hexahedron) symbolizes visible and measurable reality: the 6 squares, 8 corners and 12 edges express the perfection of the created world in the space-time-mass continuum. Inside it we find the tetrahedron, which is characterized by 4 triangles, 4 corners and 6 edges. Its edges coincide with the diagonals of the cube's planes and so it creates and maintains the whole of the cube virtually from inside. The tetrahedron in itself symbolizes the triple unity of spiritual existence and at the same time expresses the hidden law of the number four in creation: its four triangular planes almost show the surface of contact of spiritual and material world.

The common center of the two regular solids is of equal distance from the corners, which touch the spherical surface and point beyond it. The harmony of their dimensions illustrates the union of spirit and matter or the interaction of mind and body. The same harmony is indicated by the symbolic meaning of the biblical numbers: 4+3 = 7, and the sum of the six numbers determining the two regular solids is 40 as fullness of human existence. These realizations do not originate in the Greek philosophy of Platonic solids but in Ezekiel's prophetic geometry, in which analogy means more than the symbol of numbers. The symbol renders abstract notions perceptible, but by itself does not prove anything. The analogy, however, expresses certain similarities and inner accord. The prophets describe the other world by the analogy of earthly and cosmic dimensions, because the physical forms of existence are the manifestations of spiritual realities. That is what the prophets are capable of seeing and experiencing.

Although spirit and matter are not identical, but two essentially different forms of existence, they form a certain unity in living creatures. Only man is aware of this unity, because man alone is capable of realizing that his being is determined by the unity of spiritual soul and sensual body. The essence of an apple pip is determined by the nature of the apple tree latent in it. This is the spirit of the pip and will only be visible when the pip shoots up and becomes an apple tree. The apostle Paul uses this as analogy to explain man's resurrection: man's physical body will be transformed into a spiritual body, but it keeps its individual form even then (1 Cor 15:35-44). The historical proof of this is the resurrection of Jesus, to which his apostles testify.

People in ancient times believed in the immortality of the soul, but had a false conception of life in the other world. The right conception of the eternal life was rendered possible by the revelations of Christ, who compares the Kingdom of Heaven to a feast at a royal wedding held in brightly illuminated rooms with richly laid tables. To his disciples he says: "In my Father's house there are many rooms", and "you will eat and drink at my table in my Kingdom" (Mt 22:2; Jn 14:2; Lk 22:30). The apostles took these allegories literally: "So you will with all the saints have strength to grasp the breadth and the length, the height and the depth... There is one God who is Father of all, over all, through all and within all" (Eph 3:18; 4:6).

The city of the other world is the transformed or spiritualised reality of the forms known in earthly existence. What to us is everlasting and immeasurable is not empty and infinite in space. Where there are no roads, walls and definite shapes, man is unable to find his bearings and loses consciousness. In the visions of Ezekiel and John the eternal city has three dimensions, it is surrounded by walls with twelve open gates, in the middle of it there is a magnificent throne with crystal clear water gushing from it, in the streets and on the banks of the river fruit trees bring fruit twelve times, i.e., every month (Rev 21:15 - 22:5).

So everything has its own shape, place and order there, too. The numbers and dimensions demonstrate harmony and order. Ezekiel repeatedly uses subordinate clauses of cause to explain this order: "since the spirit of the living Being is in the wheels" (Ezek 10:17). Five hundred years later the author of the Book of Wisdom praises the Lord of history in the following way: "You ordered all things by measure, number and weight... For your imperishable spirit is in everything" (Wis 11:20; 12:1).

In the visions of Daniel and John events are controlled by the rhythm of the number seven, while everything is in progress. Final fulfillment in the Christocentric Universe is characterized by the proportion of twelve, which is the analogy of the period of revolution of the Sun and the constellations. Twelve squared twelve (12 × 12 = 144, and 144,000) is the human and angelic dimension, i.e., the complete unity of spiritual and physical existence (Rev 7:4; 21:17). All this is not yet quite clear to us, because we are still on the move in the stormy history of redemption. The constellations have not yet stopped revolving in the sky, and the four "living creatures" have not come to rest in the depth of human psyche. What is the origin of their extremely rich symbolic role?

Modern psychological researches could help us to understand better these "four living creatures". According to depth psychology theories the zodiacal signs are projections of some primordial images or archetypes which the Creator has placed within the human psyche. In ancient times these images were projected from the unconscious depth of the psyche on-to the screen of the firmament. Later they have been projected into the figures of the four great prophets, and finally into the four evangelists. The Hebrew word used by Ezekiel to describe the visions (*mareoth*) can indeed mean projections or reflected images. (Cf. BDB 1977).

The deepest meaning of these primordial images is shown by St. John in the Book of Revelation. The four living creatures witness to the divine and human qualities of Christ and at the same time they represent the virtues of man "created in image of God". When they praise Christ, they list seven divine and human qualities (Rev 5:12): power (Lion), riches and strength (Bull), wisdom and honor (Man), glory and blessing (Eagle). According to St. Ambrose, these qualities express the four spiritual faculties which distinguish man from the animal: intellect, feeling, memory and will; and also the four corresponding natural virtues: prudence, temperance, righteousness, and fortitude; and finally the three Christian virtues built on these four: faith, hope and love.

The first Fathers of the Church claimed to have recognized the four evangelists of Christ in the faces of the heavenly "living Creatures": Matthew is human faced, because he lists the human ancestors of Jesus starting from Abraham; Luke is bull faced, because he starts his writing with the sacrificial office of the priest Zechariah; Mark is lion faced, because he begins with the appearance of John the Baptist, who is "the voice crying in the wilderness"; and evangelist John is eagle faced, because, soaring in spiritual heights, he begins his testimony with the incarnation of the everlasting divine Word (Ireneus, *Adv. Haer.* III. 11; St. Jerome, *Comment. in Ezech.* I. 1).

In the 6th century Pope Gregory the Great interpreted the prophetic archetypes as expressions of four chapters of Christ's life and the history of redemption: Christ was born as Son of Man; he died as a sacrificial Bull; he rose from the dead as a Lion; and ascended to heaven as an Eagle (*Homilia in Ezech.* II-IV).

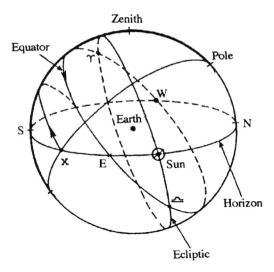

Fig. 43: This figure shows the celestial sphere for the latitude of Babylon (32°30′), around 30 July 593 BC, when the prophet Ezekiel dated his first heavenly vision. The Sun rises at 6h15m with the constellation of Leo on the northeast horizon, whilst Taurus crosses the meridian, and Aquarius sets. At the same time, Sirius (x) rises on the southeast horizon (declination -16°39′).

18. *Precession of the Earth's Axis and World Eras*

In connection with Daniel's dates we have seen the possible relation between certain cosmic cycles and historical events. The Bible is the oldest written account which presents the important eras of world history from the first moment in time to the last, from Creation to the Last Judgment. Babylonian and Greek scholars believed in history constantly repeating itself in accordance with the motions of the heavens. The Hebrew prophets, however, clearly saw and professed that the God's purpose with time is the everlasting salvation of man.

The prophet Daniel describes four historical ages within the framework of the flourishing and the destruction of four world empires. This is followed by the age of the Messiah, which definitely marks the end of earthly history. The seven periods of the Messianic Age in the Book of Revelation resembles the continuation of the seven-day account of creation described in the Old Testament. They are partly recognizable in the history of the Church, but the prophetic prototypes also suggest the era of the restoration of the universe. Christ's declaration is now being fulfilled: "Look, I am making the whole creation new" (Rev 21:5). Thus we may see the present and future events in this new light.

Heraclitus (544-480 BC) was the first Greek philosopher to determine the period of one world era as 18,000 years and to divide it into months, days and hours. For one thousand years Greek philosophers relied on this cosmic rhythm to explain the destruction and renewal of empires. At that time 18,000 was half of the period of precession of the equinoxes. According to Hipparchus' calculations, the point of the vernal equinox shifted one degree per one hundred years, so it should perform one full revolution in 36,000 years. The vernal equinox is the point where the Sun's path (Ecliptic) crosses the celestial Equator, about March 22. Hipparchus observed that the vernal equinoctial point was located on the last degree of the zodiacal sign Ram (First of *Aries*). This observation was made about 130 BC. Indeed, the point of the vernal equinox shifted out of the sign Ram (*Aries*) into the sign Fish (*Pisces*) in the century just before our era.

The most prominent astronomers of antiquity regarded the shift of the sign of the vernal equinox as the symbol of the beginning of a new world era. Even Origen, one of the most learned Fathers of the Church, accepted this view. The Book of Genesis says: "Let there be lights in the vault of heaven to divide the day from night, and let them indicate festivals, days and years...God blessed the seventh day and made it holy, because on that day he had rested after all his work of creating" (Gn 1:14; 2:3). Today every calendar divided into 52 weeks testifies to this Biblical statement. The prophet is speaking of the regular movement of the celestial bodies, the observation of which helps people to properly reckon with time and to determine their earthly age. In connection with this Origen notes:

There is a theory, according to which the circle of the zodiac moves one degree from west to east in the course of one hundred years... Although its twelfth part [i.e., the 30 degree wide sign], when interpreted by the intellect, seems very different from what we can perceive by the senses [i.e., the constellation], the intellectual approach nevertheless points to the truth of the matter, which otherwise would be very difficult to hold for certain (Origen, *Comment. in Genesim*, III. I,1:14).

Origen refers to this again, when he is interpreting the apostle Paul's statement about the future era (Eph 2:7):

As the last month is the fulfillment of the year, and after that begins a new month, likewise it is possible that there are several ages in a world era, the fulfillment of which is our age, and the following age shall be the beginning of a new era, when God will show for all ages to come, through his goodness towards us in Christ Jesus, how infinitely rich he is in grace (*De oratione* 27).

Jesus begins his public speeches by saying: "the time is fulfilled", and repeatedly urges his audience to perceive the signs of the new epoch:

When you see a cloud looming up in the west you say at once that rain is coming, and so it does. And when the wind is from the south you say it will be hot, and it is. Hypocrites! You know how to interpret the face of the earth and the sky. How is it you do not know how to interpret these times? (Lk 12:54-56; Mt 16:1-4. The "times" are the messianic age; the "signs" are the miracles worked by Jesus.)

270

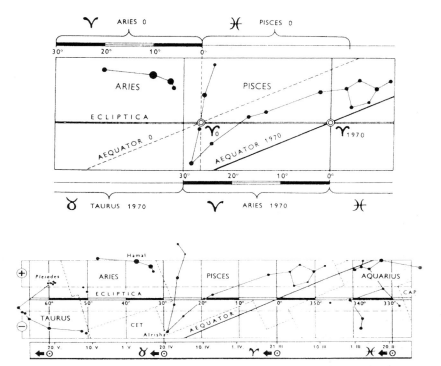

Fig. 44: The point of the vernal equinox in the sign of *Aries* and in the Constellation of *Pisces*. (Klepesta and Rükl 1973).

For two thousand years millions have recognized the signs of the new epoch in Christ's work and Church, but only a few have understood its full significance. Today many people believe that the time of the Christian Church belongs to the past and they preach a new age, which, instead of the star of Bethlehem, began perhaps with the atom bombing of Hiroshima. Many are inclined to believe that we are now living in the age of the Water Bearer, because the vernal equinox has shifted to the sign of *Aquarius*. The pseudo scientific statements made by the partisans of the New Age movement mislead young people, who long for a better world. The star maps above (Fig. 44) show that at the beginning of our age the vernal equinox, the intersection point of the ecliptic and the celestial equator, stood at the star *Omicron* in *Pisces* and the Sun rose together with it about March 22. This equinoctial point has since then precessed 29 degrees and today the vernal Sun rises with the west stars of *Pisces* which extend over the star *Omega* in *Aquarius*. That is the reason why some people think that a new age has begun in the sign of Aquarius. This, however, cannot be verified by astronomical calculations.

271

The slow westward drift of the equinoxes is 5025 arc seconds per 100 years at the present rate, that is 30 degrees in 2149 years. This is the period of a world-month or an age. According to Ptolemy's Tables, the vernal equinoctial point reached the star *Alfa Piscium* (*Alrisha*) in 146 BC and the line of *Omicron Piscium* in 11 A.D. If we take the former date as the starting point, the vernal equinox will enter into the sign of Aquarius in 2004 A.D.; starting from the other date (11 AD) it will get there in 2160 AD.

The astronomers of ancient times did not know the cause of precession, but they were aware of its symbolic meaning: they had a presentiment of its impact on the turning point of an age. They counted the beginning of each new year from the new moon of the vernal equinox, because that was the time of the renewal and blooming of nature. It was on this analogy that they thought that a new era of world history would begin when the vernal new moon entered the next constellation after several thousands of years. Today's astronomers are familiar with the cause of the precession, but they cannot accept that the zodiacal sign of the vernal equinox should characterize the historical and cultural character of each age. It has been known since Newton that the precession is caused by the Earth's specific position and motion in the gravitational field of the Sun, the Moon and the planets. The gravitational force of the Sun and the Moon would turn the ecliptic into the equatorial plane, if it were not counterbalanced by the rotation of the Earth. That is why the Earth's axis of rotation slowly draws a complete conic surface around the line joining the ecliptic poles. It is called lunisolar precession, which lasts 25,788 or 26,000 years. This great period is a Platonic year or a world era, a twelfth part of which is the world-month.

According to recent observations, as an effect of the gravitational coupling between the center of mass of the Earth and that of the other planets, the angle between the ecliptic and the equator decreases 47" and the precession of the equinox decreases 11" per 100 years. 9000 years ago the largest inclination of the ecliptic could have been 24°12' and in 9000 years it will be 22°35', then it will increase again. (Could it be that Heraclitus' presentiment was an allusion to this 18,000 year period?) The continuous changes make it impossible to reckon with equal periods in the precession of the vernal equinox for thousands of years ahead. The determination of precessional historical ages has no astrophysical basis. There are still many people who forget that the constellations are in fact not real formations existing in the sky, but the creations of human imagination. The 30 degree signs of the zodiac originally served the purpose of facilitating calculations and observations. Except for the names given to them at one time, there is no physical importance in the constellations.

Ancient astronomers repeatedly observed that historical events occurred simultaneously with such heavenly phenomena as the conjunctions of planets in certain signs of the Zodiac, i.e., in certain ecliptic longitudes. From these observations they then derived the symbolical meaning of the recurrent phenomena concerning the beginning of a new age. The Magi who went to Bethlehem did not refer to the precession of the vernal equinox, but to the star of the king, since they had observed the evening rising of that star, when it stood in opposition to the Sun and at the point of the sky where the vernal new moon usually occurred. Astronomical

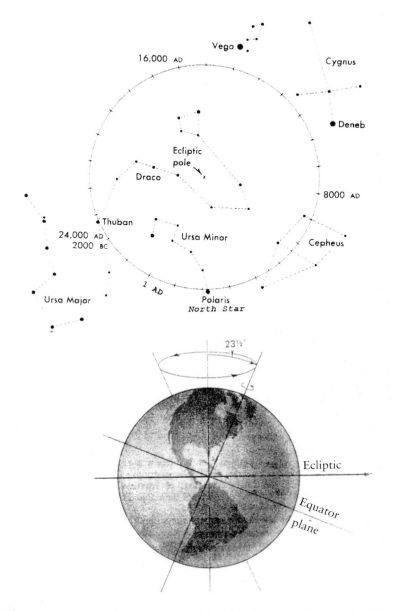

Fig. 45: Precession: Path of the North Celestial Pole. As an effect of the differential gravitational attractions of the Sun and Moon, the rotation axis of the Earth is inclined at an angle of 66°33' to the ecliptic plane. Therefore the angle between the planes of the celestial equator and the ecliptic is 23°27'. If we consider this obliquity of the ecliptic constant, in the course of 25,788 years the north celestial pole will move on the celestial sphere along a circle of 23°27' radius. In the year 2700 BC, the North Star was *Thuban* (*Alpha Draconis*), and in 14,000 AD the North Star will be *Vega* (*Alpha Lyrae*).

calculations show that the "star" mentioned was a conjunction of Jupiter and Saturn in the sign of *Pisces*. This zodiacal sign thus gained a particular significance because of this very conjunction.

The followers of Jesus have accepted his statements regarding wars and the prince of this world, who "was a murderer from the start..., a liar, and the father of lies...In the world you will have trouble, but be brave: I have conquered the world" (Jn 8:44; 16:33; Mt 24:6). Both philosophers and psychologists have tried to find a reassuring explanation for the problem of evil. That was the aim of the new theory of world-ages, which was best elaborated by two Swiss researchers: the psychiatrist Carl Gustav Jung, and the historian Alfons Rosenberg (see Jung 1971, Rosenberg 1958). They both agreed that the 6300 year long history of human civilization could be divided into approximately 2100 year periods, which show remarkable similarities to the 30 degree periods of the vernal equinoctial point and the symbolic content of the respective constellations. They accepted the assumption that the beginning of a new age, on the basis of certain historical facts, was to be counted from 1950. However, their interpretations of the phenomenon were different.

In his book on the future Rosenberg (1958) assumes that the zodiacal signs have a cosmic impact, which does not originate in the twelve constellations but in their symbolical field surrounding our solar system. He divides each 2100 year period into 12 parts and gives a detailed account of the events, the quality of which is recurrent in each age. Resorting to the method of historical parallelism, in other words by making comparative analyses, he infers what man can expect in the following thousand years, in the age of Aquarius.

Jung reckoned with the traditional constellations and claimed that the length of astrological ages was very uncertain, because it was impossible to determine the border lines of the constellations unambiguously. The development of primordial symbols, however, seems to play a decisive role in each age. For the psychologist the main area of interest is the symbol of the Fish, because "the synchronistic concomitant of the two thousand year old Christian psychic evolution is the constellation of Pisces" (Jung 1971, Aion 9). Thus there can be an obvious analogy between precessional periods and culture ages, but there is no causal relation between them. Jung does not believe in the physical influence of the stars. He treats astrology as a psychological symptom. He asserts that "astrology represents the whole psychological knowledge of antiquity". The observation of the heavens and stars awakened the primordial images or archetypes hidden in the depth of the human psyche. The constellations must, therefore, be the projections of those archetypes of the collective unconscious, since they are present in the mythology of every ancient people, from China through Egypt to Central America. The twelve constellations situated along the paths of the Sun and the planets are the ones that best reflect the unconscious desires, inclinations, strengths, ideas and presentiments of man. Jung states: "These unconscious projections took place so deeply, that a few thousand years of progress in civilization was necessary for them to be at least partly separated from the external images".

Astrologers so far have been unable to clearly differentiate between the inner contents of the human psyche and the features projected onto the sky.

The symbolic content of the constellations has become so obscure, that many people consider them to be physical forces. Those who attribute the course of their lives to the influence of the stars are following a dangerous path, because in this way they lose their sense of responsibility and with it their moral personality. This statement is also true for the precessional periods which are characterized by the symbolic content of *Pisces* and *Aquarius*. In his book entitled "Flying Saucers: A Modern Myth" Jung (1971) refers to his conscience as a doctor and feels it his responsibility to warn people of the dangers that come from a preoccupation with problems arising from the turn of the age. His book entitled "Aion" (Jung 1971) gives a depth-psychological and historical analysis of astrological symbols. In its introduction Jung emphasizes that his book is written from the standpoint "of a doctor, not from that of a confessor or a scholar". His intention is to help people who have "lost their ideological bearings in the social and spiritual chaos, and so easily fall victim to the world of dreams which is the source of contemporary mass-psychosis."

Christian symbolism has become so weak that now Buddhists and Muslims also feel that their time has come, and they are now engaged in missionary activity all over the world. The mental beggars of our age, for their part, are far too tempted to imitate them. This is the danger about which people cannot be warned often enough, says the psychiatrist and asks: What is the use of oriental wisdom and the knowledge of yoga, if we lose our own roots? What we need above all is European wisdom, which is meant for us. The road we have to follow begins with European reality, not oriental practices, which lures us from our own cultural values. From 1930 for thirty years, the Swiss doctor repeatedly stressed this and showed us the right way to follow. His ideas, however, were so new and so profound, his style so complex, that even today very few people understand and many misinterpret them. Even though the partisans of New Age in America and Europe made the very fatal mistake about which the psychiatrist had warned western society, they claimed that his theory was the basis of their movement.

In his commentary written to the book of Chinese Wisdom (*I Ching*), Jung says:

> In today's anonymous masses there is a gnostic movement, which psychologically corresponds exactly to the one observable 1900 years ago. Then, just like today, there were solitary wanderers, like the great Apollonius, who span the mental threads from Europe to Asia... Then, like today, tastelessness and inner disquietude prevailed; just like today, all the mazes of mental life were open and the ideas of pseudo prophets flourished (Jung 1971, Vol.15).

The crisis that prevailed in the 2nd century BC was just as deep as the one in the 20th century A.D. The two world wars and the victory of America are comparable to the Punic wars and the victory of Rome over Carthage (200-146 BC). The terror of Antiochus IV in the Middle East, Hannibal's campaigns conducted against Italy, Shi-Huang-Ti's cruel tyranny in China: religious persecutions, the banning and burning of books, deportations, forced labor camps, the building of roads and the

Chinese wall; all this parallels the dictatorships of Hitler, Stalin and Mao-tze-Tung, the *iron curtain* and the *death camps*.

Ethnographic and archaeological research prove that the first significant turn of age probably took place between 4300-3800 BC, when planned agricultural activity and urbanization started among certain groups of nomadic fishing and hunting societies. A new species of man seems to have appeared, a species with more highly developed mental faculties. Between 4350 and 2200 BC, the vernal equinoctial point was in the constellation of the Bull, the symbolic content of which characterizes the ideals of that period: the beauty and fertility of earthly and physical life, superhuman force and power in the shape of the bull; this was the focal point of art and religion.

The 3rd millennium before Christ was the first great period when human spirit and culture flourished. This is testified by the huge Sumerian and Accadian tower temples, the Egyptian pyramids, the enormous statues, the didactic poems carved in stone and terracotta. The people of that age were hard working animal farmers, peasants, architects, sculptors and magi. They enjoyed the fruits of the earth, wanted to live in welfare and asked for the blessing of Heaven to help them do so. They developed a mythological system of the motions of the stars, the cosmic rhythms of life, and the religious cult of the heavenly powers, which provided for a certain ordering of moral and social life. Their kings possessed the strength of the heavenly winged bull, so as to be able to defend their people from all outside invasions and natural disasters.

Both the new cult of the bull and the myth of the labyrinth developed around 2600 BC on the island of Crete. This cult and myth claimed that with the help of his own mental powers, man defeats the bull present in him and is freed from the labyrinth. The well known myth presents the complicated story through simple allegories: Zeus-Jupiter appears before the Phoenician princess *Europa* in the form of a white bull, and when *Europa* mounts the tame bull, it plunges into the sea and swims with her to the island of Crete, where he turns into a human being. Of their marriage was born *Minos*, the first monarch and lawgiver in the West, the founder of Bronze-Age culture, commerce and the Mediterranean naval force. That is why the western part of the Asian continent was named Europe, which bears the sign of the Bull even today.

The story of the princess *Europa* and the white bull is represented by a number of ancient works of art and modern paintings. The historic core of the myth could be interpreted as follows: in the Bull Age European culture developed under the influence of oriental civilization transmitted by the Phoenicians to the Greeks and the Romans. According to archeological finds, different forms of the cult of the bull were widespread in the 4th and 3rd millenniums BC from the river Nile to India and China. It will suffice to mention the idolized black bulls of the Egyptian *Apis*, with a white spot on their foreheads and the sun disk between their horns. They were buried embalmed in Memphis and the dates of their birth and death were engraved on their statues. The Semitic, Accadian and Assyrian kings, however, regarded the human faced bulls as cherubs, who symbolized their power and who kept guard at the gates of their palaces.

Fig. 46: The Bull-Cherub of Sargon II in Korsabad, 720 BC. It is 5 meters high and weighs 36 metric tons.

The peaceful and just reign of the kings ruling under the archetype of Bull is followed by a period of cruel tyranny: the Age of Aries, in which the ideal qualities are heroism, militancy and the endeavor to conquer the world (from 2200 to about 45 BC). The upheavals of the new turn-of-age begin at the end of the 3rd millennium BC. It is a period of wars, migrations and religious reforms. The civilized city-states are invaded by Semitic and Indo-European peoples coming from the northeast. The Sumerians are subdued by Sargon I who establishes the first Semitic-Accadian empire of Babylon (around 2400 BC). In the Book of Moses it is called the Land of Shinar, because of its cult of the Moon (*Shin*) and Venus (*Ishtar*). At the same time in Egypt the old feudal system comes to an end and a unified state is established by the Pharaohs of the Amenemhet and Amenhotep dynasties (2000-1350 BC). This is the age of classical Egyptian literature and religion: in its magic writings the heavenly deity *Amon-Ra* is identical with the Sun, but is often represented in the form of a ram. This is one proof of the fact that Egyptian priests were familiar with the astronomical

277

position of the vernal equinox. The Pharaoh Amenhotep IV the *Ekhnaton,* introduces the cult of the Sun as the prototype of monotheism, but it will not last long. The people return to their idols of Bull and Ram. The fertile land of the Nile falls into the hands of the Assyrians and is later subdued by cruel Persian rulers.

In the book of Daniel the two-horned Ram symbolizes the king of the Medes and Persians, and the prophet foretells that the powerful Greek He Goat will defeat the Persians (Dan 8:3-22). With the lightning war and founding of the empire by the Macedonian Alexander the Great, the Ram Age reaches its climax and comes to an end. For many centuries on it is Alexander the Great's ram-horned statue that represents the deity *Amon-Ra* in the Egyptian temples. (In astrological symbolism the He Goat was the same as the Ram.) The great historical figures of the first part of the Ram Age are Hammurabi, Abraham and Moses. Hammurabi is the first priest monarch and lawgiver, who establishes the new Babylonian empire and the religion of Marduk, the heavenly Lord of Wisdom: he is the one who restores universal order.

Abraham too is a priest monarch, but he breaks with his ancestors' cult of the Moon and Venus and leaves his native land. It is from his heritage that the monotheist religion of the chosen people will be established. Abraham's behavior reflects the Ram archetype: he is ready to sacrifice his son to the Almighty Creator, but the Angel of the Lord prevents it and shows him a ram caught by its horns in a bush: "Abraham took the ram and offered it as a burnt offering in place of his son" (Gen 22:11-13). Eight hundred years later, Moses liberates the clan of Abraham, Isaac and Jacob from the Egyptian servitude by offering young rams. This takes place in the very month in which the vernal new moon is visible in the constellation of the Ram. Henceforth the *Lamb of Sacrifice* is the ritual symbol of the Covenant; each year at the vernal full moon the priests offer one year old rams in memory of the Passover of the Lord. Moses, at the same time, fights against the old cult of the bull: he smashes the golden calf, which is again and again worshipped by his people wandering in the wilderness (Ex 12:5; 32:4-24).

Centuries later the ghost of the past still haunts: after Solomon's death, when ten Israelite tribes break with the house of David, their first king, Jeroboam has two statues of a bull made and says to his people: "Here is your God, Israel, who brought you out of Egypt" (1 Kg 12:28). And this brought about the downfall of Israel. The Assyrian Sargon II, who still had the people worship him in the form of the two thousand year old winged bull, ordered the tribes of Israel to be carried away and put an end to their kingdom. It is, nevertheless, among the sons of this oppressed people that we find, later on, the greatest religious writers and prophets. The Hebrew Bible preserves the lasting cultural values of the Bull Age and Ram Age, everything that might be necessary and useful to understand the mystery of history.

The 6th century BC is the age of great Messianic revelations, prophets and sages. We find Lao-tzu and Konfu-tze (Confucius) in China, Buddha in India, Zarathustra in Persia, Ezekiel, Daniel and Isaiah the Second in Babylon, Jeremiah in Judaea, Thales, Pythagoras, Heraclitus and the anonymous Sibyls in Greece. What strange contemporaries! They seem to be able to perceive the inspiration of the same invisible spiritual Power, who is present everywhere. Although they do not speak each other's language, they preach the same ideas: the righteous Lord of the world will come, he will create a new era and will save all those who welcome him in goodwill.

We have studied the great Hebrew prophets in the previous sections. They were the only ones capable of describing the secrets of redemption in the divine person of the Messiah, who revealed himself to them. The wise men of other, distant lands discussed the idea of redemption more vaguely, but some of their statements are worth considering. Lao-tzu, without being able to name it, mentions a certain mysterious power, which operates in the universe. Ancient drawings represent the old Sage of China riding a bull and leaving his country westwards. This can be interpreted as follows: he defeated the past and preceded his age. Only after two thousand years do his teachings become known. The Jesuit missionaries arriving in China interpret the deep message of Tao-Te-Ching by substituting the Christian concept of God. (The famous Italian astronomer and mathematician, Matteo Ricci, S.J. worked in China from 1583 to 1610 and established the first Observatory in the Peking imperial court.) Lao-tzu realizes that the source of every form of life and existence is an immaterial and immutable reality:

> That existed before heaven and earth; dependent on nothing, unchanging, all pervading, unfailing. One may think of it as the mother of the universe. But its true name I do not know; Tao is the name that I give it (Trans. by Waley 1934).

Here, heaven means spiritual, and earth material existence, and man represents the consciousness of the two; all three are pervaded and maintained by *Tao*. Existence is the tension between opposites. If good exists, so does evil. The perfect sage liberates himself from the opposites, having seen through their connection with one another and their alternation: "He whose actions are in harmony with Tao becomes one with Tao". The old Sage longs to see the heavenly Light and Reason embodied "in a powerful man, who is able to save all people and every thing" (Waley 1934, p.174). Some translators render the Chinese *Tao* into English as Way, Reason, Principle, or even as God. The idea of Tao is similar to the Greek concept of *Logos* (Word), and the Hindu *Brahman-Atman* (Supreme Self), as universal grounds from which all creation proceeds. The primordial image underlying *Brahman-Atman* and *Tao* is as universal as man, appearing in every age and among all peoples as a primitive conception of energy, or life force (Jung 1971, *Psychological Types*).

Confucius (*Konfu-tze*) supplements the Tao theory with the practical rules of The Golden Mean. In a very cruel age he preaches the principle of human cordiality: "Do for others what you desire for yourself. Do not do to others what you do not wish for yourself." The world can only be saved by the gentleman and the saint, who has self-control and follows "the will of Heaven" on the road of virtue. (Golden Mean 22-30). There are 300 rules of ritual and 3000 rules of cordiality. We have to wait for the arrival of a saint, only then will these rules be implemented:

"I have never had the pleasure of seeing a saint. If only I could see a single one, I would be satisfied" , complains the sage and remarks: "Am I a saint? I do not dare to think so. As to the never flagging practice and continuous teaching of virtue, I can say that I do justice to these" (Confucius, *Golden Mean*, 30).

That was how the advent of the Savior, the Saint was preached by Confucius. His disciples wanted him to establish a religious community for his followers, but he refused: "We had better wait for Heaven itself to reveal how we should believe and what we should believe". (At the same time the prophet Ezekiel wrote: "The heavens opened and I saw divine visions".)

The Sage of India, Siddharta Gautama Buddha, taught the way of self redemption. Buddhism has become a widespread teaching among the peoples of the northeast and west of India. Yoga and nirvana, reincarnation and karma are well-known terms, which, however, are often misinterpreted by the general public today. They are not Gautama's inventions, but ancient Hindu traditions. Initially he himself had wanted to achieve salvation through self torture and fasting, but he was disappointed in this method. Later,he decided to practice meditation and contemplation and found the truth through a right way of living. Thus he achieved full consciousness, that is the state of an awakened and enlightened man; the Buddha state. Then he established a monastery for those who wanted to get rid of the belief in reincarnation, "that senseless recurrence". His disciples noted his saying: "My road is fully determined by the intention of redemption". The only way to defeat suffering and death is to completely extinguish or transform our physical and earthly desires.

Gautama Buddha admits he is not the Savior of the world. He will be succeeded by the ultimate Enlightened One, whose name is *Maitreya,* Self-Sacrifice. The ancient Vedas talk about him: "The self-existent supreme being [Brahman] sacrifices himself: I sacrifice myself in the beings and the beings in myself" (cf. *Chataptha Brahmanam* 13:7; *Cullavagga* 9; *Dighanikaya* 16:2). In this profound awareness of Gautama we find his real wisdom. But most Buddhists have not yet understood the depth of this wisdom. However, many of them have since become aware of the redeeming self-sacrifice in Jesus Christ, who took upon himself all sufferings of our earthly existence. Just as the apostle John preached it: "Jesus Christ is the sacrifice that takes our sins away, and not only ours, but the whole world's" (1 Jn 2:2).

The teaching of Heraclitus of Ephesus is remarkably similar to the ideas of Lao-tzu. He believes that the whole physical process of the universe is maintained by the tension between opposites. Everything is in constant motion (*pantha rhei*) and opposites counterbalance each other. The purpose of existence is harmony (*harmonia*), law (*nomos*) and measure (*metron*). The cosmos as universal order is able to be comprehended by man, and this order is what man should implement in his own moral life. The source of the intelligible cosmos is the never changing and immaterial Idea, *Logos*. According to the context, *Logos* could mean mind or sense, thought or will; expressed thought and will, that is word and law. Some ancient philosophers interpreted it as mediator between God and man.

Heraclitus does not mention God, but he is the first philosopher to use the expression *Logos* in the sense of the eternal source of "universal order, which embodies objective truth and can be grasped by human intelligence". This seems so obvious to the Greek philosopher that he often complains of how blind people are: "Even though everything happens in accordance with this Logos, people behave as if they had never discovered it". Could this have been a presentiment of the future? Six hundred years after Heraclitus, the apostle St. John, the first bishop of Ephesus, begins his testimony of the Savior of the World as follows:

> In the beginning was the Word [*Logos*]: the Word was with God, and God was the Word. Through him all things came into being... He was in the world that had come into being through him, and the world did not recognise him... The Word became flesh, he lived among us, and we saw his glory (Jn 1:1-14).

Logos here is not an abstract or inanimate notion any more, but an embodied historic reality: the full unity of divine and human nature in the person of Jesus Christ. The expectation of the divine king coming from heaven was widespread during the centuries preceding the birth of Christ. Some rulers, taking advantage of this anticipation, themselves assumed the name of the Savior and made arbitrary use of the sign of the "Messiah's Star", but were again and again disillusioned and so were their peoples.

In 37 BC, when at the vernal equinox the Sun rose with the stars of the Fish, Virgil, with the help of the Muses of Sicily, once again summed up the hopes of the past and present. Some researchers believe that the fourth poem of his pastoral songs refers to the Emperor Augustus. However, the Fathers of the Church, e.g. Bishop Eusebius and St. Augustine, interpreted it as a poetic vision of Christ's age. Let us quote the translation of its most admirable sentences (Virgil, *Bucolica*, Eclogue IV. Trans. by Berg 1974):

Of Sibylline song the final era now has come,
the mighty march of centuries is born anew.
Now returns the Virgo, returns Saturnian reign,
now new offspring down from heaven on high is sent.
Do you but favour, pure Maternity, his nativity,
the boy whose coming marks
   the first retreat of race of iron,
the rise, world-wide, of golden race.
   Your own Sun god, Apollo reigns...
And he will lead the life of gods,
   and will appear to them himself;
by ancestral virtues he will rule the world at peace...
Advance to your great rank, the time will soon be here,
dear offspring of the gods, great seed of Jupiter !
See the cosmos tremble with its vaulted mass
of lands, of ocean tracts, of heaven's depths !
See how all rejoices in the age to come !
Begin, o little boy, to know your mother with a laugh,

ten months have brought your mother
  long endured disdain.
Begin, o little boy; who has not laughed for parent,
him no god deems fit for feast...

In the view the early Church Fathers it is not the Roman empire of Augustus that marks the beginning of the golden age, but the birth, crucifixion and resurrection of Christ. From a perspective of two thousand years, it is easier to see the significance of this great event: "When the completion of the time came, God sent his Son, born of a woman, born a subject to the Law, to redeem us..." (Gal 4:4). With this event begins the Age of *Pisces*. The first apostles are chosen from among fishermen by Christ. After the miraculous catch Christ says to them: "Follow me and I will make you fishers of men" (Mt 4:19; Lk 5:4-11). With a blessing he multiplies the five loaves of bread and two fish, so as to satiate the hungry people listening to his teachings all day (Mt 14:19; 15:36). After his resurrection, on the shore of Sea of Galilee, he once again offers bread and grilled fish to his apostles, who, having cast their net on his advice, catch 153 big fish (Jn 21:6-14). Bread and fish, the Lenten dish of the followers of Christ ever since the first Christians, are served as holy food at their agapes (Tertullian, *Adv. Marc.* I. 4).

Christ establishes the sacrament of baptism, which remains the permanent sign of the new generations: "unless a man is born through water and Spirit, he cannot enter the Kingdom of God" (Jn 3:5). In old Christian churches the large fonts are called fish pond (*piscina*) and an inscription says: "The christened are the divine generation of the heavenly Fish". Tertullian notes (*De baptismo*, Cap.I): "According to our fish Jesus Christ, we are little fish (*pisciculi*) born through water and we cannot escape from death unless we remain in this water". The baptized are given a small bronze fish as a keepsake. When the scribes demand that Jesus give them a heavenly sign to prove his power, he cites the case of the prophet Jonah to them. Jonah was swallowed by the whale, but on the third day he was put ashore so that he could preach repentance and save the people: "For just as Jonah became a sign to the people of Nineveh, so will the Son of Man be a sign to this generation" through his crucifixion and resurrection (Mt 12:39; Lk 11:30).

Referring to these quotations Jung remarks that the primordial image of the Savior was projected into the constellation *Pisces* centuries before Christ, but the idea that these accounts from the Gospel are transcriptions of astrological myths, is totally unfounded. The chapters in which fish and fishing form a part of the narrative, describe quite ordinary natural events. Whatever the evangelists relate, took place simply and naturally, just as they describe it. Nevertheless, the fish has kept its traditional symbolic meaning in the Gospel and, at the same time, the accounts are prophecies hinting at the future. (Cf. Jung 1971, *Aion*, pp. 98-103).

Several old Christian traditions testify that in the first centuries Christ was considered the last lamb of sacrifice of the Ram Age and the first fish of the Fish Age. (Cf. Origen, *In Genesim hom.* VIII.9; Augustine, *De Civitate Dei* XVI.32). These symbols may seem strange to us now, in the 3rd millennium after Christ, but they formed an essential part of ancient civilization; they served as a means of making Christ's person and work comprehensible and convincing. In this respect they may be helpful even today to those who are familiar with the history and psychology of cosmic symbolism.

During the centuries of the persecutions Christ's secret symbol was FISH, which is ICHTYS in Greek and which was often written in the form of a cross. The anchor with one or two fish can also be seen on some tombstones and on the walls of chapels: the hidden cross of Christ "which is the anchor our souls have, as sure as it is firm" (Heb 6:19). Another popular symbol of the Savior is the dolphin, as the savior of the shipwrecked. The anchor is the sign of hope and reminds one of the constellation of *Pisces*.

 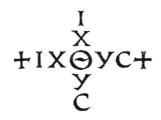 

| *Delphinus Salvator*: Christ as Savior of the shipwrecked | *Ichtys = Fish* written as a cross: a sign of Salvation | *Crux Dissimulata:* the hidden cross of the Savior |

Fig.47: Early Christian Symbols

The synchronism and symbolic correspondence between the celestial sign of the vernal equinox and Christ's cross are very significant. The assumption by the divine Person of human nature ("The Word became Man" Jn 1:14) makes man aware of the contrast between body and spirit and at the same time renders the achievement of the desired unity and harmony possible. That is what the apostle Paul preaches:

Human nature has nothing to look forward to but death, while the spirit looks forward to life and peace..., and if the Spirit of him who raised Jesus from the dead is living in you, then he who raised Jesus from the dead will give life to your own mortal bodies through his Spirit living in you (Rom 8:6-11; Phil 3:12).

The constellation *Pisces* consists of two fish: one pointing toward the north, the other one on its right, pointing toward the west. Its two branches are connected by its first and brightest star (*Alrisha* = Rosette), the early morning rising of which announced spring when Christ was born. The cross, which has been the sign of our age for two thousand years, can indeed be recognized in the form of the constellation of *Pisces*. The first three hundred years of the Christian era were a period of religious

283

persecution, the age of the martyrs of Christ. This is followed by the resurrection of Christianity, which emerges from the catacombs and expands in the west for a thousand years. The Gothic churches with their pointed arches, lines and steeples pointing up to the sky indicate the striving of medieval man for an eternal life in the next world. In the 16th century this is replaced by the ornate baroque, with its churches built on broad foundations and its cult of personality. This is followed by reformed movements, schisms and wars of religion. Finally, the last Antichristian act of the age of *Pisces* begins with the French revolution (1789): widespread religious persecutions under the guise of liberty, the lust for power and fall of bloodthirsty dictators (Napoleon, Hitler, Stalin, Mao-tze-tung).

The drama of Christ's crucifixion and resurrection is a stunning illustration of man's destiny in the age of *Pisces*. Since then mankind has been split into two opposing camps and the distance between them is constantly increasing. New social forms of sequestered life and monastic communities came into being. The founder of the first monastic order, St. Benedict (about 547), became the spiritual father and patron saint of Europe. For one thousand years, cultural development and the dissemination of knowledge was the province of people sequestered in monasteries. The evolvement of spiritual and material assets, the cultivation of religious and moral values had their sources in the depth of the mind and in divine inspiration, independent of the knowledge of cosmic rhythms.

Six hundred years before the birth of Christ the great prophets started to preach the coming of the new era. Similarly, the 16th century AD was the time of the great confessors and teaching saints, who prepared the peoples of Europe for a new turn of age. One of the most prominent saint among them was St. Ignatius of Loyola who is today referred to by psychologists as the grand master of introspection and self control. His Spiritual Exercises focus on "the meditation on Two Standards: the one of Christ, our sovereign Leader and Lord; the other of Lucifer, the mortal enemy of our human nature". He lures everybody under his standard by promising people earthly fortune and power, with no regard to God or their fellow human beings. Christ, on the other hand, leads people along the road of self-sacrificing fraternal love and shows by his own example that the guarantee of a happy life is kindness and peace (Mt 4:8; 5:3; 11:29: "Shoulder my yoke and learn from me, for I am gentle and humble in heart, and you will find rest for your souls"). From this vision of the Two Standards stemmed the famous "rules for in some degree perceiving and knowing the various motions excited in the soul; the good that they may be admitted; the bad that they may be rejected..., and to the same effect a fuller discernment of Spirits", so that they cannot deceive us (Ignatius, *Spiritual Exercises*, 146-148; 314-336).

The name of St. Ignatius is associated with the foundation of the missionary order officially called the Society of Jesus, in common speech known as the Jesuit Order. With St. Francis Xavier St. Ignatius began to organize world missions in 1540. Since then thousands of missionaries have sacrificed their lives for the Gospel, which was preached by them in every language. Today the events of Christ's life are is familiar to all people: the image of the redeeming deity merciful to man is dispersed all over the world in the age of *Pisces*. There is a desire to imitate Christian culture even among those who have not yet accepted the Christian faith.

The oldest and best known explanation of the link between the known ages of culture and precessional periods is the relation of the four elements and the signs of the zodiac. The Chaldaeans divided the circle of the zodiac into four equal triangles, in which they saw the elements of the universe. Fire (light), earth, water and air (breath) are the first four words of the Creator in the Hebrew Bible; they preach His glory to man (Dan 3:62-74). The history of our civilization began about 6300 years ago, when the vernal Sun rose with the stars of the Bull. The element of the Bull is earth; that was the age when the practice of planned agriculture started to spread. The materials of the earth were subjugated by man: he built adobe huts, made his tools and statues from wood and stone and his dishes of clay. According to Moses the Lord Almighty shaped also man's body from dust of the soil (Gen 2:7).

The element of the Ram is fire; that was the age when man learned the use of fire. By melting metals he separated them from the earth and made tools and weapons. God Almighty called to Moses from the middle of a burning bush. In the wilderness he went before the people in the form of a pillar of fire. The oil lamps were incessantly burning in the sanctuary and the high priest offered burned sacrifices (Gen 22:13; cf. "Holocaust" in Lev 1:3-9). The natural element of the Fish is water, and that was the age when man learned how to make use of the energy residing in water. The building of spas and hydroelectric power stations, the discovery of the steam engine, the steam ship and the submarine, chemical laboratories and chemicals are all characteristic features of the age of the Fish. In religion the baptismal water sanctified by Christ is the sacrament of spiritual revival and eternal life (Jn 3:5: Rom 6:4).

The Spirit present in the baptismal water characterizes the future as well. The element of *Aquarius* is namely air, the sign of the invisible soul and spiritual current. The human figure in the traditional constellation is holding a large jug, from which flows the water of life and wisdom. In the Gospel and in the Revelation of John it is the pierced heart of Jesus from which "flow streams of living water" into the heart of his faithful; that is his saving Spirit, the living water of wisdom (Jn 7:38; 19:34; Rev 22:17).

For the next two thousand years, the vernal equinox will be moving in the sign of the Fish and in the constellation of Aquarius. The experts of symbology believe that the ideal of the human being could be achieved in the forthcoming centuries. The revolutionary discoveries of recent decades from the wonders of electrotechnics to nuclear power stations make intellectual and physical work easier. Man has more time and energy left to study and perfect himself. Analytical psychology can also help in this process. Since the Second Vatican Council (1964) many people hope for a new golden age of Christian culture, some promising signs of which are already visible. For the time being, however, we are living in the crises of a transitional age. New discoveries always involve the risk of being misunderstood and misused by many. And the fight of ideologies goes on between the Two Standards.

Marilyn Ferguson and Fritjof Capra, the apostles of the New Age movement, preach that man's personality and mind are transformed by the precession of the vernal equinox and the cosmic influence of Aquarius, so the world does not need great philosophers and saints for its social and religious life to be renewed. They blame the materialistic and rationalistic attitude of western society for today's crisis. (And what about eastern society? The Chinese or the Japanese for example, are they not materialists and rationalists?)

The Pontiffs of the Church have, since the last century, repeatedly warned against the dangers of "modernism"; the idolization of the human mind and technology. The worship of machines and the use of science for its own sake delude man whose spiritual and moral development lag behind the evolution of technology and so he may easily lose control of the helm of the liberated forces:

"One would say that humanity today, which has been able to build the marvelous, complex machine of the modern world, subjugating to its services the tremendous forces of nature, now appears incapable of controlling these forces - as though the rudder has slipped from its hands - and so it is in peril of being overthrown and crushed by them" (Pius XII, Christmas Address, 24.12.1952. *Acta Ap. Sedis*, Vol.45, p.33).

The partisans of New Age have expropriated these declarations of the Pope and act as if they had discovered the real cause of the problems, but reject the right solution that comes from Christ's teaching. They turn away from the Church, "because Christians do not show any sign of being redeemed" - they say. But do they themselves show any sign of it? They reject any conscious and purposeful thinking and turn to misunderstood ancient oriental teachings to solve current problems. They think the universal spirit and cosmic rays will show us the way to a new and more honest age, "when everybody unites in a divine mind and everything is God".

This erroneous pantheism is the faith of spiritually blind men, who believe they can see. We cannot discuss here in detail the teachings of New Age. What we have said should be sufficient to make us realize their dangerous mistakes in the light of our studies of the star of Bethlehem. In the face of an erroneous concept of man and God, we cannot stress often enough that the creator Spirit pervades and sustains human spirit as well as the material world, but its omnipotence and eternity permanently surpass them and never will be identical with the created universe or the spirit of man.

19. *Cosmic Covenant*

Agreement and cooperation to implement a common goal are the essence and aims of every covenant. Some countries conclude defense and economic treaties. Different groups conclude peace pacts defining mutual rights and obligations. Marriage and the family are among the most intimate covenants. The adjective *cosmic* refers to an agreement which comprehends the entire universe. The ancient idea of the marriage of

286

heaven and earth becomes a metaphor for God's covenant with his people.

Moses and the prophets draw on general human experience to describe the relationship between God Almighty and his creatures. In the Book *Genesis* God leaves it to man to name the growing things and the animals, because their destiny is to serve man. Man, who is created as an image of God, is by nature the ally of the Creator of the universe. His duty is to "conquer the earth, and be master of all living animals", i.e., to maintain the order of creation in nature, which is originally "very good" (Gen 1:28-31). Yet man neglects this royal duty and misuses his power. He makes unjust and excessive use of the assets received in creation, disregarding God and his fellow human beings. In this way the order of nature is disrupted and the whole of mankind has to suffer. The story of the Deluge, in which the faithless and the false are punished, illustrates the law of justice and testifies to divine grace shown to the faithful and the just.

After the Deluge the world is renewed for those who remain alive in the Ark. According to the apostle Peter, this is the prophetic prototype of the faithful reborn through the water of baptism in the Church. The reference here is to the new and everlasting covenant. The Lord of the Armies obeyed by the stars and natural forces, forms alliance with the whole of creation for the benefit of man. This cosmic covenant is symbolized by the magnificent rainbow, which spans the whole sky. In the vision of Ezekiel the figure of the Lord, the Son of Man is surrounded by such a rainbow (Gen 9: 16; Ezek 1: 28).

Later in the text the Most High (*El-Shaddai*) selects a righteous and faithful man, with whom he forms a personal alliance also aimed at redeeming the whole of mankind. For the promises were addressed to Abraham and his descendants: "All nations will be blessed in you". His descendant is Christ, the Savior of the world. It is here that the idea of justification by faith is first linked to the covenant to save the world. (Gen 12:3; Gal 3:8-16). Finally, the ever present Lord (He who is) forms an alliance with the people of Israel through Moses. He liberates them from the slavery of Egypt and shows them his miraculous power. The idea of law is then explicitly linked to the covenant. The precondition of redemption is the righteousness, i.e., faithful observance of the laws of the natural, moral and religious order. According to the apostle Paul the Ten Commandments are also laws of nature, "written in man's heart". However, fallen man can only abide by them with the help of Christ the Savior (Rom 2: 15).

In addition to historical accounts, the Bible preaches that sin is not only a matter to be settled between man and God. Sin alienates man from the original order of nature and sets him against other creatures. Redemption places man into a stronger and larger order, which spans the whole created world. This basic Scriptural truth has been completely neglected by biblical scholars in recent centuries. Theologians and preachers have only talked about the redemption of man, as if God did not care about the other creatures. There is an urgent need for a more profound explanation of the account of creation and salvation, which is in accordance with the teachings of the Apostles and the Fathers of the Church. People should be made aware of the responsibility they bear to nature.

The above thoughts are stressed by Robert Murray, S.J. who is professor at the Theological Faculty of London University and president of the Society for Old Testament Study. The subtitle of his book (Murray 1992) is "Biblical Themes of Justice, Peace and the Integrity of Creation". The author offers a refreshing interpretation of the biblical texts which are about the universal order of creation, and the means and ways of its maintenance or restoration. He shows that the ideas of justification and justice, reconciliation and peace refer not only to the moral and social order, but to the order of nature as well. This recent research sheds light on the historical background of the view, according to which the heavenly sign heralding the birth of Christ was a natural star and its symbolic sense was known in the Babylonian and Hebrew traditions.

Murray amply quotes and analyzes the Hebrew prophets, comparing them to the apocryphal writings of the Old Testament (Enoch, Book of Jubilees, etc.) and the Accadian-Babylonian myths (*Enuma Elish, Erra,* etc.). The accounts relating the breach of the cosmic covenant and the rites designed to restore universal order have a common old Semitic source. The Hebrew Bible contains traces of ancient magic practices, which were appropriately rewritten but left in the text by the Israelite priests. It has often been noted, though has never been proven, that several biblical texts contain magic rituals that are aimed at maintaining order "on earth as it is in heaven" by symbolic acts. Also, in The Lord's Prayer Matthew quotes the sentence: "Your will be done on earth as in heaven" (Mt 6:10).

The idea of the Cosmic Covenant focuses on the biblical evidence for a belief which ancient Israel shared with neighboring cultures, one well documented from Babylon and Egypt: the belief in a divinely willed order harmoniously linking heaven and earth. In Israelite tradition, too, it is the visible order of the heavens that serves as a model for social and moral order, because the unchanging laws of the motion of the stars demonstrate the will of the Lord Almighty. This was established at creation, when the cosmic elements were fixed and bound to maintain the order; but the harmony was broken by demons, hostile to God and to mankind. The Book of Enoch, for example, begins with these statements:

Contemplate all the events in heaven, how the lights in heaven do not change their courses, how each rises and sets in order, each at its proper time, and they do not transgress their law...All his works serve him and do not change, but as God has decreed, so everything is done...And you have not persevered, nor observed the law of the Lord, but you have transgressed, and have spoken proud and hard words with your unclean mouth against his majesty (1 Enoch 2: 1; 5: 2-4).

The prophet Isaiah, too, predicts the judgment:

See how the Lord [He who is] lays the earth waste, makes it a desert..., because the earth is defiled under its inhabitants' feet, for they have transgressed the law, violated the decree, broken the everlasting covenant... The Lord will punish the armies of the sky above and below the king of the earth... The Moon will hide her face, the Sun be

288

ashamed, for the Lord of the Armies will be king in Jerusalem, and his glory will shine... (Is 24: 1-5 and 23).

The Armies, in Hebrew *Sabaoth*, indicate the Sun, Moon and stars, regarded as deities in Babylonia, in the Semitic pagan world. The "everlasting Covenant" (*Berit'olam*) is not that with Abraham or Israel, but God's eternal covenant with the whole of mankind, analogous to the covenant with Noah; once this is violated, judgment follows like a second flood.

The first Temple in Jerusalem was built by Solomon in honor of the Lord, who maintains the heaven and the earth (960 BC). Henceforth the anointed king (messiah) in power became the deputy of God on Earth. It was his task to assure lawful justice, order and peace and to supervise religious services. As early as Solomon's time, the cult of the stars taken from other cultures is to be found in the Temple of Jerusalem. At that time even that cult was regarded as a symbolic act of justice and law. The people needed to hold magical ceremonies in order to feel through them the power of God over frightening natural forces. That was the reason why they prayed for the king: they wanted the king to have a supernatural power, so that he may maintain justice among the peoples, in the same way as *Elohim* maintains order among the stars.

Such a prayer is, for example, Psalm 72, which recalls the ceremony of the royal enthronement: "God, endow the king with your own fair judgement, the son of the king with your own saving justice, that he may rule your people with justice..." This ensures victory, peace, welfare and order in society and in nature, and finally divine blessing. All kings will pay him homage, every race in the world will be "blessed in him", through faith in him. This prophetic Psalm pictures the cosmic covenant and the awaited age of the Messiah. The early Church Fathers saw the fulfillment of this very Psalm in the visit of the Magi of the East to Bethlehem, as related by Matthew. The ideal of the cosmic covenant in old Hebrew is always expressed by the same words: *mishpat*, i.e., law and order; *sedeq* or *sedaqah*, i.e., truth or justice. In the genre of poetry and in the prophetic style, these two concepts can be widely interpreted: as heavenly or earthly law, as divine or human justice; in another interpretation, both words express the order desired by God both in nature and in human society. An example of this is the old prayer quoted in the book of Isaiah, which also refers to the enthronement of the Messiah (Is 45:8): "Send victory like a dew, you heavens, and let the clouds rain it down. Let the earth open for salvation to spring up. Let deliverance, too, bud forth which I [He who is] shall create". (The Hebrew word *sedeq* here rendered "victory" means "righteousness", i.e., "victory of the Just One"; so also *sedaqah* here rendered "deliverance", is the justice which shall rise as the morning star with the coming of the Messiah.) Today this verse is the Entrance Antiphon of the Masses in the season of Advent, with which the Church prepares for the celebration of Jesus' birth.

In Chapter 32 of Isaiah, the virtues of the ideal king and the order of nature and society restored by the Messiah are again expressed by these two words:

A king reigns by justice [*sedeq*] and princes rule by law [*mishpat*]...Once more will be poured on us the spirit above; then shall the wilderness be fertile land, in the wilderness justice [*mishpat*] will come to live...; integrity [*sedaqah*] will bring peace, justice give lasting security (Is 32: 1 and 15-17).

If we compare the oldest Hebrew texts about the messianic age and the Accadian-Babylonian myths, we shall discover uniform religious ideas in both cults. Murray (1992) claims that the cosmic covenant is rooted in ancient oriental culture and that its ideas, expressed in different ways, appear in the age of Abraham, Moses and David. Modern interpretations of the Scriptures arbitrarily separate the ancient Semitic, Israelite and Judean traditions, because they are still afraid of misinterpreted mythology. On the other hand, the basic error of the fundamentalist exegetes is a "refusal to recognize the variety of styles and genres of statement in the Bible, and, therefore, to realize that the divine Truth comes to us in many modes, some of them essentially symbolic". Divine grace and revelation are not confined to the written letters of the alphabet. God can let us know his will through the symbols of nature, too.

The two words (*sedeq* and *mishpat*) used by the Hebrew prophets to characterize the king who restores and maintains universal order are the same as the ones in the Babylonian ceremonies (*kittu* and *mesharu*): justice and law, or right and order. In the Accadian cuneiform writings the qualities and the role of Jupiter and Saturn are indicated by these words; the two giant wandering stars represent the abstract notions of justice and law. The prophetic and poetic statements of the Bible, on the other hand, contain only pure symbols and allegories, no star is personified as liberating king. The awaited Messiah appears in a human-like form before the prophets and speaks to them in human language (Is 6:1; Ezek 1:26; Dan 10:16). Murray (1992) assumes that some of the ceremonies in the first Temple of Jerusalem were held by the king himself to maintain the cosmic covenant and order, as well as to defeat the enemy forces. They are not mentioned explicitly in the Hebrew Bible, but they can be inferred from the genre and contents of the messianic Psalms (2, 18, 20, 21, 45, 72, 110), which were obviously related to such ceremonies. The cosmic character of religion in the Old Testament is also shown by the furnishings of the Temple. The Book of Kings lists the liturgical objects without describing their symbolic meaning. The astral and cosmic character of these objects may have been so obvious and well known that the priests who recopied and re-edited the old writings after the Exile considered any explanation unnecessary.

This is testified by the philosopher Philon and the historian Josephus, the two most outstanding Israelite scholars in the first century. Quite independently from each other they draw on the same traditions when they refer to the cosmic archetype of the Temple and describe the symbolic content of the ritual objects. The ban of images by Moses did not involve symbolic representation, only idols or statues of God. The seven-branched lampstand (*menorah*) is the main symbol of religion in the Old Testament and is today part of the coat of arms of Israel. It was made by Moses according to the pattern shown to him by the Lord on the mountain (Ex 25:31-40; Zech 4:2). During the wandering in the wilderness, it stood in the tent of the Covenant, in front of the sanctuary and it became the permanent ornament of the Temple on the order of Solomon. According to Philon and Josephus, its six semicircular branches symbolize the orbits of the Moon and the five planets: the oil lamp in the middle represents the Sun, to its left stand the lamps of Mercury, Venus and the Moon, to the right those of Mars, Jupiter and Saturn. The light of the permanently burning oil lamp reminded the priests of the glory and presence of the Lord of the Universe.

The breastplate of judgement adorned the sacred vestments of the high priest. It contained the "sacred lots", two small sticks, which served to decide by a draw who was to perform the priestly services. The breastplate was adorned with four rows of three precious stones of different colors. Both writers, Philon and Josephus, also interpret the twelve stones on the high priest's breastplate in terms of the signs of the zodiac. Indeed, these indicated the twelve gates of the heavenly revelations. The account of the vestments relates the stones to the twelve tribes: "they correspond to the names of the sons of Israel" (Ex 28:15-21).

The veil of the Sanctuary was a symbol for the heavens, as it was adorned with the cardinal signs of the zodiac. The Lord said to Moses: "You are to make a veil of purple stuffs, violet shade and red; you are to have it finely embroidered with Cherubs..., and the veil will serve you to separate the Holy Place from the Holy of Holies" (Ex 26:31). This veil shuts off the Holy of Holies, dwelling place of the Lord Almighty, from the worshippers. Only the high priest entered this Sanctuary, and then only once a year, where two Cherubs guarded the Ark of the Covenant, and each of them had a lion's face and a human face. Philo thought that the Sanctuary and its furnishings had represented "the Universal Temple which existed before the holy Temple" and which was visible in heaven. All these ritual objects were charged with astral and cosmic symbolism.

Originally all these were profound and sacred symbols. Nevertheless, after Solomon the false worship of the stars was widely practiced in Judaea, too. It was King Josiah who put an end to this between 630-620 BC. He removed the statues of the star gods and "destroyed the horses which the kings of Judah had dedicated to the Sun at the entrance to the Temple..., and he burned the Chariot of the Sun" (2 Kg 23:11). The idea, according to which the whole solar system with its twelve constellations takes part in the worship of God the Creator, lived on even after the destruction of the Temple of Jerusalem. An example of this is the still extant mosaic on the stone floor of the Beth Alpha Synagogue, which represents the triple pattern of *sedaqah*, the justice and order of God's will: in each faithful man, in the religious community and in the whole of nature.

Fig. 48: The seasons and the constellations of the zodiac in the Beth Alpha Synagogue.

As we observe in the mosaic, at the entrance of the temple we find the Book of Law (*Torah*) guarded by the two Cherubs, the Bull and the Lion. The next scene represents the justice of Abraham the faithful (Gen 22:1-18): he is ready to sacrifice his only legitimate son, because he recognizes that each man belongs to God the Creator, who must be given everything he possesses, including his life. However, divine justice is merciful to man and it does not desire the child to be killed, so it gives the father an innocent lamb to be sacrificed instead. The stars above Abraham's head indicate the number of his descendants. In the center of the pavement is the cosmic order, symbolized by the twelve signs of the zodiac and the four seasons, framing the Sun, which the artist did not hesitate to picture as the Sun god in his chariot. In the back of the temple we can see the drawn veil of the sanctuary with two seven-branched lampstands in front of it and the Ark of the Covenant guarded by two lions.

A remarkable feature of this mosaic is the exact setting of the zodiac: the sign of the Cancer is at the top, because that is where the Sun culminates at the time of the summer solstice. The central point is not the Earth but the

Fig. 49: Cosmic symbols of the Old Covenant in the Beth Alpha Synagogue built in the fifth century AD (Sukenik 1934)

Sun, *Helios*, with its carriage and four, similar to the seven-branched *menorah* which also has the lamp of the Sun in the middle. The artists did not know the heliocentric system, but had a presentiment that the Sun radiating light and heat had to be in the center. They seem to have referred the symbol of Sun god to the awaited Messiah. The first Roman Christians did the same: on the sepulchre of the apostle Peter we find the carriage and four of Helios with the figure of Christ standing on it. The sepulchre uncovered in 1950 was found 50 meters deep under the high altar of St. Peter's Basilica in Rome.

The all embracing cosmic covenant is implemented in Jesus Christ. The direct continuation of creation is redemption which comprehends the whole of nature. It is in this light that the Apostle Paul sees man's place in the universe: since the sin of man has disrupted the order of nature, it is restored by divine justice through Jesus, who, as Son of God and Son of Man, is ready to associate himself with the descendants of the fallen Adam and obtains reconciliation for the whole world through his self-sacrifice. This, therefore, can only be attained through community with Christ. The followers of Christ are new human beings; born again through the sacrament of baptism they are God's children. With this rebirth begins the universal adoption as sons and the restoration of the universe. This idea belongs to the new and eternal covenant, and its laws are revealed in the inaugural discourse of Jesus (Mt 5-7). The Apostle Paul gives a concise explanation of this mystery in his letter to the Church in Rome:

> I think that what we suffer in this life can never be compared to the glory, as yet unrevealed, which is waiting for us. The whole creation is eagerly waiting for God to reveal his sons. It was not for any fault on the part of creation that it was made unable to attain its purpose, it was made so by God; but creation still retains the hope of being free, like us, from its slavery to decadence, to enjoy the same freedom and glory as the children of God. We are well aware that the whole creation, until this time, has been groaning in labour pains. And not only that: we too, who have the first fruits of the Spirit, even we are groaning inside ourselves, waiting with eagerness for our bodies to be set free. In hope, we already have salvation..., we are able to wait for it with persevering confidence (Rom 8: 18-24).

That is how the apostle sees the reality of the new heaven and earth, which was prophesied by Isaiah seven hundred years before (Is 65:17), and the fascinating pictures of which were revealed to the elderly John (Rev 21). This is also described by St. Peter: "What we are waiting for is what he promised: the new heavens and new earth,where righteousness will be at home" (2 Pet 3:13).

Paul encourages the faithful to wait patiently while they are fighting against evil with Christ's spiritual armor, "for it is not against human enemies that we have to struggle, but against the principalities and the powers of darkness, the spiritual army of evil in the heavenly altitudes" (Eph 6,12). These expressions refer not only to evil spiritual beings, but also to cosmic influences which make man prone to certain crimes or diseases. Such harmful influences, however, cannot come from heaven, which is the dwelling place of God and his angels. The Jerusalem Bible notes that St. Paul is here referring to the invisible forces and powers which, according to the ancient concept, live in certain celestial bodies (*in caelestibus*) and in the atmosphere (in the air), i.e., between the surface of the earth and the heavens. That is why the apostle says that in Jesus God has shown "the power which he exercised in raising him from the dead and enthroning him at his right hand, in heaven, far above every principality, ruling force or power...The purpose of this was, that now, through the Church, the principalities and powers should learn how comprehensive God's wisdom is" (Eph 1:21 and 3:10).

The apostles and the early Church Fathers mention these cosmic forces and powers as ones that are fully under the sovereignty of the Risen Christ. Their influence is perceptible but they no longer have power over the faithful souls reborn through the sacrament of baptism.

20. *Kepler's "Astronomia Nova"*

We have learned and have become accustomed to the fact that we together with our Earth are rotating and flying very fast in interstellar space. This is something we accept as quite normal and we never even think of it. However, four hundred years ago the author of *Astronomia Nova* took great pains to explain this to all those who considered themselves scholars and religious believers. Both scholars and ordinary people had been proud and happy to live with the idea that our Earth stood at the center of the universe. They instinctively rejected the new theory which disturbed their happiness and sense of security.

Johannes Kepler had to start his epoch-making work by refuting the philosophical and theological objections to the heliocentric theory. His predecessor and master, Tycho Brahe, had previously realized the considerable difference between the observational results and Ptolemy's calculations and that Copernicus' method was more accurate. Nevertheless, in order to save the geocentric system Brahe assumed that the planets revolved around the Sun, which itself, accompanied by all the planets, revolved round the Earth. This model, however, did not square any better with the observations.

While looking for the cause of the revolution of the planets, i.e., for a common driving force, Kepler found that it was physically impossible for the motion of large planets to be maintained by the attraction of the Earth. So the common driving force could only originate in the Sun. Venus performed a complete revolution in 225 days and Mars in 687 days; the 365 day period was between these two periods, therefore it could not be that of the Sun, but had to be that of the Earth, which should move around the Sun in an orbit between Mars and Venus.

This statement was supported by the observation that the Earth and the planets moved faster or slower at stated intervals, because their distances from the Sun varied. Kepler asserted that this was the strongest geometrical proof of the physical conclusion that the source of the planets' motion was in the Sun itself. He believed that the attractive force of the Sun decreased with increasing distance.This was the first step toward the right definition of the law of gravitation. Many people developed a false concept of the gravitational force and argued against Copernicus' theory by stating that it is impossible for a mathematical point to set bodies in motion and that there is need for an animate faculty. That induced Kepler to formulate the basic principles of the right theory of gravity. He described it as a corporeal faculty of all material objects to attract each other. He argued that when a body was separated from kindred bodies, that corporeal faculty brought into action a force which moved them back together; there was no need for an animate faculty. (Seventy years after the publication of *Astronomia Nova*, Isaac Newton discovered and mathematically defined the universal law of gravitation on the basis of Kepler's laws.)

Before the law of gravitation was known many scholars had believed that, if the Earth moved, it would have to move at a very high speed owing to the immensity of the heavens. This would be unbearable to living creatures, and the yearly revolution of the Earth would be unnatural. Kepler, on the other hand, showed that these worries were unfounded, since the Earth's speed was in correct proportion with the distance of the Sun, and that the speed of the celestial sphere would become disproportional and unnatural "were the Earth ordered to remain quite motionless in its place".

We now quote the most important paragraphs of Kepler's introduction to his *Astronomia Nova* in a new English translation (Donahue 1992). He writes:

There are, however, many more people who are moved by piety to withhold assent from Copernicus, fearing that falsehood might be charged against the Holy Spirit speaking in the Scriptures if we say that the Earth is moved and the Sun is still. But let them consider that since we acquire most of our information, both in quality and quantity, through the sense of sight, it is impossible for us to abstract our speech from this ocular sense. Thus, many times each day we speak in accordance with the sense of sight, although we are quite certain that the truth of the matter is otherwise. This verse of Virgil furnishes an example: "We are carried from the port, the land and cities recede". It does seem so to the eyes, but Optics shows the cause of this fallacy. Thus, we call the rising and setting of the stars ascent and descent, though at the same time that we say the Sun ascends, others say it descends. The Ptolemaic astronomers even now say that the planets are stationary when they are seen to stay near the same fixed stars for several days, even though they think the planets are then really moving downwards in a straight line, or upwards away from the Earth. Thus writers of all nations use the word *solstice*, even though they in fact deny that the Sun stands still.

Now the Holy Scriptures, too, when treating common things (concerning which it is not their purpose to instruct humankind), speak with humans in the human manner, in order to be understood by them. They make use of what is generally acknowledged, in order to weave in other things more lofty and divine. No wonder, then, if Scripture also speaks in accordance with human perception when the truth of things is at odds with the senses, whether or not humans are aware of this. Who is unaware that the allusion in Psalm 19 is poetical ? Here, under the image of the Sun, are sung the spreading of the Gospel and even the sojourn of Christ the Lord in this world on our behalf, and in the singing the Sun is said to emerge from the tabernacle of the horizon like a bridegroom from his marriage bed, exuberant as a strong man for the race.

The psalmist was aware that the sun does not go forth from the horizon as from a tabernacle (even though it may appear so to the eyes). On the other hand, he considered the Sun to move for the precise reason that it appears so to the eyes. In either case, he expressed it so because in either case it appeared so to the eyes. He should not be judged to have spoken falsely in either case, for the perception of the eyes also has its truth, well suited to the psalmist's more hidden aim, the adumbration of the Gospel and also of the Son of God. Likewise Joshua makes mention of the valleys against which the Sun and Moon moved, because when he was at the Jordan it appeared so to him...He meant that the Sun should be held back in its place in the middle of the sky for an entire day with respect to the sense of his eyes, since for other people during the same interval of time it would remain below the horizon. But thoughtless persons pay attention only to the verbal contradiction, *the Sun stood still* versus *the Earth stood still*, not considering that this contradiction can only arise in an optical and astronomical context, and does not carry over into common usage...

Now God easily understood from Joshua's words what he meant, and he responded by stopping the motion of the Earth, so that the Sun might appear so to him to stop. For the gist of Joshua's petition comes to this, that it might appear so to him, whatever the reality might meanwhile be. Indeed, that this appearance should come about was not vain and purposeless, but quite conjoined with the desired effect. But see Chapter 10 of the *Astronomiae pars optica*, where you will find reasons why, to absolutely all men, the Sun appears to move and not the Earth: it is because, owing to its apparent slowness, the Sun's motion is perceived, not by sight, but by reasoning alone, through its change of distance from the mountains over a period of time. It is therefore impossible for a previously uninformed reason to imagine anything but that the Earth, along with the arch of heaven set over it, is like a great house, immobile, in which the Sun, so small in stature, travels from one side to the other like a bird flying in the air.

What absolutely all men imagine, the first line of Holy Scripture presents: In the beginning, says Moses, God created the heaven and the earth, because it is these two parts that chiefly present themselves to the sense of sight. It is as though Moses were to say to man: 'This whole worldly edifice that you see, light above and dark and widely spread out below, upon which you are standing and by which you are roofed over, has been created by God'. In another passage, Man is asked whether he has learned how to seek out the height of heavens above, or the depths of the earth below (Jer 31,37), because to the ordinary man both appear to extend through equally infinite spaces. Nevertheless, there is no one in his right mind who, upon hearing these words, would use them to limit the astronomer's diligence either in showing the contemptible smallness of the Earth in comparison with the heavens, or in investigating astronomical distances. For these words do not concern measurements arrived at by reasoning. Rather, they concern real exploration, which is utterly impossible for the human body,fixed upon the land and drawing upon the free air. Read all of Chapter 38 of Job, and compare it with matters discussed in astronomy and in physics.

Suppose someone were to assert, from Psalm 24, that the Earth is founded upon the Ocean, in order to support the absurd philosophical conclusion that the Earth floats upon waters. Would it not be correct to say to him that he should regard the Holy Spirit as a divine messenger, and refrain from want only dragging Him into physics class ? For in that passage the psalmist intends nothing but what men already know and experience daily, namely, that the land has great rivers flowing through it and seas surrounding it. If this be easily accepted, why can it not also be accepted that in other passages usually cited in opposition to the Earth's motion we should likewise turn our eyes from physics to the aims of Scripture?

A generation passes away, and a generation comes, but the Earth stands forever, says Ecclesiastes (1:4). Does it seem here as if Solomon wanted to argue with the astronomers? No, rather, he wanted to warn men of their own mutability, while the Earth, home of the human race, remains always the same, the motion of the Sun perpetually returns to the same place, rivers flow from their sources into the sea.., and finally, as these men perish, others are born. Life's tale is ever the same; there is nothing new under the Sun.

You do not hear any physical theorem here. The message is a moral one, concerning something self evident and seen by all eyes but seldom pondered. Solomon therefore urges us to ponder. Who is unaware that the Earth is always the same ? Who does not see the Sun return daily to its place of rising, rivers perennially flowing towards the sea, and men succeeding one another? But who really considers that the same drama of life is always being played, only with different characters, and that not a single thing in human affairs is new? So Solomon, by mentioning what is evident to all, warns of that which almost everyone wrongly neglects. It is said, however, that Psalm 104, in its entirety, is a physical discussion, since the whole of it is concerned with physical matters: God is said to have fixed the Earth on its foundations, unshakable for ever and ever. But in fact, nothing could be farther from the psalmist's intention than speculation about physical causes; he has composed a hymn to God the Creator, in which he treats the world in order, as it appears to the eyes. If you consider carefully, you will see that it is a commentary upon the six days of creation in Genesis....

The psalmist relates everything to the Earth and to the things that live on it, because, in the judgment of sight, the chief parts of the world are two: Heaven and Earth. He therefore considers that for so many ages now the Earth has neither sunk nor cracked apart nor tumbled down, yet no one has certain knowledge of what it is founded upon. He does not wish to teach things of which men are ignorant, but to recall to mind something they neglect,namely,God's greatness and potency in a creation of such magnitude, so solid and stable. If an astronomer teaches that the Earth is carried through the heavens, he is not spurning what the psalmist says here, nor does he contradict human experience... The fourth part of the Psalm 104 begins with verse 19, and celebrates the work of the fourth day, the Sun and the Moon, but chiefly the benefit that the division of times brings to humans and other living things. It is this benefit that is his subject matter: it is clear that the author is not writing as an astronomer here. If he were,he would not fail to mention the five planets, than whose motion nothing is more admirable, nothing more beautiful, and nothing a better witness to the Creator's wisdom, for those who take note of it...At the end, in conclusion, he declares the general goodness of God in sustaining all things and creating new things. So everything the psalmist said of the world relates to living things. He tells nothing that is not generally acknowledged, because his purpose was to praise things that are known, not to seek out the unknown. It was his wish to invite men to consider the benefits accruing to them from each of these works of the six days.

I, too, implore my reader, when he departs from the temple and enters astronomical studies,not to forget the divine goodness conferred upon men, to the consideration of which the psalmist chiefly invites. I hope that,with me, he will praise and celebrate the Creator's wisdom and greatness, which I unfold for him in the more perspicacious explanation of the world's form, the investigation of causes, and the detection of errors of vision. Let him not only extol the Creator's divine beneficence in His concern for the well being of all living things, expressed in the firmness and stability of the Earth, but also acknowledge His wisdom expressed in its motion, at once so well hidden and so admirable. But whoever is too dull to understand astronomical science, or too weak to believe Copernicus without affecting his faith, I would advise him that, having dismissed astronomical studies and having damned whatever philosophical opinions he pleases, he mind his own business and betake himself home to scratch in his own dirt patch, abandoning this wandering about the world. He should raise his eyes (his only means of vision) to the visible heaven and with his whole heart burst forth in giving thanks and praising God the Creator. He can be sure that he worships God no less than the astronomer, to whom God has granted the more penetrating vision of the mind's eye, and an ability and desire to celebrate his God above those things he has discovered. (Kepler's Introduction to "The New Astronomy", translated by Donahue 1992).

21. *Galileo: Truth and Error*

On 8 December 1613 the Grand Duchess Christina of Tuscany invited the professors of the Academy of the Medici to luncheon. During the conversation at the richly laid table, they mentioned Galileo, who, being ill, had been unable to accept the invitation. The guests talked about his new telescope, with which they, too, had had the chance to observe the moons of Jupiter and the phases of Venus. Could this really mean that the Earth was orbiting around the stationary Sun?

One of the philosophers remarked it was impossible to empirically prove the Earth's motion; moreover, that would be contrary to the Bible, which was another reason why one should not believe it. According to the Book of Joshua, the Sun revolves, but at that time it "stood still in the middle of the sky and delayed its setting for almost a whole day" (Jos 10: 12).

The Duchess Christina said the Bible was never wrong. She wondered, however, whether that miracle of the Sun could be accounted for by the temporary halt of the revolution of the celestial spheres, as suggested by Galileo. The theologian Don Antonio and the mathematician Father Benedetto Castelli tried to give a correct answer to the question. They explained that the Bible was infallible in religious and moral questions, which should be interpreted literally; its descriptions of natural phenomena, however, were in most cases allegorical or symbolic, which did not exclude the validity of scientific observations.

A few days later Father Castelli sent a letter to Galileo telling him about the discussion, and one of the professors gave the physicist a detailed account of the arguments put forward against his assumptions. Galileo took this so seriously that he immediately wrote a treatise, and he sent it as a letter to Castelli on 21 December. This was the first time he discussed his ideas about the heliocentric theory of Copernicus and the interpretation of Scripture.

Thus began the famous Italian drama, which, associated with the name of Galileo Galilei, has been for centuries one of the most popular productions of the world theater. In addition, some clever journalists staged an amusing final scene to the drama in recent years: "The Vatican finally recognized that the Earth moves!" and "Galileo was rehabilitated by the Pope!". Unfortunately, many people believe newspaper headlines in bold print without a second thought. Very few have the time to draw on primary sources and study authentic documents. Nevertheless, it is worth reading at least the most important paragraphs of the letter addressed to Benedetto Castelli. They illustrate quite clearly where Galileo was right and where he was wrong. He wrote the following:

> In regard to the Grand Duchess' first question, I agree, that it is not possible for Sacred Scripture to err…Nevertheless some of its expositors can sometimes err, in various ways. The most serious and most frequent of these errors occurs when they wish to retain only the direct or literal meaning of the words, because from this there results not only various contradictions but even grave and blasphemous heresies. Accordingly it would be necessary to attribute to God feet and hands and eyes and even

human feelings like anger, regret, hatred, and even occasional forgetfulness of the past and ignorance of the future. Many propositions are found in the Scriptures which, in respect to the bare meaning of the words, give an impression which is different from the truth, but they are stated in this way in order to accommodate the common man. Consequently, it is necessary that wise expositors provide the true meanings and indicate the particular reasons why the Scriptures are expressed in such words.

Granting then that in many passages the Scriptures not only can be, but necessarily must be, interpreted differently from the apparent meaning of the words, it seems to me that in matters concerned with the world of nature Scripture ought to be relegated to the last place. For both Sacred Scripture and Nature are derived from the Divine Word, the former as inspired by the Holy Spirit and the latter as most carefully ordered by the laws of God. Moreover it is agreed that, to accommodate itself to the understanding of everyone, Scripture says many things which are different from absolute truth in the impression it gives...So who would wish to maintain with certainty that Scripture abandons this characteristic when it speaks of the Earth or the Sun choosing rather to restrain itself within the limited meaning of the words ?...

Granting this, and also granting that it is even more obvious that two truths can never be contrary to each other, it is the task of skilled exegetes to find the true meaning of certain passages by taking into account the conclusions reached by natural science through experience and the required demonstration. I believe that it would be prudent to agree that no one should fix the meaning of passages of Scripture and oblige us to maintain as true any conclusions which later experience and necessary demonstrations show to be contrary to truth. Who would wish to place limits on human understanding? Who would wish to assert that everything which is knowable about the world is already known ?...

I believe Sacred Scripture has the sole aim of teaching those truths of faith which, being necessary for salvation but being beyond all human discourse, cannot come to be believed by any means other than by the inspiration of the Holy Spirit. God himself is the source of all truth, discourse and of the intellect itself. I believe that there are some things which God decided to give us the knowledge of through science, thus putting aside as it were the use of revelation in these areas. The science of Astronomy is an example of this. Scripture indeed touches so little on Astronomy that not even the names of the planets are to be found there.

I come now to a consideration of the particular passage from Joshua... Let it be conceded to an opponent that the sacred text should be taken in its literal meaning; namely, that God was asked by Joshua to make the Sun stand still and to prolong the day so that he could obtain the victory. I ask now my opponent to observe the same rule that I observe, that is, that one must be ready to accept an alteration of the meaning of the words. I say, then, that this passage shows the falsity and impossibility of the Aristotelian and Ptolemaic world system, and that it is very compatible with the Copernican system. First I ask my opponent if he knows by what motions the Sun is moved. If he knows, he must reply that the Sun has two motions; namely, an annual motion towards the east and a daily motion towards the west. Next I ask him whether both of these motions, which are different and contrary to each other, belong to the Sun and are both proper to it. He must reply *no*, for the only proper motion of the Sun is its annual motion. The other motion is not proper to it, but belongs to the highest heaven, that is, the first celestial sphere, which in its rotation carries along the Sun and the planets and the fixed stars and which is ordained to give a revolution around the Earth in twenty-four hours [in the Ptolemaic system]...

I come then to the third question, and I ask him which of these two motions of the Sun causes day and night; namely, its own proper and real motion, or the revolution of the first sphere [of the fixed stars]. He must reply that day and night are caused by the revolution of the first celestial sphere, and that the proper motion of the Sun does not produce day and night but rather the various seasons and the year itself. Now if the day depends not on the motion of the Sun but only on the revolution of the first celestial sphere, it is obvious that in order to lengthen the day, one needs to stop the first sphere, and not the Sun. Thus if someone understands these elements of Astronomy, does he not also recognize that if God had stopped the motion of the Sun, then instead of lengthening the day, he would have shortened it ?...

Hence either one must say that the motions are not arranged as Ptolemy said, or one must alter the meaning of the words. When the Scripture says that God stopped the Sun, it really wished to say that He stopped the first celestial sphere... Let me add that it is not credible that God would have stopped the Sun without paying attention to the other spheres [i.e., the orbits of the planets]. For without any reason He would have changed all the laws and positions of the other stars in respect to the Sun, and would have disturbed the whole course of nature. But it is credible that He stopped the whole system of celestial spheres which, after an intervening period of rest, returned consistently to their functions without any confusion.

But since we have already agreed not to alter the meaning of the words of the text, we must have recourse to another arrangement of the celestial bodies, and then see if it agrees with the bare meaning of the words. Now I have discovered and have proven and demonstrated [by the observation of the motion of the sunspots] that the Sun rotates on itself, making one full rotation in about one lunar month. Moreover it is quite probable and reasonable that the Sun, as if it were the heart of the world, gives not only light, but also motion to all the planets which revolve about it. Therefore, if in agreement with the theory of Copernicus we attribute the daily rotation primarily to the Earth, then it is obvious that in order to prolong the time of the daylight, it is sufficient to make the Sun stop, as the literal meaning of the sacred text says. In this way it is possible to lengthen the day by stopping the rotation of the Sun, without introducing any confusion among the parts of the world and without altering the words of Scripture. (The Italian original of the Letter to Castelli is to be found in the *Opere* V. 275-288 [Favaro 1968]. Trans. by Blackwell 1991).

Benedetto Castelli was pleased to read Galileo's letter and with his permission made copies of it for those who were interested in the subject. Some young Dominican scholars misunderstood Galileo and, accusing him of heresy, sent a copy of his letter to the Ecclesiastical Tribunal, which then had the frightful name of Inquisition. The Inquisitor, however, found that Galileo's letter contained no false teachings, except for "a few inappropriate words and offending statements".

When Galileo had been informed of the charges brought against him, he wrote a very detailed treatise to verify his views outlined in his letter, and he addressed it to the Duchess Christina. With the help of his theologian friends, he accumulated the exegetical arguments of the Fathers of the Church and quoted amply from them. He also tried to show the possibility of the Bible being interpreted in accordance with the heliocentric theory.

The Council of Trent had ruled that nobody should interpret Scripture according to their personal views in "questions concerning faith and morals", but should keep strictly to the traditional teachings of the Church and the Fathers. Galileo accepted this but remarked that the motion of the Sun and Earth did not belong to the subject of faith and morals. Moreover, the Fathers of the Church had no teachings concerning the subject, because the heliocentric theory had been unknown in the first centuries. On the other hand, he agreed with the idea that there was no contradiction between the truths of Scripture and Nature. Consequently, the Biblical texts were to be interpreted in accordance with the laws of nature. The movement of the Earth had already been sufficiently proven by observations.

This treatise of the Florentine physicist, which had been sent as a private letter to *Madama Cristina Gran Duchessa di Toscana,* was never reproved by the Inquisition. A year later, however, the propagation of Copernicus' theory was banned in order to put an end to the fruitless disputes about the Bible. Following this, Galileo's triumphant career continued for another fourteen years. Festive receptions were held in his honor by the Pope Paul V and the Roman cardinals, who listened to and enjoyed his lectures.

Cardinal Maffeo Barberini wrote a poem in praise of the work of Galileo and encouraged him to continue his scientific researches. In 1623 the same Cardinal was elected Pope, in history known as Urban VIII. He also was a mathematician and physicist, and he received his friend from Florence in his Palace at Rome for three weeks, to discuss the theory of Copernicus. Galileo then asked the Pope to lift the ban on the book of Copernicus and not to condemn the heliocentric system which, in his opinion, was already proven by the tides and the motion of the sunspots. They were in agreement that Copernicus's theory was a good mathematical assumption and made calculations easier. However, the Pontiff stressed that from a purely physical point of view and leaving even biblical passages out of consideration, the sunspots and the tidal phenomenon did not prove the motion of the Earth. So he asked the physicist not to circulate the controversial view until it had been sufficiently founded, because it would merely confuse the faithful.

Galileo promised to do as the Pope requested, but on his return to Florence he decided to write a treatise about his discussions with the Pope in the form of a dialogue. He sent the manuscript of his Dialogue Concerning the Two Chief World Systems to Rome in 1630, to obtain the authorization of the Church for the publication, which was compulsory even for the members of the Academy of the Medici. He obtained the permission with the help of his friends. The book was published in 1632 in Florence and was read by many people, who recognized the author's talent as a writer and physicist.

The three main characters of the Dialogue represent Aristotle, Ptolemy and Copernicus. The follower of the geocentric system is called *Simplicio* (Simpleton), whom the author uses as the mouthpiece of the Pope's statements, which are often distorted. Galileo's adversaries managed to convince Urban VIII that the author had publicly made fun of him and, contravening the previously accepted ban, had defended the theory of Copernicus. The Pope had to consent that his physicist friend be brought before the Inquisition, although he distanced himself from the trial and asked the inquisitors to handle the case with indulgence and avoid mentioning the offenses committed against his person.

After three hearings, the Inquisition banned Galileo's book on the "suspicion of grave error and heresy" and Galileo himself was made to vow never again to defend the heliocentric theory. As for the justification of the ruling it was declared that, according to a 1616 decree of the Holy Office, the doctrine of "the Sun being stationary in the center of the universe was false and contradicted the Holy Scripture". Moreover, the assumption that the "Earth was not the center of the universe and was not stationary, but performed a daily movement", although not conflicting with the Scripture, "was at any rate false concerning faith".

Galileo's behavior was thus considered a crime against the Faith. His arbitrary interpretation of the Bible was regarded as a serious offense. He was also accused of misleading the ecclesiastical authorities, by having concealed the ban imposed ten years before, when he asked for permission to publish his book. As a penance he was commanded to read the penitential psalms every week for three years.

The belief in Scripture as the safeguard of eternal salvation was taken extremely seriously in the 17th century. The Cardinals had the best of intentions when they imposed penitence on the seventy-year old physicist on June 22nd, 1633: they had his salvation in mind. Galileo himself admitted his mistakes, signed the oath and accepted the penance. He spent the rest of his life in his Florentine villa in house arrest. That was where he wrote his most significant studies in physics and natural philosophy or, to be more precise, dictated them to his disciples, as by that time he had gone almost completely blind. Until the end of his life he was looked after by his loving two daughters who lived in a nearby convent.

This is the very least one ought to know about Galileo's story. Unlike the plots of all the overdramatized plays and legends, he was not imprisoned and was not threatened with torture. During the interrogation in Rome he lived in a three room flat with two servants and he was fully provided for.

He was not excommunicated from the Church, and he was not excluded from the Academy of Medici. He died in pace on 8th January 1642, at the age of seventy-seven.

Pope Alexander VII lifted the ban on the books discussing Copernicus' theory as early as 1664. The Benedictine Guido Grandi published his writing "In Defense of Galileo" with the approval of the Church in 1712. In the 18th century 254 books were published by academic and ecclesiastical writers in appreciation of the great physicit's work. When he was entombed in the family crypt of the church *Santa Croce* in Florence, Pope Clement XII had an adorned monument built over his tomb in 1734.

One of the most prominent scholars of that time, the Jesuit Joseph Boscovich, taught Galileo's theory concerning the reliability of astronomical observations (*De observationibus astronomicis*, pp.22-25. Roma 1742). In 1744 the professors of the Academy of Padua published Galileo's major works, including the complete text of the Dialogue, with the Inquisitor General's judgment on the first page. It said: "This writing is not in conflict with the theological and moral teaching of the Church". In 1757 Benedict XIV ordered the retraction of the "decree which banned books preaching that the Sun was stationary and the Earth moved" (Cf. Poupard 1984, pp. 181-194). With a decree of 16th August 1820, Pius VII gave his approval to Joseph Settele's textbook of astronomy "which professes the ideas of our age concerning the daily and yearly movement of the Earth", and ruled that "in future nobody should forbid the defense of Copernicus's theory". (Cf. Brandmüller & Greipl 1992, p.300). But unfortunately, very few people knew about this. All the general public remembered was that, though the learned Galileo had been right, the Church had unjustly condemned him. An unbridgeable gap was formed between the medieval religious world view and modern scientific views.

But why is it that nobody realized how unjust this generalization is? Why should medieval philosophy still be regarded as the basis of Christian theology? Why should the Church be reprimanded because of the mistake made by a few of its representatives at that time? In order to clear up these questions, the Galileo case was put on the agenda by Pope John Paul II soon after he had been elected. The centenary celebrations of Albert Einstein's birth organized by the Pontifical Academy of Sciences on November 10th 1979 proved the most appropriate opportunity to do so. The Head of the Church then called the attention of scholars and cardinals to the fact that Galileo in his time was just as important as Einstein is in our century. While we are celebrating the latter today, said he, the former had to go through considerable suffering because of the ecclesiastical authorities. The Second Vatican Council had expressed its regret that certain Christians in the past "had not appropriately recognized the rightful independence of science, which led to conflicts and disputes, making the impression on many people that science and faith were in conflict with each other" (*Gaudium et Spes*, 36). The Pope expressed his wish "that theologians, astronomers and historians, animated by a spirit of sincere collaboration, will study the Galileo case more deeply and, in loyal recognition of wrongs from whatever side they come, will dispel the mistrust that still opposes, in many minds, a fruitful concord between science and faith".

The work of an international research committee, called by the Pope, began in 1981 and ended in 1992. Its members pointed out that throughout their work they had endeavored, according to the wish of the Pontiff, to "testify to the possibility of a fruitful concord between theologians and scientists". They did not mean to review the trial or rehabilitate Galileo, but wished to make serious and objective studies, which would facilitate mutual understanding. (Cf. Poupard 1984, pp. 5-9). The majority of ecclesiastical and secular scholars disagreed with the ruling of the Inquisition in the first place, but avoided speaking of it for the sake of peace. Some prelates in high positions expressed their disapproval, as for example, the Archbishop of Siena. (Cf. Favaro 1968, *Opere* XIX. 293). By publicly recognizing Galileo's merits and the mistake of the ecclesiastical authorities who had condemned him, Pope John Paul II merely summed up the testimony of the past 350 years. Galileo was right in establishing that the biblical texts describing natural phenomena were not religious doctrines and their literal interpretation in most cases could not be reconciled with scientific facts. The principles he had taken over from the Fathers of the Church and had applied to interpret Scripture were correct, but he did not always apply them consistently. While stressing that exegetes could sometimes be wrong, he forgot that scientists could also be wrong and had often been so.

The 17th century was the age of great wars of religion and rampant false beliefs. These circumstances rightfully induced the theologians of Rome to act in both self defense and in defense of the faith. They exaggerated, however, when they demanded that all the passages of Scripture should be taken literally and the interpretations of the early Fathers of the Church should always be followed. They wrongly believed that the statements about the motion of the Sun and the state of the Earth could be taken as eternal physical laws. They were mistaken when they wanted to interpret these statements in terms of the geocentric formulas of traditional philosophy.

Galileo was right in assuming that the heliocentric system could be proved, but he was wrong to believe that the Sun was the center of the universe and that a new interpretation of the biblical terms would support that. Pope Urban VIII, on the other hand, was right in assuming that neither the movement of the sunspots nor the seven day rhythm of the tides in the Oceans were proof of the motion of the Earth. Yet these had been Galileo's decisive arguments in his Dialogue; moreover, he had rejected Kepler's correct theory which stated that the tides were caused by the gravitational force of the Moon and Sun. (Cf. Favaro 1968, *Opere* VII, 486).

The work of the Committee was repeatedly praised by John Paul II, who said that the study of the Galileo case had helped the leaders of the Church to better exercise their office. He affirmed that divine revelation, of which the Church is the keeper, does not give us the scientific theory of the physical universe. It should not surprise anybody today, he noted, that theologians of that time made such slow progress in that difficult domain and that we should draw a lesson from the mistakes made in the past to deal with similar events, which may well occur both now and in future. (Cf. *Osservatore Romano*, 11.1.1992; 5.10.1993).

22. Foscarini: Interpretation of Scriptural Expressions

The Carmelite theologian, Paolo Antonio Foscarini, was the first to continue and supplement the work of Copernicus in 1615. In his exegetical and philosophical treatise he showed that the heliocentric system could be reconciled with the passages of Sacred Scripture and the theological propositions which had been adduced against it. (Foscarini's treatise is preserved in the National Library of Paris, R 12953. Bellarmine's letter to him is to be found in Galileo's *Opere* Vol.XII.171. English translations of both texts by Blackwell 1991, 217-251 and 265-266.) The opportuneness of Foscarini's exegetical principles is justified by the latest document of the Pontifical Biblical Commission, which emphasizes the importance of an exegesis in accordance with the needs of our age. Besides the inspired character of the Scripture, we must take into account that

> ... the biblical texts were written by authors who had a specific terminology of their own and used the means available in their surroundings at the time. We need therefore to resort to scientific methods which reveal the meaning of those texts against their linguistic, literary, social, cultural, religious and historical background... We have to approach the Scriptures from a standpoint which can reconcile the modern scientific culture with the religious tradition of Old Testament and Early Christianity. This method begins within the Bible itself and proceeds in the life of the Church (Pontifical Biblical Commission 1993, II. A).

Antonio Foscarini divided the passages of Sacred Scripture which were apparently in conflict with the heliocentric view into the following groups:
(1) The passages describing the stability of the Earth do not refer to its immobility in space but to the immutability of its created character or its nature in general (Ecclus 1:4; Psalms 93:1; 104:5);
(2) The passages about the motion of the Sun describe an apparent movement, in accordance with the general concept (Jos 10:12; Ps 19:7; Is 38:8);
(3) The passages which say that heavens are above (as at the top) and the Earth is below (at the bottom) are in accordance with the general usage in every language. Thus it is said that Christ descended from heaven in the incarnation, and ascended into heaven after the resurrection (Acts 2:19; Jn 3:13; Jer 31:37). Some people erroneously believe that if the Earth were to revolve round the Sun, the Earth would be in the heavens above, and we should say that Christ ascended to Earth;
(4) The most difficult passages are the ones which contrast Heaven to Earth, and also Earth to Heaven, as having a relation like a circumference to its center and a center to its circumference. Thus, e.g., it is said in Genesis 1:1, "In the beginning God created the heavens and the earth"; in Psalm 115:16, "Heaven belongs to God, he gave the earth to the sons of men", and in many other places he is called, "He who made heaven and earth". Many have drawn from this the false conclusion that the Earth could not move in the third orbit around the Sun, because it is the center of the universe and that was the reason why Christ descended to Earth and

not to another planet. Again, the misinterpretations stem from the fact that the biblical statements were taken literally, i.e., as if they referred to the external physical world and not the spiritual world of man;

(5) The same external and materialistic view led some theologians to the misunderstanding of the words of the Creed about Hades, the dwelling place of the dead. Taken in the strict sense of the word, Hades ought to be in the lowest part of the world, and since in a sphere no part is lower than the center, it follows that Hades or hell is in the center of the Earth. Thus the descent of Christ to Hades (or to the dead in the new translation) is one of the articles in the Apostles' Creed; he went there to liberate the faithful souls of the Old Testament, who were waiting for salvation (1 Pet 3:19; Mt 12:40; 16:18; Rom 10:7). Some philosophers argued then against the heliocentric view: if the Earth actually were to revolve round the Sun, it would necessarily follow that Hades would be in the Sun, or hell together with the Earth would be in the heavens, which would obviously be a contradiction. But such a distortion of words reflects complete ignorance or malevolence.

In order to avoid these errors Foscarini lists the most important practical principles of interpretation. The parts of Sacred Scripture which attribute something to God or another creature, which would otherwise be improper and incommensurable, should be interpreted and explained in one of the following ways:

(A) in a figurative sense or as imagery (allegory, metaphor, symbol);

(B) according to the common human way of thinking (as it is usually put in Latin *secundum nostrum modum considerandi, apprehendendi, concipiendi, intelligendi, cognoscendi*);

(C) according to the vulgar opinion and the common way of speaking, since the inspiration of the Holy Spirit is often adapted to the common way of speaking;

(D) according to what is suggested by appearance or some human viewpoint. For instance the Moon is constantly moving and changing while the Earth is apparently stationary and unchanged.

Foscarini asks: "But why is it that the Sacred Scriptures are so often adapted to the common and vulgar opinion, and do not instruct us in the truths of the secrets of nature?" He gives the answer: "This happens because of the exquisite distribution of divine wisdom, which adjusts itself to each person according to his nature and capacity. This wisdom is associated with salvation, because the Scriptures have no other purpose than the attainment of salvation." It follows that only the dogmas of the faith, that is to say truths contained in divine Revelation, are certain and unchanging, whereas scientific theories change with time.

Foscarini testifies that the heliocentric system and the biblical terms were correctly interpreted by the most learned theologians since Copernicus. Contradictions can be avoided, if we distinguish between the two different ways of approaching and expressing things, namely the scientific and the Scriptural or common way. Either way can in itself be correct. This is illustrated by the following example: When we rotate an apple in front of a burning candle which is at rest, the light will pass across the surface of the apple, while the source of light is motionless. It is therefore correct to say that the Sun apparently revolves around the Earth, because the Earth rotates on its own axis in the opposite direction of the Sun's movement, and the sunlight rises on one part of the Earth's sphere and sets on another. Consequently the Sun itself (which does not move except by supposition) is said to rise and set only by extrinsic denomination. With this one can interpret the command of Joshua: "Sun, stand still" (10:12).

According to the Psalm 148, all things have been given by God the Creator an immutable and inviolable law of their being and nature: "He has fixed them in their place for ever, by an unalterable law". By this law things always maintain a perpetual structure in their being and functions. It is in this sense that the Scripture says that Heaven and Earth are stable and immobile, in other words the laws of their movements are constant. Copernicus showed that the Earth in its own nature contains a triple local motion: a daily rotation on an axis, a yearly revolution around the Sun and a precessional motion because of the inclination of the Earth's axis to the ecliptic plane. This natural process is unchanging: "The Earth is moving constantly and immutably in all three species of motion just mentioned."

The third practical rule derives from the relationship between parts and the whole. A whole system can remain unchanged while parts of it can move or change. This principle can very well be applied to the passages which infer that the Earth stands still. What the Scripture in fact means is that the Earth as a whole is unchanged while certain parts of it change. This is the true sense of the text of Ecclesiastes 1:4, which says this very thing: "A generation goes, a generation comes, yet the earth stands firm forever." Such passages of Scripture do not speak of local motion but of other types of change; namely, in substance, quantity, and quality of the earth.

The fourth rule enables us to interpret determined spatial movements. Each material thing, whether it be mobile or immobile, has its own natural place. Taken as a whole, neither the Earth nor the sea nor the atmosphere can be removed from its designated place. If they are removed violently by some external force, they always return to their original position. Nor can celestial bodies be displaced from their determined paths. The Earth does not change its natural orbit. In this sense we can interpret the verse of Psalm 104:5, "You fixed the earth on its foundations, unshakeable for ever and ever". This is not in conflict with Copernicus' theory. The Earth always has the same fixed orbit which it never leaves.

Furthermore, the Scripture speaks of the stability of the Earth. Anything that consists of separable parts cannot be stable. The Earth is stable in the sense that its parts can be separated neither from each other nor from the center of the terrestrial sphere. In this way then the Earth is said to be immutable. Foscarini is here alluding to the gravitational force, the notion of which he has guessed in certain Scriptural expressions. With reference to observational evidence, he refutes the geocentric theory of Aristotle, according to which: "Circular motion, which is around the center, belongs to the heavens, which contain neither heavy nor light elements" (*De Coelo* I. 3). The Carmelite scholar displays amazing accuracy when discussing Kepler's theory on the mutual attraction of celestial bodies:

According to the principles of this new opinion, heaviness [*gravitazione*] properly speaking is simply a certain natural inclination of parts to reunite with their whole. This was established by divine providence not only for the Earth and the bodies on it, but also for celestial bodies (as is credible) and for the Sun, the Moon, and the stars. Because of this inclination the parts of all these bodies gather together and joined so firmly that no one of them could find any place of rest other than the center of the body of which it is a part. The striving of all the parts from every direction toward the center, and their consequent compression, causes the spherical and round figure of the celestial bodies and preserves them always in this shape and in their being... As a result heaviness and lightness are found not only in our terrestrial globe and in the bodies on it, but also in the bodies which are said to be in the heavens. Both heavy and light parts exists in the Sun, the Moon, and the stars. Consequently, the heavens are not composed of a matter which is different from the elements. Nor are they immutable in their substance, quantity, and quality. Nor are they of such an unusual condition as Aristotle insistently portrays them to be. Nor are they as solid and impenetrably dense as everyone commonly believes them to be... And if some passages to the contrary were to be found in Sacred Scripture, it is excluded by the principles given above, proportionally applied. Thus solidity of the heavens can be understood as not admitting a void, or any break in which a void might occur, i.e., an unbroken extension (Blackwell 1991, Appendix IV).

How can we determine whether something is located high up or deep down? The position of things cannot be simply determined in relation to one or two objects, only in relation to their whole environment. Thus we can say that the Earth is in the center or in the depth of the world only if we determine its position in comparison with the starry sky, which surrounds everything. In this way theological propositions can be quite properly justified. The apostles are speaking of the ascension of Christ because "he was lifted up while they looked on" and "he was taken up to heaven" (Acts 1: 9). Here the word "heaven" is in the singular and means the dwelling place of God, the angels and saints, beyond all material existence. And if they speak of heavens, in the plural, they refer to everything without distinction, i.e., both the visible starry sky and the spiritual existence beyond it. In the teaching of Jesus the Kingdom of the Heavens is the same as the Kingdom of God, and he is Our Father in the heavens, that is to say, he is everywhere present. (In the Greek original and the Latin Vulgate the word heavens is always in the plural form with the definite article; cf. Mt 5:3; 6:9.)

In conclusion, the final solution of this question according to the Carmelite scholar lies in the concept of the Christocentric order of world: God the Creator is the center of spiritual things; the Sun is the center of corporeal things; Christ (the Word become man) is the center of both spiritual and corporeal things. Each of these centers supports the things corresponding to them, as the heart is in the center of living beings and supports them.

The Apostle Paul preaches that Christ arose and ascended into heaven and is the one who is "sustaining the universe by his powerful command" (Heb 1:3). The order of the universe is therefore neither geocentric nor heliocentric but Christocentric. Ever since the time of the prophets this has been the original teaching of the Scripture. The geocentric interpretation taken in a physical sense was an unfortunate misunderstanding resulting from medieval Greek natural philosophy.

Antonio Foscarini concludes the discussion with the following statements:

> From these principles and their delineation it is very clear that the opinion of Pythagoras and Copernicus is so probable that it is perhaps more likely than the common opinion of Ptolemy. For from it one can derive the hidden constitution of the world in a way which is much more solidly based on reason and experience than is the common opinion. It is also quite clear that the new opinion can be explained in such a way that there is no longer any need to be concerned whether it is contrary to passages of Sacred Scripture or to the justification of theological propositions... Finally Sacred Scripture on various occasions presents other passages, which are worthy of long and mature consideration, dealing with the issue of the order of the heavens and the arrangement of both material and spiritual creatures. The Holy Spirit has presented all this enigmatically in symbols, parables, and images, lest he completely dazzle us with the immense splendor of such excellent things. From this I conclude that in this same way we can philosophize (on doctrinal matters which are ambiguous) by means of the Sacred Scriptures, especially if we try to understand the prophesies, which otherwise are most obscure. They will be fully understood and grasped only when they have already been fulfilled, and not before. Likewise when the true system of the universe has come to be known and to be established as true, only then will the meaning of these images and enigmas be understood (Trans. by Blackwell).

When the Jesuit Cardinal, Robert Bellarmine (1542-1621), had read Foscarini's treatise, he answered its questions in a cordial manner. He approved the principles of the Carmelite scholar, but he pointed out the existing difficulties. In addition to the views of the Church's Magisterium of the time, he also briefly outlined his own opinion. It is worth reading some of the most important paragraphs of his letter:

> To the Very Reverend Father Paolo Antonio Foscarini, Provincial of the Carmelite Order of the Province of Calabria.

> My Very Reverend Father,

I was pleased to read the letter in Italian and the treatise in Latin which Your Reverence sent to me. I thank you for both of them, which indeed are quite full of ingenuity and learning. And since you have asked for my reactions, I will state them briefly,for you now have little time to read, as you yourself say, and I have little time to write.

Firstly I say that it appears to me that Your Reverence and Mr.Galileo have acted prudently in being satisfied with speaking in terms of assumptions (*ex suppositione*) and not absolutely, as I have always believed Copernicus also spoke. For to say that the assumption that the Earth moves and the Sun stands still saves all the appearances better than do eccentrics and epicycles is to speak well. This is enough for the mathematician, and contains nothing dangerous. But to wish to assert that the Sun is really located in the center of the world and rotates only on itself without moving from east to west,and that the Earth is located in the third celestial orbit and revolves with great velocity around the Sun, is very dangerous thing, not only because it irritates the philosophers and scholastic theologians,but also because it is damaging to the Holy Faith by making the Sacred Scriptures false. Although Your Reverence has clearly exhibited the many ways of interpreting the Sacred Scriptures, still you have not applied them to particular cases, and without doubt you would have encountered the very greatest difficulties if you had tried to interpret all the passages which you yourself have cited.

Secondly I say that, as you know, the Council [of Trent] has prohibited the interpretation of Scripture contrary to the common agreement of the Blessed Fathers...They all agree on the literal interpretation that the Sun revolves around the Earth, and that the Earth stands immobile in the center of the world... Nor can one reply that this is not a matter of faith, because even if it is not a matter of faith because of the subject matter [*ex parte objecti*], it is still a matter of faith because of the speaker [*ex parte dicentis*], ...for the Holy Spirit has said both of these things through the mouths of the Prophets and the Apostles.

Thirdly I say that whenever a true demonstration would be produced that the Sun stands in the center of the world and the Earth in the third celestial orbit, and that the Sun does not revolve around the Earth but the Earth around the Sun, then at that time it would be necessary to proceed with great caution in interpreting the Scriptures which seem to be contrary, and it would be better to say that we do not understand them than to say that what has been demonstrated is false. But I do not believe that there is such a demonstration, for it has not been shown to me... And in case of doubt one should not abandon the Sacred Scriptures as interpreted by the Blessed Fathers..., and the eye is not mistaken when it judges that the Sun moves, just as it is not mistaken when it judges that the Moon and stars move. And this is enough for now.

With cordial greetings, Reverend Father, and I pray for every blessing from God,

12 April 1615, as your brother, Cardinal Bellarmine.

(Bellermin's letter is to be found in the *Opere* XII. 171. [Favaro 1968]. Trans. by Blackwell 1991, Appendix VIII).

23. *Dialogue and Scientific Concordism*

A dialogue between people can only be successful, if they have a common language, topic and purpose. Unfortunately we still live in a Babel of languages. Even though the magi of different nationalities have agreed to use English as their common language, they have problems in understanding each other. Some scholars create new technical terms or use the old ones in a different sense. The initial confusion of concepts is unavoidable. This difficulty is already manifest within certain special fields of science, but the real danger lies in people trying to translate physical truths expressed in the language of mathematics into the language of philosophy or theology.

Exchanges of view are always aimed at synthesis: the reconciliation of opposing views at a higher level and the synthesizing of scientific results. As a matter of fact, this is the aim of any thinker. The common grounds for this is provided by the fact that we are aware of having the same human nature, of living in the same world and of seeking the same truth, because our destiny is the same from the moment we are born until we die. The dialogue between physicists and theologians began with heated disputes at the beginning of the 17th century, but came to a halt after the age of Enlightenment. Religious and philosophical considerations were totally excluded from the work of modern natural scientists. Those who are ready to resume the dialogue today, quote the saying of the exegete Saint Jerome: "To err is human, but to stick to the error is dishonest". Both sides have since tried honestly to admit their errors, at least in the fields where the errors proved obvious.

The European Society for the Study of Science and Religion was formed in 1986 and counts at the moment 110 regular members. It organizes a one-week conference every two years. The subject of the 4th conference in 1992 was the origin of time and the universe; 140 participants discussed the ideas of 67 lectures in seven work groups. Part of the conference material was published in a book (Coyne et al. 1993). These conferences testify to common good will, but we are still a long way from the goal. Though a number of lecturers at the conference, who were doctors of both physics and theology, have found the appropriate synthesis, it is not acceptable to everyone. Some feel it lacks the appropriate terminology, others refute it on psychological grounds.

The British scientist, Stephen Hawking, has addressed these matters. One of the work groups of the above mentioned conference pointed out that Hawking had often mentioned the idea of God the Creator in his book, "A Brief History of Time" (Hawking 1988). This is indeed one of the demands of logical thinking, but a physicist cannot go beyond the boundaries of his own special field. He passionately seeks a generally valid theory of the universe. He reckons with the possibility of the universe being infinite, which means that it has no beginning, so the difficult problem of the moment of creation can be excluded. In Hawking's opinion scientists have been so preoccupied with describing what the Universe is, that they have not posed the question of why. Why does the Universe exist at all? Every man is able to ponder over why the Universe and we ourselves exist. "If we find the answer to that, it would be the ultimate triumph of human reason, for then we would know the mind of God." (Hawking 1988). Could it be that in seeking the answer, he wants to rely on his own intellect and science only? Then he tacitly acknowledges that he, as a physicist, is unable to find the answer. He gives the floor to the philosopher, who will go a longer way by inference and can reconcile the purposefulness or the teleological order experienced in the universe with cosmological theories. The field of research of theology is even broader: it seeks the full and ultimate purpose of creation in the light of historically verifiable divine revelations.

It follows that the possibility of a unified cosmology is to be found in human nature itself. The complete reality of the universe can be perceived in three ways according to man's physical, intellectual and spiritual faculties:

(1) with our senses we perceive the world as a series of natural effects;

(2) with our intellect we perceive the world as the order of expedient phenomena;

(3) with our faith we see it as the creative activity of an omnipotent Being.

Viewed from outside, man's work appears to be no more than a physical process, but we know that it is a purposeful activity. In other words, man consciously utilizes his physical faculties to perform purposeful work. Similarly one might say that God utilizes the natural laws and causes to maintain and direct the universe according to his purposes. These comparisons are taken from human life, but without them it is hardly possible to speak about creation of the cosmos.

One of the results of the new dialogue between physicists, philosophers and theologians is that we can regard the essential teaching of the Scripture as philosophical and theological cosmology; philosophical, since it raises the human soul to the knowledge of the Creator's wisdom from the contemplation of the phenomena and the heavens; theological, because, through divine inspiration, it shows the ultimate purpose of the creation of the world and the meaning of life in it: the possibility of man's eternal salvation.

From the dialogues carried on so far we can draw the following conclusions. Both science and theology follow their own way, neither is a prerequisite of the other. The right explanation of natural phenomena prevents the development of false beliefs; the knowledge of articles of faith shields physicists from the dangers of materialism. Scientific discoveries open up new perspectives for the religious approach to the world, while theology gives answers to the ultimate questions of existence. Learning from past mistakes, we should never try to prove the existence of God from the insufficiency of scientific hypotheses. The existence of God is not a hypothesis. Laplace was right in this respect. When Napoleon asked him where God was in his scientific theory, he answered: "Sir, I do not need such a hypothesis." In connection with the primeval explosion, George Lemaître had remarked that those who want to fill in the gaps in physical research with the hypothesis of God, do a disservice to the Creator. Such a picture of God who fills gaps causes disappointment when the missing natural evidence and explanations are actually found.

When we wish to reconcile physical, metaphysical and theological formulas, we should make an effort to define accurately the notions covered by individual words. We should, on the one hand, carefully avoid interpreting certain physical terms in a theological sense and, on the other hand, we should avoid the erroneous scientific interpretation of certain biblical texts, which leads to false concordism. Popular scientific books and textbooks sometimes tend to identify the cosmological theory of the primeval explosion with the theological view of creation. Michael Heller, professor at the Pontifical Theological Academy of the Jagellonian University, Krakow, has clearly discussed this problem in his treatise on the "Theological Interpretations of Physical Creation Theories" (Russell et al. 1996, pp. 91-102). With respect to the mathematical structure of a physical theory a theological or philosophical comment must be neutral, otherwise it would be inconsistent with or even contradict it.

An example of the interpretations which are inconsistent with the mathematical structure of cosmological theories is Robert Jastrow's book entitled "God and the Astronomers". Commenting on the Big Bang theory he writes:

> For the scientist who has lived by his faith in the power of reason, the story ends like a bad dream. He has scaled the mountains of ignorance; he is about to conquer the highest peak; as he pulls himself over the final rock, he is greeted by a band of theologians who have been sitting there for centuries (Jastrow 1980, p.125).

The point is that both scientists and theologians are aiming at the same peak. This is clearly stated in the epilogue to the Jastrow's book:

> We see then, that the resemblance between our cosmology today and that of the theologians of the past is not merely accidental. What they saw dimly, we see more clearly, with the advantage of better physics and astronomy. But we are looking at the same God, the Creator (Jastrow 1980, p.158).

This is a beautiful statement, but unfortunately not quite true. Such a confusion of concepts can be avoided if we take account of the essential difference between the subjects and methods of physics and theology. After all, every physical theory is a mathematical description of a part of the material world, a description made possible by certain suppositions and observations. Yet no physical theory is quite complete; all mathematical descriptions have been gradually developed, and mathematical structures of many recent theories still evolve. Moreover, philosophical and theological comments are usually written in the everyday language which is inadequate for the advanced mathematical models. Consequently, a theological interpretation of cosmological theories can only be right, if it is neutral with respect to the mathematical models.

It is correct to ask the following question: Does the physical process of the universe have a temporal origin, and, if so, what can physical cosmology tell us about it? It is, however, wrong to ask the following question: Was there a creation of the universe, and, if so, how can it be explained by physical theories? This question contains a contradiction, because it identifies a physical concept with a metaphysical or theological one and expects the physical theory to prove the metaphysical truth. This, however, is impossible. The following statement has no scientific value: "God created the world in a state of initial singularity, so the theory of the primeval explosion is identical with the doctrine of creation". Any good physicist and theologian knows that a statement like this cannot be proven, and physical theories cannot explain the theological doctrine of creation. Nevertheless, it is possible to find a correct solution showing a compatibility of these two doctrines, because they do not exclude each other.

For the physicist the world is comprehensible in so far as its structure, including everything from elementary particles to clusters of galaxies, can be described by mathematical models. However, he asks himself: How can it be that the structure of the universe is mathematical to this extent and is comprehensible in this way? As for the theologian, he will answer: It is precisely by creation that the existence of the world and its mathematical structure is comprehensible. In other words, the comprehensibility of the world and its existence are but two aspects of the act of creation. The wisdom or rationality of the Creator is reflected in the created cosmos. The creative action always has a geometric, or more generally mathematical character. Professor Michael Heller finishes his treatise by remarking that such interpretations are useful insofar as they help us to make our theology and our cosmology consonant in the contribution they make to our world view.(Heller 1993).

This is how the exchange of views between theology and science begins, but it is not at all as simple as that, as shown by this brief survey. New discoveries always open up new perspectives. It is today clearer than ever to physicists and theologians that both the Book of Nature and the Bible are inexhaustible fields of research. We outlined previously how Kepler, Galileo and Foscarini tried to explain apparent contradictions and how they wanted to show the harmony between certain biblical passages and scientific theories. A similar apologetic method called natural scientific concordism was developed later in history.

In the last century some biblicists and scientists supposed that the "six days" of creation agreed with the known geological and paleontological ages, at least in broad outline. According to others, the light before the creation of the stars is in concord with the primeval nebula of Kant-Laplace, from which the Solar System evolved. This seemingly successful concordism has become disputable and unacceptable with the progress of science. It is a false concordism which wants to turn the Bible into some kind of a scientific textbook so that today's generation might also believe in God. In order to avoid misunderstandings, it should be remarked that this concordism has nothing to do with what we tried to show about the star of the Magi, the astronomical expressions and the visions of Ezekiel and Daniel in this book. We pointed out as an important fact of the history of civilization, how accurately biblical writers had preserved the science of their own age, excluding from it all ancient superstition and idolatry. In this respect they are very close to the accepted scientific approach of our age. The prophets fully reconciled the science of their age with the truth of pure monotheism and their religious world view. They are, accordingly, the models of true concordism.

Since the days of St. Augustine scholars have repeatedly insisted on a correct principle for the concordist interpretation of Scriptures. For instance, in the Encyclical *Providentissimus Deus* (1893) Pope Leo XIII cites the same principle which was used by Antonio Foscarini:

No real disaccord can exist between the theologian and the physicist provided each keeps within his own limits and follows the warning of St. Augustine to beware of affirming anything rashly, and the unknown as known. If nevertheless there is disagreement, the same Doctor proposes a summary rule for the theologian: Whatever they [the physicists] are able to demonstrate about nature by true proofs, let us show that it is not contrary to our scriptures. But whenever they propose in any books of theirs which is contrary to our Scriptures, let us also show, if we are at all able, that it is false. In order to understand the justness of this rule we must remember that the sacred writers did not seek to penetrate the secrets of nature, but rather described things in more or less figurative language, or in terms which were commonly used at the time, and which in many instances are in daily use at this day, even by the most eminent men of science (*Acta Sanctae Sedis*, 26/1893. Trans. by Carlen 1981).

According to Pope Pius XII the latest scientific discoveries help to elucidate the meaning of certain biblical texts, if we have a number of sufficiently proven facts at our disposal. We cannot, however, accept scientific theories which are contrary to the religious and moral teaching of the Scripture (*Divino Afflante Spiritu*, 1943). It was Pius XII who modernized the Vatican Observatory at Castel Gandolfo in the 1950's with the installation of a Schmidt wide angle telescope and the addition of a modern computing facility. Research was extended to the structure of our Galaxy (see Maffeo 1991). The Pope was a learned astronomer himself and welcomed Eddington's and Lemaître's new cosmological theory. In his lecture given at the Pontifical Academy of Sciences in 1951, he used the new discoveries to strengthen the classical proofs of God's existence. The expansion and transformation of the universe, i.e., its mutability at all levels, requires the existence of a Mover itself unmoved, a *Primus Motor Immobile*, according to St. Thomas Aquinas' philosophy. Moreover, modern cosmology can testify to both a beginning and a cessation of material processes in the cosmos, thus confirming its contingency. This postulates the existence of a Necessary Being, a Creator of the universe. Nevertheless, let us quote the Pope's words which caused a sensation worldwide at the time:

If the primitive experience of the ancients could provide human reason with sufficient arguments to demonstrate the existence of God, then with the expanding and deepening of the field of man's experiments, the mark of the Eternal One is discernible in the visible world in ever more striking and clearer light ... Everything seems to indicate that the material universe had in finite terms a mighty beginning, with an indescribably vast abundance of energy reserves ... The mind in its eagerness for truth insists on asking how matter reached this state, which is so unlike anything found in our everyday experience; it wants to know also what went before it. In vain do we interrogate natural science, which declares honestly that it finds itself face to face with an insoluble enigma ... It is undeniable that when a mind enlightened with modern scientific knowledge weighs this problem calmly, it feels drawn to break through the circle of completely independent or self explanatory matter and to ascend to a Creator Spirit. With the same clear and critical look with which it examines judgment on facts, it perceives and recognizes the work of creative omnipotence, whose power, set in motion by the mighty *Fiat* pronounced billions of years ago by the Creating Spirit, spread out over the universe, calling into existence with a gesture of generous love matter bursting with energy. In fact, it would seem that present day science, with one sweeping step back across millions of centuries, has succeeded in bearing witness to that primordial *Fiat lux* [Let there be light!] uttered at the moment when there burst forth from nothing a sea of light and radiation, while the particles of chemical elements split and formed into millions of galaxies. It is quite true that the facts established up to the present time are not an absolute proof of creation in time, as are the proofs drawn from metaphysics and Revelation in what concerns simple creation, or those founded on Revelation if there be question of creation in time. The pertinent facts of the natural sciences are awaiting still further research and confirmation, and the theories founded on them are in need of further development and proof, before they can provide a sure foundation for arguments which of themselves are outside the proper sphere of the natural sciences (*Acta Apostolicae Sedis*, pp.31-43, 44/1952; Trans. McHugh 1959).

Physicists and astronomers had probably misunderstood the Pope's words at the time, because they later accused him of false concordism, as if he had tried utilize the theory of primeval explosion to provide a reasonable verification for the Scriptural account of creation. It is true that the Pope had emphasized that possibility, but he had not identified the primeval explosion with creation like Jastrow and many others did. The Pontiff's intention was to emphatically call the attention of scientists, both believers and non believers, to the fact that God the Creator can be known with certainty from his works, by the natural light of human reason. That is what was preached by the Sage of the Old Testament and the apostle Paul: "ever since the creation of the world, the invisible existence of God and his everlasting power have been clearly seen by the mind's understanding of created things" (Rom 1:20; Wis 13:5).

The dialogue goes on. The theologians who claim that neither the Bible nor the faithful need a scientific explanation may, to some extent, be right. Others, however, keep on looking for the right form and extent of concordism, since the effect of the rapid progress of science and technology on religious attitudes cannot be neglected. This circumstance was taken extremely seriously by the theologians of the Second Vatican Council, who regarded the reconciliation of physical and spiritual sciences as one of the most important tasks of the future. Mathematics and technology play an ever increasing role in everyday human work and culture, and natural sciences gradually transform our way of thinking. Under the influence of changed conditions many people feel the increasing need for religion and divine service, but at the same time many others give up practicing their religion. It is false, however, to say that technical progress necessarily leads to the decline of religious faith. Besides philosophy, history and arts it is important to cultivate the natural sciences, which can prepare people to accept the articles of faith. (Cf. *Gaudium et spes*, 7; 57, Vatican 1965).

Every scientific theory which denies spiritual existence and the Creator of the world is obviously in conflict with the doctrines of Scripture. Real science, however, (mathematics, physics, astronomy, psychology etc.) is in itself neutral with respect to the exercise of religion, i.e., independent of professions of faith. The Scripture, therefore, is not contrary but supplementary to natural science. The practical unification of these two sources of knowledge is the result of the thinking man's free choice. Talks and dialogues can lead to conceptual agreement, but the reconciliation of religious and scientific views of life depends on the personal, free choice of the individual.

The theoretical question of science versus the Bible emerges as follows: Is it possible to reconcile the biblical doctrines about the origin of the world and life with the proven formulas of modern cosmology and the theory of evolution? The answer depends on how we interpret the inspired character of the Scripture and the original text of the Hebrew Bible. The participants in these dialogues recommend two ways of resolving this apparent contradiction.

The Scriptural account of creation does not give a scientific description of the origin of the world and life but one which has implications on man's religious and moral life. The description of natural phenomena agrees with the ideas of ancient times and does not belong to divine inspiration in the strict sense. The theologian can therefore separate the contents of Revelation from outdated human ideas and can interpret them so that they can be understood by people today. Thus the only thing that remains to be shown is that the theory of evolution is not contrary to the biblical doctrines and does not endanger the basic dogmas of faith. The notion of evolution presupposes the notion of creation. This solution simply accepts the traditional view and in no way tries to prove that the biblical account is compatible with modern cosmology.

The other suggestion is opposed to this one: The biblical description of natural phenomena must be in accordance with reality because it was written under divine inspiration, albeit not as a dictation rendering the inspiration word for word, but as one expressed in the authors' own words. Nevertheless, the linguistic analysis of old Hebrew words and the correct translation of the texts should show that the Scriptural doctrine about the origin of the world and life is quite compatible with modern scientific results. This is the view of the proponents of scientific concordism. They would like to interpret the above mentioned texts strictly in accordance with the original meaning of the Hebrew words,on the basis of new proper translations. This is a very difficult task, though not so much from the linguistic but from the traditional exegetical point of view. We ought to admit that we have misinterpreted quite a few important biblical expressions, which have become clear only now in the light of scientific discoveries. Even if this were possible to some extent, theologians would remain doubtful about this method because the scientific picture of the world changes with time and some of its formulas become outdated. Concordists would therefore always have to adjust the interpretation of the Bible to the latest discoveries.

One of the most original representatives of scientific concordism in our century is the Dutch linguist and physicist, Karel Claeys (1914-1989). In his view it is not discoveries made by physicists which should verify biblical revelations, but the other way round. As if trying to reassure those who have doubts about new cosmology, he attempts to show that "The Bible Verifies the World View of Natural Science". This is the title of his 700 page book (Claeys 1979). By means of etymology of Hebrew and Greek words and detailed grammatical analyses, he uncovers the literal meaning of the texts in question. In the light of his findings, he rejects the view that the authors of the Old Testament adopted the primitive image of the world of their age and surroundings and merely applied it to their own religion.

Who was it who believed that the Earth was a flat disc and the sky was moving above it like a stretched tent, with the stars attached to it? Not the prophets. In their original writings they describe some facts of nature which are well known today. For example, the spherical shape of the Earth and the formation of its surface and atmosphere; the evolution of the universe from a single nucleus; the geometrical structure of space and its expansion; gravitation, nuclear energy, and many other physical facts.

Karel Claeys claims that this is the best proof of divine inspiration, through which the prophets found the right expressions to describe the laws of nature without knowing their scientific explanation. In this respect it is a significant observation that the prophets speaking of the creative activity use four specific words which, in most cases, occur in the following order: to create, to firm by design, to arrange, and to expand or to enlarge. (In usual translations the respective Hebrew words are rendered as to make, to fashion, to stretch or to spread). According to the etymology of the Hebrew words and in the Scriptural context, these can be interpreted as follows:

bara: to create, to produce something from nonexistence;
jasar: to implant the design of the whole cosmos into the primeval element already created (which could refer to the natural constants known today);
asah: to arrange matter according to the design, (forming progressively more complex structures: atoms, celestial bodies, galaxies);
natah: to expand, or to enlarge the system thus arranged.

These expressions occur in the present participle, which means that they indicate continuous activities or processes. Apart form the allegory of the "stretched tent", these expressions are compatible with the modern cosmological theory of an expanding universe. To prove this Claeys quotes and analyses twelve passages from the Hebrew Bible. He remarks that the Hebrew *hashamaïm*, the heavens, in several contexts denotes the entire universe consisting of innumerable galaxies, each with billions of stars. Thus, for instance, in the prayer of Nehemiah: "You, He who is, by yourself have arranged (*asah*) the heavens, the heaven of the heavens, with all their array [of stars]" (cf. Neh 9: 6; Ps 33: 6).

Accordingly, several passages of Isaiah can be rendered into English as follows:

I am the Lord [He who is] creating [*bara*] and expanding [*natah*] the heavens; firming the light by design [*jasar*]... He is ruling above the sphere of the Earth, and he is expanding [*natah*] the heavens like a dust cloud [*doq*] (cf. Is 40:22; 42:5; 45:7,12; 51:13; Job 9:8; 26:7).

The same words can be found in the Book of Jeremiah: "By his power he created the Earth, by his wisdom set the world firm, by his discernment expanded the heavens" (Jer 10:12).

Theologians who have studied Claeys's work have formed different opinions about it. Some believe that his linguistic analyses are in most cases correct and his new interpretations are partly possible and acceptable. However, those who only accept the religious and moral doctrines of the Bible and exclude any science, reject Claeys's proposals.

We shall conclude this discussion with a remark that calls for caution formulated by two professors of philosophy at the University of London:

> Some theologians seem to think that since the biblical teaching of creation is not a lesson in cosmogony, scientific questions about the origin of world and man are completely irrelevant to it. This seems to be an extreme position and a mistaken one at that. The fact that several scientific theories of cosmology and biology are compatible with the biblical notion of creation does not warrant the conclusion that none is incompatible with it. It is quite conceivable that some scientific theories, not in themselves but by implication, are opposed to the position which is expressed in the Bible. If, for instance, a scientific theory allows only a purely materialistic view of man's nature it would by implication be contrary to the teaching of the Bible. Moreover, the total separation of the scientific field from the theological one raises serious questions about the cognitive status of religious beliefs and their relevance in the present world. (Nemesszeghy and Russell 1972).

24. Natural Science and Theology

The world drama about Galileo has been going on for 350 years now. The strangest thing about it is that neither the characters, nor the audience seem to be bored. Both learned and unlearned people seem willing to rewrite the scenario and are pleased to take the various roles. From a psychological point of view all this demonstrates a general need to overcome the split personality aspect in scientific life and achieve a unified view of the world, to reconcile our knowledge acquired through scientific research with the theological doctrines based on divine revelations. Scientifically proven knowledge can be reconciled only with the theological faith which is in no way opposed to reason.

The world drama about Galileo seems to have come to its final act in our days. We are living in the age of landmark discoveries, when the real value of natural sciences and at the same time the true meaning of the Sacred Scripture become more and more obvious to large numbers of people all over the world, and not only a few privileged persons.

To err is human, but to cling to an error is dishonest. The gravest error is to generalize, or to assign a mistake made by some individuals to the whole of the community. Anybody who blames Christianity or the Church because Copernicus' theory was condemned by some of its representatives lacks common sense or is malevolent. Similarly, it is unreasonable to infer that scientific thinking excludes all religious belief, because some modern scientists refute religion.

Even today many people argue about the contradictions of religion and science without finding a solution. This is because the way they formulate the questions is basically wrong. Unfortunately even recently published writings use some old and abstract notions, which lead the unlearned to false generalizations. Is it faith and religion that are in conflict with science? Was it the Church that condemned Copernicus and Galileo? Is the Bible contrary to natural sciences?

The original text of the Bible is not identical with its various translations nor with the erroneous interpretations of some exegetes. It is never faith and religion or for that matter the Church which are in conflict with certain views. It is almost always the individual. It was not the Church that condemned Galileo, but some of its officials, who, in those troubled times felt it their duty to protect the integrity of the Scripture and its traditional teaching. The cruel Inquisition, introduced against heresy by the kings of Spain in the 16th century, was not in accordance with the original and traditional procedure of the Church.

In the 17th century all the statements of the Bible were considered infallible divine revelations. Prior to that period there had been no scientific method or system which could have shown the mistakes of the geocentric view of the world. That was the reason why the responsible theologians of the time felt that, being in possession of complete knowledge, they were entitled to and had to prescribe what could be accepted as science. When the mistakes of the old theologians concerning some natural phenomena had later become obvious, young physicists felt entitled to determine what one could and should believe.

Science and theology can never contradict each other, because they are like two trains running along two parallel tracks, which can never collide unless somebody shifts the points. Unfortunately a similar mistake was made when some people used biblical quotations to refute the heliocentric theory and when others resorted to the theory of evolution to refute the Scriptural doctrine of the creation of man. Even though the comparison might not be perfect, the work of theologians and scientists is indeed progressing along parallel lines which meet in infinity. The direction and final goal are common: the full and true knowledge of reality. Researchers on both sides agree that the objective reality of the world can be correctly interpreted by means of appropriate models and analogies, with respect to its quantitative and qualitative relations. Both groups of scholars verify their theories and make a certain system of them.

We have already shown the basic differences between the subject matter and methods of physics and theology. It is easier to define and empirically verify physical theories than the theses of religion, but physical formulas also demand belief, if they are to be convincing. For instance, Kepler, Galileo, and Newton had found convincing circumstancial evidence in favor of a rotating Earth, but it was not until the 19th century that direct proofs of the Earth's rotation were devised. It was first demonstrated by the French physicist Jean Foucault in 1851. Under the dome of the Panthéon in Paris he suspended an iron ball by a 67 meter long wire and started it swinging. The plane of oscillation of this pendulum slowly turns in clockwise direction every day, because the Earth rotates in the opposite direction at the same time. The fact that the Foucault Pendulum changes its direction of swing with respect to the earth is proof that the Earth itself rotates and that it is not the sky which revolves around the Earth. However, those who are not able to understand this connection of the pendulum and the Earth's rotation, are not obliged to believe in it.

The sources of the truths of faith are historical revelations; not only the revelations once put down in the Bible by trustworthy witnesses, but also those which are silently experienced even today in the community of the faithful, in Christ's Church and in the fulfillment of the prophets' visions. They cannot be reproduced by experiments; anyway, that would be unnecessary. It is a truth of faith, for example, that Jesus Christ possesses two natures, one divine and the other human, united in the one person of God's Son. Jesus himself has proven this by his deeds. He has repeatedly declared: if you do not believe what I am saying, believe what I am doing: "Even if you refuse to believe in me, at least believe in the work I do" (Jn 10:38; 14:11). Jesus does not insist that his disciples believe him without reserve. They can see his miracles which persuade them of his divine power. There is no possibility for parapsychological explanations. His miracles are not intended to satisfy people's curiosity or desire for magic, but to invite belief in him as God's Son. And the convincing final evidence of his real human and real divine nature is his death on the cross and his resurrection on the third day.

All this is an empirical and historical fact, to which the apostles themselves testify: "Something which has existed since the beginning, that we have heard, and we have seen with our own eyes; that we have watched and touched with our hands: the Word, who is Life, this is our subject" (1 Jn 1: 1). This sounds more convincing than any scientific evidence. However, the individual is again free to choose. You are not obliged to believe what journalists write, unless you really want to accept it.

The question we asked ourselves above was this: how and to what extent can scientific formulas come near to the revealed truths of faith? The answer is to be found in the type of relationship which exists between the Christian scholar's belief and the system of scientific truths which he is examining. Experience shows that a sound relationship can exist in spite of all the differences which we may encounter. Indeed, the truths of Revelation can only be interpreted in terms of what we know about ourselves and the world, at the same time that they help us to better understand the meaning of the laws of nature.

Christian faith is not strictly tied to any definite conception of the world. However, any believer who wants to understand and unfold the truths of religion, needs a certain conception of the world which one usually takes from that of the age he is living in. This conception, however, changes with the progress of science, usually slowly, but sometimes dramatically. When this happens, believers feel the tension between the interpretation of certain religious doctrines and the new scientific discoveries. It is actually not the truth of faith which is in contradiction with the truth of science, but the new view of the world with the old one, by means of which certain dogmas were interpreted. It is therefore the task of the theologian to reconsider the dogmas which have been interpreted traditionally and give a new formulation which is in accordance with the new scientific view. By this latter we mean the well founded system of scientific truths, not hypotheses or the world of science fiction.

As we have seen, man's many fold activities, knowledge and experience are unified by the sphere of theological truths which fill them with meaning and purpose. Theology is always open toward scientific discoveries. A theologian who fails to take account of the scientific knowledge concerning the world and man can hardly be regarded as competent. It follows that only a fruitful cooperation between theologians and natural scientists can insure the progress of culture.

Before concluding, let us look back once more and try to form an integral picture of our whole existence. From so many details this may be the only thing remembered at the end of the long journey we have covered from Babylon to Bethlehem. The illustration below is a symbolic representation of the order of creation as revealed in the first and last chapters of the Bible. This coincides with the ideas of the great scholars and philosophers in the first centuries of our era, those who are today called the Fathers of the Church. However, let us again quote the last words of "A Brief History of Time" by Stephen Hawking, a famous physicist of this century who, in reply to the question as to why is it that the universe and we ourselves exist? "If we find the answer to that, it would be the ultimate triumph of human reason, for then we would know the mind of God" (Hawking 1988).

We would like to comfort the physicist who is so passionately seeking the truth. The ultimate triumph of human reason was brilliantly shown by the military officer, who, while defending the royal castle, was hit by a cannonball which broke his leg. He later told his friends that "his greatest consolation was to look at the heavens and the stars, which he contemplated often and for long periods of time, because from this there was born in his heart an extremely strong impulse to serve our Lord" (Ignatius, *Autobiography*, 11). St. Ignatius of Loyola gives a brief and clear answer to the physicist's question: "We are created to praise, reverence and serve the Creator, our Lord, and by this means to save our souls, so that we may attain our goal of everlasting happiness with him. All the things in this world are created for us to help us in attaining the goal for which we are created" (*Spiritual Exercises*, 23).

Man is the only being in this universe, who, with the help of his five senses and reason is capable of knowing everything which exists, every visible and invisible existence. We can, first of all, see the difference between the Creator and the creature, between the everlasting and the mortal being. We can also discern the shape and nature of things. We know that there is physical and spiritual existence, and that there are inanimate-inorganic and animate-organic beings. We discover among them the increasing perfection and order of existence and the strong relationship between them.

The elements and minerals are completely unconscious and helpless by themselves although they are the components of every vegetable and animal organism. The consciousness of corporeal existence gradually increases from the light sensitivity of the vegetables to the consciousness of human existence. Vegetables support the existence of both animals and humans. Domestic animals have no personal consciousness, but serve man in many ways. Human beings possess also the power of spiritual consciousness and self-knowledge (intellect, memory and will), which exists at an even higher level in purely spiritual creatures, the angels.

The Supreme Being is the Almighty Creator who names himself "I Am Who I Am" before man (Ex 3:14), which in the usage of the oriental Fathers means "the eternal consciousness of spiritual existence" (*Noésis noéseôs*). This first recognition and distinction is of vital importance to us. Those who misuse their reason and freedom confound or identify the material world with some permanent deity. Therefore they do not reverence the Creator our Lord, and they do not seek the mind of God. So they cannot save their souls, because disintegration is the final destiny of all material beings.

Let us now regard the order of existence in Fig. 50 as a line which returns to its starting point: every existence originates in an eternal Spirit; everything is the creation of that Spirit and in a fully developed form returns to that Spirit as to its final goal. Where is the human being itself in this order of existence? Where does he and she live and evolve? Between pure and eternal spirit and mere perishable matter! It is in us that spiritual-angelic and material-animal nature are united. Our great task is to consciously unite in ourselves these two natures and thus sustain the harmony of the order of existence. Thus we all feel that we have to live between two opposing forces: while the material sensate world pulls us down, spiritual existence attracts us upwards. It is in man that the two currents cross each other and in the tension formed between them man is almost crucified. This is the special cross of human existence which was dramatically demonstrated by the crucifixion of Christ the Savior.

How difficult it is for us to accept and to fulfill this central position and duty in the universe! We instinctively flee from the tension of the cross, many of us repress it below the threshold of consciousness. We do not want to know about it. However,this only increases our sufferings,because we fail to see the sense and goal of life. It is no use envying the life of animals, because man is not capable of living like them, without personal consciousness and without thought.

Every man craves for eternal life and happiness, but few are striving consciously for it. Only those who observe the laws of spiritual nature too are capable of striving for perfection. The creatures which are below us can only help in attaining our goal if we use them in a correct way: according to the laws of both physical and spiritual nature. There is a mean in all things. The fate and success of the individual as well as the life of the community (family and society) depend on how we use things: reasonably and in moderation or unreasonably and immoderately with regard to the Creator and his works, or unjustly, with blind egoism?

When a physicist, after having solved difficult mathematical problems, contentedly looks up at the stars and sky with relief, he seeks the mind of God in the right place. From the order of creation it is clear that every other creature came into being before him: the whole material world, the Sun and the Earth with the Moon, air and water, minerals and vegetables, fruit

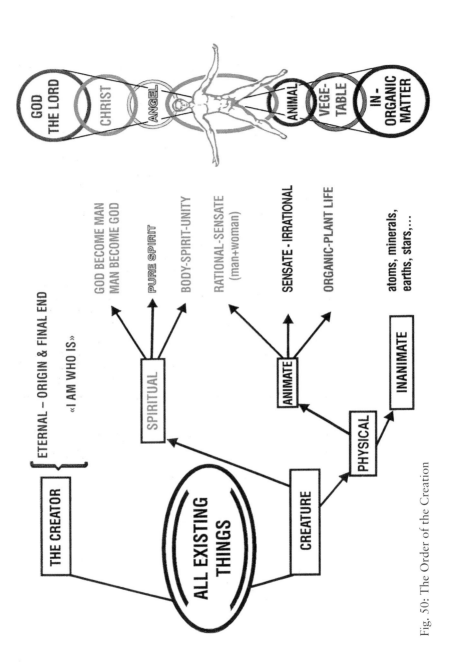

Fig. 50: The Order of the Creation

trees and animals, everything that is necessary for the maintenance of human life was ready before the appearance of man. The will of God the Creator is manifest in this, the will to make every creature serve man to attain his goal.

Spiritual creatures also play an important role in the order of existence. Even before having read about the visions of the prophets, Greek philosophers assumed the existence of angels, messengers from the other world, by way of logical inference. As purely spiritual creatures they have intelligence and will. By logical necessity angels are intermediaries between spiritual and material existence. As for the "Angels of the Lord", trustworthy writers testify to the significant role they played in the account of Jesus Christ's life, from his birth to his resurrection. The mind of God here becomes even clearer to those who read the Gospels of Matthew and Luke.

A solution of the great mystery is visible in the general effect of Fig. 50. While the unity of the material and spiritual world is fulfilled in man, the unity of human and divine nature is fulfilled in Christ. Thus the creatures in the universe will attain their final goal through man, and man will do so through Christ: it is through Christ that perfect unity between man and woman, body and soul, heaven and earth will be attained.

"God saw all he had made, and indeed it was very good" (Gen 1:31). The rules of grammar allow us to interpret this as a statement referring to the future: everything will be very good, because the creation of the world is still in progress. As for our part, we are trying to collaborate with the Creator knowing that *there are no evil forces, only forces used in an evil way.*

With this hopeful idea we take leave of the good Magi, who, overcoming every difficulty, found the person they had been looking for in Bethlehem. Are they the first or the last ones to convince us of the harmony between natural science and theological science?

REFERENCES

NB. The critical editions of the works of the Church Fathers, which are quoted in this book, will be found in the Volumes of *Patrologia Latina* and *Patrologia Graeca*, (Paris: Migne, J.P. 1844-1891)

Abarbanel, I. 1497, *Le Sorgenti della Salvezza* (Venice)

Abell, G. 1969, *Exploration of the Universe* (New York: Holt, Rinehart & Winston)

BDB 1977, Brown - Driver - Briggs - Genesius, *The New Hebrew and English Lexicon* (New York: Hendrickson)

Bauer, W. 1988, *Griechisch-Deutsch Wörterbuch zu den Schriften des N.T. und der frühchristlichen Literatur* (Berlin - New York: Walter de Gruyter)

Berg, W. 1974, *Early Virgil*. Eclogue IV. pp.48-51. (London: The Athlone Press)

Blackwell, R. J. 1991, *Galileo, Bellarmine and the Bible*. Translations: Appendix II-VIII (Notre Dame: University of Notre Dame Press)

Brandmüller, W. and Greipl, E. J. 1992, *Copernico, Galilei e la Chiesa. Fine della controversia, 1820*. Gli atti del Sant' Uffizio, pp. 299-480. (Vatican City: Pontifical Academy of Sciences)

Brown, L. W. 1956, *The Indian Christians of St Thomas*, pp.43-64. (Cambridge: University Press)

Brown, R. E., et al. 1968, *The Jerome Biblical Commentary (JBC)*, (London & New Jersey: Prentice-Hall Inc. Publications)

―――― 1977, *The Birth of the Messiah. A Commentary on the Infancy Narratives in Matthew and Luke* (New York: Doubleday)

Brunt, P. A. and Moore, J. M. 1973, Res Gestae Divi Augusti. *The Achievements of the Divine Augustus*. The complete Latin text of the Monumentum Ancyranum with an English translation and notes (Oxford: University Press)

Bultmann, R. 1948, *Neues Testament und Mythologie. Kerygma und Mythos* I., 5. (Hamburg: H. Reich Evang. Verlag)

―――― 1958, *Jesus Christ and Mythology*. (New York: Scribner's Sons)

Carlen, C. 1981, *The Papal Encyclicals* 1878-1903, Providentissimus Deus, pp.334ff; 1939-1958, Divino Afflante Spiritu, pp.52ff (Wilmington, N.C.: McGrath)

Carter, B. 1974, *Large Number Coincidences and the Anthropic Principle in Cosmology*, IAU Symposium No. 63, 290ff (Dordrecht: Reidel)

Cassiodorus, F. M., *Computus Paschalis*, in *Patrologia Latina*, lxix, cols 1249-1250 (Paris: Migne, J.P. 1855)

CCC 1994, *Catechismus Ecclesiae Catholicae* (Vatican City: Libreria Editrice Vaticana) English Edition: *Catechism of the Catholic Church* (London: Chapman)

Christern, E. 1960, *Johannes von Hildesheim, Die Legende von den Heiligen Drei Königen*, Übertragung und Nachwort von E.Christern (Cologne: J.P.Bachen)

Claeys, K. 1979, *Die Bibel bestätigt das Weltbild der Naturwissenschaften. Neues Beweisverfahren aus Etymologie, Kontext, Konkordanz und Naturwissenschaft* (Stein am Rhein: Christiana)

Clemens Alexandrinus, *Stromata*, I.21, §§ 144-147. The Greek text with French translation will be found in *Sources Chrétiennes*, No. 30 (Paris: Ed. du Cerf, 1951)

Corbishley, T. 1975, "Chronology of New Testament Times" in *The New Catholic Commentary on Holy Scripture* (London: Thomas Nelson & Sons Ltd)

Coyne, G. V. et al. 1993, *Origins, Time and Complexity*. Proceedings of the 4th Conference of the European Society for Study of Science and Religion (Geneva: Labor et Fides)

Coyne, G. V. 1999, "Science and Religious Belief. 4. Unifying Knowledge", in International Symposium on Astrophysics Research and Science Education, Vatican Observatory 1999, C. D. Impey editor (Vatican City State; distributed by the University of Notre Dame Press, Notre Dame, IN., USA)

Daniélou, J. 1961, *Les symboles chrétiens primitifs*. (Paris: Ed. du Seuil), translated into English by D. Attwater, *Primitive Christian Symbols*, Chapter 7: The Star of Jacob (London: Compass Books, 1964)

Dionysius Exiguus, *Liber de Paschate; Cyclus decemnovennalis. Argumenta Paschalia; Epistola prima scripta Anno Christi 525*, in *Patrologia Latina*, lxvii, cols 19-23; 483-508 (Paris: Migne, J.P. 1855). The quoted passages translated by G. Teres.

De Strycker, E. 1961, *La forme la plus ancienne du Protoévangile de Jacques*. Subsidia Hagiographica No. 33 (Bruxelles: Société des Bollandistes)

Degrassi, A. 1952, *I Fasti Consulari dell' Impero Romano dal 30 avanti Cristo al 613 dopo Cristo* (Rome: Edizioni di storia e letteratura)

Donahue, W.H. 1992, *Johannes Kepler, New Astronomy*, translated by W.H. Donahue (Cambridge: University Press)

Eddington, A. 1928, *The Nature of the Physical World* (London: Dent & Sons)

Eliade, M. 1957, *Das Heilige und das Prophane II* (Hamburg: Rowohlt)

Fairbridge, R. W. 1961, *Solar Variations, Climatic Changes, and Related Geophysical Problems*. Annals of the New York Academy of Sciences, Vol. 95. (New York: Published by the Academy)

Fantoli, A. 1996, *Galileo: For Copernicanism and for the Church*, Second Edition (Vatican City: Vatican Observatory Publications); distributed by the University of Notre Dame Press, Notre Dame, IN., USA.

Favaro, A. 1968, *Edizione Nazionale delle Opere di Galileo Galilei*, original edition 1890-1909, reprinted 1968 (Florence: Giunti Barbèra)

Ferrari d'Occhieppo, K. 1965, *Jupiter und Saturn in den Jahren -125 und -6 nach babylonischen Quellen* (Vienna: Österreichische Akademie der Wissenschaften)

———— 1977, *Der Stern der Weisen. Geschichte oder Legende* (Vienna: Herold)

———— 1978, "The Star of Bethlehem" in the *Quarterly Journal of the Royal Astronomical Society*, Vol. 19, 517-520 (London: Blackwell Scientific Publications)

———— 1991, *Der Stern von Bethlehem aus der Sicht der Astronomie. Babylonische Astronomie*, pp.109-133 (Stuttgart: Franckh-Kosmos)

Frank, Ph. 1947, *Einstein, His Life and Times* (New York: Knopf)

Geminos, *Eisagogé eis tá phainoména. Gemini Elementa Astronomiae*. Ad Codicum fidem recensuit C. Manitius (Lipsiae: Teubner 1898). The quoted passages translated by G.Teres.

Gordis, R. 1978, *The Book of Job. Commentary, New Translation and Special Studies* (New York: Doubleday)

Grundmann, W. 1968, *Das Evangelium nach Matthäus*. Theol. Handkommentar zum Neuen Testament (Berlin: Evangelischer Verlagsanstalt)

Guitton, J. and Bogdanov, G. 1991, *Dieu et la science* (Paris: Grasset & Fasquelle)

Hawking, S. W. 1988, *A Brief History of Time* (New York & London: Bantam)

Heller, M. 1993, "Creation Interpretations in Cosmology", in *Quantum Cosmology and the Laws of Nature*, pp.96-101, eds. R. J. Russell et al. (Vatican City: Vatican Observatory Publications), distributed by the University of Notre Dame Press, Nortre Dame IN., USA.

Hennecke, E. and Schneemelcher, W. 1963, *The New Testament Apocrypha. Evangelium Infantiae Arabicum*, Vol. I (London: Lutterworth)

Herodotus, *Histories Apodexis*, I. 101-185. Greek text with an Italian translation by A.I.D'Accini, *Erodoto, Storie*, Vol. I (Milano: Rizzioli 1984). The quoted passages translated by G. Teres.

Hildegard Gesellschaft, 1982, Hildegard von Bingen, *Liber Compositae et Simplicis Medicinae. Scivias*, in *Patrologia Latina*, cxcvii (Paris: J.P.Migne 1865), German translations: *Heilkunde, Leib und Seele, Scivias*, by M. L. Portmann (Basel: Baseler Hildegard Gesellschaft)

Hildesheim, J.von, 1370, *Vita trium Regum. Liber de trium Regum corporibus Coloniam translatis.* (Coloniae); see also Christern, 1960

Holzmeister, U. 1933, *Chronologia vitae Christi. Chronologia mortis Domini* (Rome: Pontifical Biblical Institute)

Hoyle, F. 1962, *Astronomy* (New York: Doubleday & Co.Inc.)

Hughes, D. 1979, *The Star of Bethlehem Mystery. An Astronomer's Confirmation* (New York: Walter & Co and London: Dent & Sons)

Jastrow, R. 1980, *God and the Astronomers* (New York: Warner)

Josephus Flavius, "The Antiquities of the Jews" and "The Jewish War" in *The Works of Josephus*, Complete and Unabridged, translated by W. Whiston (New York: Hendrickson 1960; New Updated Edition, Grand Rapids, Michigan: Kregel 1980)

JBC 1968, *The Jerome Biblical Commentary* (London: Prentice-Hall Inc.)

Jung, C. G. 1971, *The Collected Works of C. G. Jung* in Bollingen Series XX (Princeton: Princeton University Press; paperback printing, with corrections, 1976, trans. by H. G. Baynes, revised by R. F. C. Hull): *Psychological Types*, Vol. 6.; *Synchronicity: An Acausal Connecting Principle*, Vol. 8.; *The Archetypes and the Collective Unconscious*, Vol. 9.I.; *Aion. Researches into the Phenomenology of the Self. The Sign of the Fishes*, Vol. 9.II.; *Flying Saucers: A Modern Myth*, Vol. 10.; *Psychology and Religion. Answer to Job*, Vol. 11.; *Psychology and Alchemy, Introduction to the Religious and Psychological Problems*, Vol. 12; *In Memory of Richard Wilhelm*, who translated the Chinese *I Ching* into German, Vol. 15.

Kähler, H. 1958, *Rom und seine Welt. Bilder zur Geschichte und Kultur* (Munich: Kähler)

Kepler, J. 1606, *De Stella Nova in Pede Serpentarii: II. De Jesu Cristi Servatoris Vero Anno Natalitio; Sylva chronologica*, pp. 1-35. (Pragae: Officina P. Sessii). The quoted passages translated by G. Teres.

———— 1619,. *Weltharmonik*, "Harmonices Mundi" translated by Max Caspar (Munich: Oldenbourg 1939)

———— 1870, *Gesammelte Werke*, "Opera Omnia" (Frankfurt: Frish 1870) translated by Max Caspar (Munich: Oldenbourg 1953)

Knibb, M.A. 1978, *The Ethiopic Book of Enoch: A New Edition in the Light of the Aramaic Dead Sea Fragments*, edited and translated by M.A. Knibb (Oxford: Clarendon Press)

Klepesta, J. and Rükl, A. 1973, *Taschenatlas der Sternbilder* (Hanau Main: Dausien)

Koldewey, R. 1913, *Das wieder erstehende Babylon* (Leipzig: Teubner). The quoted passages translated by G. Teres.

Küchler, M. 1989, "Vidimus stellam eius" in *Bibel und Kirche*, 44 (Fribourg: Institute Biblique)

Kugler, F. X. 1907-1935, *Sternkunde und Sterndienst in Babel. Assyriologische, astronomische und astralmythologische Untersuchungen*, I-III (Münster in W.: Aschendorffsche Verlagsbuchhandlung)

———— 1912, Sternkunde und Sterndienst in Babel, II.Buch, 2.Teil: *Babylonische Zeitordnung und ältere Himmelskunde* (Münster in W.: Aschendorffsche Verlagsbuchhandlung)

Lampe, G.W. 1961, *A Patristic Greek Lexicon* (Oxford: University Press)

Laurentin, R. 1982, *Les évangiles de l'Enfance du Christ, vérité du Noël au-delà des mythes*, pp.464-469 (Paris: Desclée)

Lemaître, G. 1950, *The Primeval Atom. An Essay on Cosmology* (London & New York: D. van Nostrand Co. Inc.)

Léon-Dufour, X. 1963, *Les Évangiles et l'histoire de Jésus*, pp. 343-351 (Paris: Ed. du Cerf)

———— 1970, *Vocabulaire de théologie biblique* (Paris: Ed. du Cerf)

Maffeo, S. 1991, *In the Service of Nine Popes: 100 Years of the Vatican Observatory*, trans. by G.V. Coyne (Vatican City: Vatican Observatory Publications)

Manilius, *Astronomica*, with an English Translation by G. P. Goold (Cambridge MA: Harvard University Press and London: Heinemann 1977)

Manitius, C. 1974, *Gemini Elementa Astronomiae*. (Leipzig: Teubner; reprint of 1898 edition)

Marik, M. 1989, Csillagászat (Budapest: Akadémia Kiadó)

Maunder, E. W. 1908, *The Astronomy of the Bible* (London: Sealey Clark & Co.Ltd; reprinted by Dent & Sons 1935)

McHugh, L.C. 1959, *Two Addresses of Pope Pius XII*, "Science and the Existence of God", 22.11.1951, and "Science and Philosophy", 14.09.1955 (New York: America Press)

Murray, R. 1992, *The Cosmic Covenant. Biblical Themes of Justice, Peace and the Integrity of Creation* (London: Heythrop Monographs)

Nemesszeghy, E. and Russell, J. 1972, "The Theology of Evolution", in *Theology Today*, No.6, p.38 (Cork: Mercier Press)

Neugebauer, O. 1955, *Astronomical Cuneiform Texts (ACT), Babylonian Ephemerides of the Seleucid Period*, 3 Volumes (London: Humphries)

——— 1975, *A History of Ancient Mathematical Astronomy. In Three Parts with 9 Plates and 619 Figures.* Sexagesimal Computations, Tables, pp. 1113-30 (New York: Springer-Verlag)

——— 1983, *Astronomy and History, Selected Essays* (New York: Springer), The Astronomy of the Book of Enoch, p. 470 ff.

Paffenroth, K. 1993, "The Star of Bethlehem Casts Light on its Modern Interpreters", in *Quarterly Journal of the Royal Astronomical Society*, Vol. 34, 449 - 460 (London: Blackwell Scientific Publications)

Palacios, L. and Camps, V. 1954, *Grammatica Syriaca* (Paris & Rome: Desclée)

Pannekoek, A. 1961, *A History of Astronomy*. Chaldaean Tables, pp. 63-81 (New York: Interscience Publications, Inc.)

Parker, R. A. and Dubberstein, W. H. 1956, *Babylonian Chronology*. (Providence, Rhode Island: Brown University Press)

Paulus, W. 1928, *Marduk, Urtyp Christi?* (Rome: Pontifical Biblical Institute)

Pedersen, O. 1992, *The Book of Nature* (Vatican City: Vatican Observatory Publications); distributed by the University of Notre Dame Press, Notre Dame, IN., USA.

Payne Smith, R. 1957, *A Compendious Syriac Dictionary* (Oxford: University Press); see also *Thesaurus Syriacus I - II.* (New York: Hildesheim 1981)

Pontifical Biblical Commission 1993, *The Interpretation of the Bible in the Church* (Vatican City: Libreria Editrice Vaticana)

Poupard, P. et al. 1984, *Galileo Galilei, 350 anni di storia, 1633 - 1983. Studi e ricerche* (Rome: Marietti)

Pritchard, J.B. 1969, *Ancient Near Eastern Texts Relating to the Old Testament*, Third Edition (Princeton: Princeton University Press)

Ptolemy, C. *Tetrabiblos*, translated into Italian by M. Candellero: Claudio Tolemeo, *Tetrabiblos o i quattro libri delle predizioni astrologiche* (Carmagnola: Arktos 1979); see also C. Ptolemäus, *Handbuch der Astronomie I-XII*, Deutsche Übersetzung und Anmerkungen von K. Manitius. Vorwort und Berichtigungen von O. Neugebauer (Leipzig: Teubner 1963)

Rabban, R. 1955, *Shahîd al-Ittahad, Martyr of Union*, a Biography of Yohanan Sulâqâ (Mosul: Rabban-Hormizd)

Ratzinger, J. 1989, *Schriftauslegung im Widerstreit* (Freiburg: Herder)

Rienecker, Fr. 1950, *Sprachlicher Schlüssel zum Griechischen Neuen Testament* (Basel: Brunnen-Verlag)

Rosenberg, A. 1958, *Durchbruch zur Zukunft. Der Mensch im Wassermannzeitalter* (Munich: Barth)

Rosenberg, R. A. 1972, "The Star of the Messiah reconsidered", *Biblica* 53, 105-116

Russell, R.J.et al. 1993, *Quantum Cosmology and the Laws of Nature, Second Edition* (Vatican City: Vatican Observatory Publications); distributed by the University of Notre Dame Press, Notre Dame, IN., USA.

Sachs, A. J. 1955, *Late Babylonian Astronomical and Related Texts* (Providence, Rhode Island: University Press)

Schaumberger, J. 1925, "Textus Cuneiformis de Stella Magorum", *Biblica* 6, 444 ff., 1943, *Biblica*, 24, 165-168.

Schiaparelli, G. V. 1903, *L'Astronomia nell'Antico Testamento;* reprinted in *Scritti sulla Storia della Astronomia Antica*, Tomo I. pp.147 - 321 (Bologna 1925: Zanichelli)

Schröder, W. et al. 1992, *Solar-terrestrial Variability and Global Change.* Symposium of IAGA in Vienna 1991 (Bremen: Interdivisional Commission on History of IAGA)

Seilo, B.E. 1971, *Astronomi* (Oslo: Schibsteds)

Sheen F. J. 1977, *Life of Christ.* (New York & London: Doubleday)

Smith, G. 1876, *The Chaldaean Account of Genesis* (Oxford: University Press)

Speiser, E.A. 1969, "The Creation Epic" in *Ancient Near Eastern Texts Relating to the Old Testament*, ed. J.B. Pritchard (Princeton: Princeton University Press)

Strassmaier, E.L. and Epping, J, 1889, *Astronomisches aus Babylon* (Freiburg: Herder)

Sukenik, E.L. 1934, *Ancient Synagogues in Palestine and Greece* (Oxford: University Press)

Tanquerey, A. 1956, *Brevior Synopsis Theologiae Dogmaticae* (Paris: Desclée)

Testuz, M. 1958, *Papyrus Bodmer V, Nativité de Marie* (Cologny - Genève: Bibliotheca Bodmeriana)

Unger, E. 1931, *Babylon, die heilige Stadt, nach der Beschreibung der Babylonier* (Berlin: Walter de Gruyter)

Virgil, P.M. *Bucolica, Ecloga IV*, Latin text with English translation by William Berg, *"Early Virgil"* (University of London: The Athlone Press 1974)

Waley, A. 1934, *The Way and Its Power, a Study of the Tao-Tê-Ching*, English translation pp.141-244 (London: Allen & Unwin)

Weinberg, D.J. 1977, *The First Three Minutes* (New York: Basic Books; updated edition New York: Basic Books 1988)

Williams, D. J. 1976, *Physics of the Solar Planetary Environments*, Vol.II. International Symposium on Solar-Terrestrial Physics (Boulder: American Geophysical Union)

Woolley, C. L. 1954, *Excavations at Ur* (London: Exploration Society)

Wright, A.G. 1967, *The Literary Genre Midrash, Are the Infancy Narratives Midrash?* pp.139-145 (New York: Society of St. Paul)

Zannoni, G. 1948, *Arato di Soli, Fenomeni e pronostici* (Florence: Sansoni) Greek text of Aratus with an Italian translation by G. Zannoni.

INDEX

p 11
p 49

p 32, bottom
 37, bottom
 48 "Chaldean dynasty"?
 48 very bottom
 60, 1, 2 bottom
 84, 1 'NO!

p 103—111

175
182: middle
192 top
193 middle, bottom
194 top

(191)

256